Korean War Heroes

Korean War Heroes

Edward F. Murphy

★

PRESIDIO

Unless otherwise stated, all incidents of heroic action related here resulted in the award of the Medal of Honor to the person involved.

Published by Presidio Press
505 B San Marin Drive, Suite 300
Novato, CA 94945-1340

This edition printed 1997

Library of Congress Cataloging-in-Publication Data

Murphy, Edward F., 1947–
    Korean war heroes / Edward F. Murphy.
        p. cm.
    Includes bibliographical references (p. 297) and index.
    ISBN 0-89141-636-6 (paperback)
    ISBN 0-89141-404-5 (hardcover)
    1. Korean War, 1950–1953—Campaigns. 2. United States—Armed Forces—Biography. 3. Medal of honor. I. Title.
    DS918.M9 1992
    951.904'2—dc20   91-29472
                                                        CIP

All photographs not otherwise credited are from the author's collection.
Printed in the United States of America

To Kay: third time's a charm!

Acknowledgments

I would like to offer a special thanks to the following Medal of Honor recipients and relatives of recipients without whose friendship and support this book would not be possible: William E. Barber, Lloyd L. Burke, William R. Charette, Jessica Commiskey, Raymond G. Davis, Eva Gilliland, Raymond Harvey, Robert E. Kilmer, Lewis L. Millett, Hiroshi Miyamura, Ola L. Mize, Raymond G. Murphy, Ronald E. Rosser, Edward R. Schowalter, James L. Stone, Harold E. Wilson.

Contents

N

MANCHURIA

• Hoenyong

Changjin •

• Hyesanjin

Yalu R.

Manpojin   • Kanggye   Kilchu •

Unsan   Chongchon R.   • Mupyong-ni   Iwon
                                    Yudam-ni
• Anju   Tokchon   Hamhung

             •   Hungnam

Sukchon • • Sunchon
      • Pyongyang   • Wonsan   Sea of
                                            Japan

Sariwon •

                Kumchon
Haeju •   Kaesong   Pyonggang   PUNCHBOWL
                              Chorwon •   HEARTBREAK
                                    Kumhwa   RIDGE   Yangyang
              Uijongbu   Chunchon
Yellow Sea   • Seoul   38th Parallel
      Inchon   • Suwon   Wonju
              • Osan
                              • Chechon
             Chonan
                    Chungju

              Kum R.
                    Taejon
      Kunsan   Naktong R.
                                    Pohang-dong
                              • Taegu
                    Nam R.
Mokpo   Masan
                         Pusan

                              Korea Strait

                                    MILES
                                    0   50

NORTH AND
SOUTH KOREA

Map by Edward F. Murphy

Hamchang

Andong

Naktong R.

Sangju

Naktong-ni

Yongdok

Sea of Japan

Kumchon

Yongchon

Waegwan

Songju

Yonil

Taegu

Koryong

Changnyong

Yongson   Miryang

Agok   *Naktong R.*   Samnangjin

Nam R.

Saga

Chinju   Haman

Masan

Pusan

Muchon-ni

Hadong

Kosong

Korea Strait

N

MILES

10   0   10

Pusan Perimeter

July - September 1950

Map by Edward F. Murphy

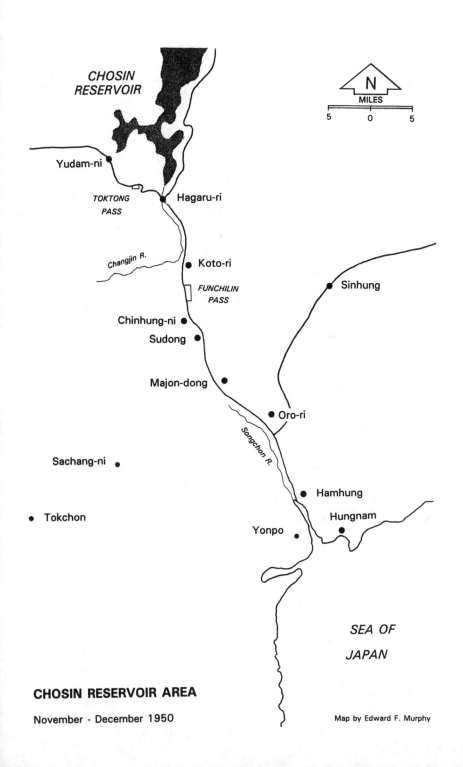

CHOSIN RESERVOIR

CHOSIN
RESERVOIR

N
MILES
5   0   5

Yudam-ni

TOKTONG
PASS

Hagaru-ri

Changjin R.

Koto-ri

FUNCHILIN
PASS

Sinhung

Chinhung-ni

Sudong

Majon-dong

Oro-ri

Songchon R.

Sachang-ni

Tokchon

Hamhung

Hungnam

Yonpo

SEA OF

JAPAN

CHOSIN RESERVOIR AREA

November - December 1950

Map by Edward F. Murphy

Introduction
Medal of Honor History

Amerca's highest award for combat valor is the Medal of Honor. Only 3,399 men have earned this high award since it was first presented during the Civil War. Its prestige is so high that President Harry S. Truman once told a Korean War hero, "I'd rather have this medal than be president." Gen. George S. Patton told one World War II recipient as he placed the coveted medal around the hero's neck, "I'd give my immortal soul for that medal." Though he was an outstanding combat soldier, Patton never earned the Medal of Honor.

To earn the Medal of Honor a member of the Armed Forces must perform an act of the most conspicuous gallantry and intrepidity, far above and beyond the call of duty, in the presence of an armed enemy. The deed must involve a clear risk of life. It must be the type of voluntary act which, if the hero did not do it, would not subject him to undue criticism. In addition, at least two eyewitnesses must attest to the deed. By adhering to these strict criteria the Armed Forces have reserved the Medal of Honor solely for the "bravest of the brave."

The Medal of Honor traces its roots to the early days of the Civil War when, in December 1861, Iowa Senator James W. Grimes introduced a bill in Congress "to promote the efficiency of the navy." One of the bill's minor paragraphs authorized a "medal of honor" for sailors and marines who distinguished themselves by their gallantry in action. President Abraham Lincoln signed the bill, and the Medal of Honor, into law on December 21, 1861.

A few months later the army prevailed upon Massachusetts Senator Henry Wilson to introduce a similar bill for it. The law creating an army Medal of Honor was signed into effect on July 12, 1862.

The medal itself was designed by a Philadelphia silversmith firm, Wm. Wilson & Son. They described the medal as:

> A five-pointed star, one point down. On the obverse the foul spirit of Secession and Rebellion is represented by a male figure in crouching attitude holding in his hands serpents, which, with forked tongues, are striking at a large female figure representing the Union or Genius of our country, who holds in her right hand a shield, and in her left, the fasces. Around these figures are thirty-four stars, indicating the number of states in the Union.

Both medals were suspended from identical ribbons—a blue horizontal top band above alternating vertical stripes of red and white—with only the suspension devices differing. The navy's medal connected to the ribbon with a rope-fouled anchor; the army's via an eagle, wings spread, astride crossed cannon and cannonball stacks.

Since that beginning the 3,399 recipients have earned 3,418 medals. The most recent was awarded by President Bush in April 1991 for World War I service. Nineteen Americans have earned the Medal of Honor twice. Heroic acts performed during the Civil War account for 1,520 medals, nearly half of all those awarded. But there were no other medals then. It was the Medal of Honor or nothing.

Today, the Medal of Honor is the most prestigious of all decorations. A strict review process ensures that the medal will not be conferred on unworthy candidates. The standards are so high that over fifty-five percent of the medals awarded since World War I have been posthumous. Nearly seventy percent of the Medals of Honor awarded for the Korean War and the Vietnam War went to heroes who lost their lives as a result of their bravery. Those who wear the Medal of Honor are truly a special breed.

The first man to earn a Medal of Honor was army Lt. Bernard J. D. Irwin. On February 14, 1861, the young surgeon volunteered to lead a relief expedition to the aid of a patrol of cavalrymen trapped by Indians at Apache Pass, Arizona. Fighting Apaches and a raging blizzard, Irwin broke the siege, saving the beleaguered command from certain death.

The first Medals of Honor actually awarded went to six soldiers from Ohio who survived the legendary "Great Locomotive Chase" through Georgia in April 1862. Twenty-one volunteers under the command of civilian spy James J. Andrews set out from Shelbyville, Tennessee, with the mission of capturing a Confederate locomotive near Atlanta. Once they had the train they planned to run it north to Chattanooga, burning bridges and cutting telegraph wires along the way. The resulting confusion would prevent the Confederate Army from reinforcing Chattanooga during an upcoming Union attack.

Unfortunately, bad weather and the stubborn determination of the Confederate train's conductor spoiled the mission. All the "engine thieves" were captured. They languished in prison for nearly a year, during which time eight of the band, including Andrews, were tried and executed by their captors. Eight more men escaped a few months later, eventually making their way back to Union lines. In March 1863 the remaining six were taken to City Point, Virginia, to be exchanged for Confederate prisoners.

They arrived in Washington, D.C., on March 25 with orders to report to the Judge Advocate General so that they could revise and qualify evidence concerning the raid. When Secretary of War Edwin M. Stanton heard they were in the capital, he sent word he wanted to see them.

After listening to the group recite the horrors of their imprisonment, Stanton offered praise for their courage and devotion to duty. Then he said, "Congress has recently created a special medal to honor the brave defenders of the Union. None have yet been awarded. I have the honor of presenting you the first." He then pinned the first Medal of Honor to the tunic of the group's youngest member, 19-year-old Jacob Parrott. The others receiving medals that day were William Bensinger, Robert Buffum, Elihu Mason, William Pittinger, and William H. Reddick.

A few days later the navy awarded its first medals. Unlike the army, it held no formal ceremony for its heroes. Instead, the medals were forwarded to the intended recipient's commanding officer who handled the presentation ceremony on an individual basis.

When the Civil War ended in April 1865, 1,196 soldiers, 307 sailors, and 17 marines had performed deeds of valor that brought them the Medal of Honor.

Both the army and navy continued to award the Medal of Honor after the Civil War. Medals went to gallant soldiers who fought Indians as America expanded westward—423 in all. Sailors and marines were cited primarily for heroism involved in rescuing drowning men, although a few medals were awarded to men for combat heroics in isolated skirmishes around the world. Between the Civil War and the Spanish-American War, the navy awarded 128 medals to gallant sailors and marines.

As America began establishing herself late in the 19th century as a global power, the men filling the ranks of her Armed Forces were called upon to exhibit new heights of courage and daring. Medals of Honor went to brave men who stormed San Juan Hill, to sailors who faced Spanish cannon at

Manila Bay, and to those heroic men who marched to relieve Peking from the hordes of religious fanatics surrounding the Chinese capital in 1900. While the military circumstances might have changed in the years since the Civil War, the need for heroic action had not diminished.

In 1904 the army adopted a new design for its Medal of Honor. The change was prompted by various Civil War veterans groups issuing membership badges that too closely resembled the Medal of Honor. Horace Porter, U.S. ambassador to France and a Civil War recipient of the Medal of Honor, commissioned the Parisian jewelry firm of Messrs. Arthur, Bertrand, and Berenger to prepare several designs for a new medal. One was approved by both the members of the Medal of Honor Legion and the secretary of war. On November 22, 1904, a patent was issued to protect the new medal.

The chief feature of the old medal, the five-pointed star, was retained in the new design. The head of Minerva fills the medal's center, surrounded by the words *United States of America*. An open laurel wreath, enameled in green, encircles the star. Green oak leaves fill the prongs of the star. Above the star is a bar bearing the word *VALOR*. An eagle with wings spread sits atop the bar.

The Medal of Honor also gained a new ribbon. It now hung from a light blue, watered-silk material spangled with thirteen white stars, representing the original colonies. Initially, the medal was worn on the recipient's left breast. Later, a neck ribbon was added.

Because the navy awarded its Medal of Honor for both combat and noncombat heroism it adopted a second Medal of Honor to be reserved for combat heroism. In 1919 the navy introduced a gold cross pattee-style medal designed by the New York City jewelry firm, Tiffany & Co. The old five-pointed star design was used for noncombat heroism. The two-medal system proved cumbersome, though, and the navy dropped it in 1942, going back to the original Medal of Honor design.

During World War I the army, in order to recognize various degrees of bravery, created several new decorations. The Distinguished Service Cross (DSC) would rank immediately below the Medal of Honor, recognizing combat heroism not justifying the Medal of Honor. Below the DSC was the Silver Star. The navy introduced the Navy Cross, equivalent to the DSC, and also used the Silver Star.

The introduction of these new decorations ensured that the Medal of Honor would be reserved only for those doughboys exhibiting the highest degrees of heroism. So exacting were the standards that only 119 members of the Allied Expeditionary Force (AEF) received the Medal of Honor: ninety-one army, twenty-one navy, and seven marines (five of whom also received the army Medal of Honor for the same deed). For the first time posthumous awards accounted for a large percentage of the total. Thirty-two of the heroes died performing the act which earned them the award.

In the years immediately following the "Great War" both the army and the navy continued to award the Medal of Honor for exceptional heroism. Most of the navy's went to men who bravely fought fires aboard ships. Others went for exceptional accomplishments, the most notable being the army award to Charles A. Lindbergh for his epic flight across the Atlantic.

It was in World War II that the Medal of Honor achieved the prominence it holds today. To assure that only the most deserving heroes received this ultimate recognition, both the army and navy created internal decorations boards to review recommendations for awards. There were various levels of boards each award recommendation had to pass, beginning at the divisional level. The higher the proposed medal, the longer the review process. Recommendations for the Medal of Honor went all the way back to Washington, D.C., where senior, combat-tested officers reviewed the supporting documentation. They, as well as any of the intermediate boards, could downgrade the Medal of Honor recommendation to a lesser award, or, conversely, upgrade a recommendation for another medal to the Medal of Honor.

While this was a lengthy, time-consuming process, it did uphold the highest traditions of the Medal of Honor. Over thirteen million men served in the military during World War II. Only 433 of them earned the Medal of Honor (294 army, fifty-seven navy, eighty-one marines, and one lone coast guardsman). For the first time posthumous awards outnumbered awards to living heroes—only 190 men survived to have their medals placed around their necks.

Less than five years after the end of World War II the United States found itself enmeshed in its first limited commitment war. The Soviet-sponsored and Chinese-supported North Korean invasion of South Korea in June 1950 put America's military forces in a war they not only could not win, but which was largely ignored by most Americans. Regardless of the lack of support, the fighting man in Korea proved himself to be a tenacious combatant. One hundred thirty-one Americans earned the Medal of Honor fighting in North and South Korea (seventy-eight army, forty-two marine, seven navy, and four members of the newly created air force).

As evidence of the savage fighting experienced by U.S. troops in Korea, over seventy percent of the Medals of Honor were awarded posthumously. Only thirty-seven heroes survived their deeds.

In the mid-1960s the sons of World War II's veterans were called upon to fight their own war. Unlike Korea, the U.S. military had no clear-cut military objectives in Vietnam. Instead, it adopted a policy of attrition. Wear the enemy down, kill more of them than they did of us, and we could declare a victory. As a result, America became entrenched in her longest, most controversial war.

Though the Vietnam War was widely and actively opposed by various factions across the United States, America's fighting men, mainly young draftees, proved themselves to be as formidable as their fathers in World War II, and their older brothers in Korea. Two hundred thirty-eight Medals of Honor went to Vietnam veterans (155 soldiers, 14 sailors, 57 marines, and 12 airmen). One hundred fifty of Vietnam's Medal of Honor heroes died performing the deed that brought them this supreme recognition.

In the 125-plus years that the Medal of Honor has been awarded it has proven to be as democratic as the great country that presents it. It has been earned by presidents' sons and sharecroppers' sons. Blacks, whites, Indians, and Hispanics have all shared in its glory. College professors and grade school dropouts have worn the medal with equal pride. Some heroes were rich, others poor. They came from farms and city neighborhoods.

Yet, in spite of their differences, their men share a common trait: uncommon courage. A courage worthy of the ultimate recognition—the Medal of Honor.

Chapter One
South Korea Invaded

At precisely 4:00 A.M. on Sunday, June 25, 1950, ninety thousand men of the North Korean People's Army—NKPA—attacked across the Thirty-eighth Parallel, which divided their country from South Korea. Seven infantry divisions, one armored brigade, a separate infantry regiment, a motorcycle regiment, and a brigade of border constabulary, backed by 130 aircraft and dozens of artillery batteries, poured across the border in a drizzling rain. The attack started on the Ongjin Peninsula, west of the South Korean capital of Seoul, which itself lay some fifty miles south of the Thirty-eighth Parallel. It unrolled eastward over the next hour, culminating in an NKPA amphibious assault on South Korea's eastern shore, just below the Thirty-eighth Parallel.

On the south side of the Thirty-eighth Parallel four Republic of Korea (ROK) infantry divisions were deployed. Normally, this would have been a sufficiently large force to stem the flood of NKPA troops. However, only one of each division's three regiments manned its defensive positions. The other regiments occupied reserve areas which lay ten to forty miles south of the parallel. And, since it was a weekend, many of the regiments' officers, and a good number of enlisted men, were on pass to Seoul or other nearby towns.

The armored spearheads of the NKPA thus found not a poised South Korean opponent, but a surprised and ill-prepared ROK army. As a result, the NKPA forces flowed over the ROK defenders like rushing floodwaters over weakened dikes.

Within hours of the opening attack the survivors of the ROK 17th Regiment defending Ongjin Peninsula were evacuated by LSTs (landing ship, tank) to Inchon, eighteen miles west of Seoul. North and west of Seoul at Kaesong it was even worse. Only two shattered companies of the ROK 1st Infantry Division's 12th Regiment were able to flee south of the Imjin River to safety; hundreds of their comrades were killed or captured.

Down the Uijongbu Corridor, north of Seoul, two NKPA infantry divisions, each led by forty Soviet-built T-34 tanks, struck toward the capital city. Taking the full force of the brutal assault was the ROK 7th Infantry Division. With its three regiments scattered over a wide area, the 7th could offer only minimal resistance. By 8:30 that morning the 7th was radioing army headquarters in Seoul for reinforcements. But there were few reinforcements, and there was no way to stop the steel monsters—no rivers, no mountain ranges to stop the advancing NKPA from reaching Seoul.

By nightfall of June 25, the ROK 7th Division had fallen back to the town of Uijongbu. If it fell, Seoul lay wide open.

Farther east, NKPA forces fell on Chunchon. Although the ROK 6th Infantry Division fought valiantly for three days, it, too, was finally forced back.

On the east coast, near the seaport city of Samchok, a flotilla of junks and sampans were landing North Korean soldiers north and south of the city.

All along the Thirty-eighth Parallel ROK units reeled under the tremendous onslaught of the NKPA. The key was Uijongbu. ROK headquarters rushed whatever reinforcements it could find to the corridor. They were not enough. On June 26, the NKPA overran Uijongbu. They barely paused to celebrate their victory. Seoul lay ahead.

On Tuesday, June 27, the government of South Korea abandoned Seoul, moving to Taejon, ninety miles south. ROK Army headquarters also fled Seoul, heading fifteen miles south to Suwon. All that day North Korean airplanes flew over Seoul dropping leaflets urging surrender. Already thousands of civilian refugees were fleeing over the Han River bridges on Seoul's south side, joined by thousands more defeated ROK troops.

By midnight, advance elements of the NKPA had reached the northern outskirts of Seoul. Gallant ROK infantrymen drove them off, but it was a futile effort. Seoul's fate was sealed.

At 2:15 A.M., June 28, a panicked ROK engineer ignited demolition charges set under the Han bridges. The resulting explosions killed thousands of refugees. But even worse, over forty thousand ROK soldiers were left stranded north of the Han. Along with their vitally needed equipment and armament, most of them would disappear forever.

By nightfall of June 28, the NKPA held Seoul. South of the Han the ROK Army Command mustered only twenty-two thousand of the ninety-eight thousand men on its rolls just three days earlier. The South Korean Army, which three weeks previously had been called by *Time* magazine the best outside of the United States, had been destroyed.

Word of the North Korean attack arrived in Washington, D.C., because of the International Dateline, on the morning of Saturday, June 24. The attack caught the Americans by surprise. Though the U.S. government recognized the threat to South Korea from its northern neighbor, it had not anticipated an attack. After all, the United States, the strongest nation on earth, was the protector of South Korea. Communist North Korea wouldn't dare challenge the U.S.

The United States had assumed responsibility for South Korea in the waning days of World War II. Though the Allies had urged the Soviets to declare war against Japan throughout World War II, they did not do so until August 8, 1945, two days after the first atomic bomb was dropped on Hiroshima, sealing Japan's fate. The Soviet Union immediately sent an army of 120,000 men across the Yalu River, Korea's northern boundary with Manchuria, and headed south. Stalin had agreed at the Yalta Conference of the Big Four Allied Powers in 1944 to some form of international trusteeship for Korea, and had reaffirmed that commitment at the Potsdam Conference in 1945. But, an outright occupation of the little country by the Soviets is not what the other Allies had in mind. The government of the United States, as the dominant force in the Pacific, decided to send its own occupation forces to Korea.

The potential volatility of having two armed forces occupying the same territory did not escape the U.S. The State-War-Navy Coordinating Committee was given the task of developing occupational zones for the two powers, within which each would accept the surrender of the Japanese. Because the Thirty-eighth Parallel of latitude conveniently divided the peninsula nearly in half it was decided to use it as the dividing line.

Thus were formed North and South Korea.

The alliance was never an easy one. The U.S. soon concluded that Russia had very different ideas from its own for a solution to a divided Korea and would not cooperate. They further understood that without massive quantities of American military and economic aid Korea would not survive. And, from a purely military standpoint, any U.S. troops stationed there would be unavailable for use in the event of a large-scale war elsewhere in the world.

In fact, the last point was so significant the Joint Chiefs of Staff issued a report on September 26, 1947, that said, "From the standpoint of military security, the United States has little strategic interest in maintaining the present troops and bases in Korea."

A solution had to be found. A solution that would release the U.S. from a military liability yet hold out the promise for stability in Korea.

The solution was found in the United Nations. At America's urging, the U.N. accepted full responsibility, voting Korea a U.N. mandate. As part of the proposal the U.N. promised free elections in South Korea. They were held on May 10, 1948. Syngman Rhee, a conservative candidate backed by the U.S., was elected. The Republic of Korea was established on August 15, 1948.

Naturally, the USSR was unhappy with the U.N. proceedings. Not to be outdone, it established the Korean Democratic People's Republic with Kim Il Sung, a Soviet citizen and army officer, as premier. Sung quickly announced that his regime's primary objective was the reunification of Korea.

On January 1, 1949, the U.S. formally recognized the Republic of Korea. An ambassador was sent to Seoul and the remaining U.S. occupation forces were withdrawn. The U.S. did agree, however, to provide military assistance and training to the ROK armed forces.

One year later, on January 12, 1950, Secretary of State Dean Acheson, in a speech before the National Press Club in Washington, revealed that neither Korea nor Taiwan was included in the United States' security cordon for the Far East. According to overall U.S. policy, he said, the main Communist threat was to Europe. Moreover, the U.S. was ready and willing to accept another global war to defend it. Korea and Taiwan were of little use in a global war focusing on Europe.

Acheson's remarks were seen as a green light by the Soviets, who were convinced the U.S. had abandoned any interest or power position in Korea. Along with Chinese and North Korean leaders, they concluded the U.S. would not come to South Korea's aid if it were attacked by North Korea; the U.S. would stand aside as it had during the fall of Nationalist China.

Almost immediately the Communist leaders began planning for the invasion and capture of South Korea.

In Washington on June 24 and 25, government leaders did not fully grasp the implications of the NKPA attack. Most were convinced the action was a feint, designed to draw off U.S. military forces while the Soviet Union planned to overtake Europe. Only gradually, over several years, did American planners realize the Soviets might be willing to achieve their worldwide domination objective in small steps rather than in giant leaps.

At his home in Independence, Missouri, President Harry S. Truman was informed of the attack. He immediately made preparations to return to Washington and meet with the secretaries of state and defense on Sunday night, June 25.

In New York City U.N. Secretary General Trygve Lie received the news by telephone. Declaring "This is war against the United Nations," Lie called an emergency meeting of the U.N. Security Council for 2:00 P.M., Sunday.

At the U.N. meeting Sunday afternoon Lie swiftly proposed a resolution on the Korean crisis. Only one fact allowed the U.N. to move with such haste. On January 10, 1950, the Soviets had walked out of the Security Council over the issue of seating Red China. They had boycotted all subsequent meetings.

Without the Soviets to cast a veto the U.N. Security Council passed the resolution condemning the North Korean attack as a breach of peace. The resolution called for:

1. an immediate cessation of hostilities
2. North Korea to withdraw its forces north of the Thirty-eighth Parallel
3. all members of the U.N. to render every assistance to the U.N. in executing the resolution and to give no assistance to North Korea.

The resolution passed at 6:00 P.M.

Two hours later President Truman commenced his meeting in Washington. By 10:30 P.M., the U.S. government had also agreed to provide South Korea with whatever assistance it required.

A message was immediately sent to Gen. Douglas MacArthur, commanding general of the Far East Command in Tokyo, to send munitions and equipment to Korea. He was also authorized to provide needed air and naval support to assure its arrival and to evacuate American citizens.

Within hours jet fighters from Japan were flying reconnaissance missions over Seoul. When fired upon by three Soviet-built Yak fighters, the Americans blew them out of the sky. Four more Yaks were destroyed later that day.

Just five years after emerging victorious from World War II, the United States again found itself in a shooting war. A war it would not win.

General MacArthur personally visited the battleground, arriving at Suwon on June 29. He was given a briefing on the tactical situation, then was driven north toward the Han River to see, first-hand, the situation. What he saw of the decimated ROK Army left a vivid impression.

That night, back in Japan, he wired the Joint Chiefs of Staff a request for U.S. ground combat forces. He wanted the immediate deployment of a regimental combat team, to be followed by a two-division force. President Truman concurred.

On July 1, the 1st Battalion, 21st Infantry Regiment, U.S. 24th Infantry Division, under Lt. Col. Charles B. Smith, was alerted for immediate airborne movement from its garrison in Japan to Korea. The rest of the 24th Division, scattered throughout Japan, would follow in bits and pieces as transportation became available.

Task Force Smith began arriving at the Korean port of Pusan on July 2. It was supposed to be an intimidating display of U.S. military might. After all, America was at the very peak of being America. Nearly everyone in the U.S. government sincerely believed the mere appearance of American troops would cause the NKPA to recoil. Who would dare challenge the great United States of America?

That same aura of overconfidence had prevailed in Washington, D.C., in June 1861, when the Union forces under Gen. Irvin McDowell marched forth to meet the rebels at Bull Run. The same disastrous results that befell them awaited Task Force Smith.

Occupation duty in Japan had been a cushy assignment. A good time was had by all, with training more symbolic than actual. Little physical activity challenged the U.S. troops. There were just too many benefits to be enjoyed in Japan to bother with rigorous training. The men of Task Force Smith were not ready for a shooting war.

Four days after being alerted, the two infantry companies of Task Force Smith were dug in on the hillsides along the road running from Suwon to Osan, a few miles south. At 7:30 A.M., July 5, Colonel Smith spotted eight Soviet T-34 tanks moving south out of Suwon in a driving rain. Thirty minutes later Smith's artillery support opened fire. The four hundred men of TF Smith fully expected the tanks to turn and run once they faced the might of the U.S Army.

Instead, the T-34s paused momentarily, then continued forward.

"Jesus Christ," exclaimed one young infantryman, "they're still coming!"

Unperturbed by the thin line of American soldiers, the tanks rolled right past them. The T-34s advanced upon an artillery battery dug in several hundred yards behind the infantrymen and opened fire on the howitzer crews. A young machine gunner fell dead, the first American to die in Korea.

He would soon have a lot of company.

Ten minutes after the first platoon of tanks cruised past TF Smith, more rumbled down from the north. This time the American infantry engaged the tanks, but their light weapons did not faze the armored vehicles. The T-34s simply turned their cannons and machine guns on the soldiers. Within minutes twenty Americans lay dead or wounded. Then the tanks continued south.

An hour later two columns of NKPA infantry appeared on the road. Colonel Smith estimated the column to be six miles long, complete with more tanks and supply trucks. When they were just one thousand yards away Smith ordered, "Open fire!"

For seven hours the battle raged. But it was a vain attempt. The poorly trained and equipped Americans were no match for the tanks and well-disciplined infantrymen of the NKPA.

By late afternoon Smith concluded his situation was hopeless. He ordered the survivors of his companies to fall back to Osan. The withdrawal started smoothly but soon deteriorated into a panicked flight.

Frightened men left their weapons, equipment, and wounded buddies behind in their run for safety. Under heavy fire from the North Koreans the Americans broke into small groups, scattering across the rugged countryside. Those who managed to reach Osan found it already occupied by the T-34s. Some GIs headed east, others went west. Survivors straggled into American lines for days.

When it was all over Colonel Smith could only account for 250 of his men.

During the time TF Smith was advancing to Osan and fighting its battle, the rest of the 24th Infantry Division had been arriving in Korea by dribs and drabs.

WILLIAM F. DEAN

While Colonel Smith was loading his men aboard planes at Itazuke Air Base in Japan his division commander, Maj. Gen. William F. Dean, arrived with his final instructions. Dean, a tall man with close-cropped red hair, grimly shook hands with Smith. "When you get to Pusan, head immediately to Taejon. We want to stop the North Koreans as far from Pusan as possible. Go to Taejon and beyond, if you can. Sorry I can't give you more information, that's all I've got. We'll be there as soon as we can. Good luck, and God bless you and your men!"

By the time Smith's men saw their first T-34s Dean had moved his two remaining infantry regiments, the 19th and 34th, and the balance of the 21st to Korea. It hadn't been an easy task. Dean had commandeered every available seagoing transport in Japan in order to have the majority of his men in Pusan within two days. There they boarded trains for movement to Taejon and points north.

After establishing his division command post at Taejon, Korea's sixth largest city and a rapidly growing commercial center with a population of 130,000, Dean sent his regiments north. The 34th Infantry went to Pyongtaek, about fifteen miles south of Osan. He backed it up with a battalion of the 21st Infantry. Farther south, Dean set the 19th Infantry Regiment in positions on the south side of the Kum River at Taepyong-ni, just eight miles north of Taejon.

Dean told his regimental commanders, "By God, we must hold them. I don't want to have to fight for every mile of this ground again!"

Dean hoped to hold the NKPA back until promised reinforcements arrived. The U.S. 25th Infantry Division was already on its way from Okinawa and Japan, with the U.S. 1st Cavalry Division soon to follow. If his troops could hold the Taejon salient the arriving units might be enough to stall the North Koreans.

His troops did try but the green infantrymen, accustomed to the luxuries of occupation duty in Japan, were no match for the combat-proven NKPA. One after another the U.S. regiments were pushed back. Pyongtaek, Chonan, Chochiwon, then Taepyong-ni fell to the North Korean onslaught. For two weeks the regiments of the 24th Division were chewed up and pushed back. By July 17, Dean had had to pull the remnants of his division back to Taejon. On the 18th, Gen. Walton Walker, commander of the newly arrived Eighth Army, flew into Taejon.

"I need two days, Bill," Walton said. "In two days I can have the First Cav and the Twenty-fifth Infantry Division in positions east of here. I have every confidence you can do it." General Walker knew what he was doing. He couldn't have picked a better man for the job.

That afternoon, after Walker flew back to his headquarters at Taegu, forty miles north of Pusan, Dean sent his division headquarters and all but the 34th Infantry to Yongdong, twenty miles southeast of Taejon. He elected to remain with his combat troops in Taejon.

There were three reasons why Dean decided to stay put. First, he wanted to help boost the crumbling morale of the 34th Infantry; second, he wanted to set an example for the ROK troops fighting alongside the Americans; and, third, he wanted to see up close just what kind of a fighter the North Korean was.

The front lines were familiar territory to General Dean. As commander of the 44th Infantry Division battling the Nazis across France and Germany in World War II, Dean frequently took command of small units at the front. "I'm just a frustrated platoon leader," Dean jokingly told his corps commander after being cautioned about risking himself on the front lines.

During the December 8, 1944, attack on Echenberg, France, Dean found his division's timetable frustrated by a stubborn enemy artillery battery. Making his way to the front lines, he assumed command of an infantry platoon whose officer had been killed. He led the platoon forward through heavy gunfire to overrun the battery and get his division rolling again. When the company commander caught up with the platoon he was quite surprised to find his division commander as a member of his unit. The corps commander again chewed Dean out, then prepared a recommendation for the Distinguished Service Cross, which was awarded.

Dean was born in Carlyle, Illinois, on August 1, 1899. His father, a dentist, moved his family to Berkeley, California, when Dean was a youngster. From an early age Dean wanted to attend West Point. His failure to pass the tough competitive exams and win an appointment to the academy was a lifelong disappointment. "I just wasn't smart enough to pass the tests," he said later. But that failure didn't deter Dean from pursuing a military career. When he enrolled at the University of California in 1918 he also enlisted in the California National Guard.

Dean put himself through college by working at a variety of jobs, ranging from stevedore to policeman. In 1923, a year after he graduated from college, he passed an exam for a direct appointment as a second lieutenant, infantry, in the Regular Army. Promotion in the peacetime army came slowly. Dean spent twelve years as a lieutenant and five as a captain, but he was happy. Army life was for him.

Once the pre–World War II U.S. Army expansion began, promotion came quickly for the capable Dean. He was promoted to major in 1940, colonel two years later, and in 1943 received his first star and a post as assistant division commander of the 44th Infantry Division. By the time the division crossed the Normandy beaches in September 1944 Dean was its commander, sporting two stars.

After the war Dean was sent to the Far East, where he became military governor of South Korea in 1947. Two years later he went to Japan to command first the 7th Infantry Division, then the 24th Infantry Division. Now he was back in Korea. Since bringing his division to Korea on July 4, Dean had seen it nearly destroyed as he fought a series of delaying actions, trying to buy time for the Eighth Army to establish a firm perimeter along the Naktong River around Pusan, the seaport on the southeast coast of Korea. Dean didn't want to retreat anymore. He wanted a fight.

He got it beginning the next morning, July 19. The North Koreans announced their all-out assault on Taejon that morning with a tremendous artillery bombardment on U.S. positions north of the city. Dean told the officers at the 34th Infantry's CP that the barrage was worse than anything he'd seen in World War II. That didn't keep the feisty general from visiting the front lines throughout the day. Wherever the fighting was heaviest, Dean appeared. At one point, even though enemy rifle fire pocked the ground around him, Dean stood alongside an American tank, directing its fire against enemy positions.

That evening Dean appeared at his forward command post in Yongdong. His assistant division commander, Brig. Gen. Pearson Menoher, pleaded with Dean to stay at the CP. Dean refused. "I'll be okay," he said. "I want to be up there myself. I'll see you later." At 6:00 P.M. he drove back into the battle at Taejon.

Heavy gunfire awoke Dean before dawn the next morning. The NKPA had launched a determined two-division assault on the single understrength American regimental combat team still clinging to Taejon.

By 5:30 that morning defenders of the outlying U.S. positions began straggling back into town. The sound of enemy gunfire grew louder. Soon word reached Dean at the 34th's CP that enemy tanks were in Taejon. Dean wasn't content to sit idly by doing nothing. He gathered up some stragglers, armed them with bazookas, and took them tank hunting.

In a field west of town Dean spotted a disabled T-34. He directed the fire of a 75mm recoilless rifle against it but missed four times. Determined to hurt the enemy, Dean grabbed a hand grenade and started crawling down a furrow toward the tank. Halfway to his target enemy small-arms fire pinned him down. While he hugged the foul-smelling earth, two more enemy tanks arrived to cover the withdrawal of the disabled vehicle. Dean crawled away in disgust.

Dean spent most of the rest of the morning at the front lines, encouraging the men to hang on. He also spotted targets for his air cover and radioed precise bombing instructions to the pilots so his own men wouldn't be hit.

Around 11:30 Dean was again at the 34th's CP, nibbling at a C ration. At the time there wasn't much else for him to do. While he ate, a T-34 rolled defiantly by. Dean rounded up a bazooka crew and took off, yelling as he left, "I'm going tank hunting!"

Dean and his crew pursued the tank down the street, dodging sniper fire along the way. They ran down a side street parallel to the tank, snuck through several backyards, then climbed up to the second story of a Korean house facing the street. Dean peaked out the window. The muzzle of the tank's 85mm cannon pointed directly at him, only a dozen feet away.

The bazooka gunner aimed where the general pointed, and fired. The blowback from the rocket nearly knocked everyone in the room off his feet, but the round hit the tank dead on.

"Hit 'em again!" Dean roared.

Two more rounds streaked toward the tank, turning it into an inferno. As jubilant as a high school quarterback scoring his first touchdown, Dean whooped, "We got us a tank!"

Later Dean, his aide, Lt. Arthur Clarke, and another bazooka team found two more tanks on a street, just behind a burning American ammo carrier. Machine-gun fire from the tanks forced the hunters into a building fronting the street. The North Koreans thought they had driven Dean and the others away but the smoke and haze of the battle allowed the team to creep around to the tanks' rear.

With Dean again directing the fire and Clarke loading, the bazooka gunner took aim. But he was shaking too badly to hold his aim for long. When he pulled the trigger the rocket hit the street a few yards in front of him, exploding harmlessly.

Then he told Dean that he only had the one round.

The tanks now reversed, rolling right past Dean and his small party. Dean lost his temper. He pulled his .45-caliber automatic from its holster and emptied a full clip at the side of the first tank. The fat slugs bounced ineffectively off the thick armored hide. Then Dean and the others ran like hell.

Despite General Dean's heroic personal efforts and the last-ditch stand of the beleaguered 34th Infantry Regiment, it was apparent to everyone by mid-afternoon, July 20, that Taejon must fall. Dean ordered all available vehicles formed into convoys for the withdrawal. Just before the withdrawal began, several light tanks from the U.S. 1st Cavalry Division fought their way into Taejon. Dean ordered them to lead the first column out. Only moments after they left the assembly area the sound of a bitter firefight reached Dean and the others. Soon after, Dean helped organize the remaining regimental headquarters' vehicles into a rough column. They started to the east, the way the tank-led column had gone, hoping to reach Okchon and the 21st Infantry positioned there.

Dean's convoy quickly ran into the tail end of the first column, which had been ambushed. Many of its trucks were ablaze, while others stood askew along the street. Flimsy Korean buildings on both sides of the street burned furiously. U.S. infantry, on one side of the street, exchanged gunfire with NKPA infantry on the other.

The driver of Dean's jeep, careening around the burning and stalled trucks, floored the vehicle's accelerator. The heat from their flames was so intense it seared Dean and the others as they drove past. A few blocks farther on, Dean's driver roared through an intersection. Lieutenant Clarke yelled out, "We missed our turn." In the confusion the driver had driven right by the tricky turn to Okchon. Enemy gunfire prevented Dean and his escort jeep from turning around. Dean looked at a map and decided to continue on the road, heading south and east to Kumsan. American troops were supposed to be there, too.

Several times Dean stopped his jeeps to load wounded soldiers aboard. They were soon filled. Dean sent the two vehicles ahead. He'd walk out. Within minutes an artillery half-track rumbled by. It, too, was jammed with wounded soldiers but Dean managed to climb aboard.

Presently they came upon his two jeeps. NKPA machine gun fire from a roadblock had driven their occupants into a roadside ditch. Dean and the others joined them there. After a head count Dean gathered up all the men in the area, about twenty, and led them into a nearby field to await nightfall. Dean started them moving again about 7:30. Lieutenant Clarke scouted ahead. He quickly scurried back to tell the general he had stumbled upon an American soldier badly wounded in both legs. Dean said the man had to be carried out. By this time, most of the others had slipped away in the dark to fend for themselves. Only Dean, Clarke, and a handful of others remained. Clarke hoisted the man on his back but managed only a short distance before his own wounds weakened him. Dean loaded the man on his back.

The little band proceeded cross-country, struggling over the rugged terrain. Korea is a mountainous land. One hill after another stretches to the horizon wherever one looks. The slopes were difficult enough for an able-bodied man; for the fifty-year-old general carrying a delirious, wounded man they were near torture. Near the peak of a small hill several miles south of Taejon the group paused to rest. It was around 10:30 P.M. As they sat resting, Dean heard the gurgling of a mountain stream at the base of the hill. He grabbed a couple of empty canteens and headed for the water.

Halfway down the slope General Dean stumbled. Weak from hunger and the rigors of the battle, he was unable to break his fall. He plunged down the steep hill, struck his head on a rock, and lost consciousness.

When Dean didn't return after a reasonable time the others began to search frantically for him. In the darkness they failed to see his prostrate form by the stream. After awhile, hearing North Korean troops approaching, they abandoned the search. They continued south, reaching safety the next day. Clarke reported Dean missing in action. On January 9, 1951, the army announced that General Dean had been awarded the Medal of Honor for his intrepid leadership and outstanding valor. The medal was presented to Dean's wife by President Truman in the presence of Dean's mother and his two children. Since no report of Dean as a prisoner had been received from the North Koreans, the general's fate was still unknown. It was feared he was dead.

But Dean wasn't dead. He had regained consciousness at 2:30 A.M., though he wasn't sure if he had been out for four hours or twenty-eight. He managed to crawl to the stream and swallow a few gulps of water before passing out again. When he came to, his watch read 4:30. He soon became aware of severe pain. He had broken his left shoulder and several ribs in the fall.

At dawn Dean crawled into some nearby bushes and stayed there all day, only barely conscious. As darkness fell he started walking. Movement up the steep hill was difficult, as his one shoulder was nearly useless. He managed to gain the summit, then followed a ridge line until it ended in a sheer cliff. After painfully making his way to the base of the cliff, Dean fell asleep there. He was still lying there in the morning when approaching footsteps sent him scrambling behind a large rock. He pulled his .45. In the faint light Dean recognized the outline of an American helmet. It was an officer from the 34th. The men hugged in the dark, then resumed walking south.

They struggled through the countryside for several days, foraging for vegetables in native gardens. One night hunger drove them to seek refuge in a Korean village. They were given food and a bed to sleep on, in an apparent friendly gesture. In the middle of the night they heard shots and a voice calling, "Come out, Americans. We will not kill you."

The two officers emerged with their pistols blazing and managed to elude capture. In the darkness they became separated. Dean called to his comrade several times but his only answer was gunfire. Though he hated to do so, Dean finally had to proceed alone.

Two days later, his fifty-first birthday, Dean had his last solid food for three weeks. His weight dropped from 190 to 130 pounds while he wandered through the Korean countryside, sustained only by water he found in streams. His sole protection was his .45 and twelve rounds of ammo. Eleven for the enemy and one for himself, he decided.

Several times during his ordeal Dean was nearly captured by members of village "home guards" but managed to break away each time. From then on he traveled only at night.

Finally the inevitable happened. Dean fell into the company of two Koreans, one of whom spoke English, who promised to lead him to safety. Instead, they betrayed him. When one of the guides beckoned Dean around a bend in the road North Koreans rushed forward. Dean reached for his pistol, but the other guide knocked it from his hand. It was August 25, 1950.

Dean's ordeal at the hands of his North Korean and Chinese captors would last three years. Throughout his captivity he was denied access to other Americans. He was moved frequently; the sites ranged from a house in Manchuria to a cave in North Korea. So closely did the North Koreans guard knowledge of Dean's imprisonment that word of his capture did not leak out until December 1951.

In September 1953 Dean was repatriated. Dressed in an ill-fitting suit, orange shirt, red tie, and gold cap provided by his captors, he walked slowly and painfully to the American side of Freedom Village, the repatriation site at Panmunjom. During his captivity he had suffered much illness and hardship. His captors had never given him proper medical attention for his broken shoulder and other injuries. He was fifty-four but looked at least ten years older.

Following a bath, a medical exam, and a hot meal, Dean was told his gallantry at Taejon had earned him the Medal of Honor. He stared in disbelief. "I expected to be court-martialed," he said. "I don't understand it."

General Dean never accepted himself as a hero. "Anyone who's dumb enough to get captured doesn't deserve to be a hero," he said later. He remained in the army a few more years, retiring in 1955. He settled in Berkeley where he took an active role in local Boy Scout activities. There he died on August 24, 1981.

Another hero emerged during the frightful flight from Taejon on the night of July 20, 1950. Enemy gunfire at a roadblock east of town disabled the truck on which Sgt. George D. Libby rode, killing or wounding everyone on it except him. The thirty-year-old member of Company C, 3d Engineer Combat Battalion, crawled into a roadside ditch and took the enemy under fire. Twice he rushed across the bullet-swept road to aid wounded buddies. He stopped an M-5 artillery tractor approaching the roadblock and put the wounded on it. Once they were loaded, he took up a position on the outside of the truck, on the enemy side of the driver. Libby deliberately elected to expose himself to the vicious enemy fire, protecting the driver, as he realized no one else present could operate the tractor.

In this position Libby, a World War II veteran of the fighting in Europe, rode "shotgun" for the tractor and its load of wounded, returning the enemy's fire. The tractor stopped several times so Libby could help other wounded aboard. While passing through the first roadblock Libby was hit by enemy fire several times in the body and arms. At a second roadblock he was hit again. Now too weak to fire his carbine, Libby pulled himself erect in order to give the driver as much protection as possible. Struck several more times by enemy rounds, Libby collapsed and subsequently died from loss of blood, but his selfless actions allowed the driver to get his load of wounded through to safety.

At noon on July 22, the U.S. 1st Cavalry Division relieved the U.S. 24th Infantry Division at the new front line east of Yongdong. In its seventeen days of combat the 24th Infantry Division had been driven back a hundred miles, lost enough matériel to equip a full-strength infantry division, and suffered in excess of thirty percent casualties. Over two thousand of its members were listed as missing in action.

But had it not been committed to battle, the rest of the U.S. forces under the Eighth Army could not have been established in Korea. Besides the 1st Cavalry, the 25th Infantry Division had also recently arrived from Japan. The 2d Infantry Division came directly from the States, as did the 1st Marine Provisional Brigade. Two separate regimental combat teams, the 29th from Okinawa and the 5th from Hawaii, had been sent to Korea, too.

In spite of the persistent loss of terrain and men, these fresh units brought new optimism to the embattled peninsula. General Walker continued the withdrawals, but now they were for sound tactical reasons—the need to buy time and reorganize. Walker's forces broke contact with the NKPA on July 31, 1950. By August 4, all units had withdrawn behind the new Naktong River line in southeast Korea.

The new U.N. perimeter had the Korean Strait at its back on the east and on the south; the Naktong River formed its western boundary. Then it cut east to the coastal town of Yongdok, ninety miles north of Pusan. The entire front stretched 170 miles. If Walker could hold the North Koreans at bay it would allow time for more U.S. and U.N. forces to be assembled and brought to Korea. But first he had to hold the NKPA.

The strongest enemy drive against the Pusan Perimeter came at its southern edge, along the Chinju-Masan corridor. Walker concentrated his reinforcements there as quickly as they arrived in Korea. Because of his strength in this area, Walker decided to launch a counterattack there. Task Force Kean, named for the 25th Infantry Division's commander, Maj. Gen. William B. Kean, consisted of two regiments of the 25th Division, the 5th RCT, and the 1st Marine Brigade. The attacking regiments would drive westward toward Chinju, twenty-seven miles from Masan. TF Kean was set to jump off on the first U.N. offensive of the war on August 7, 1950. But first some pockets of North Korean infantry isolated within the American lines had to be handled. For this task Kean selected his all-black 24th Infantry Regiment.

Although President Truman had ordered the desegregation of the armed forces in 1947, the U.S. Army had not fully complied with that edict by the time of the Korean War. As a result, the 25th Infantry Division still had one of its regiments, the 24th Infantry, staffed entirely with black enlisted men. As was the custom, most of its officers were white.

One of the oldest of the army's regular infantry regiments, the 24th had been formed at Fort McKavitt, Texas, in 1869. The 24th Infantry Regiment fought Indians throughout the American West of the 1870s and 1880s. In 1898 it fought in Cuba and later saw duty in the Philippines. Two of its black enlisted men earned Medals of Honor during the Indian Wars.

Members of the 24th Regiment were not allowed to fight for their country in World Wars I or II. Following stevedore service in the Pacific during the Second World War, the 24th was sent to Japan as part of the occupation forces.

Along with the rest of the 25th Infantry Division, the 24th Regiment deployed to Korea from its bases in Japan between July 10 and 15, 1950. It was quickly rushed to the front lines north and west of Taegu where it fought a series of withdrawals into the Pusan Perimeter. Walker subsequently assigned the 25th Division to the southernmost sector of the perimeter, an area west of Pusan. During the withdrawals the 24th Infantry Regiment performed no better or worse than its sister regiments. However, the regiment's fighting retreats were described as panicked routs by racially prejudiced observers. As a result, the 24th Regiment now received only a secondary role in TF Kean's counterattack. It was to clear enemy troops from the mountainous area in and around Sobuk-san, about ten miles west of Masan.

WILLIAM THOMPSON

After a platoon from Company M, the heavy weapons unit of the 24th Regiment, had provided support to a rifle company clearing out the hamlet of Haman, a few miles north of Sobuk-san in a mountain valley, it was ordered back to a rear assembly area. It had no sooner reached there when the NKPA viciously fell on it. Enemy automatic-weapons fire racked the men.

Many of them panicked, fleeing into the night. Those that didn't were organized into a tight defensive perimeter by 2d Lt. Herbert H. Wilson. He ordered two machine guns into action. Almost immediately one of them was knocked out by an exploding enemy grenade. The other, manned by Pfc. William Thompson, continued sending out bursts of fire. It quickly became the focal point of the enemy's return fire.

Little is known of Thompson's early life. Born out of wedlock in Brooklyn, New York, on August 16, 1927, he had dropped out of school at an early age. Most of his teen years were spent roaming the streets of his tenement-filled neighborhood. With an unsure future he sought the best opportunity.

As were many of his peers, Thompson was drawn to army life. Not only did the army provide the security he had not known in New York, it was one of the few niches in American society of the 1940s where a black youth could feel some degree of comfort. Thompson enlisted in the army in October 1945. He spent his two-year tour in Adak, Alaska.

Thompson reenlisted in January 1948. He was sent to the 6th Infantry Division, then on occupation duty in Korea. When that outfit transferred to the United States, Thompson was sent to the 24th Infantry Regiment in Japan.

A thin, hollow-eyed, quiet soldier, Thompson was typical of the many anonymous men who make up the Regular Army. He never aspired to rank or responsibility; he was far more satisfied with taking orders than giving them. He did take a fierce pride in his ability to adhere to the peacetime army's high standards. He kept his uniform and equipment spotless. His machine gun was always one of the cleanest in the company. And he was considered one of the best shots in the regiment. Rarely was he in any trouble. He was just one of those men who find a home in the lower ranks of the military.

When the NKPA soldiers renewed their attack on the Americans' small position, Thompson moved his machine gun directly into their path. He began mowing them down with deadly accurate bursts of fire. Belt after belt of .30-caliber ammo disappeared into Thompson's gun. His fire drove the attackers to cover.

In the lull Lieutenant Wilson ordered his remaining men to pull back to higher ground. Wilson then crawled out to Thompson. He saw the man had been wounded several times; Thompson was bleeding heavily. "Let's go," Wilson said. "We can get out of here now."

Thompson refused. He told the lieutenant he knew he was dying and was not going to move back. He kept triggering short bursts of fire at any enemy soldier foolish enough to expose himself. Wilson now ordered Thompson to withdraw but he again refused. "I may not get out," he told the lieutenant, "but I'll take a lot of them with me."

Wilson called forward two noncommissioned officers. One of the NCOs, Corporal Washington, grabbed Thompson. He managed to pull the machine gunner off his weapon, but Thompson broke away.

"Get out of here!" he screamed to the others. "I'll cover you!" Then he began firing again at the advancing NKPA. Reluctantly, Wilson ordered the rest of his platoon to retreat. As they headed into the hills they could hear Thompson's gun chattering away. They could also hear the *karumpf* of exploding NKPA grenades. Finally, after one sharp grenade explosion, Thompson's machine gun fell silent.

A few days later Company M retook the area. Scattered around Thompson's lifeless body was the evidence of his gallant one-man stand. He had taken a lot of them with him.

Private First Class William Thompson's posthumous Medal of Honor was presented to his mother by General of the Army Omar N. Bradley on June 21, 1951.

As for TF Kean, it quickly ground to a halt as it ran headlong into stubborn NKPA resistance. After a series of seesaw battles over a two-week period TF Kean was disbanded.

Air support, both tactical and strategic, played a major role in preventing North Korean forces from overrunning all of Korea during the first weeks of the war. Beginning with the first seven Yaks destroyed over Seoul on the opening day of the war, the Far East Air Force, by early August, had been credited with destroying some one hundred ten enemy planes, leaving the NKPA with an air force of about twenty planes.

In addition to winning superiority in the sky, the pilots of the FEAF provided close-air support to their brothers on the ground, helping gain the time necessary to bring in reinforcements and supplies to make the Pusan Perimeter a reality. By the time General Walker consolidated his troops along the Naktong, the air force had all but stopped the movement of enemy troops, armor, and supplies during daylight hours. This imposed the greatest of difficulties on the already overextended North Korean supply lines and helped slow the NKPA advance.

Sometimes the air force pilots went to extraordinary lengths to help their ground-pounding buddies.

LOUIS J. SEBILLE

Twelve days after the Japanese bombed Pearl Harbor, Louis J. Sebille enlisted in the U.S. Army Air Corps at Chicago, Illinois. Born November 21, 1915, at Harbor Beach, Michigan, on the shores of Lake Huron, Sebille earned his wings and fought as a P-51 fighter pilot with the 9th Air Force in Europe. He was demobilized in the fall of 1945. He found he missed flying the powerful Mustang and returned to active duty in the summer of 1946. Two years later he was assigned to Clark Field in the Philippines.

Major Sebille had been ordered to bring his squadron, the 67th Fighter-Bomber Squadron, 18th Group, to Japan on August 1, 1950, to support the U.N. forces. In the next five days his men flew dozens of sorties against the NKPA.

Around noon on August 5, a forward air controller spotted a target near Hamchang, the point where the Pusan Perimeter line turned east to meet the sea. At a river crossing about five miles southwest of Hamchang, the FAC saw a large convoy of enemy trucks, horse-drawn artillery, and supporting troops trying to cross in broad daylight.

He immediately reported the target to the Joint Operations Center at Taegu. They in turn relayed the data to the ready flight on standby in Japan. Within minutes of the sighting Major Sebille was leading a flight of four P-51s to the scene.

Halfway across the 160 miles of the Korean Strait Sebille's wingman suffered an engine malfunction. He turned back to Japan. Sebille and the two others, Capt. Martin H. Johnson and his wingman, Lt. Charles R. Morehouse, bore on through the nearly cloudless sky. Once in the vicinity of Hamchang they radioed the FAC for further instructions.

The FAC was orbiting two thousand feet above a camouflaged NKPA truck he had picked as the focal point of the attack by the P-51s. Sebille, followed by the two others, dropped down for a look. In addition to the trucks, they spotted horse-drawn artillery hung up on a sandbar in the middle of the river.

Sebille radioed Johnson, "This'll be like shooting fish in a barrel."

He roared in on a low pass and dropped a five-hundred-pound bomb. It exploded with devastating effect among the enemy. While Johnson and Morehouse strafed the NKPA along the river's banks to keep their heads down, Sebille dived down for another pass. He pushed the bomb release lever. Nothing happened. He zoomed into the air, rolled over, and dropped back down again. Once again the bomb failed to drop.

In the meantime Johnson had spotted a group of ammo trucks on the river's west bank, all but obscured by trees. Sebille decided these would make good targets for the P-51's rockets. He called his team in for an attack.

Sebille went in first. It was quickly apparent the North Koreans had some antiaircraft weapons concealed in the woods. The Mustangs were drawing heavy fire.

After Johnson completed his run he pulled in alongside Sebille. He didn't like what he saw. Sebille's plane was trailing smoke. It was either on fire or rapidly losing engine coolant. Frantically, Johnson tried to raise Sebille on the radio. Finally he got through.

"They hit me," was all Sebille said.

Johnson advised his boss to head for an emergency landing strip near Taegu. "You can make it," he said. "It's only five miles away."

During this conversation the planes had completed two full circles high above the targets. To Johnson, Sebille seemed to have full control of his aircraft, although it was now obvious Sebille's plane was rapidly losing coolant.

It was only five minutes' flying time to safety, or, at worst, a crash landing behind friendly lines.

Johnson was startled when Sebille came back on the radio. "I can't make it back," the calm, but strained, voice said. "I'm going down there and getting those SOBs."

The words were no sooner out of Sebille's mouth than he made a tight turn, went into a thirty-degree dive, and headed toward the ammo trucks at better than 350 miles per hour. Sebille never wavered from the course he set for himself.

The FAC looked down just in time to see the final phase. As Sebille drew into point-blank range he opened up on the ammo trucks with his six wing-mounted .50-caliber machine guns. He flew squarely into the truck compound with all six guns blazing. He was still carrying a number of rockets and the five-hundred-pound bomb when he hit his target.

Johnson and Morehouse watched in stunned horror and fascination as a huge fireball exploded across the ground, engulfing nearby trucks and dozens of NKPA troops. The pilots could do nothing more. Sadly, they headed their planes back to their base at Ashiya.

A few days later General Walker expressed his appreciation for the air force pilots who had helped him in Korea. He must have been thinking of Sebille when he said, "Their effort has been of tremendous value to our forces and has saved many, many lives of our infantry troops."

Sebille's Medal of Honor was awarded on August 24, 1951.

Chapter Two
Pusan Defense

Once secured within the Pusan Perimeter, General Walker could finally form a continuous, solid battle line. His Eighth Army was spread thin, but both his flanks were firmly anchored on the sea, denying the NKPA the opportunity to turn them. Along the perimeter's northern edge Walker placed five ROK divisions: the 3d, Capital, 8th, and 6th, from east to west, and, along the northern end of the north-south line running along the Naktong River, the 1st Infantry Division. Next in line came the U.S. 1st Cavalry Division, then the U.S. 24th Infantry Division, and, at the southern end of the Naktong, the U.S. 25th Infantry Division with the U.S. 5th Regimental Combat Team attached, and the U.S. 1st Marine Provisional Brigade.

At the southeastern tip of the perimeter the port city of Pusan witnessed a flurry of activity in the first weeks of August. Working around the clock, transportation and quartermaster personnel poured in tons of supplies and equipment to replace those lost in the rout down the Korean peninsula. More importantly, thousands of American replacements came ashore. Some came from Japan where Operation *Flushout* had separated GIs from their desks and motor pools and rushed them to Korea as infantry replacements. Some came directly from the States because in July President Truman had authorized calling up the reserve forces. He asked for four National Guard divisions, hundreds of support units, and thousands of individual reservists. World War II veterans suddenly found themselves once again donning their uniforms.

By August 5, 1950, Walker's U.N. force—the United Nations had given the command of its efforts in South Korea to the United States, and the

Republic of Korea, though not a member, had placed its armed forces under U.N. command—had a strength of 141,800. About eighty-two thousand of these were ROKs. American combat ground strength alone stood at forty-seven thousand. By the end of the month American replacements and rein- forcements would bring their forces to over seventy thousand.

Against the Pusan Perimeter the North Koreans mounted eleven divisions totaling about seventy thousand men. Their push into South Korea had cost them between forty thousand and fifty thousand casualties. But replacements were hurriedly fed into their lines, some impressed from the overrun popu- lation of South Korea. These conscripts were hardly soldiers, but they were led by battle-hardened sergeants who did not hesitate to shoot reluctant re- cruits. Before long the NKPA divisions were near full strength.

Despite its successes, North Korean Premier Kim Il Sung was not satis- fied with his army's progress. All of Korea was not yet in his possession. The tenacious hold of the ROKs and Americans around Pusan frustrated his desire to control the entire peninsula. He ordered his commanders to crush completely the pesky defenders.

Marshal Choe Yong Gun, the field commander of the NKPA, ordered his subordinates to launch a massive blow against the Pusan Perimeter on Sep- tember 1, 1950. His two corps commanders, Lt. Gen. Kim Ung heading the NKPA I Corps from Taegu south and Lt. Gen. Kim Mu Chong leading the NKPA II Corps from Taegu east, prepared five major attacks against the U.N. forces.

Two NKPA divisions would penetrate the U.S. 25th Infantry Division in the south. Four NKPA divisions were allocated to destroy the U.S. 2d Infan- try Division west of Yongsan and capture the important road junction at Miryang twelve miles farther east. Three divisions would break through the U.S. 1st Cavalry and ROK 1st Infantry Divisions around Taegu. Two NKPA divisions would attack the ROK 6th and 8th Infantry Divisions at Taegu, while two more would smash the ROK 3d and Capital divisions along the east coast. If all went well, the hated Americans and their South Korean puppets would be driven into the sea in a matter of days.

A preview of the main attack occurred on August 25, as NKPA units moved into position. Company C, 5th Infantry Regiment, 24th Infantry Di- vision, manned a ridge line near Sobuk-san, a few miles south of Haman. At approximately 11:00 P.M., one of the company's outposts reported that about a hundred North Koreans were making their way toward the company's lines. Immediately, the GIs went on full alert. Within minutes an intense barrage of enemy mortar rounds and artillery shells fell on the American company. The infantrymen crouched deep in their holes. Overhead, murderous shards of shrapnel cut through the darkness. Small-arms fire from the attackers soon added to the din.

Determined to halt the onslaught against his understrength company, Master Sgt. Melvin O. Handrich of Manawa, Wisconsin, voluntarily crawled out of his foxhole. Making his way across the fire-swept ground, Handrich took an exposed position at the base of an outcropping of rocks. From there he had a clear view of the enemy's advance. Giving crisp and precise instructions, the thirty-one-year-old World War II veteran radioed firing directions to his supporting mortar and artillery batteries.

For the next eight hours Handrich fearlessly held his exposed position. When a squad of NKPA infantrymen snuck to within fifty feet of Handrich's position he calmly took them under fire with his carbine. Six North Koreans soon lay sprawled on the rocky hillside.

Just past 6:00 A.M. another enemy force of about 150 men stormed the beleaguered company's position. Still at the forefront of the American resistance, Handrich left what little cover he had and climbed atop a large boulder. From there he continued to call down salvo after salvo of deadly accurate artillery fire. When some North Koreans escaped the artillery bursts, Handrich boldly stood up and coldly cut them down with rifle fire.

In spite of Handrich's valiant efforts the enemy overran a portion of the company's battered perimeter. A group of American GIs panicked and broke for the rear. Handrich was on them in an instant. "Get back up there, dammit!" he exhorted. "This fight's not over yet."

Handrich got the rattled men back on the line. As he took a position among them, enemy bullets tore into his back and leg. Though suffering excruciating pain, Handrich refused treatment or evacuation. Instead, he made his way back to his previous position where he continued calling in the artillery.

Just after 7:00 A.M. the NKPA succeeded in overwhelming Handrich's position. He went down, firing his carbine into the mass of enemy soldiers rushing him. When the remnants of his company retook the position later that morning, seventy-one enemy dead lay in and around the position Handrich had so valiantly defended.

Around 9:00 P.M. on the evening of August 31, 1950, the main NKPA offensive began when artillery unexpectedly crashed down on American and ROK positions all along their thinly held line. At first the artillery bursts were sporadic; the North Koreans were simply getting the range. Over the next hour the exploding 76mm shells built in intensity. Soon the individual bursts were indistinguishable from one another.

Deep in their foxholes the weary GIs and ROK soldiers trembled with each concussion. Behind the wall of crashing artillery shells the NKPA soldiers advanced. The North Korean skirmishers moved out of the night, rifles blazing, chanting, "Manzai! Manzai!" (This was the Korean equivalent of "Banzai," used by Japanese troops in World War II suicide charges.)

By midnight nearly every position along the perimeter was under attack.

Bitter, bloody fighting erupted as the two desperate forces clashed. Here and there the NKPA flowed between the thinly spaced U.N. positions. In some places the NKPA ran headlong into the U.N. defenders and was stalled. At other sites the NKPA quickly rolled over the panicked defenders.

A major breakthrough anywhere at the five attack points would have resulted in disaster. However, the most serious threat developed near the southern end of the perimeter, at the Naktong Bulge, a natural attack route into the Pusan Perimeter. A breach here and the NKPA had a straight shot at Miryang.

A few miles north of the confluence of the Naktong and the Nam Rivers, the Naktong takes a wide bow to the west. It runs for several miles in that direction before turning first north then back east, where it finally continues its north-south run. The resulting bulge encloses a loop of land stretching four miles by five miles. The ground enclosed on three sides by the Naktong is hilly along the river, then flattens as it moves east. The town of Yongsan anchors the bulge's eastern edge. Major roads run in all four directions out of Yongsan.

The NKPA had previously breached the Naktong Bulge in early August. A surprise attack in the early morning hours of August 5 caught the defending U.S. 24th Infantry Division by surprise. Weakened by its fight into the perimeter, the 24th rapidly gave ground under heavy pressure. Only the timely arrival of units of the fresh U.S. 2d Infantry Division and the 1st Marine Provisional Brigade halted the NKPA just five miles west of Yongsan. Not until nightfall of August 17 was the NKPA driven back across the Naktong.

The 2d Division's 9th Infantry Regiment stayed and took over the defense of the southern portion of the bulge. Because of the near desperate shortage of manpower, the regiment was forced to defend a twenty-thousand-yard front, an area normally held by a full division. The GIs of the 9th Regiment only occupied the strategic high ground facing the Naktong, leaving huge gaps in the line. On the night of August 31, these were quickly discovered by the attacking NKPA 9th Infantry Division, which rushed through them headed eastward. Only the gallant conduct of individual soldiers prevented a disaster.

On the left flank of the 9th Infantry Regiment's southernmost company, Company A, two Pershing tanks from Company A, 72d Tank Battalion, and supporting tracked antiaircraft vehicles, stood guard at the little Korean town of Agok.

ERNEST R. KOUMA

Commanding one of the Pershings was Sgt. 1st Class Ernest R. Kouma. Born in Dwight, Nebraska, on November 23, 1919, Kouma had enlisted in the army in June 1940. As an infantry staff sergeant Kouma had led a squad of the 1st Infantry Division across the beaches of Normandy on D-Day. Ten months of near constant combat followed as the Allies chased the Germans across France, into Belgium, Germany, and, finally, Czechoslovakia.

After returning to the States in the fall of 1945, Kouma decided to make the army a career. He enjoyed the camaraderie among the NCOs and the sense of purpose and accomplishment that came to victorious soldiers. In March 1946 he drew an assignment with the occupation troops in South Korea. He remained there for a year and a half. Then he went to Fort Lewis, Washington, and the command of a tank in the 72d Tank Battalion.

On the night of August 31, Kouma had the early evening watch. A thick blanket of fog obscured the Naktong, a scant forty yards away. He strained to hear or see something in the night but all he could hear was the barking of dogs from the cluster of huts comprising Agok.

Starting around 8:00 P.M., light mortar fire began falling in the area. The shells crashed down only sporadically, so Kouma ignored them to maintain his vigil. Then just before midnight the fog lifted.

Kouma was startled to see a pontoon bridge already reaching two-thirds of the way across the Naktong. Enemy soldiers were cleary visible, moving along the bridge's length.

"Fire!" Kouma instantly ordered his gunner.

Seconds later the tank's 90mm cannon roared. Kouma manned the tank's turret-mounted .50-caliber machine gun. Thick fingers of red-hot lead sliced through the night, tearing into the North Koreans. Soon the second tank, commanded by Sfc. Oscar V. Berry, added its cannon to the carnage. Then the antiaircraft vehicles joined in with their dual 40mm's and quad .50-caliber machine guns.

Under that fusillade of fire the bridge collapsed, the pontoons drifting downstream with the current. Scores of enemy soldiers foundered in the water. But the NKPA had already crossed the river elsewhere. Sudden firing erupted around the infantry positions on the slopes above Agok.

Under intense pressure the infantry pulled out. One of the soldiers called out to Kouma as he fled, "We're pulling out, tankers."

"We're not," Kouma called back. If he left now the NKPA would slaughter the infantrymen. He had to hold.

About that time seven Koreans, wearing U.S. uniforms with 2d Infantry Division patches and speaking English, approached Kouma's tank. The American sergeant was up top, feeding a fresh belt of ammo into the .50 caliber. "The North Koreans have broken through. Company A's gone," one of them announced.

Before Kouma could respond, the Korean who spoke gave a signal. All seven tossed grenades at the tank, then scattered. At the same time a machine gun in the hills, recently occupied by the American infantry, opened fire on the tanks.

With bullets splattering off the tank's hull, Kouma instantly swung his gun around and returned the enemy's fire. The enemy grenades exploded. Hot shards of metal tore into Kouma's foot. He ignored the pain to keep up his fire.

Several hundred yards behind Kouma the antiaircraft vehicle armed with quad .50s suddenly erupted in a ball of fire. The bogus ROKs had snuck up on that vehicle and destroyed it, killing its crew. All the members of the half-track mounting the twin 40mm's were wounded in the same attack. They retreated.

Buttoned up inside his Pershing, Kouma radioed instructions to Berry. Together the two huge armored vehicles moved into open ground, blazing away with all weapons, cutting wide swaths through the charging NKPA. Under Kouma's skillful leadership the two tanks beat off repeated waves of North Koreans.

After about an hour of heavy fighting Berry radioed to Kouma. His engine was overheating; it had taken a round from a North Korean rifle. Berry was pulling out. Was Kouma coming?

No, Kouma told him. He'd stay put, holding off the NKPA and covering Berry's withdrawal. Berry wished him well and headed for Yongsan. A mile down the road his engine caught fire. The crew abandoned the vehicle, reaching safety after daylight.

Back along the Naktong, Kouma continued his gallant stand. For seven hours he held his position, battling the invaders. Repeatedly, he exposed himself on the tank's rear deck to man the .50-caliber machine gun. Under his deadly accurate fire the North Koreans fell in droves. Even though he took a round through his shoulder, Kouma held his position, firing his machine gun and tossing grenades.

Finally, at 7:30 A.M., with the enemy attacks waning and his tank running low on ammo, Kouma decided it was time to pull back. He guided his Pershing through eight miles of enemy-infested territory. Three separate times NKPA machine guns took him under fire. Calmly, Kouma aimed the tank's big 90mm gun, then fired. When the smoke cleared each machine gun lay ruined, its crew sprawled dead.

When he reached his company's CP, Kouma immediately headed for the ammo dump. He wanted to return to the fight. Instead, his CO ordered him to the aid station. Once patched up, Kouma headed right back to his tank. Again his CO intercepted him. This time he ordered Kouma to the evacuation station. His war was over.

After the Naktong Bulge was retaken, over 250 enemy bodies were counted in the area where Kouma made his stand. His fearlessness had been largely responsible for delaying the enemy's timetable and allowing the American infantry time to regroup.

President Truman presented Sergeant Kouma the Medal of Honor on May 19, 1951. The hero remained in the army, retiring as a master sergeant.

In the hills above Agok the positions of Company A, 9th Infantry Regiment, were instantly threatened by the hordes of North Koreans pouring across the Naktong. In the nightmarish confusion of that bullet-swept night the actions of one man stood out.

Pfc. Luther H. Story, manning an observation post overlooking the river, was among the first to spot the advancing enemy. At about the same time Kouma opened fire, Story unlimbered a machine gun and fired down on the NKPA soldiers. His fire allowed his company to reorganize for a better defense. Comrades estimated Story cut down over a hundred North Koreans in the brief, but bitter, action.

Later, after the remnants of the battered company had been ordered to withdraw, Story boldly destroyed a soldier-filled enemy truck by standing square in the middle of a dirt road and flipping a grenade into it as it roared past.

A short time later Story's luck ran out when he stopped a chestful of enemy bullets. Rather than retreat, the twenty-one-year-old resident of Americus, Georgia, volunteered to cover his buddies' withdrawal. Cpl. Charles O. Courtney tried to talk Story out of it. "Hell no, I'm staying," Story told him.

When last seen, Story was on his knees firing every weapon available at the swarm of North Koreans closing in on him. Courtney said, "Story was the bravest soldier I ever knew."

About five miles north of where Kouma and Story fought, Company B, 9th Infantry Regiment, held Hill 209, overlooking a ferry site across the Naktong. It was here that the 2d Infantry Division had coincidentally planned an offensive of its own. Dubbed Operation Manchu, the mini-offensive called for Company E to make an aggressive foray west of the Naktong while Company B provided cover. The heavy weapons company, Company H, would furnish additional supporting fire.

The NKPA attack caught the GIs flatfooted. Earlier that evening, while Company E was still forming up near Yongsan, Lt. Edward Schmitt took his Company H up Hill 209. By 8:00 P.M. Schmitt had his weapons emplaced where they could most effectively lay down a base of fire for the crossing. An hour later they were desperately fighting for survival as the North Koreans swarmed up the rocky slope.

Schmitt led a withdrawal onto a wide knob of Hill 209. By the time they got there only seventy-five of his men remained. The survivors had only a jumble of weapons—a radio, three light machine guns, a Browning Automatic Rifle (BAR), a handful of M-1s and about two dozen carbines and pistols. They used them as effectively as they could against the NKPA which streamed by them throughout the night.

When daylight finally broke Schmitt and his men realized they were surrounded. Where Company B had been the night before, only North Koreans were now visible. Below them to the west they could see long columns of enemy troops moving eastward. And the enemy saw them. The NKPA began a series of attacks against the small force of Americans that would last three days.

JOSEPH R. OUELLETTE
TRAVIS E. WATKINS

Because he thought there still might be some Americans trapped at Company B's position, Lieutenant Schmitt decided to send a patrol to reconnoiter the area. One of the four volunteers was Pfc. Joseph R. Ouellette. A native of Lowell, Massachusetts, Ouellette had enlisted in the army on his eighteenth birthday, January 30, 1948. Following basic training, the youngster joined the 2d Infantry Division at Fort Lewis, Washington. He went with them to Korea in July.

When Schmitt asked for volunteers to try to contact any Company B survivors, Ouellette was one of the first to step forward. As soon as it was light enough to see, the patrol set out across the four hundred yards of rocky terrain. No sooner had it reached the foot of the knoll where they believed the Americans might be holed up than enemy machine-gun fire laced the area. The patrol members dove for cover. Unwilling to abandon the mission, Ouellette crawled over to M. Sgt. Grover L. Bozarth, the patrol leader.

"Cover me," Ouellette told him. "I'll sneak up the hill and see if anyone's there."

Before Bozarth could even consider the proposal, Ouellette was gone. Bounding from one cluster of rocks to the next, Ouellette made his way upward. Bursts of enemy machine-gun fire slammed into the ground near the youth, but miraculously missed him.

Ouellette made the top of the knoll unscathed. The only Americans there were dead, their corpses already bloated in the summer heat. Ouellette spent several minutes alone on the knoll searching foxholes for any survivors. He even snuck down the far side of the knoll but found no one. After he rejoined the patrol it returned to Schmitt's position.

One of the mainstays of Schmitt's small group was M. Sgt. Travis E. Watkins of Gladewater, Texas. Born in Waldo, Arkansas, in 1921, Watkins grew up in Turnertown, Texas. After graduating from high school in May 1939, Watkins enlisted in the army. He served in the South Pacific where his valor on Guadalcanal earned him a Bronze Star.

Watkins arrived in Korea with the rest of the 2d Infantry Division. His combat experience quickly made him a valuable member of Company H. He made it his responsibility to calm the inexperienced men when they first faced enemy fire. Lieutenant Schmitt depended upon him to be a stabilizing force in the company.

When it became apparent the men were trapped behind enemy lines, Watkins labored hard to encourage them and keep them from despair. All during the day he moved around the small perimeter, offering cheerful words to the GIs. Throughout the day, under repeated attacks by the NKPA, Watkins courageously rallied the men. Under his bold, forceful leadership the band beat off the North Koreans.

During the night Watkins advised his men, "If you see the enemy don't use your rifle. The muzzle blast will give your position away. Instead, toss a grenade." They listened to the wise veteran. No North Koreans penetrated the perimeter.

By the morning of September 2 the group was nearly out of grenades. Watkins provided a solution. Rifle in hand, he roamed the edge of the perimeter, eyes straining against the sun's glare for some sign of the enemy. About 9:00 A.M. he spotted two North Koreans behind some rocks. Carefully sighting in, he fired. Both enemy soldiers dropped.

Insisting he needed no help, Watkins left the perimeter, gingerly making his way across the fifty yards of open ground to where the North Koreans lay.

While other Americans watched breathlessly, Watkins covered about half the distance. Suddenly, three more North Koreans popped from cover. Watkins whipped his rifle up, his finger squeezing the trigger three times in rapid succession. The three fell heavily. With this threat removed, Watkins casually gathered up the enemy weapons, ammo, and grenades. With his booty he returned to the defensive lines where the others were immeasurably cheered by his courage.

Less than an hour later Watkins spotted six enemy soldiers who had snuck to within twenty-five yards of one of his machine guns. They rained a shower of grenades on the nest, driving the crew to cover.

Watkins came out of his foxhole, rifle blazing. Before he'd taken a step a spent round tore a gash in his forehead. He wiped the blood from his eyes and continued forward. A few steps later an enemy machine gun opened up on his solitary figure. The heavy slugs tore into Watkins's body, severing his spine.

From his crumpled position on the ground, bravely ignoring the intense pain, Watkins continued firing on the enemy. Not until all six were killed did the intrepid NCO pull himself back into his hole.

His wounds were serious. He was paralyzed from the waist down. But he never gave up. He shouted encouragement to his men. "Hang on, fellows. Help will be here soon. Now kill one for me."

Despite the searing heat, Watkins refused all rations and water, telling the others he didn't deserve them because he could no longer fight.

During this time Lieutenant Schmitt had been in radio contact with his battalion headquarters at Yongsan. He learned the entire area between him and Yongsan was swarming with enemy. The entire 9th Regiment line was shattered. Company E had been sent to make contact with Schmitt, but was pushed back, its commander killed. There was little hope for immediate relief.

Schmitt asked for an airdrop of supplies. His band of men were desperate for water and needed rations, ammo, and medical supplies. A light plane made a drop that afternoon, but most of the supplies fell outside the perimeter. One five-gallon can of water could be seen lying about six hundred yards away.

Pfc. Ouellette volunteered to retrieve it. Though his route was covered by two enemy machine guns and two enemy tanks, Ouellette safely made his way through their fire to the can. Upon reaching it he found the can shot full of holes and empty of water.

On his way back to the perimeter Ouellette stumbled upon a brackish water hole. He quickly filled his helmet with the precious liquid and started crawling back to his lines. The enemy fire became so intense he was unable to avoid spilling the badly needed water. Although he returned empty-handed, his gallant attempt greatly inspired the others.

A little later one of Ouellette's buddies downed five North Koreans just twenty-five yards outside the perimeter. Again Ouellette slipped from the line, intent on retrieving the enemy's grenades.

But one of the North Koreans wasn't dead. As Ouellette reached for the man's grenades he lunged at Ouellette with a knife. The two wrestled across the exposed ground, locked in mortal combat. Ouellette finally got the knife away from the North Korean, then plunged it deep into his chest.

When he crawled back into his own lines the five enemy grenades he carried were covered in blood.

Late that afternoon the NKPA launched a determined attack against the trapped Americans. Human wave assaults charged up the slopes. Most of the North Koreans fell under the Americans' fire. Some got close to the perimeter where they threw grenades.

Six times enemy grenades landed in Ouellette's foxhole. Six times he leapt to safety. Then he'd jump back in his hole, continuing the fight.

A seventh grenade landed in Ouellette's hole and exploded before he could get out. The blast shattered his legs. Rapidly weakening from loss of blood, he gallantly remained at his battle post, firing his rifle, throwing the last of his grenades. Then an eighth grenade dropped in his hole. Ouellette died in its blast.

That same afternoon an exploding mortar shell killed Lieutenant Schmitt. The next senior officer took command; he, too, was determined to hold out until relief arrived. From the ridge line above the battered band of men, the North Koreans unleashed a constant barrage of small-arms, automatic-weapons, and mortar fire. That night the skies mercifully poured buckets of rain. Not only did the Americans gather much-needed water, but the rain also kept the enemy at bay.

By the end of the next day the Americans were at the end of their rope. Ammo was critically low, rations nonexistent. The intense heat had made several of the men delirious. The two surviving officers decided to break through to friendly lines. They agreed to divide the remaining men, now only about thirty, into small groups of four or five and scatter through the hills.

They had one major problem—Sergeant Watkins, still alive, still paralyzed.

Watkins told the others to leave him; he did not want to be a burden to those who had a chance to escape. The man who had done more than anyone else to defend the hill was still brave, still cheerful.

As the Americans prepared to pull out under cover of darkness someone lay a carbine on Watkins's chest, the barrel pointed at his chin. "Thanks," he muttered through cracked lips. The men filed past. Watkins waved. "Good luck," he called weakly, "Good luck. Hope you make it."

When last seen, Watkins was still smiling.

The incredible courage displayed by both Watkins and Ouellette resulted in Medals of Honor for both of them. Watkins's widow accepted her husband's award from President Truman on January 9, 1951. Gen. Omar Bradley, Chairman of the Joint Chiefs of Staff, made the presentation to Ouellette's mother on April 3, 1951.

Of the seventy-five men who had taken up positions on the knob three days earlier, twenty-nine were able to escape on September 4. Eventually, twenty-two would safely reach American lines.

The shattered American defensive perimeter was filled with stragglers when dawn came on September 1. By mid-morning Maj. Gen. Lawrence B. Keiser, CG of the 2d Infantry Division, realized his division had been cleaved in two. His two northern regiments, the 23d and 38th, were out of contact with his headquarters, while the survivors of the 9th Infantry Regiment were reeling backwards toward Yongsan. He reported the situation to Eighth Army HQ.

Additional reports streamed into General Walker's headquarters that morning. He learned not only had the NKPA driven an eight-mile-deep by six-mile-wide wedge into the 2d Infantry Division, but farther south the U.S. 25th Infantry Division had also given ground under heavy pressure. On the east coast the ROK divisions, too, had come under heavy attack. Only the timely arrival of American armor and air support prevented a rout there. And near Taegu the U.S. 1st Cavalry Division faced some of the most vicious fighting of the war.

As he reviewed the situation General Walker realized the key area was the Naktong Bulge. He quickly ordered the Fifth Air Force to make a maximum effort in front of the 2d Infantry Division. They were to destroy the supply lines feeding the NKPA forces east of the Naktong.

In reserve Walker had only three weakened regiments: the 19th and 27th Infantry Regiments, and the 5th Marine Regiment. He placed all three on alert and ordered the 5th Marines into the bulge. When he finished issuing these orders, Walker proceeded to the 2d Infantry Division's front. Riding up and down in his jeep, with its special guardrail fitted so he could stand while traveling, Walker told the men of the 2d to stand or die.

He had good reason to issue such an order, for a major crisis was developing in front of Yongsan. NKPA forces approached the tiny crossroads village from the north, west, and southwest. To resist them, General Keiser had only the remnants of Company E, a company of tanks from the 72d Tank Battalion, some engineers, and the division recon company. With no other choice he sent them into the rice paddies and rolling hills west of Yongsan.

The composite force inflicted heavy casualties on the enemy, but by nightfall of September 1 the NKPA were in Yongsan. During the fighting around Yongsan a mortar man in Company E elected to sacrifice himself to save his buddies.

Twenty-three-year-old Pfc. David M. Smith of Livingston, Kentucky, was manning a 60mm mortar with five others when the enemy suddenly launched a surprise attack. In the opening minutes an enemy grenade sailed into the mortar pit. Smith saw it. Yelling "Grenade coming!", Smith pushed aside two men and dived on the lethal missile.

The resulting blast killed Smith instantly, but his actions saved five others, allowing them to drive off the enemy soldiers.

Around 5:30 that evening an enemy force estimated at two hundred swept toward Yongsan from the south. In the NKPA's path stood the tanks of the 2d Reconnaissance Company, 2d Infantry Division. If they didn't at least slow the North Koreans, the Americans still fighting at Yongsan would be trapped.

CHARLES W. TURNER

Commanding the 2d Recon's Scout Squad was twenty-nine-year-old Sgt. 1st Class Charles W. Turner. Turner's section consisted of lightly armored vehicles capable of ranging ahead of the company's tanks and locating the enemy. Once enemy forces were found, the heavier vehicles would engage them, holding them in defensive positions until air strikes or infantry units could arrive to destroy them.

Turner had enlisted in the Massachusetts National Guard from his home in Boston in June 1939, when he was eighteen years old. In February 1941 his unit was called into federal service as the 191st Tank Battalion. Turner went ashore with his unit at Salerno, Italy, on September 9, 1943. He saw considerable combat around Salerno and during the struggle up the Italian boot toward Naples.

Turner's combat days ended on November 19, 1943, when he and the others in his tank's crew were captured by the Germans. He remained a POW until returned to American control on May 8, 1945.

Like many other veterans of World War II, Turner opted to make the army a career. He enjoyed being around the machinery found in a tank unit. Besides, he already had six years in—fourteen more and he could retire.

Promotion came rapidly for a natural leader such as Turner. By the time he joined the 2d Infantry Division at Fort Lewis, Washington, in late 1949, he was wearing the stripes of a sergeant first class. Eight months later he boarded a ship at Bremerton, Washington, with the rest of the division for the trip to Pusan.

Turner was appalled by the stories he heard of GIs fleeing the enemy. In his mind one American was worth at least ten North Koreans. When he got into combat he'd show the enemy how an American could fight.

He got his chance late that September 1 afternoon.

As soon as word of the advancing enemy force reached Turner, he set his men and vehicles into position. Under his careful guidance they were well prepared to meet the enemy. A short time later Turner realized the attack's main thrust was coming at a point about one hundred yards to his left. There, his platoon sergeant's tank was coming under a savage attack.

"Cover me," Turner told his squad. "I'll be right back."

Completely ignoring the crash of artillery and mortar shells hitting all around him, Turner crossed the hundred yards of open ground lying between him and the other tank. Several times the sharp explosions drove him to the ground, but he never faltered in his self-appointed mission.

At the tank, Turner unhesitatingly climbed up onto its exposed rear deck. While enemy bullets splattered the tank's heavy armor plating he manned the .50-caliber machine gun. Back and forth he swept the heavy weapon, its deep staccato reports filling the air. Enemy soldiers fell by the score. Around him other American soldiers, inspired by Turner's action, added their fire to the battle. Soon a veritable hail of American lead was flying toward the enemy.

It didn't take the enemy long to realize Turner was the key to the American defense. The North Koreans turned their attention on him.

In the next ten minutes over fifty enemy rounds slammed into the tank. Its periscope and antennae were shot off. In positions around the tank four GIs were wounded and one killed by the retaliatory fire. But none of it bothered Turner.

He continued sending a stream of deadly rounds into the enemy's ranks. In addition, he yelled out firing instructions to the tank's gun crew.

"Ten to the left," he barked after a shot missed an NKPA machine-gun nest. The next shell flew right into the nest, scattering the gunners.

Altogether, Turner called down the tank's fire on seven enemy machine-gun nests. All seven were blown up.

On two occasions Turner's elevated perch gave him a clear view of an attempted enemy flanking movement. He called out to Lt. Ralph Decker, his platoon leader, "On the left, lieutenant. A breakthrough on the left!"

Decker quickly scraped together a reaction squad and sent it to plug the hole in his line. Without Turner's instructions the thin line would have been breached.

The fierce battle raged for over twenty minutes. Through it all Turner held his position. Even when the enemy advanced to within ten yards of his tank Turner never gave up. The bodies of more than fifty North Koreans lay around Turner, bloody testimony to his telltale accuracy.

But Turner's luck couldn't last forever. Under ever-increasing enemy fire the gallant sergeant kept fighting until at last an enemy rifleman brought him down.

Without Turner's courageous example the line faltered. Ammo was low. Lieutenant Decker had no choice. He ordered his men to pull back. As the remnants of the 2d Recon moved down the road toward Miryang, the North Koreans entered Yongsan.

Later, in recognition of Turner's great heroism, Lieutenant Decker prepared a recommendation for the Medal of Honor. Turner's widowed mother, Hazel, received the medal from President Truman on January 9, 1951.

Surprisingly, the North Koreans made no effort to move east of Yongsan. Their current offensive had been dramatic but quickly revealed major weaknesses. Because of their poor communications and a badly overextended supply line, they could break through the U.N. lines but could not exploit their successes, especially in the face of superior air power and artillery. And, with their greater mobility, the U.N. forces could regroup and counterattack faster than the NKPA could press their advantage. Finally, the huge number of casualties the NKPA had suffered had largely been replaced by conscripted South Koreans, reluctant combatants at best.

The commander of the 9th Infantry Regiment, Col. John G. Hill, spent the night of September 1 organizing a reaction force to retake Yongsan the next day. Most of the men came from the various rifle companies shattered in the fighting west of Yongsan. Just after noon on September 2, about eight hundred men, supported by tanks, stepped off in the attack.

Yongsan itself was but a collection of thatched houses clustered around the crossroads. The fighting to reclaim the strategic hamlet was bitter. American tanks battled with North Korean T-34 tanks. Brave GIs crept forward to blast the enemy armor with bazookas. Infantrymen flushed out the enemy in savage house-to-house fighting. After awhile, rather than risk casualties taking enemy positions this way, tanks were called. Their heavy 90mm cannon quickly reduced the buildings to rubble.

By 3:00 P.M. the Americans had regained possession of the town. By evening the NKPA had been pushed into the low hills west of Yongsan. The attacking Americans quickly took up positions about one-half mile beyond Yongsan. For the time being the enemy drive on Miryang had been smashed.

The next morning the 9th Infantry, with two battalions of the 5th Marines fighting alongside them, launched a counterattack into the Naktong Bulge. In daylong heavy fighting the soldiers and marines pushed the North Koreans back three miles. The U.N. forces resumed their attack the next day, bathed in warm sunshine after a night of torrential rains. Against an oddly passive enemy the Americans made three more miles before digging in for the night.

That evening, after spreading his platoons out over a hilltop, Lt. Frank Muñoz, commander of Company G, 9th Infantry, saw enemy troops assembling to the west, just out of rifle range. His request for an artillery barrage was denied. Muñoz put out extra listening posts on the rocky fingers leading west from his defensive positions atop a hill. He hurried along the line telling his men to prepare for a night attack. "Those people are getting ready," he said.

At 10:00 P.M., without any of their usual yelling and screaming, the North Koreans hit Company G's lines. The Americans reacted with a wall of rifle fire. Within a few minutes the enemy pulled back. Then it started to rain. The North Koreans came back. This time Muñoz's first platoon fell back, withdrawing over the hill's crest to the reverse slope. There, supporting Pershing tanks blasted the North Koreans off the hill. The platoon went back up. A third enemy attack pushed them off again. Muñoz led a bayonet charge back up the hill, again succeeding in forcing the enemy back.

Panting, Muñoz radioed his third platoon, dug in farther down the ridge, to join him. He didn't want them cut off by the enemy and he needed every man he could muster to hold his position against another enemy attack.

LOREN R. KAUFMAN

Because the third platoon leader was experiencing his first combat, Muñoz told him to be guided by his platoon sergeant, Sfc. Loren R. Kaufman. Born in The Dalles, Oregon, on July 27, 1923, Kaufman had first enlisted in the army the week after Pearl Harbor. Assigned to the 3d Infantry Division at Fort Lewis, Washington, he spent three years with them, fighting the Nazis in North Africa, Sicily, Italy, and France. His consistent valor as a member of an artillery battery's forward observer team earned him a Bronze Star. In the August fighting around the Naktong Bulge Kaufman had added an oak leaf cluster to that decoration.

The new platoon leader quickly recognized Kaufman's talents and deferred to his judgment. Now, after he passed on Muñoz's message, Kaufman said, "Okay, let's saddle up and move out."

In minutes the platoon was moving up the ridge line toward Muñoz. The rain cut visibility to scant yards. Kaufman took the lead. Halfway up the ridge he spotted a large group of men moving up a draw in the same direction. He couldn't tell if they were friendly. He halted the column of men and went forward alone to investigate. Not until he was three feet from the lead man in the group did Kaufman realize they were North Koreans.

Kaufman swung his M-1 like a club, bashing the enemy soldier in the head. Then he ran his bayonet into the man's chest. He then turned and raced back to his platoon, yelling, "North Koreans! Open fire!"

Ahead of him the Americans hit the dirt, rifles blazing. While they fired, Kaufman stood in full view of the enemy, firing his rifle and throwing grenades into their ranks. Unable to reach Muñoz, the platoon fought its way to the position held by the second platoon, with Kaufman covering their movement.

At the new position Kaufman quickly took charge. Sgt. Leonard N. Miller saw Kaufman in action. "He immediately started giving encouragement to the men by running back and forth all along the top of the hill firing his rifle and throwing grenades," Miller said. "When one fellow got hit, Kaufman stopped to tell him everything would be okay and then he grabbed the fellow's rifle and started firing back at the enemy."

At one point Kaufman spotted two North Koreans who, in the rain, had nearly worked their way to the top of the hill. Bounding forward, he slammed his bayonet first into one, then the other.

Once back inside his lines Kaufman moved to a .30-caliber machine gun whose crew had been wounded by a bursting enemy grenade. He fed a fresh belt of ammo into the automatic weapon, then sent a sweeping burst of bullets flying downhill. North Koreans nearby recognized the threat of this weapon, so they concentrated their fire on Kaufman. Behind him one of the wounded gunners cried out in pain as an enemy round opened a new wound. Rather than cause them more injury, Kaufman picked up the weapon and moved it to a new position.

A short time later Kaufman led the survivors of the two platoons into Muñoz's position. When the North Koreans came again Company G pulled back down the hill's reverse side. As before, the heavy firepower from the tanks, unable to move closer because of the steep terrain, blasted away at the enemy.

In the counterattack Kaufman's platoon went up the hill's right side. Sergeant Miller again saw Kaufman in action: "We got about halfway up the hill when heavy enemy fire broke out. There was hardly any cover on the hillside. Sergeant Kaufman moved up the hill as far as he could and began throwing grenades as fast and in as many directions as he could, trying to knock out the enemy positions in order for the platoon to advance."

Kaufman used his bayonet on two more North Koreans, then turned his attention to a mortar crew. Braving intense enemy rifle fire and exploding grenades, he boldly ran right up to the crew. He emptied a full clip from his M-1 into the three enemy, killing them all. Next, he went after a North Korean machine-gun nest, killing its crew with a well-placed grenade.

That was the way it went until morning. Fighting, clawing viciously at the enemy, Company G retook the hill. In hand-to-hand fighting, Kaufman went after the North Koreans wherever they threatened the lines. His unheralded bravery was primarily responsible for Company G's victory.

At first light the North Koreans pulled off the hill, taking up positions in a small village at the base of the hill. Kaufman rounded up a band of volunteers and went after the enemy. His small band hunted down the North Koreans, killing a score and sending the rest fleeing. Atop the hill, Muñoz finally got his artillery barrage. The heavy shells drove the enemy farther west.

Kaufman's incredible valor would be rewarded with the Medal of Honor. Regrettably, it would be awarded posthumously. He was killed in action on February 10, 1951.

While Company G tended to its wounded the morning of September 5, the rest of the 9th Infantry and the 5th Marines, both relatively untouched the previous night, resumed their push west. In a driving rainstorm the Americans fought their way up Obong-ni Ridge and Cloverleaf Hill, the same ground they'd battled for in early August. Here they halted their counteroffensive, for General MacArthur had other plans for the 5th Marines. General Walker released them to the newly activated X Corps on September 6.

At the same time the 2d Infantry Division was battling for Yongsan, other sites along the Pusan Perimeter erupted in heavy combat. Some of the fiercest action occurred along the thirty-five-mile front held by the U.S. 1st Cavalry Division near Taegu, site of General Walker's Eighth Army headquarters. For two solid weeks the 1st Cavalry Division lived in a constant state of crisis. At one point the situation became so critical Walker sent his headquarters staff to Pusan. General Walker, however, remained in Taegu, prepared to fight it out as General Dean had two months earlier.

At the beginning of the North Korean offensive, when they had cracked the Naktong Bulge, General Walker ordered the 1st Cavalry Division to the attack. He wanted to divert to that sector some of the enemy strength in the south. Accordingly, the 7th and 8th Cavalry Regiments launched simultaneous attacks against key enemy-held positions just east of the Naktong River on September 2.

The attacks were doomed to failure. Heavy air and artillery bombardments had failed to dislodge the enemy from their positions on the hill. At the same time, the North Koreans initiated an attack of their own. They quickly swept through gaps between the American units. By the end of September 3 there were as many North Koreans behind the attacking cavalrymen as there were in front of them. Maj. Gen. Hobart R. Gay, the 1st Cavalry Division's commander, called off the attack that evening. The cavalrymen began a fighting withdrawal.

A major North Korean threat developed in a northern section of the Naktong Bulge, known to the Americans as the Bowling Alley, above Taegu. An NKPA infantry and armored attack sent elements of the 8th Cavalry Regiment reeling. Lost in the battle was a dominant mountaintop ten miles north of Taegu, Hill 902, locally called Kasan. Hill 902 provided an unobstructed view all the way south into Taegu, and, in enemy hands, could be used for general intelligence purposes and would provide an excellent location for an artillery spotter.

Kasan differed from most peaks in Korea in that it had a large oval-shaped level area on its summit. It varied in width from two hundred to eight hundred yards and ran from the peak of Hill 902 to Hill 755, nearly a mile to the southeast. On all sides of this ridge crest the mountain slopes dropped precipitously. Ancient Koreans had constructed a thirty-foot-high stone wall around the crest and turned it into a fortress. Most of the summit was covered with a dense growth of scrub brush and small pine trees.

General Gay ordered Company D, 8th Engineer Combat Battalion, under

Lt. John T. Kennedy, and Company E, 8th Cavalry, to recapture Kasan. They set off in trucks in a driving rain the evening of September 3. After waiting in their assembly area for several hours the troops returned to their respective camps. The next morning at breakfast the engineers received orders to move immediately to Kasan. Without waiting for Company E they set off.

About noon the ninety men of Company D started up the steep path running up the ridge's south end. Enemy sniper fire harassed the engineers as they moved upward. By the time they were halfway up two men had been killed and eight wounded. Not until 5:00 P.M. did Lieutenant Kennedy lead his company into the bowl-shaped summit of Hill 755. He placed his men into positions around the area.

Before he started up the ridge Kennedy had been told about seventy-five disorganized enemy soldiers held Kasan. Actually, an entire enemy battalion occupied the summit. They came at Company D about 5:30 P.M.

MELVIN L. BROWN

The main attack hit the second platoon commanded by Platoon Sgt. James N. Vandygriff. Its thirty members held the northwest corner of the summit, facing north-northwest, its left flank anchored along the stone wall. Vandygriff had no sooner set up and loaded his platoon's two machine guns when the enemy hit. Supporting the automatic weapons next to the wall on the platoon's extreme left was BAR man Pfc. Melvin L. Brown.

Though not yet twenty years old, Brown already had nearly two years' service, enlisting from his home in Mahaffey, Pennsylvania, in October 1948. After his basic training, Brown drew an assignment with the 8th Engineer Combat Battalion in Japan. Though intended to be primarily construction troops, all members of the combat engineers are cross-trained as infantry. When the need arises they can drop their tools and fight.

When the North Koreans attacked, Brown quickly took them under fire. With short, deadly accurate bursts he dropped five enemy soldiers as they rushed one machine gun from its blind side. With heavy losses the North Koreans pulled back, leaving one dead and two wounded in the second platoon. That night, enemy mortar and small-arms fire kept the GIs deep in their foxholes.

It rained most of the night and September 5 dawned wet and foggy on top of Hill 755. Just past dawn the enemy came again. A squad of North Koreans tried to come over the wall next to Brown. Each time they appeared on the stone wall Brown calmly shot them off.

Between 10:00 and 11:00 A.M. a platoon from Company E, 8th Cavalry, entered the position. Kennedy quickly fed them into his line. Within a few minutes the North Koreans attacked again. Brown stood up in his foxhole, sweeping the attackers with fire from his automatic rifle. For nearly thirty minutes the fight raged. Not until Sergeant Vandygriff fired a bazooka into their midst did the North Koreans pull back.

Upon checking with his men, Vandygriff found they were low on ammunition. He sent his men out to collect weapons and ammo from the enemy dead. As he distributed this, Vandygriff passed by Brown's position. At the bottom of the wall lay fifteen to twenty dead North Koreans. Vandygriff asked what happened.

Brown shrugged his shoulders. "Every time they came up I knocked them off the wall."

Vandygriff noticed a bloody bandage on Brown's left shoulder. To his question Brown replied, "One of them got a little close. It's nothing."

Vandygriff told him to see the medics. Brown refused. "It's nothing," he repeated.

Soon the NKPA came again. They seemed to be everywhere now. A group of enemy soldiers started over the wall. Brown sprayed them with fire from his BAR. They screamed in agony as they disappeared. More came. Brown continued his fire, holding them back. Then he ran out of ammo. He dropped his few grenades over the wall, disrupting their attack.

Brown realized the vital necessity of holding his position. Calling to his buddies in nearby foxholes for more grenades, he caught them in midair, pulled the pins, and dropped them over the wall. Several times the grenades were thrown short of his position. Completely ignoring the heavy enemy fire directed at him, Brown scampered into the open, retrieved the missiles, and dropped them over the wall.

In spite of Brown's heroic efforts the enemy continued their effort to breach the wall. Out of ammo, out of grenades, Brown reached for his one remaining weapon. He pulled his entrenching tool from his pack.

Each time a North Korean popped up over the wall, Brown slammed him in the head with the little shovel. For nearly half an hour Brown maintained his lonely vigil. He delivered a skull-crushing blow to at least ten enemy soldiers.

Brown's gallant one-man stand so inspired his buddies they rallied and drove back the attack.

By this time Kennedy recognized his force could no longer hold its position. Low on ammo and with nearly a score of wounded, he ordered a withdrawal.

Vandygriff was overseeing the destruction of excess weapons when Brown's squad leader reported the youngster had been killed. By this time enemy fire was falling in the platoon area from nearly all directions. It was time to get out.

When Company D came off Hill 755 the afternoon of September 5 it was at half strength: eighteen were wounded and thirty were missing, presumed dead, including Melvin L. Brown.

In a White House ceremony on January 9, 1951, Brown's father, Edward B., received his son's Medal of Honor from President Truman.

By September 5 the threat along three-quarters of the Pusan Perimeter had eased. West of Yongsan the men of the U.S. 2d Infantry Division continued pushing the enemy back to the Naktong. To the south heroic efforts by the U.S. 25th Infantry Division ground the NKPA to a halt.

Only near Taegu did the enemy pressure continue. They had driven to within a few miles of this important town. A brilliant attack by the 3d Battalion, 7th Cavalry Regiment, on September 12 threw the NKPA off Hill 314, overlooking Taegu. Though heavy fighting continued, the situation around Taegu, and elsewhere, never seemed so bleak again.

U.N. and North Korean forces remained locked in close combat all around the perimeter through mid-September. But the tempo of the fighting was easing. Both sides were nearing exhaustion. The embattled U.N. forces had dealt the North Korean timetable a serious blow. It had originally called for the conquest of South Korea by August 15.

The NKPA had all but shot its bolt. Only about half of the original battle-hardened invaders remained. The NKPA leadership still wondered how they could throw the U.N. forces completely out of Korea. While they contemplated their options, General MacArthur settled the issue for them.

Chapter Three
Hammer and Anvil

It came as no surprise to those who knew him that General MacArthur thought an amphibious landing at the enemy's rear would win the Korean War. During his campaigns in the southwest Pacific during World War II MacArthur had frequently jumped his troops past enemy strongholds in order to strike at their vulnerable rear areas. A bold, water-borne sweep around the North Koreans' flanks to attack their supply and communications lines greatly appealed to MacArthur's sense of grand tactics. Though the course of the war in its first weeks forced him to repeatedly postpone his plan, he never wavered from its concept.

As early as the first week of July 1950, with the war little more than a week old, MacArthur instructed his chief of staff, Maj. Gen. Edward M. Almond, to prepare plans for an amphibious landing on Korea's west coast. The first meeting, attended by representatives of the army, navy, and air force, was held at MacArthur's Tokyo headquarters. Almond's initial proposal called for the U.S. 1st Cavalry Division to make the landing on July 22. This plan was dropped a week later due to Eighth Army's inability to stop the NKPA's southward advance. The 1st Cavalry Division, instead, was fed into the line east of Taejon.

Next, MacArthur informed the Joint Chiefs of Staff he planned a mid-September landing using the 5th Marine Regiment and the army's 2d Infantry Division. Further advances by the North Koreans, however, necessitated the use of both these units in the defense of the Pusan Perimeter. Their loss did not mean a cancellation of MacArthur's grand plan, though. Instead, he would substitute his sole reserve unit in Japan, the 7th Infantry Division.

In the meantime, General Almond's staff had finalized several plans for the amphibious landing. The one that MacArthur approved was labeled 100-B. Plan 100-B called for an amphibious landing at Inchon along with a simultaneous breakout from the Pusan Perimeter by the Eighth Army. It was a classic hammer and anvil maneuver.

MacArthur selected Inchon because it was Korea's second port, his intelligence reported it lightly defended, and it sat only eighteen miles from Seoul. Seoul in U.N. hands would isolate the North Koreans hammering the Pusan Perimeter from their bases in the north. A successful operation at Inchon would cause the disintegration of the NKPA and bring a quick end to the war.

Inchon was not without problems, though. Between Inchon and the open sea lay great expanses of mud flats, crossed by a treacherous channel. Most formidable, however, were Inchon's extreme tides. They ran from thirty-one feet at flood to minus six inches at ebb. Landing craft had only a few hours each day to approach the beaches. In mid-September, because of the tides, the attackers would have to land against a sixteen-foot-high seawall with only two hours of daylight remaining.

After the JCS approved Plan 100-B, MacArthur activated the X Corps on August 24 to command the assault. When General Almond asked who would command the corps MacArthur surprised him by saying, "It is you." MacArthur surprised Almond again when he told him he would also retain his position as his chief of staff. MacArthur planned for Almond to oversee the Inchon landing and the recapture of Seoul and then, with the war over, return to his old position in Tokyo. Both Almond and General Walker, commanding the Eighth Army, would report directly to MacArthur.

The major ground units of X Corps were the U.S. 1st Marine Division and the U.S. 7th Infantry Division. The 1st Marine Division was ordered to full combat strength on July 25 and told to be ready to sail for the Far East from the States between August 10 and 15. In those two weeks fifteen thousand men and their equipment were assembled into two regiments. From all over the United States reserves flooded into Camp Pendleton, California. The marines met their deadline: By September 6 most of the 1st and 7th Marine Regiments had assembled in Japan; the 5th Marines were already waiting at Pusan to join the invasion fleet.

In Japan the 7th Infantry Division had to be rebuilt to full strength as over nine thousand of its officers and men had been sent to Korea in July and early August as replacements. Though Eighth Army screamed during the last week of August and the first week of September, all infantry replacements to the Far East Command were allocated to the 7th Infantry Division. By September 4, nearly fifty-eight hundred men had joined the division. To further augment its ranks eighty-six hundred South Korean conscripts were sent to join the division. Though of dubious quality, packs of one hundred scared, bewildered South Korean men unable to speak English were assigned to each infantry company and artillery battery.

The marines sailed from Kobe, Japan, on September 11. The 7th Infantry Division left Yokohama the same day. On the 12th the 5th Marines departed Pusan for a rendezvous at sea. On September 13 MacArthur and his staff boarded the command ship *Mt. McKinley*. The seventy thousand men of X Corps were at sea. Against all odds, facing every known logistical problem, MacArthur had put together a force that embodied the best of American military capability.

Because of the extreme tides prevailing on D-Day, September 15, the Inchon invasion had to be made in two stages. Wolmi-do Island, about a thousand yards across and rising to a height of 335 feet, connects to the mainland via a causeway. Bristling with troops and guns, it had to be captured before the seawall protecting Inchon could be attacked. Thus, a battalion of marines would assault Wolmi-do early in the morning; they would secure the island and hold it while the falling tide forced the fleet to retire. Then, at five o'clock that afternoon, the fleet would return, throwing its landing craft against the seawall.

Marine Corsairs struck Wolmi-do at 5:00 A.M. Following a heavy naval bombardment, a battalion of the 5th Marines hit Wolmi-do's beaches at 6:30 a.m. Within thirty minutes an American flag was flying from the island's highest point. In the fighting the marines killed 108 enemy and captured 136. About three hundred more fled to Inchon. Marine casualties were light— only seventeen wounded.

Covered by marine and naval air which roamed over Inchon all day, the marines on Wolmi-do spent an anxious day waiting for the tide to allow the return of the invasion fleet. The ships finally sailed back at 3:00 P.M. At 3:30 P.M. the infantrymen of the 1st and 5th Marines boarded their landing craft. Behind them the fighting ships loosed an intense barrage of gunfire against the beaches. Rocket ships moved in close and launched two thousand rockets toward the landing area.

At 5:32 P.M. the assault elements of the 1st Marines touched shore at Blue Beach, south of Inchon. After climbing the high seawall, the marines moved inland, gaining a mile before halting and digging in just past midnight.

Red Beach sat at the northwest edge of the peninsula containing the city of Inchon. The first wave of the 5th Marines landed there at 5:33 P.M. Using scaling ladders, the marines quickly climbed up and over the seawall. Against sporadic enemy fire the marines moved inland.

Heavy firing broke out on the left flank of Red Beach. Enemy troops in a trench line and a pillbox just behind the seawall pinned down the marines in

Company A, 1st Battalion, 5th Marines. First Lt. Baldomero Lopez, a twenty-five-year-old regular officer from Tampa, Florida, led his third platoon forward. Under his skillful leadership the marines killed a dozen North Koreans in the trench. Then, realizing the heaviest fire came from the pillbox, Lopez ordered his men to cover him while he crawled forward to throw a grenade. As he lifted his arm to throw the grenade a burst of enemy fire caught him in the shoulder, ripping into his flesh. Lopez tumbled backwards. The grenade fell from his hand.

Lopez groped anxiously for the missile, hoping still to get it off. He picked it up. His weakened fingers dropped it. Determined to protect his men from danger, Lopez yelled, "Get back!" He reached out with his good arm, gathered the grenade in the crook of his arm, and rolled over on top of the deadly missile. He took the full and tremendous blast himself, dying to save his men. Lopez was the first marine to earn the Medal of Honor in Korea.

Soon after Lopez died marines fired a flare indicating they had captured Cemetery Hill, one of two significant hill masses at Inchon. The second, Observatory Hill, fell to the 5th Marines by midnight. Marine casualties for D-Day were 20 killed, 174 wounded, and one missing.

With their beachhead secure, the marines left the mopping up around Inchon to the ROK Special Marines and began their drive to Seoul. Against stubborn resistance the two marine regiments moved east along the Inchon-Seoul highway. The 5th Marines advanced on the road's north side while the 1st Marines moved astride the road and to its south. A few miles beyond Inchon the boundary left the highway and slanted northeast. This turned the 5th Marines toward Kimpo Field and the Han River just past it. The 1st Marines moved toward Yongdungp'o, the large industrial Seoul suburb on the south bank of the Han.

On the night of September 16–17, the 2d Battalion, 1st Marines, occupied positions near the hamlet of Sosa-ri. Shortly before dawn the NKPA sent forth its first foray to challenge the American invaders. The 2d Battalion of the 1st Seoul Defense Division, accompanied by a tank platoon of the 42d Mechanized Regiment, moved west out of Yongdungp'o toward Sosa-ri. They planned to push across the narrow band of ridges east of Inchon, destroying the marines, and retaking Inchon. The marines had other plans.

WALTER C. MONEGAN

Though he wouldn't be twenty until Christmas Day, Walter C. Monegan already had nearly two and one-half years of military service. Blessed with an adventuresome spirit and fired by stories of glory from relatives who had served in World War II, Monegan lied about his age and joined the army in his hometown of Melrose, Massachusetts, in November 1947 when he was just sixteen. Less than six months later, when the army discovered his fraudulent enlistment, he was discharged.

Still determined to satisfy his quest for adventure in the military, Monegan persuaded his parents to sign his marine corps enlistment papers. He reported to Parris Island, South Carolina, for boot camp in March 1948. He spent a year with the 3d Marine Regiment in Tsingtao, China, before the Communist takeover forced the withdrawal of all U.S. forces. Monegan completed his two-year hitch at Camp Pendleton, California.

When the North Koreans crossed the Thirty-eighth Parallel Monegan found himself in a turmoil. Newly married and settled in Seattle, Washington, he felt torn between his obligation to his wife and a desire to continue the pursuit of adventure. He pondered his circumstances for several weeks. Then his pregnant wife, Elizabeth, encouraged him to reenlist. She knew he wouldn't be happy unless he went back in. Monegan re-upped on July 20, 1950.

Less than two months later he came ashore at Inchon with Company F, 2d Battalion, 1st Marines. He was carrying a new weapon in addition to his M-1 carbine: a 3.5-inch rocket launcher, known as a bazooka. The weapon had its supporters and detractors. The bazooka had proven itself in training; combat would make or break the weapon. Monegan believed in the weapon. He had earned an expert's badge with it during training at Camp Pendleton. All he wanted was a chance to show its worth in action.

Through the patches of swirling, early morning fog just before dawn on September 17, the unmistakable clank of T-34 tanks could be heard approaching the marines' position. Pfc. Monegan's loader, Pfc. Robert F. Perkins, woke the sleeping bazookaman with a nudge in the ribs. "Here they come," he warned.

As the two young marines peeked over the edge of their foxhole, six T-34 tanks came into view along the road. Squads of North Korean infantry crowded atop the armored vehicles.

"Come on," Monegan told Perkins.

Together, the men stealthily made their way down the scrub-covered hillside. Unobserved, they crept into a roadside ditch. Perkins slipped a rocket into the six-foot-long tube. He tapped Monegan on the helmet, signaling the bazooka was loaded and ready.

Calmly, Monegan drew a bead on the lead tank. It clanked closer. Perkins waited for Monegan to fire. But still he held his fire. The lead T-34 drew closer. One hundred yards. Seventy-five. Fifty! Perkins wanted to yell "Fire!" but held his tongue.

At just forty yards Monegan fired. The rocket whooshed down the road. It slammed into the tank, exploding with a roar. The T-34 burst into flames, then skewed sideways across the road. Behind it the other five tanks ground to a halt.

While Perkins loaded another round an NKPA soldier popped from the burning tank's escape hatch. Monegan dropped the bazooka, grabbed his carbine, and drilled the enemy soldier with one shot.

Monegan then picked up his loaded bazooka and aimed at the second tank. That vehicle burst into flame with another accurate hit.

By this time the marines behind Monegan and Perkins had opened fire on the enemy column. The enemy infantry tumbled from the tanks, seeking refuge along the road. Marine 75mm recoilless rifles dropped their deadly shells on the NKPA, spreading death among their ranks. Pershing tanks from the 1st Tank Battalion pumped their powerful rounds into the T-34s, destroying or disabling them.

Monegan got off two more bazooka rounds, further disrupting the enemy's attack, before he and Perkins made their way back up the hill.

Behind them the NKPA force was torn to shreds. The Pershing's 90mm shells had a devastating effect. Within fifteen minutes it was over. All six enemy tanks lay in smoldering ruins. Nearly two hundred North Koreans lay dead or dying along the road. It was a gruesome sight.

Monegan's company encountered continued heavy fighting on the road to Yongdungp'o over the next two days. On September 19 Company F dug in on a slight rise several hundred yards north of the road, about three miles from Yongdungp'o. Company D sat between them and the road. The marines set up a fifty percent watch with half the men sleeping while the others stayed on watch, alternating every two hours.

Starting at 1:00 A.M., September 20, the marines on watch started hearing the sounds of armored vehicles coming from the direction of Yongdungp'o. In anticipation of an attack by T-34s, the marines' supporting tank platoon was ordered forward. The Pershings started to roll but, in the darkness, the lead tank slid partly off the road and bogged down in the mud. It blocked the movement of the following tanks. If the NKPA did attack, the marines would have to fight them without armored support.

The attack came at four in the morning.

The North Korean force consisted of an ammo truck followed by four T-34s, a troop carrier, and a company of infantry on foot.

The brunt of the attack hit Company D. One of its marines tossed a grenade into the ammo truck. It erupted with a tremendous roar. Flaming pyrotechnics fell for hundreds of yards. The blast alerted Monegan to the attack.

In an instant he was out of his hole, lugging his bazooka down the fire-swept hillside. Behind him Cpl. William Cheek carried three rounds of ammo. Perkins busied himself breaking out more rockets. Then he, too, raced across the three hundred yards of open ground to where Monegan and Cheek had gone into action.

Monegan knelt atop a small knoll that gave him a clear view of the road, but also made him a highly visible target.

Cheek slid a round into the tube and slapped Monegan's helmet. Monegan sighted on a tank and fired. The rocket missed by ten yards.

"We gotta get closer!" Monegan hollered to Cheek over the sound of battle. They looked around for a spot. Monegan pointed to a water tower about one hundred yards distant. The two men raced to the base of the tower. Perkins joined them there.

In the light of the burning truck Monegan drew a bead on the tank behind the truck. "Fire!" Cheek yelled.

The rocket scored a direct hit on the tank, stopping it dead.

In response, the enemy infantry and one of the tanks sprayed the water tower with fire. The three marines hit the dirt. Perkins loaded the bazooka. Once again Monegan stepped out of the shadow thrown by the water tank. In full view of the enemy he sighted carefully on yet another tank. Just as Perkins started to yell at him to hurry and fire, Monegan sent the rocket on its way. He scored another direct hit.

One of the two remaining tanks turned and fled. Monegan barked at Perkins to hurry and reload him. He stepped back into the open and sighted on the lone remaining tank. Enemy machine-gun fire splintered the wooden structure supporting the water tank. Monegan ignored it to continue tracking the T-34.

Before Monegan could fire, a burst of enemy machine-gun fire stitched up his body. He slumped to the ground.

By this time marines from Company D had taken the last tank under fire. It soon erupted in flames. Other marines hunted down the NKPA infantry, killing them where they found them. Soon the survivors were streaking back to Yongdungp'o.

As the rising sun lighted the battleground a corpsman reached Monegan. He ripped open the youngster's bloody shirt, but it was too late. With the corpsman's help, Perkins and Cheek pulled Monegan's body under the water tank, then made their way back up the hill.

In a solemn ceremony in Washington on February 8, 1952, Monegan's widow and his infant son accepted his posthumous Medal of Honor.

Simultaneously with their attack down the Seoul-Inchon highway, the North Koreans sent an attack group against marine positions northwest of Yongdungp'o. On September 19, the 1st Battalion, 5th Marines, had occupied three key positions on the northwestern edge of the city: Hills 80, 85, and 118. Because the rest of the 5th Marines were preparing to cross the Han River on September 20, their 1st Battalion was pulled off the hill positions the evening of September 19 to be replaced by the 1st Battalion, 1st Marines. Due to darkness the relieving marines occupied only Hill 118.

The NKPA attack thus found Hills 80 and 85 undefended. Part of its force dug in on the twin hills while the rest continued on to challenge the marines on Hill 118. While Pfc. Monegan bravely attacked the enemy tanks three miles to the south, Companies A and C of the 1st Battalion, 1st Marines, on Hill 118 struggled for two hours in the predawn darkness to repulse the charging enemy. After fighting all night, the two companies next had to wrest Hills 80 and 85 from the North Koreans. This attack started at 9:00 A.M., September 20, 1950.

Company C first had to clear a small village at the base of Hill 85 held by a company of NKPA. That fight took until nearly noon. Next the marines turned their attention to the hill mass. At least two companies of North Koreans were deployed on the hill in a horseshoe formation. Well concealed, the NKPA offered only minimal resistance as the marines moved up the hill. Only as they approached the top did the enemy open up from three directions with everything they had.

HENRY A. COMMISKEY

Henry A. Commiskey came from a family of fighters. His father served as a machine gunner with the army in World War I, then volunteered for World War II. An older brother fought on Guadalcanal with a marine raider battalion. A second brother saw service with the 187th Airborne Regiment in Korea.

Born January 10, 1927, in Hattiesburg, Mississippi, Commiskey grew up in a strict Catholic environment. He attended the local parochial school, where he was a favorite altar boy of the pastor. While in high school, he spent his summers working as a brakeman on the Illinois Central Railroad.

Like many youngsters of his age, Commiskey itched to join the action of World War II. Deeply patriotic, he begged his father to allow him to enlist before he was seventeen, but his father refused. At one point he told his son, "You can't go into the service until I do."

When the senior Commiskey entered the army in late 1943, he told his son he would sign his enlistment papers as soon as he turned seventeen. On January 12, 1944, Henry Commiskey enlisted in the U.S. Marine Corps.

Pfc. Commiskey celebrated his eighteenth birthday aboard a transport carrying him and the rest of the 27th Marines, 5th Marine Division, to Iwo Jima. The brutal fighting on the volcanic island matured young Commiskey far beyond his years. He fought throughout the twenty-six-day battle, earning his first Purple Heart and a commendation for his "high quality of leadership and courage in the face of a stubborn and fanatical enemy."

Following World War II Commiskey opted to remain in the Marine Corps. He served tours in Hawaii and Japan before being selected for drill instructors' school. In 1949, while serving as a DI at the Marine Corps Recruit Depot, Parris Island, South Carolina, Staff Sergeant Commiskey was selected for Officer Candidate School. He was commissioned a second lieutenant in September 1949.

Lieutenant Commiskey was on orders for a marine corps school at Quantico, Virginia, when the North Koreans launched their invasion. He immediately requested the orders be canceled and he be assigned to a line company. His request was approved. He joined the 1st Marine Regiment, under the legendary Col. Lewis "Chesty" Puller, forming at Camp Pendleton, California.

Held in reserve during the Inchon landing, Commiskey's 1st Battalion followed the rest of the 1st Marines ashore on September 16. During the advance toward Yongdungp'o, Commiskey fearlessly led his platoon against scattered, but determined, enemy resistance. He rallied his marines when the NKPA attacked Hill 118, helping to throw off the attackers.

When Capt. Robert P. Wray sent his Company C up Hill 85, he put Commiskey's platoon in the lead. The husky twenty-three-year-old Mississippian placed his squads in position and then, picking up an abandoned Browning Automatic Rifle, started up the hill.

Only sporadic enemy fire harassed the marines as Commiskey led them up the rocky, barren hillside. Stopping every few yards, he brought his BAR up to his shoulder and sent quick bursts of lead flying into enemy positions. At his urging, his platoon swept up the hill, killing more than a dozen North Koreans. Just short of the hill's crest, and deep within the U-formation of the NKPA, the marines received a blistering hail of rifle and automatic-weapons fire. Marines all along the line fell, some writhing in agony, others laying silent in death.

Commiskey hit the dirt, his eyes quickly scanning the ground above and ahead of him. He spotted a heavy machine gun manned by five North Koreans. It seemed to be the key to the enemy's defense. If he could knock it out. . . .

Scrambling to his knees, Commiskey fired his BAR. The thick slugs drove the crew to cover. As he rose to his feet, a marine nearby yelled in frustration at his jammed M-1 rifle. Commiskey knew the heavy BAR would only slow him down, so he tossed it to the man.

"Cover me!" he screamed as he pulled his .45 automatic pistol from its holster.

Commiskey bounded forward in great leaps, oblivious to the enemy bullets snapping past his head. He covered the thirty yards in seconds, firing his pistol at the machine-gun crew. With a great leap, he jumped right into the middle of the enemy emplacement.

The startled North Koreans scrambled backwards, fumbling for their side arms. Commiskey fired four times. Four North Koreans collapsed, gaping holes in their chests testifying to Commiskey's deadly accuracy. He turned to the fifth man. He pulled the trigger. Nothing. The automatic's slide was in its rearmost position. He was out of ammo.

At that point the North Korean jumped on Commiskey. The two men grappled in the bottom of the dirt pit, trading punches. Commiskey fought his way to the top of his enemy, battering his face with his fists. Just then another marine appeared at the lip of the emplacement, rifle at the ready.

"Gimme your pistol!" Commiskey barked.

With the new weapon in hand, he placed its barrel against his enemy's head. A shower of bone and brain tissue flew across the emplacement in answer to Commiskey's squeeze on the trigger.

Still determined to eliminate the threat to his platoon, Commiskey hurried forward, pistol in hand. A few yards away another enemy machine gun spat bullets at the marines still caught on the hillside. Ignoring its fire, Commiskey boldly attacked it. He stood atop the bunker, firing down on the crew. He killed two of the gun crew while another marine finished off the other two.

Now that the two major threats to the marines were removed, Commiskey rallied the survivors from his platoon and led them forward. They swarmed over the hill, attacking and killing the NKPA soldiers. Always at the forefront, Commiskey guided his men, offering encouragement by his fearless display of leadership.

In another ten minutes the fight was over. A handful of enemy soldiers fled back to Yongdungp'o. Nearly fifty enemy bodies littered the top of Hill 85. The way to Yongdungp'o was open.

Miraculously, Commiskey survived his gallant assault unscathed. A week later, though, while leading his platoon in the house-to-house fighting in Seoul, he was wounded. After a brief period of hospitalization Commiskey rejoined his platoon. He led them in the X Corps invasion of eastern North Korea and through the Chosin Reservoir debacle.

During the retreat from North Korea, Commiskey received a third wound. The bitter cold left him with badly frost-bitten feet. That, combined with his three Purple Hearts, earmarked him for evacuation back to the United States.

After his recovery Commiskey received word of his Medal of Honor award. President Truman made the presentation on August 1, 1951, while Commiskey's wife, Jessica, and his family watched with pride.

Because of the damage to his feet, Commiskey applied for flight school. He entered aviation training at Pensacola, Florida, in the fall of 1951. After receiving his wings in June 1952, Commiskey once again returned to Korea.

By that time, though, the war was rapidly winding down. He flew only a few combat missions before the truce was signed.

In 1955 Commiskey requested he be taken off flight status and returned to the ground forces. His request was granted.

The intervening years passed slowly for Commiskey. With peacetime budgets promotion came slowly. When the Vietnam War started Commiskey volunteered to serve there. The Marine Corps, however, was initially reluctant to send one of its heroes back into combat. Commiskey persisted in his requests and, finally in late 1969, received orders for Vietnam.

During a routine physical examination prior to his departure overseas, doctors discovered a brain tumor. Further tests proved the tumor to be malignant. Commiskey spent eighteen months at Bethesda Naval Hospital in Washington, D.C., before dying on August 5, 1971. At his request his remains were cremated and scattered over the Gulf of Mexico. Commiskey was survived by his wife, a daughter, and a son, who carried on the family tradition of military service.

After the capture of Hill 85 marine artillery shelled Yongdungp'o for the rest of September 20th. Marine Corsairs added their bombs to the chaos. At 6:30 A.M. the next day, the 1st Marines attacked the industrial city. Heavy barrages of enemy artillery and mortar rounds peppered the advancing marines. The two flank companies took heavy casualties, forcing them to falter.

Good fortune, however, awaited the middle assault company. Company A, 1st Battalion, 1st Marines, forded a small creek and entered Yongdungp'o undiscovered. Fighting well behind enemy lines they resisted repeated enemy attacks throughout the rest of September 21 and into the night. After failing to dislodge this small group of marines the NKPA abandoned the city, leaving over four hundred dead behind. The rest of the 1st Marines occupied Yongdungp'o on September 22.

In the meantime, after capturing Kimpo Airfield on September 18, the 5th Marines quickly advanced to the Han River. They boarded landing craft just before dawn on September 20 and started across the river. Enemy automatic-weapons and small-arms fire caused heavy casualties among the leading assault waves, but they were soon reinforced on the east bank by succeeding boatloads of marines.

By noon that day two battalions of marines were across the Han and moving southeast along a railroad track toward Seoul. Resistance, at first light, steadily increased. The marines pushed forward, capturing several key hill positions. By nightfall, now supported by tanks, they were within three miles of the main railroad station in Seoul. There they ran smack into the 25th NKPA

Brigade moving out of Seoul. The marines settled down for a bloody struggle along a line of low hills ringing Seoul on the west.

By this time elements of the army's 7th Infantry Division had crossed the Inchon beachhead. They moved east, taking over positions from the 1st Marines south of the Seoul-Inchon highway. The 32d Infantry Regiment cut the Seoul-Suwon highway, isolating the NKPA units in Seoul from reinforcements in the Naktong area. They then drove northeast, securing the southern approaches to Seoul.

Heavy fighting raged all along the western approaches to Seoul throughout September 22 and 23. The newly arrived 7th Marine Regiment joined the battle alongside the 5th Marines on September 23. The 1st Marines began crossing the Han River on September 24, then took up positions on the south flank of the 5th Marines.

The stalemate along Seoul's western perimeter broke when Company D, 2d Battalion, 5th Marines, captured Hill 66 in the center of the enemy's line of resistance on September 24. At a cost of 36 killed and 142 wounded out of an original force of 206, the marines threw the North Koreans off the hill. Its capture broke the back of the NKPA defense. The next day the entire North Korean hill line collapsed. They left over twelve hundred dead behind when they withdrew.

As the 7th Marines moved along the northern flank of Seoul to secure it and block escape routes there, the 1st and 5th Marines moved into the western edge of Seoul on September 25. Heavy street fighting broke out, slowing the marines' advance. The 32d Infantry Regiment crossed the Han that same day, moving alongside the marines' right flank.

Just prior to midnight September 25, because he wanted to send the message exactly three months from the date of the start of the war, General Almond announced the liberation of Seoul. The very next day General MacArthur signed and released United Nations Communique 9, stating: "Seoul, the capital of the Republic of Korea, is again in friendly hands. United Nations forces . . . have completed the envelopment and seizure of the city."

Both pronouncements were premature. Less than half the city was actually in U.N. hands. Over twelve thousand NKPA soldiers had been ordered to make a last-ditch stand in Seoul. The marines and soldiers faced four more days of savage house-to-house fighting before the last fanatical defenders were pried loose. The marines would suffer their heaviest losses of the campaign during the final four days of the battle for Seoul.

Snipers harassed the advancing marines and GIs every step of the way. Chest-high barricades, made of rice- and earth-filled bags, stretched across the streets from side to side. From behind them, and at their flanks, enemy soldiers fired antitank guns and swept the streets with deadly machine-gun fire. Other NKPA soldiers held positions in nearby buildings. Antitank and personnel mines filled the streets in front of the barricades.

The marines quickly established a routine for reducing the barricades. Aircraft would bombard the barricade; artillery and mortars would lay down a base of covering fire while combat engineers exploded the mines; Pershing tanks would rumble up, take the barricade under fire; and once it was destroyed, infantrymen would swarm over the rubble, killing survivors, hunting down snipers, and clearing the area. Then it was on to the next barricade where the brutal process would be repeated.

Company G, 3d Battalion, 5th Marines, moved down a Seoul street early on the afternoon of September 26. While General MacArthur sent his optimistic message around the world, Company G's marines dived for cover when twin enemy machine guns spat out hot lead from behind a barricade. A half dozen men sprawled in the street, writhing in death's painful grip.

Nineteen-year-old Pfc. Eugene A. Obregon of Los Angeles, California, saw a buddy lying in the debris-filled street. The cries of pain from the man with a gaping hole in his chest drowned out the machine guns' chatter. Though safe behind a brick wall, Obregon couldn't bear to see his friend in agony. He had to get him out of the line of fire and into the hands of the medics.

Completely disregarding the enemy fire and the warnings of other marines, Obregon burst from cover into the bullet-swept street. Blazing away at the enemy with his M-1, Obregon reached his buddy's side. While bullets cut the air around him, the young Californian placed himself between the casualty and the North Koreans, shielding him from further injury.

After calming the man, Obregon grabbed his shirtfront and started pulling him to safety. While other marines placed effective fire on the enemy, Obregon inched his way to safety. He was just ten yards from cover when another enemy machine gun spoke. Its bullets tore into Obregon's body, spinning him around.

Mortally wounded, Obregon still thought only of the other marine. He deliberately crawled back to the casualty and threw himself on top of the man, using his torn body to protect his buddy. Another blast of enemy fire ended Obregon's life. His actions saved the casualty and resulted in his being awarded a posthumous Medal of Honor.

Not until September 29 did the 1st Marines sweep through the northeast corner of Seoul. By evening they had taken the two main hills in that area, effectively completing the capture of the city. Enemy resistance in Seoul had finally ended.

At noon, September 29, General MacArthur escorted Republic of Korea President Syngman Rhee into the National Assembly Hall. Before the assembled dignitaries MacArthur said, "In behalf of the United Nations

Command I am happy to restore to you, Mr. President, the seat of your government that from it you may better fulfill your constitutional responsibilities."

Little Syngman Rhee rose to speak. Nearly overcome with emotion, the old man, who had spent much of his life in exile, could not make his prepared speech. Instead, he said, in English, to the assembled Americans, "How can I ever explain to you my own undying gratitude and that of the Korean people?"

The ceremony ended. MacArthur returned to Tokyo to receive plaudits from the president, the Joint Chiefs of Staff, and world leaders.

That night, on Hill 132 just outside the northeastern edge of Seoul, Company E, 2d Battalion, 1st Marines, settled into their foxholes. They were expecting a quiet night. The marines had been told of MacArthur's speech. Many felt the war was over. In a few more weeks they'd be home. It was a false hope.

STANLEY R. CHRISTIANSON

The South Pacific is a long way from central Wisconsin, but that's where Stanley R. Christianson wanted to go. From his parents' farm near Mindoro, Wisconsin, he enlisted in the Marine Corps on January 25, 1943, the day after his eighteenth birthday. Following boot camp and advanced infantry training, Christianson joined the 2d Marine Division in New Zealand.

Ten months after his enlistment Pfc. Christianson found himself storming the coral bastion of Tarawa. Three days of brutal combat quickly indoctrinated the tough youngster into the ways of war. He saw enough fighting in the next seventy-two hours to last any man a lifetime. But he faced more war. Christianson made three more amphibious landings, fighting with the 6th Marine Regiment on Saipan, Tinian, and Okinawa.

Wearing sergeant's stripes, Christianson spent four months in Japan on occupation duty before being discharged just before Christmas 1945. But after his experiences in World War II, life on the family farm was too tame for him. Just ninety days after his return home he reenlisted in the marines.

Because of his combat experience Christianson applied for duty as a drill instructor. He felt if his training could help one marine survive in combat he'd done his job. As a sergeant Christianson spent two years at Parris Island, South Carolina. He probably would have stayed there longer but he had a run-in with a superior. He was busted back to private and removed from the DI program. When the Korean War broke out, Pvt. Christianson joined the 1st Marine Regiment in Japan.

Christianson performed so well in the fighting between Inchon and Seoul his company commander promoted him to private first class.

On the night of September 29, Christianson and Pfc. Al Walsh were ordered to man a machine gun in a listening post about three hundred yards in front of Hill 132. Grabbing only their rifles and a supply of hand grenades, they took their post at dusk. Behind them the other members of Company E, confident their fighting days were all but over, prepared for a quiet night.

Shortly before midnight Christianson heard movement in front of his foxhole. As he listened he realized it was a group of North Korean soldiers bent on attacking the marines in one last gesture of defiance. He quickly woke his partner.

"Listen," he told Walsh. "There must be a hundred of them."

Walsh agreed.

Knowing he would have little chance of survival once he opened up on the NKPA, but knowing also his sleeping comrades would need time to set up, Christianson told Walsh, "You warn the others. I'll hold 'em off."

Walsh hesitated. He didn't want to leave his friend behind.

"Go! I'll be okay," Christianson said.

Reluctantly, Walsh crawled out of the foxhole to warn the company. Christianson waited until he was sure Walsh was well on his way. Then, with the enemy less than fifty yards away, he opened fire. Swinging the machine gun back and forth on its tripod, Christianson sent a deadly stream of bullets into the NKPA's ranks. The enemy fell under his onslaught. More than a dozen North Koreans died in the initial burst of fire. The others scattered for cover.

At the top of the hill Walsh turned at the sound of the firing. He could see the muzzle blast from Christianson's machine gun splitting the inky blackness. Screams from the enemy wounded reached his ears. He raced into the perimeter, shouting for help. In minutes Walsh and a squad of marines tore down the hill.

Only ominous silence awaited them as they neared Christianson's position. They found him dead, slumped over his gun. Around him were the bodies of several dozen North Koreans. The surviving attackers had fled north.

Christianson's heroic self-sacrifice had saved his company from a potentially devastating surprise attack. His parents accepted his posthumous Medal of Honor on August 30, 1951.

In the days after Seoul's fall the marines and soldiers pushed out of the city, establishing blocking positions north at Uijongbu and south at Suwon. The U.S. X Corps was now firmly entrenched in the enemy's rear, sitting astride his communication and supply routes. The anvil was in place. Now all that remained was for the hammer to fall.

General MacArthur's grand scheme for ending the war in Korea included a massive offensive by the Eighth Army, coinciding with the Inchon landing. United Nations' troops in the Pusan Perimeter would break out, drive north, and link up with the X Corps in Seoul, destroying the NKPA forces trapped between them.

The enemy forces encircling Pusan numbered around seventy thousand men, of whom less than thirty percent were original veterans of the initial invasion. Low on supplies, including food and ammunition, the NKPA still presented a formidable opposition. From their positions atop the high ground surrounding the perimeter, they would have to be pried out in close combat.

Opposing the NKPA the U.N. forces numbered more than 150,000 men, including sixty thousand American troops. Though the U.N. troops were also short on some critical supplies, including artillery ammunition needed to support an offensive, cargo ships from the United States were arriving every day. In addition, the U.N. held the air and could deliver the massive firepower that control of the air implied.

The breakout began at 9:00 A.M., September 16. All along the U.N. line, units that had been on the defensive suddenly started attacking. Under murky skies and in heavy rain, the U.N. soldiers pushed forward against stubborn resistance. The most spectacular success occurred in the U.S. 2d Infantry Division's zone at the Naktong Bulge. Attacking with all three regiments abreast, the division overcame a brutal defense to cross the Naktong River on the morning of September 18. By the end of the day they had poured across the river in strength, sending several NKPA divisions fleeing.

The real collapse of the NKPA around Pusan came on September 19. At the north end, along Korea's east coast, ROK units advanced. In the center, the U.S. 1st Cavalry Division continued to meet fanatical resistance around Taegu. Only when the enemy realized the ROKs were circling behind them from the east did the NKPA in front of the cavalrymen start pulling back.

The U.S. 2d Infantry Division continued its advance west of the Naktong Bulge. Before them enemy units fled in terror. In the far south the U.S. 25th Infantry Division, after spending the first two days of the breakout fighting enemy forces in its rear, went on the offensive. To the surprise of the division's infantrymen, the enemy abandoned several key hill positions, allowing the division to make major advances.

On the right of the division's line the 35th Infantry Regiment met only light resistance in its attack near Chungam-ni until it reached the high ground near a small village called Saga. A steep, saw-toothed ridge was so well-fortified and the enemy fire was so heavy the regiment's 1st Battalion was forced to withdraw. After regrouping, Company C moved out for the attack.

WILLIAM R. JECELIN

Lt. John Hayduk considered Sgt. William R. Jecelin the best squad leader in his platoon. The twenty-year-old from Baltimore, Maryland, had joined the 25th Infantry Division in March 1949 in the Far East Command, nine months after enlisting. He quickly demonstrated himself to be a competent soldier who aggressively attacked every task he was assigned.

When the 25th Division landed in Korea, Jecelin proved his talents extended to the battlefield. He always placed himself right at the front, fearlessly battling the enemy. After Jecelin's squad leader became a casualty, Lieutenant Hayduk appointed him to the job, jumping him over two more senior men.

Hayduk's wisdom was proven on September 19, near Saga. After an artillery barrage and air strike peppered the ridge, Company C stepped off. Jecelin led his squad through heavy enemy fire and bursting shells across rice paddies and rocky ground to the base of the ridge. There an intense fusillade of enemy machine-gun fire enveloped the squad, driving it to cover.

After being pinned down for several minutes, Jecelin took the initiative. Rising to his feet in full view of the enemy, he shouted for his men to follow him up the hill. Firing his rifle and pausing only to yank grenades from his belt, Jecelin charged. Inspired by his tremendous display of courage, the rest of his squad joined in the attack.

Miraculously, in the face of the furious enemy fire, Jecelin and a handful of his men reached the crest of the hill unharmed. A virtual wall of enemy fire again drove them to cover behind rocks.

Jecelin quickly rallied his men. "Come on," he yelled. "We've come this far. We're not stopping now!"

The small band of men fixed bayonets and, behind Jecelin, stormed an antitank gun. Cold steel flashed as the infantrymen slashed their way through the position. Five enemy soldiers died as the result of the charge.

Again enemy fire drove the men to cover. Again Jecelin rallied his men. Using rifle butts and bayonets they jumped into another enemy position. Fierce hand-to-hand fighting overcame the enemy. As Jecelin prepared to lead his squad toward another enemy position, a North Korean soldier in a nearby spider hole tossed a hand grenade into the small group.

Jecelin saw it first. "I got it!" he yelled.

He elbowed aside one of his squad members and threw his body over the grenade. The tremendous blast picked Jecelin off the ground and tossed him several feet. His squad members instantly surrounded Jecelin, trying to save his life. But it was too late. Half his chest was gone. He had died the instant the grenade went off.

Seconds later Lieutenant Hayduk came upon the scene. "There's nothing we can do," he said after a minute. "Don't let him die in vain."

Inspired by Jecelin's bold initiative and incredible courage, the rest of Hayduk's platoon surged forward. Within minutes they had overwhelmed the remaining NKPA, destroying them all.

Seven months later, on April 3, 1951, Gen. Omar N. Bradley, Chairman of the Joint Chiefs of Staff, presented Jecelin's father his posthumous Medal of Honor.

The rout of the NKPA continued. Opposite the Naktong Bulge three enemy divisions streamed westward in full retreat. The U.S. 1st Cavalry Division suddenly found the hills in front of them clear of all but dead North Koreans and abandoned equipment. Now it was North Koreans rather than Americans who staggered through the hills broken, demoralized, weaponless, and hungry. American soldiers found the taste of revenge very sweet.

United Nations aircraft had a field day attacking the fleeing NKPA troops. They slaughtered literally thousands of enemy soldiers with their bombs, rockets, and machine guns.

During the last week of September the Americans regained many of the towns they'd lost in the first week of the war. Taejon, turned into a major supply base for the North Koreans, fell to the U.S. 24th Infantry Division on September 28. The U.S. 1st Cavalry Division swept through Waegwan parallel to the U.S. 24th Infantry Division and seized Sangju.

A special task force of tanks from the U.S. 1st Cavalry Division spearheaded the division's advance toward Osan. They started forward on September 26. Stopping only when necessary to engage the enemy, they reached Osan the next day. There they met units of the U.S. 7th Infantry Division. The linkup between Eighth Army and X Corps was complete.

To the south, the U.S. 25th Infantry Division advanced to Chinju near Korea's south coast on September 28. From there they moved north to Chonju, already captured by the U.S. 2d Infantry Division on September 29. The two divisions headed north, reaching the Kum River the next day.

By October 1 most of the NKPA had been expelled from South Korea. ROK units on the east coast had driven to within five miles of the Thirty-eighth Parallel. The rapid sweep of the U.N. forces bypassed thousands of enemy troops in the rugged mountains of South Korea. It would be several months before ROK troops mopped them up.

The bulk of North Koreans fled north of the Thirty-eighth Parallel. There they assembled in an area that would come to be known as the Iron Triangle. Best intelligence estimates indicated not more than thirty thousand enemy soldiers made it across the parallel. For all practical purposes the NKPA had been destroyed.

Chapter Four
To the Yalu

With the North Korean Army all but destroyed and expelled from South Korea, with Seoul securely in U.N. hands, and U.S. and ROK forces assembled along the Thirty-eighth Parallel, the big question was whether U.N. forces should cross into North Korea. The Joint Chiefs of Staff sent General MacArthur a lengthy communique on September 27 governing his future actions. It stated that his first objective was the destruction of North Korean forces. If possible, he was to unite all of Korea under Syngman Rhee. But he was to be particularly alert to any intervention by Soviet or Chinese forces and report them to the JCS immediately. MacArthur was specifically told that no U.N. forces were to cross the Manchurian or Soviet borders of Korea under any circumstances. Finally, he was to submit his plan for operations north of the Thirty-eighth Parallel to the JCS for approval.

MacArthur immediately requested the JCS lift the restriction requiring their specific approval before he proceeded north. He wanted to be able to move north immediately if the North Koreans failed to surrender in accordance with a proclamation he intended to issue. Two days later Secretary of Defense George C. Marshall agreed to MacArthur's request.

On October 1, 1950, MacArthur issued his surrender demand to the NKPA commander. There was no response. The surrender demand was repeated on October 9. Though there was no official response to this demand, either, Premier Kim Il Sung rejected the demand in a radio speech monitored in Japan. The U.N. attack across the Thirty-eighth Parallel would proceed.

MacArthur planned a two-pronged attack north through North Korea to the Yalu River. The Eighth Army would move along Korea's west coast, capture the North Korean capital of Pyongyang, then proceed to the Yalu. In the meantime, the X Corps would make an amphibious landing at Wonsan, an important seaport on Korea's east coast about 110 miles north of the Thirty-eighth Parallel. From there they would move to the Yalu where they would link up with the Eighth Army.

The terrain of North Korea caused General MacArthur to operate his two northward attacking columns as separate field commands. The rugged Taebaek mountain range rises to dizzying heights in the east central part of the peninsula north of a line between Seoul and Wonsan. The range runs generally north-south in a near trackless wasteland. Only one road, from Pyongyang to Wonsan, bisects the range from east to west. The Taebaeks not only provided a monumental logistical problem, but made a coordinated attack to the north all but impossible. Accordingly, MacArthur reasoned that supplying the two armies and coordinating their movements could best be done from his Tokyo headquarters. It was a fateful, disastrous decision.

General Walker prepared for his move across the Thirty-eighth Parallel by assembling his Eighth Army along the Imjin River. He designated the U.S. 1st Cavalry Division to lead the attack. The U.S. 24th Infantry Division would protect the Eighth Army's left flank, while the ROK 1st Infantry Division moved on the right. The first objective of the cavalrymen was Kaesong, north and west of Seoul, nearly astride the Thirty-eighth Parallel. Elements of several NKPA divisions held the high terrain north and northeast of the town. On October 7 a battalion of the 8th Cavalry Regiment easily secured Kaesong. The rest of the division moved into position the next day.

On the morning of October 9 all three regiments of the U.S. 1st Cavalry Division were deployed abreast just below the parallel. In the center, the 8th Cavalry Regiment was to attack frontally along the main highway from Kaesong to Kumch'on, about fifteen miles north. On the right, the 5th Cavalry Regiment would first attack east, then swing westward in a circular flanking movement designed to envelop enemy forces south of Kumch'on. The 7th Cavalry Regiment was to move west, crossing the Yesong River about five miles west of Kaesong, before turning north to capture the hamlet of Hanp'ori, six miles north of Kumch'on, where the main Pyongyang road crossed the Yesong River.

Patrols from the U.S. 1st Cavalry Division had crossed the parallel on the afternoon of Saturday, October 7, and others crossed on Sunday night. But they were not the first to move across the line. The ROK 3d Infantry Division, operating on the east coast, crossed the Thirty-eighth Parallel on September 30. Three days later they and the ROK Capital Division established command posts in Yangyang, nine miles north of the parallel.

At 9:00 A.M., October 9, the U.S. 1st Cavalry Division moved across the parallel and began fighting its way northward. The NKPA 19th and 27th

Divisions strongly resisted the Americans. The advance proved very costly. In the center of the line the 8th Cavalry Regiment almost immediately ran into an enemy strong point defended with tanks, self-propelled guns, and antiaircraft weapons.

Company E, 8th Cavalry, leading the attack, received intense mortar and accurate automatic-weapons fire from its front, as well as from both sides of the road along which it was advancing. Mortar fragments tore into the face of twenty-one-year-old Pfc. Robert H. Young, sending him reeling. But the Vallejo, California, resident refused evacuation. He quickly advanced to the front line and placed effective M-1 rifle fire on advancing enemy troops.

Forty-five minutes later, Young was again hit by enemy fire which severely injured his right hand. While awaiting first aid at the company command post, Young heard the North Koreans were attempting to flank his company. He jumped up and returned to the fight. He killed five enemy soldiers, halting their attack, before he was wounded a third time. This time the enemy fire slammed into his head, knocking him down and destroying his helmet.

Lesser men might have quit at this point, but not Young. He ran through a concentration of enemy fire to the rear of a tank. He tried to reach the tank commander via the tank's exterior telephone. Failing that, he climbed aboard the armored vehicle where, completely exposed to hostile fire, he beat on the hatch with his rifle butt until a crew member responded. Young then directed the tank's fire on nearby enemy gun positions, destroying three, which enabled Company E to advance.

During a lull in the fighting Young helped evacuate other wounded. An exploding enemy mortar round mortally wounded the youth while he was so engaged. Despite his grievous wounds Young insisted other casualties be treated first. He died that night at the evacuation hospital.

On the division's right the 5th Cavalry Regiment also ran into stubborn resistance. Its initial attacks on October 9 and 10 had quickly overrun the hills flanking and dominating both sides of its line of advance out of Kaesong. Fifteen miles northeast of Kaesong, however, they bumped into a large enemy force holding a long ridge dominating an important pass. The regiment's 1st Battalion ground to a halt. Reinforced by the 2d Battalion the next morning, the cavalrymen drove the NKPA from the ridge the afternoon of October 12. It was during this action that a brave infantry officer gave his life to save one of his soldiers.

SAMUEL S. COURSEN

The West Point class of 1915 is often referred to as the Class of Generals because it produced Dwight D. Eisenhower, Omar Bradley, James Van Fleet, and a host of other one-, two- and three-star generals. The Class of 1918 is sometimes referred to as the Class of Jokers because it produced a flock of brand-new second lieutenants just a few short months before the Armistice ended World War I.

The West Point Class of 1949 will forever be known as the Korean Class because one out of every six members became a casualty in Korea. No less than twenty-one died in the far-off country. The first fell on August 12, at a roadblock near Taejon just a few weeks after the war started. One of those who died did so earning his country's highest award.

Samuel S. Coursen was born on August 4, 1926, at Madison, New Jersey. After completing grade school in Madison he graduated from Newark Academy in Newark. In July 1945 he entered the U.S. Military Academy at West Point. At six foot five inches and a lean 190 pounds, Coursen excelled at track, lacrosse, and football. He did well academically, too, attaining the rank of cadet sergeant.

Coursen graduated from West Point on June 3, 1949, sporting the gold bars of a second lieutenant and the crossed rifles insignia of an infantry officer. Three weeks after graduation he married Evie Sprague of Virginia Beach, Virginia. Then it was off to more school at Fort Riley, Kansas. In April 1950 the Coursens moved to Georgia where Lieutenant Coursen attended the advanced infantry course at Fort Benning. It was there his son, Samuel S., Jr., was born.

The Benning course ended in July and all talk among the students concerned prospective assignments in Korea. Coursen drew one in Japan and it seemed like a good deal. Evie and his son could join him there in just a few months.

But by the time Coursen finally headed overseas in August all talk of his family joining him in Japan had ended. Coursen's orders had been changed to Korea and the 1st Cavalry Division. He arrived in Pusan a few days after his 24th birthday. Within a week he took over a platoon in Company C, 5th Cavalry.

Coursen led his platoon in the breakout from the Pusan Perimeter and started the drive north to Seoul. He linked up with the 7th Infantry Division near Suwon, south of Seoul, and, after a brief rest and refitting, headed for Kaesong.

On October 12, Coursen's platoon was one of two assigned the task of eliminating the NKPA on Hill 174, one of the three knobs overlooking the 5th Cavalry's route of advance. On his right Coursen's West Point classmate, Lt. Lewis W. Zichel, led another platoon.

Zichel remembered that morning. "It was a gloomy, foggy day, with visibility limited to mere yards," he said. "Our platoons were about twenty-five yards apart, with Lieutenant Coursen's just a few yards forward of mine."

The two platoons crested the hill and headed down into a wide depression. Sporadic enemy small-arms fire harassed the GIs as they walked across the rocky landscape.

Suddenly, Coursen's platoon received heavy fire from a well-concealed enemy strong point. Reacting instantly, Coursen put his platoon on line and started through the fog toward the enemy.

As the enemy fire increased in volume several of Coursen's platoon members dived for cover. One private jumped into a bunker he thought was unoccupied. It wasn't. Nearly a dozen North Korean soldiers fell on the hapless American.

Coursen heard the man's screams for help. Without a second of hesitation, he plunged into the emplacement.

It was a savage hand-to-hand battle. Coursen was outnumbered at least ten-to-one, but he fought like a cornered tiger. He couldn't fire his carbine for fear of hitting his own man. It was too close for the bayonet to be effective. Instead, the lanky officer used his carbine as a club, slamming it into enemy heads. The fight lasted only a few minutes.

After Lieutenant Zichel led his platoon in wiping out the enemy position he returned to where Coursen had gone to his comrade's aid. Seven dead enemy soldiers littered the floor of the bunker. Several had had their skulls crushed by Coursen's rifle. The lieutenant lay dead on top of one of the enemy soldiers, shot in the back as he killed this last enemy soldier. Huddled unconscious in a corner of the small emplacement was the soldier Coursen had died to save.

In a solemn ceremony at the Pentagon on June 21, 1951, Gen. Omar Bradley presented the posthumous Medal of Honor to Evie Coursen and her fourteen-month-old son.

Heavy fighting continued north of Kaesong in what became known as the Kumch'on Pocket for five days. Not until the 5th and 7th Cavalry Regiments made wide enveloping attacks to the east and west of Kumch'on did the North Koreans finally withdraw. The road to the North Korean capital, Pyongyang, was open.

The drive on Pyongyang began at daybreak on October 16. The three Eighth Army units comprising the U.S. I Corps moved toward the enemy capital: the U.S. 1st Cavalry Division from the southeast, the U.S. 24th Infantry Division from the south, and the ROK 1st Infantry Division from the east. Various degrees of enemy resistance met the U.N. units as they closed on the North Korean capital. At times the NKPA defenders fought ruthlessly to hamper the U.N. forces; only heavy artillery barrages and air strikes destroyed the enemy. At other locations the NKPA made only token efforts to halt the attackers before heading north in disarray.

As the Eighth Army units neared Pyongyang on October 18, intelligence reports made it clear the NKPA planned no last-ditch defense of its capital. The North Koreans not only had to contend with the U.S. I Corps approaching from the south, but the ROK II Corps now closing from the east and southeast. All together seven U.N. divisions were converging on Pyongyang.

Eighth Army intelligence concluded that less than eight thousand NKPA soldiers would defend the city. The balance of the NKPA was withdrawing northward across the Chongchon River, about fifty miles north of Pyongyang, regrouping for further operations.

Battling their way north, the 5th and 7th Cavalry Regiments leapfrogged along the road leading to Pyongyang. While one unit held in place to destroy NKPA positions, the other would push past them to continue attacking north until it, too, encountered resistance.

At 5:00 A.M., October 19, the 2d Battalion, 5th Cavalry, passed through the 7th Cavalry. Sporadic fire greeted these troops as they advanced toward Pyongyang. Just past 11:00 A.M. that day, Company F, 2d Battalion, 5th Cavalry Regiment, entered the southwestern edge of the capital. At almost the same time the ROK 1st Division entered the city from the east. A few hours later another ROK division entered the city from the northeast. Minor skirmishes with the remaining NKPA defenders raged throughout the night and into the next morning. At 10:00 A.M., October 20, the city was declared secure.

At the same time Pyongyang fell, General Walker launched an operation designed to cut off North Korean officials and enemy troops he believed were fleeing north from the city and simultaneously rescue American POWs presumably being evacuated northward. The 187th Airborne Regiment had been held in Eighth Army reserve at Kimpo Field near Seoul. When the fall of Pyongyang appeared imminent Walker alerted the parachute unit to prepare for an airdrop into two zones thirty air miles north of the capital.

Two highways run north out of Pyongyang, forming a 'V'. The main highway to the Yalu River forms the left-hand side of the 'V' and passes through the town of Sukch'on. The right-hand road runs to Sunch'on, about seventeen air miles east of Sukch'on. The 187th Airborne Regiment would air assault into drop zones adjacent to these two towns.

At 2:30 in the morning of October 20, the airborne troopers at Kimpo Field turned out in a heavy rain. After a hearty breakfast they waited until noon for the downpour to end. At last airborne the 113 troop-laden C-119s and C-47s headed for the drop zones. Just before 2:00 P.M. the first paratroopers hit the silk over Sukch'on. Within minutes nearly fifteen hundred men were on the ground. At 2:30 P.M. the jump over Sunch'on began. Soon nearly two thousand paratroopers occupied the commanding ground near that town. By evening these paratroopers made contact with ROK troops coming north from Pyongyang.

Though General MacArthur termed the airborne assault an "expert performance" that "closed the trap on the enemy," no sizable North Korean units were caught. The main enemy body had already crossed the Chongchon River and was headed for an assembly area along the Yalu River near Kanggye. North Korean government officials had fled the capital on October 12 and were near Manpojin on the Yalu.

The 187th Airborne Regiment did meet the North Koreans in battle, however. After dropping near Sukch'on, the regiment's 3d Battalion headed south and set up blocking positions near Opa-ri, about eight miles south. At 9:00 A.M. on October 21, two companies of the battalion continued the advance south toward Pyongyang. Just as they passed through Opa-ri they ran headlong into the NKPA 239th Regiment, the last enemy force to leave Pyongyang.

Company I was moving down a narrow valley flanked on three sides by high hills when the enemy sprang his trap. From all three sides the North Koreans rained down an incessant barrage of mortar, automatic-weapons, and small-arms fire. Dozens of paratroopers fell, dead or wounded. The survivors scrambled for available cover.

RICHARD G. WILSON

While the able paratroopers hurriedly returned the enemy's fire, the company's medic busied himself caring for the wounded. Though only nineteen years old, Pfc. Richard G. Wilson was as respected among the troopers of Company I as a venerable country doctor among his patients. He was their main source of medical care and took his responsibilities very seriously. That had always been his nature.

Born in Marion, Illinois, Wilson moved with his family to Cape Girardeau, Missouri, when he was eight. At his new school he quickly earned a spot with the school patrol boys. As his mother, Alice Wilson, remembered years later, "He was very proud of his white belt. He always made sure the other children safely crossed his street."

Wilson later joined the Boy Scouts, earning a large number of merit badges. When he was fifteen he entered the area Golden Gloves championship. Though his mother objected, he did quite well, advancing all the way to the finals in St. Louis where he lost in a decision.

If Wilson did well at boxing, he excelled at football. "It was his great love," Alice Wilson recalled. As a freshman he played on the junior varsity team; the next year he made the varsity team. In his junior year he was picked for the Southeast Missouri High School All Star Team. "It was one of the proudest moments in his life," according to his mother.

Though he had a good future ahead of him as a college football player—

scouts had already approached him in his junior year—Wilson had a stronger interest in the military. He satisfied it by enlisting in the army on his seventeenth birthday.

After basic training at Fort Knox, Kentucky, Wilson received an assignment to the Field Medics School at Fort Sam Houston, Texas. He took an instant liking to the training and was one of his class's outstanding students.

The lure of more pay, combined with the excitement and adventure, led Wilson to volunteer for the paratroopers after medics school. Training at Fort Benning, Georgia, was rugged but Wilson's athletic background helped him make it through. His first jump was quite an experience. To his mother he wrote, "Don't let anyone kid you, we were all scared." But he, and the others, jumped. Four jumps later he received the coveted wings of a paratrooper.

Wilson ended up being stationed at Fort Campbell, Kentucky, just 150 miles from home. He spent many weekend passes in Cape Girardeau, hanging around with his high school buddies. On one such weekend he met a soft-eyed high school coed named Bonnie. It was instant love for both. From that point on they spent every possible moment together and planned to marry as soon as Wilson's hitch was up.

The North Korean invasion of South Korea changed all that. When the 187th Airborne was alerted for movement to the Far East the two married on Wilson's last weekend pass. They were together as man and wife for less than a week before the 187th Airborne left Fort Campbell for Japan.

The paratroopers flew into Kimpo Field on September 24. Though most of the fighting for Seoul was over, a few companies of the regiment saw limited action in the mopping-up around the capital. Pfc. Wilson spent most of his time treating blistered feet and other routine ailments. It wasn't very exciting but Wilson felt needed and did his best to take care of the men in his charge.

The paratroopers remained in garrison at Kimpo Field, anxious to get into the war, while other Eighth Army units headed for Pyongyang. They were starting to feel the war would be over before they really had the chance to fight when they were alerted for the airdrop north of Pyongyang. At last, they'd have a chance to carry the war right to the enemy.

The airborne landing at Sukch'on was unopposed by the enemy, but twenty-five paratroopers were injured in the drop. Wilson and other medics splinted the broken bones and bandaged the cuts, then prepared the men for evacuation. The next day Wilson and Company I headed south to set up a roadblock to trap NKPA fleeing Pyongyang. The NKPA found them first.

The paratroopers returned fire while Wilson patched up several of his wounded comrades. He then carried them to a sheltered location. A number of casualties still lay in the open, fully exposed to the enemy. Several attempts had been made to retrieve them but had been beaten back by vicious bursts of enemy fire.

Sfc. James Hardin watched in awe as Wilson left his sheltered aid station to go to them. Through the murderous fire Wilson calmly made his way to one wounded man's side, knelt beside him, and started treatment. Bullets clipped the air around him and plowed into the ground within inches of the two men, but miraculously none found flesh. After applying first aid, Wilson carried the man to safety. He then repeated his heroic actions until he'd pulled all the casualties to safety.

The firefight raged for two and one-half hours. Sergeant Hardin continued to be amazed at Wilson's disregard for his own safety to reach and treat the wounded. "All during the fight," Hardin said, "Wilson continued these acts of bravery, incessantly exposing himself to assist others in distress."

When it became obvious the paratroopers could not dislodge the North Koreans, Company I's commander, Capt. Glenn Q. Ganow, ordered his company to withdraw to better defensive positions on a nearby hill.

During the withdrawal Wilson helped the wounded to the new position, paying no heed to the enemy fire. At the new site a quick inventory of personnel was taken. One man was reported as dead, but then another soldier spoke up and reported he'd seen the soldier wounded but alive and moving. Upon hearing this, Wilson immediately prepared to rescue the man. Sergeant Hardin told him not to go. It was just too dangerous. Enemy soldiers already could be seen approaching the Americans' former positions. Wilson slung his medical bag over his shoulder.

Hardin grabbed Wilson. "You can't make it out there," Hardin warned. "Look. Already the North Koreans are closing in."

Wilson shrugged off Hardin's grasp. "I can't leave him there," was all he said.

Wilson knew all soldiers had a fear of being wounded and left to the mercy of a ruthless enemy. The men of Wilson's company trusted him to take care of them. He could not let them down. He started after the missing man. He carried no weapons. His fellow paratroopers provided covering fire but soon Wilson was out of sight. That was the last anyone saw of him.

The NKPA kept the pressure on the paratroopers all through the rest of the day and into the night. Not until the next day, when they were reinforced by a detachment of Australians from the 27th British Commonwealth Brigade, were the paratroopers able to go on the offensive. Caught between the Americans and the Australians, the NKPA 239th Regiment was nearly destroyed.

On October 23, 1950, a patrol from Company I made its way back to where they'd been ambushed. Among the dead GIs they found Pfc. Wilson. He was crouched beside the body of the soldier he'd gone to save. A morphine syrette was still clutched in his hand. He'd been shot at close range while trying to shield his comrade.

On June 21, 1951, Wilson's grieving widow accepted her husband's Medal of Honor. Also present were Wilson's parents, brother, and three sisters.

After the enemy was cleared from the ground between the airborne troopers and the U.N. forces coming out of Pyongyang, the drive to the Yalu River resumed.

Eighth Army had two corps driving north. The U.S. I Corps, consisting of the U.S. 24th Infantry Division and ROK 1st Infantry Division, held the left half of the front. On the right, the ROK II Corps had the ROK 6th and 8th Infantry Divisions moving north.

The last natural barrier before the Yalu was the Chongchon River, forty-five air miles north of Pyongyang and about the same distance south of the Yalu. The Chongchon River was crossed as early as October 23. Little opposition was expected from the decimated enemy and a speedy advance to the border was anticipated. Several uncoordinated columns from both corps areas headed north. Each column was free to advance as far and as fast as it could without respect to advances made by the other.

On October 26, 1950, the Recon Platoon from the 7th Regiment, ROK 6th Division, entered the town of Chosan on the Yalu River. As they approached the river, scores of fleeing North Koreans could be seen struggling up the river's north bank into Manchuria. The Recon Platoon spent several hours in the town, collected a bottle of Yalu River water for President Rhee, then pulled back in anticipation of the entire regiment occupying the town later.

As events would prove, this would be the only unit under Eighth Army control to reach the river.

While the Eighth Army was advancing on Pyongyang, General MacArthur and President Truman met on Wake Island on October 15, 1950. Amazingly, this would be the first meeting between these two powerful men. During Truman's five-year presidency MacArthur had always been overseas. Though there was no hostility between the two, there existed a sense that the government in Washington and the general were on increasingly divergent wavelengths. MacArthur acted as if he were miffed at being reminded he did not have the independence he would like to have.

In the conference among Truman, MacArthur, General Bradley, and Secretary of State Dean Rusk, little time was spent on the fighting in Korea. Everyone assumed the conflict was all but over. MacArthur even went so far as to state he felt most of the troops would be back in Japan by Thanksgiving. In fact, he was readying orders for some units to turn in their arms and ammo by the end of October before their departure from Korea. He even had begun planning a massive victory parade in Japan. Bradley wanted to know how quickly one or more divisions could be released for duty in Europe, where the real threat lay.

Near the end of the conference Truman almost casually asked MacArthur, "What are the chances of Soviet or Chinese intervention in Korea?"

Without hesitation, MacArthur responded, "Very little."

He went on to explain that if the Chinese had intervened during the conflict's first two months it would have been decisive. "But we are no longer fearful of their intervention. We no longer stand hat in hand," he said.

MacArthur acknowledged the Chinese did have three hundred thousand men in Manchuria, of which about two hundred thousand were along the Yalu. He thought maybe sixty thousand could get across the river. "But the Chinese have no air force," he said. "If the Chinese try to get down to Pyongyang there will be the greatest slaughter."

MacArthur might have been one of America's greatest generals, but on this count he was as wrong as he could be.

Evidence had been mounting for some time that the Chinese would directly involve themselves in the Korean conflict. However, as flush with the headiness of victory as they were, American military leaders in Japan believed what they wanted to believe.

As early as October 1, Chinese leader Mao Tse-tung had warned, "The Chinese people will not tolerate foreign aggression and will not stand aside if the imperialists wantonly invade the territory of their neighbor."

Since Red China had no diplomatic relations with the United States, Chinese foreign minister Chou En-lai made his views known through India's ambassador. On October 3, Chou En-lai told Sardar K. M. Pannikar, "If the United States, or United Nations forces cross the Thirty-eighth Parallel, the Chinese People's Republic will send troops to aid the People's Republic of Korea. We shall not take this action, however, if only South Korean troops cross the border."

Pannikar immediately relayed the message to New Delhi. From there the word went to Washington and London. London expressed alarm, but all Washington did was pass the word to MacArthur's headquarters in Tokyo. As more warnings filtered into Tokyo from around the world MacArthur's intelligence officers studied and analyzed the data. On October 14, MacArthur's intelligence chief issued the following opinion, "Recent declarations by Chinese Communist Forces (CCF) leaders, threatening to enter North Korea if American forces cross the Thirty-eighth Parallel, are probably in a category of diplomatic blackmail."

If only he had been right.

The first American troops had crossed the Thirty-eighth Parallel on October 9. Five days later four Chinese armies of the Fourth Field Army started across the Yalu River. By moving only at night, maintaining strict discipline, and staying covered during the day deep in the rugged mountains south of the Yalu, the Chinese remained undetected.

The U.N.'s first clash with the CCF came on October 26, near Onjong against the ROK 7th Regiment, the same unit whose Recon Platoon had reached the Yalu River. In fighting that raged throughout the night and into the next day the regiment was virtually destroyed. Over the next two days three more ROK regiments were chewed apart by the Chinese.

A prisoner taken by the ROK 6th Division on October 25 seemed to speak only Chinese. He was hastily flown to the rear. Though this POW, as well as others captured during the last days of October, spoke of the Chinese armies hidden in the mountains north of the Eighth Army, American intelligence officers again discounted the tales. They refused to believe so many troops could have snuck into North Korea without them being aware of it.

Reality began to sink in when the ROK 1st Division battled the Chinese on October 29 near Unsan, a small mountain town near the center of the Eighth Army's front. When the Chinese surrounded the ROK division, the U.S. 1st Cavalry Division was rushed forward to extricate it. After allowing the 8th Cavalry Regiment to reach Unsan on October 30, the Chinese again slammed the door shut. Over the next two days the Chinese 39th Army not only decimated the ROKs but virtually annihilated the trapped 8th Cavalry.

General Walker finally recognized the situation. He ordered his forces to pull back south to positions along the north bank of the Chongchon River. Next, he ordered north two more U.S. divisions, the 2d and 25th Infantry. Walker would use them to buy himself some time to analyze his position and solve some logistical problems.

On November 1, the Eighth Army held the lower Chongchon River valley from Won-ni and Kunu-ri westward to the Yellow Sea. Relative quiet prevailed on the battlefield for the next few days, but between November 3 and 6 the CCF launched a series of near-constant attacks against U.N. positions along the Chongchon. North of the river above the town of Anju, the 2d Battalion, 19th Infantry Regiment, U.S. 24th Infantry Division, had been almost constantly engaged with the Chinese since November 3. On the night of November 5, after finally pushing the CCF back, Companies E and G occupied Hill 123 which overlooked a little valley near the hamlet of Chonghyon, about four miles north of the Chongchon River. Though weary from forty-eight hours of combat, the infantrymen were in good spirits. They had bloodied the seemingly invincible Chinese and felt good about it. Tomorrow they would launch a local counterattack to regain lost ground. The GIs felt confident they'd be successful.

MITCHELL RED CLOUD

Company E's commander, Capt. Walter E. Conway, sent out several listening posts. His brief experience in fighting the Chinese taught him they would send nighttime probes against his position, looking for a soft spot to exploit. He didn't want them to find one.

At the point of the ridge where a trail led to his command post, Conway put one of his most experienced men, Cpl. Mitchell Red Cloud, a full-blooded Winnebago Indian from Friendship, Wisconsin.

Life in rural Wisconsin did not offer much hope for success for an Indian youngster in the years before World War II. Seeking the best opportunity, seventeen-year-old Mitchell Red Cloud enlisted in the Marine Corps in August 1941.

Red Cloud spent nearly two years in the South Pacific fighting the Japanese. He served with the elite marine raiders on several expeditions before they were disbanded. Then Red Cloud joined the 5th Marine Division for the brutal fighting at Iwo Jima.

Only twenty-one when discharged in November 1945, Red Cloud returned to his family home. He soon found life in Wisconsin boring compared to his adventures in World War II. As did many other veterans, Red Cloud rejoined the military. This time he signed on with the army, enlisting in October 1948.

Red Cloud joined the 24th Infantry Division in Japan in 1949. Occupation duty was easy, almost leisurely. Daytime schedules were light and nearly every evening was free to enjoy all that Japan had to offer. Then came Korea.

Red Cloud and the 24th Infantry Division were among the first troops rushed to Korea. He survived the withdrawal into the Pusan Perimeter, all its fighting, the breakout, then the drive north toward the Yalu. To Red Cloud and his buddies it was satisfying to witness the NKPA fleeing.

Capt. Conway had considerable confidence in Corporal Red Cloud. His years of combat experience with the marines made him more dependable than others of higher rank. Conway knew if anyone could protect the vulnerable route to the CP, Red Cloud could.

At 6:15 in the morning, November 6, Red Cloud detected movement on the brush-covered hillside below him. In the freezing morning air he strained to see through the darkness. His eyes swept the ground in front of him. His ears picked up foreign sounds but he could see nothing. Then, suddenly, emerging from the brush less than a hundred feet away, a line of Chinese soldiers came up the hill.

"Here they come!" he hollered to the men around him. Then he pulled the trigger of his BAR.

Below him half a dozen Chinese fell. The others kept coming. Red Cloud fired heavy bursts from his BAR, knocking down the enemy, but there were too many. They kept coming.

At the CP Conway quickly realized this was no ordinary attack. Word from his outposts indicated the Chinese were on him from all directions, including his rear. Only Mitchell Red Cloud's shouted warning had kept the company from being completely surprised.

Red Cloud continued his duel with the Chinese. Clip after clip of .30-caliber rounds disappeared through his BAR. Around him other members of his platoon rallied to the fight. The bark of M-1s and the chatter of light machine guns filled the morning air. Still the Chinese came.

Lt. John Anderson, Red Cloud's platoon leader, saw him take a burst of "burp" gun fire from a Chinese soldier. The corporal slumped in his foxhole.

For the next fifteen to twenty minutes Anderson busied himself with the defense of his position. Red Cloud's BAR fire was sorely missed.

Just as it seemed the position might be overrun, Anderson heard the deep pounding of Red Cloud's BAR. The mortally wounded soldier had regained consciousness. Pulling himself out of his foxhole, he wrapped one arm around a small tree, and again delivered point-blank BAR fire on the Chinese.

He remained erect for perhaps five minutes. Then Chinese soldiers swarmed around him. They cut him down.

The time Red Cloud bought for his company allowed Conway to reorganize his perimeter and tighten his defenses. The company held. The Chinese attackers were repulsed. After the fight more than a score of dead Chinese were counted on the ground where Red Cloud made his last stand.

When President Truman presented Nellie Red Cloud with her son's posthumous Medal of Honor on April 3, 1951, he told her, "Your son has joined the spirits of his forefathers. He will take his place among the other great Indian warriors who have died bravely on the field of battle."

Eighth Army forces met the CCF in battle all day November 6 and until past dawn on November 7. Unable to dislodge the U.N. forces, the Chinese scurried back into their daytime hiding spots, safe from the prying eyes of U.N. airplanes. On the battlefield U.N. troops cared for the wounded, evacuated the dead, and reorganized their defenses for another night of battle.

But the Chinese didn't come that night or the next. Leaving just as silently as they had arrived, the CCF simply melted northward into the rugged mountains. General Walker and his staff concluded the Chinese "volunteers" had faded away because they had expended their effort. Since they believed less than sixty thousand Chinese were fighting in North Korea it is easy to see how they arrived at their conclusion. As a result, Walker had the Eighth Army begin preparations for a renewed drive to the Yalu.

In the meantime, General Almond's X Corps on Korea's east coast had been undergoing an ordeal of its own. MacArthur had decided the U.S. 1st Marine Division would move to Wonsan via ship from Inchon. At the same time the U.S. 7th Infantry Division would move by truck from Seoul all the way south to Pusan, then board ships for movement north to Wonsan. The marines departed Inchon on October 17, 1950. That same day the 7th Infantry Division loaded aboard ships at Pusan.

MacArthur's original plans envisioned a marine assault at Wonsan. However, the rapid advance of the ROK I Corps, consisting of the ROK 3d and Capital Divisions, up Korea's east coast negated these plans. Even before the X Corps had boarded ship the ROK forces had captured Wonsan and were continuing north. MacArthur now directed the X Corps to make an administrative landing at Wonsan. The 7th Infantry Division would follow the marines ashore. The marines would then advance northwest through the port of Hungnam to the Chosin Reservoir, about sixty air miles from Hungnam. From there the marines would move west through Yudam-ni, effecting a linkup with the Eighth Army. The 7th Infantry Division would secure the Fusen Reservoir, some twenty air miles east of Chosin. They would also move to the Yalu River on the west, or left, flank of the ROK I Corps.

The flotilla carrying the 1st Marine Division arrived off Wonsan October 19. They then learned Wonsan Harbor had been extensively mined. For the next week the flotilla steamed slowly north and south while the mines were cleared. They finally landed on the morning of October 26, after the troops ashore had enjoyed a rollicking Bob Hope USO show the night before.

In the meantime, the 7th Infantry Division had spent ten miserable days afloat in Pusan harbor. Finally, they were directed to land at Iwon, a hundred miles north of Wonsan and that much closer to their objective. They started ashore on October 29.

From Wonsan the marines moved by rail to Hamhung, eight miles inland from the port of Hungnam. From Hamhung they would begin their move to Yudam-ni, seventy-eight miles away. These would prove to be the most difficult seventy-eight miles in marine corps history.

The road to Yudam-ni, or Main Supply Route (MSR) as the Marines would call it, was narrow and treacherously winding. Ox carts found it difficult to traverse; for tanks and trucks it was just short of impossible. The road was mostly dirt or gravel. On one side were towering cliffs; on the other sheer drops of several hundred feet.

The most difficult stretch of road was at Funchilin Pass, an eight-mile, twenty-five-hundred-foot climb to Koto-ri, a little more than halfway to

Yudam-ni. From Koto-ri, the MSR crosses a high plateau to Hagaru-ri, eleven miles distant.

At Hagaru-ri the road forks. One branch runs north to the east side of the Chosin Reservoir. The other snakes west and north up through Toktong Pass, at four thousand feet above sea level, before dropping into Yudam-ni, fourteen miles away.

On the last day of October the 7th Marines led the way out of Hamhung to Sudong, twenty-nine miles away. They found the 26th Regiment, ROK 3d Division, emplaced on a series of ridges south of Sudong. The marines learned the ROKs had captured a number of Chinese prisoners a few days before. As a result the ROKs were very anxious to depart the area. "Many, many Chinese up there," the ROKs told the marines, pointing to the hills. Even before the marines completed the takeover the ROKs were headed south to safety.

On the night of November 2 the 7th Marines occupied a series of hills and ridges about one mile south of Sudong. They suspected the Chinese were in the hills around them but had no evidence to support that notion. Patrols had searched for the enemy but located no sign of them. Even aerial reconnaissance had failed to reveal the CCF.

But they were there. Three divisions of the Chinese 42d Army were hidden between the marines and the Chosin Reservoir. While the marines consolidated their position preparatory to their move to Yudam-ni, the CCF 124th Division slipped into the area around Sudong. As the sun disappeared to the west marine outposts began reporting strange sounds in front of their positions. It was Chinese sappers seeking a weak spot in the marines' lines.

ARCHIE VAN WINKLE

When Seattle marine reservist S. Sgt. Archie Van Winkle reported for active duty at Camp Pendleton, California, in July 1950, he found himself standing in one line after another to process in. Finally, he found himself in the line where unit assignments were handed out. At the desk at the head of the line, a bored tech sergeant would try to see that each reservist's training, talent, and World War II combat experience, if any, were put to the best use.

Van Winkle's turn came. "What were you doing in civilian life?" the tech sergeant asked routinely.

"College student—University of Washington," Van Winkle answered.

"Oh, a college boy!" The tech looked up with some interest. He saw a burly, dark-haired marine about five feet eleven inches tall. His uniform sported a number of campaign ribbons signifying extensive service in the Pacific. And the top ribbon was a Distinguished Flying Cross!

"And a fly-boy, too," the tech sergeant observed wryly. He shuffled through the papers on his desk.

"Okay, fly-boy, you're all set. You're in the infantry now," said the tech sergeant. He handed Van Winkle a slip of paper that read, "Company B, 1st Bn, 7th Marines."

Van Winkle, a former dive-bomber gunner in the Solomon Islands and the Philippines, hurried off to find his new unit. His new CO, Capt. Myron E. Wilcox, assigned him to 2d Lt. Harrol Kiser's third platoon as the platoon sergeant.

Those marines who chuckled at an aviator running infantrymen soon changed their attitude. Husky Van Winkle was all marine. "You fall in at attention," he barked at his platoon. "You don't wait for someone to tell you. Get your eyes front and can the chatter." Soon, there was little "fly-boy" talk in the third platoon.

Van Winkle was born on March 17, 1925, in Juneau, Alaska, the only Medal of Honor recipient born in the forty-ninth state. Van Winkle attended high school in Darrington, Washington, where he captained the football and boxing teams. He entered the University of Washington but dropped out to enlist in the Marine Corps in December 1942.

Resuming his college career after his discharge in 1945, Van Winkle majored in physical education. For the extra money he joined the Marine Corps Reserve in March 1948. In July 1950 his battalion was called to active duty. Less than two months later he was climbing a scaling ladder at Inchon. Through the fighting to capture Seoul, Sergeant Van Winkle's daring leadership dispelled any remaining concerns his platoon might have had about how the "fly-boy" would do in ground combat.

Now, on the bitterly cold night of November 2, Van Winkle's platoon was stretched out for a hundred yards along a narrow ridge on the west side of the MSR south of Sudong. Lieutenant Kiser had more ground to cover than men so he anchored the left of the line with his .30-caliber machine gun. An outpost with four men sat about eighty yards in front of the machine gun.

As soon as it got dark Van Winkle hurried from position to position, reassuring and calming the jittery marines. About 11:30 P.M. he crawled out to the outpost. The marines there were the most vulnerable so he wanted to spend a little time with them. The outpost had a sound-powered telephone. Van Winkle used it to monitor the rest of the company. Suddenly, the phone went dead.

The very next instant a tremendous roar erupted all along the ridge as the Chinese opened their attack. Fire seemed to be coming from everywhere. "We were there to warn the platoon if the Chinese came," Van Winkle said. "Hell, they didn't need any warning from us."

"Let's get out of here," he called to the four others as the Chinese swarmed around them.

Moving backwards up the hill the four men fired their M-1s into the attacking enemy. Then a flare ignited overhead, illuminating the entire area. "Don't move," Van Winkle yelled to his men as he hit the dirt. When he looked up they were gone.

As the Chinese closed to within yards of him, Van Winkle fought his way through them to the .30-caliber machine gun. Van Winkle added the fire of his rifle to the battle. He didn't even have to sight his weapon, he just pointed and fired. "Everywhere I looked there was a Chinaman," he said.

When the Chinese threatened to overwhelm the position Van Winkle rose out of the hole, swinging his rifle like a club. He cracked several Chinese heads before his weapon broke in half.

About this time a heavy push by the Chinese threatened the center of the platoon's line. On his own initiative Van Winkle quickly gathered around him as many marines as he could. Rearmed with a discarded rifle, he boldly led his ragtag group right into the center of the Chinese.

Screaming words of encouragement to his men, Van Winkle slashed his way into the mass of Chinese. He shot the enemy when he could, used his bayonet when he couldn't. A Chinese bullet slammed into his left elbow, spinning him to the ground. Undaunted, his left arm limp at his side, Van Winkle returned to the fight. Some of his marines were down, but enough remained standing to battle the Chinese to a halt.

Once the platoon's center was relatively secure Van Winkle saw that his former position at the machine gun was now cut off by a wall of Chinese. He couldn't leave his fellow marines to be captured or killed. He charged through forty yards of bullet-swept hillside, leading a squad to rescue the stranded men.

At the machine gun he directed its fire into the masses of enemy. Wherever he saw a knot of Chinese he had the automatic weapon mow them down.

About that time shrapnel from an exploding grenade tore a hole in Van Winkle's left shoulder blade. A few minutes later a bullet struck him in the back. Still he fought on. Using his good arm he alternately fired his M-1 and a pistol he'd picked up. His actions not only encouraged and heartened the others, but bought enough time for Kiser to reorganize his badly hurt platoon so he could patch the line.

Van Winkle was kneeling alongside the machine-gun pit, trying to put another magazine into his rifle when he saw it coming. It was a Chinese grenade, the potato-masher variety, coming end over end. Van Winkle could see the missile's fuse burning as it arced toward him.

He swiped at it with his good hand. He missed. The grenade hit the left side of his chest, then exploded. Van Winkle remembered the blinding flash and stabbing pain. He went down, thrashed about on the ground, and tried to clear his head. Wavering like a punch-drunk fighter he staggered upright. Barely able to breathe (the grenade had broken every rib on his left side) and hunched over in pain, Van Winkle still encouraged those around him to fight on. Then he collapsed.

The Chinese overran the machine gun about 4:00 A.M. Less than an hour later a counterattack regained it. When dawn finally came the marines still held the ridge. Great numbers of bodies, both Chinese and American, lay sprawled everywhere. When the medics found Van Winkle he lay covered in blood. When he came to he was in an evac hospital filled with wounded. He remembered being amazed at the large number of casualties.

Van Winkle spent over six months in hospitals recovering from his wounds. He was released from active duty in July 1951. Back home in Washington he resumed his education, pushing the horrors of the fighting in Korea from his mind. When the Marine Corps called him in January 1952 to tell him he'd been awarded the Medal of Honor, Van Winkle thought it was friends pulling a prank. He hung up. Even when a telegram arrived bearing the news he refused to believe it. As far as he was concerned he'd just been doing his job that night, like the other marines on that ridge.

The Marine Corps felt differently. Van Winkle accepted his Medal of Honor on February 6, 1952. The next day he went back on active duty after receiving a direct commission to second lieutenant. He remained on active duty until 1974 when he retired as a full colonel. He then moved to Davis, California, as the inspector general of the California Department of Corrections.

While in Davis, Van Winkle built a fifty-five-foot sailboat. He planned to sail it to, and around, Alaska when he retired for good. He did. It was an idyllic life for a man who'd seen and suffered so much pain.

Archie Van Winkle died of a heart attack on May 20, 1986. He was found aboard his sailboat in the harbor at Ketchikan, Alaska.

The Chinese attacked the marines around Sudong on the next two nights. Several marine units were overrun. Only the resourcefulness of a few marines turned the tide of battle. One such marine was Cpl. Lee H. Phillips, a twenty-year-old from Ben Hill, Georgia, serving with Company E, 2d Battalion, 7th Marines. After being thrown off Hill 698, west of the MSR and about two miles south of Sudong, on November 4, the survivors of Company E made five separate attempts to regain the hill. Each was beaten back.

On the sixth try Phillips took his squad forward, bayonets fixed. Charging through mortar fire, small-arms and machine-gun fire, the squad, with only five members still on their feet, regained the crest. Immediately coun-terattacked, Phillips led his men forward into the enemy's midst. They drove the Chinese off. Though down to three men, Phillips bravely led them against an enemy machine gun sited on a rocky and nearly inaccessible portion of the hill position. Phillips used one hand to climb up while he threw gre-nades with the other. The enemy position was destroyed.

Counterattacked again and down to only two squad members, Phillips skillfully directed their fire and employed his own rifle to drive off the Chi-nese. The hill was at last firmly in American hands. Amazingly, Phillips escaped this battle unscathed. But he would be killed in action on Novem-ber 27, 1950.

Less than a mile from where Corporal Phillips led his attack, Company A, 1st Battalion, 7th Marines, found itself under attack the same night. Although he'd already been critically wounded, Sgt. James I. Poynter, a thirty-three-year-old from Downey, California, used his bayonet to fight the intruders in hand-to-hand combat. When he saw the Chinese had set up three machine guns about twenty-five yards away, he gathered up as many gre-nades as he could carry and went after them. His singlehanded attack de-stroyed all three of the threatening positions, but cost Poynter his life.

The fighting around Sudong cost the marines over sixty dead and nearly three hundred wounded. Chinese deaths were put at almost eight hundred. The area quieted on November 6, allowing the marines to resume their advance to the Chosin Reservoir. The 7th Marines continued to lead the advance, followed by the 5th Marines. The 1st Marines garrisoned Koto-ri, turning the small town into a massive supply base.

When the 7th Marines reached Hagaru-ri on November 15, they turned left, along the Chosin Reservoir's southern shore, and headed for Yudam-ni. Behind them the 5th Marines passed through Hagaru-ri and continued along the reservoir's eastern shore. This plan split the formidable marine division into three separate pockets, each only barely able to support the others in the event of an attack.

But there were no attacks. After the fighting around Sudong, the Chinese had pulled back on November 7, just as they had in front of the Eighth Army. The disappearance of the Chinese mystified the marines as much as it did their army counterparts. Had the Chinese been beaten? Were they pulling back across the Yalu?

Or were they sending MacArthur a message? Stop. Enough is enough. Go no further. A good number of soldiers and marines felt this was the case.

Their opinion didn't count for much. MacArthur planned a final push for the day after Thanksgiving that would capture all of North Korea, drive the remaining NKPA forces and Chinese "volunteers" across the Yalu, and unite Korea into one nation.

Chapter Five
The Chinese Attack

By Thanksgiving Day, November 23, 1950, the U.N. forces of the Eighth Army were in position for the final drive to the Yalu. As there had been no contact with the Chinese Communist Forces since earlier in the month, the general feeling among the soldiers was that the way north would be easy. To boost the GIs' morale thousands of turkey dinners, with all the trimmings, were served. As they enjoyed the meal most of the men were confident they'd be home by Christmas.

The Eighth Army had nearly 225,000 men in three corps arrayed along the Chongchon River from Anju eastward through Tokchon into the high mountains around Maengsan. There the gap between Eighth Army and X Corps caused by the formidable Taebaek mountain range began. The Eighth Army's left flank was held by the U.S. I Corps. On its left the U.S. 24th Infantry Division would drive almost due west to the Yellow Sea and the mouth of the Yalu River at Sinuiju. On its right the ROK 1st Division would move north through Taechon to the Yalu.

In the center of the Eighth Army's line of advance the U.S. IX Corps had two U.S. infantry divisions, the 2d and 25th. On the corps left the 25th Infantry Division stood poised to move north via Ipsok to the Yalu. To the right the 2d Infantry Division would attack northeast following the road from Kunu-ri through Sinhungdong to Huichon on the Yalu. Eighth Army's right flank was held by the two ROK divisions of the ROK II Corps, the 7th and 8th Infantry Divisions. Their mission was to move generally east via Tokchon and eventually link up with units of the X Corps coming up from the Chosin Reservoir area.

General Walker's plan dictated a slow, deliberate advance to the Yalu. Each corps would follow a specific set of phase lines. Walker wanted close control of his units. He didn't want any one unit out in front of the others where it would be vulnerable. He had developed a keen respect for the CCF after their attacks in early November. Though Walker's intelligence officers reported only a relatively small enemy force in front of him, he was still leery.

He had plenty of reason to be concerned. In the hills north of the Chongchon River, about ten miles north of the Eighth Army line, the Chinese lay in hidden assembly areas. Facing General Walker's men were six Chinese armies with nineteen divisions. Around 180,000 Chinese soldiers waited to do battle with the Americans and ROKs. And almost all were available for frontline duty. Unlike the Americans, the Chinese Army had a very short supply line. Individual soldiers were expected to carry rations and ammo with them. When they ran out of supplies they could either live off the land or use captured stores. In contrast, no more than seventy-five thousand frontline troops were available to the Eighth Army.

The CCF tactical plan was initially to penetrate the ROK II Corps, then get into its rear areas before turning westward to roll up that corps. At the same time other Chinese forces would slam head-on into the IX Corps, penetrating the border between it and the I Corps. Essentially, the Chinese planned to roll up the Eighth Army from east to west and pin it against the west coast or force it to withdraw southward.

The area between the Chongchon and Yalu Rivers was typical of most of Korea. A seemingly endless array of hills and valleys undulated northward. From the air the ridges resembled a washboard. Only a few roads ran through this area. Most were simple dirt and gravel affairs connecting isolated towns and villages. But the high hills dictated that an army as mobile as the Eighth Army would be restricted to the road network. The U.N. forces could send patrols into the hills but they were dependent upon the road for survival. The Chinese owned the hills away from the road net and would use them to great advantage.

Another major factor in the fighting in North Korea in late November was the weather. Icy cold arctic winds from Siberia blew incessantly. Temperatures fell to well below zero at night and rarely exceeded freezing during the day. Snow squalls and blizzards not only added to the discomfort of the troops but reduced visibility for air support. Ground frozen solid for eighteen inches made digging foxholes difficult, if not impossible. The bitter cold also froze rations, water, medical supplies, and weapons.

Eighth Army struggled to issue winter clothing to its troops but was only successful in outfitting about two-thirds of the GIs. Those units that did not receive a winter clothing issue improvised as best they could.

Across the Korean peninsula the X Corps made final preparations for its attack, scheduled to commence November 27, three days after the Eighth Army stepped off. ROK troops still held the east coast to just past Chongjin. Just to their west U.S. 7th Infantry Division troops started pulling back from Hyesanjin on the Yalu. The main mission of the X Corps had changed from reaching the Yalu to linking up with Eighth Army units near Kanggye. The 1st Marine Division would make that main advance from the Chosin Reservoir; the 7th Infantry Division would cover their right flank.

On Thanksgiving Day the 1st Marine Division was concentrated at three main points along the MSR. At the southern end, at Koto-ri, sat the 1st Marine Regiment with some forty-two hundred troops. Twelve miles north at Hagaru-ri were the headquarters of the 1st Marine Division. Protective and support troops in that area amounted to about three thousand people.

The point of the division was fourteen miles farther north along the western side of the Chosin Reservoir. Originally the 5th Marine Regiment had gone around the reservoir's eastern shore while the 7th Marines headed to Yudam-ni. A change in plans brought the 5th Marines into Yudam-ni where it would pass through the 7th Marines and lead the drive to join with the Eighth Army. The 5th Marines' place on the Chosin Reservoir's east side was taken by a battalion each of the 7th Infantry Division's 31st and 32d Infantry Regiments. Supporting artillery units brought that task force's strength to around three thousand.

Northeast Korea had been relatively quiet since the engagement near Sudong early in November. Only occasional scrapes with the Chinese marred the marines' advance to the Chosin Reservoir. Again, though, the Chinese were merely biding their time, waiting for the marines to position themselves where they'd be most vulnerable. Hidden in the mountains around the X Corps units in the Chosin Reservoir area were two Chinese armies consisting of twelve divisions. These 120,000 Chinese would swoop down on the marines and give them their worst defeat in their history.

Winter struck North Korea with a fury in November 1950. The bitterly cold winds screamed down from the frozen Yalu, engulfing the X Corps in the worst winter seen in twenty years. Sitting at elevations between thirty-five hundred and forty-five hundred feet above sea level, the marines and soldiers were unprepared for the frigid blast of cold. The first real cold snap hit the night of November 10. The mercury dropped to minus ten degrees without warning. The cold was so intense men became dazed and incoherent. Some went numb, others cried in pain. Though X Corps rushed winter clothing to the troops, the weather would prove to be as formidable a foe as the CCF. More men would fall from frost-bitten and frozen limbs than bullets.

Friday morning, November 24, 1950, dawned clear and cold in Korea.

Temperatures hovered around freezing. By mid-afternoon the temperatures would rise to the mid-fifties, one of the last warm days of 1950.

All along Eighth Army's front men were moving forward. With few exceptions the advance was relatively unopposed. Only sporadic enemy fire harassed the U.N. forces. The only serious fighting was against the ROK II Corps on the right flank. Actually, the fighting there was the continuation of a day-old battle that had begun when the ROKs moved into position for their new offensive. While the rest of Walker's forces advanced several miles that first day, the ROKs made a scant one thousand yards.

The night of November 24–25 was cold enough to freeze the many small streams feeding the Chongchon. Walker's GIs resumed their advance at dawn, again against light resistance. The ROK 1st Division moved through Taechon, while the U.S. 25th Infantry Division passed through Ipsok. The U.S. 2d Infantry Division passed through Sinhungdong and sent elements to garrison Hill 219, about one mile north of the little village. Here, for the first time, the enemy put up a stiff resistance. The attacking infantrymen were unable to capture Hill 219. They withdrew with heavy casualties. Their advance up the southern slopes of Hill 219 would mark the northernmost penetration of Eighth Army in its ill-fated offensive.

Without warning, the Chinese fell on the ROK II Corps just after darkness on November 25. In a matter of hours the ROKs were sent reeling. At nearly the same time the CCF launched a series of frontal attacks against Walker's other corps. About the only unit spared was the U.S. 24th Infantry Division on the far left.

So intense was the CCF attack entire companies were destroyed, wiped out. Sitting isolated on hills and ridges astride their line of advance, the soldiers were unprepared for the fury of the CCF attack. Literally tens of thousands of Chinese swarmed over the Americans. The GIs fought desperately to stem the onslaught, but the only thing that would halt the Chinese was victory or daylight.

When dawn finally came on November 26 uncounted hundreds of Chinese bodies lay in and around U.N. positions. The CCF survivors moved back into the hills, hiding from American aircraft. The Americans and ROKs tended their casualties, pulled back into better defensive positions, and prepared to face another night.

The Chinese didn't disappoint the U.N. troops. As the temperature hovered near zero the CCF unleashed another human wave attack all along the line. They hit the U.S. 2d Infantry Division's 23d Infantry Regiment holding positions south of Sinhungdong about 8:30 P.M. A two-pronged attack threw two U.S. companies off commanding ground.

Sgt. John A. Pittman, Company C, 1st Battalion, 23d Infantry, led a counterattack to regain lost ground. The twenty-two-year-old from Tallula, Mississippi, was hit by mortar fragments in the swirling fight but stayed on the line. As he crossed onto the hill's crest a retreating Chinese soldier threw a grenade. Pittman instantly threw himself on the missile. He absorbed the full blast in his own body, shielding those around him from danger.

When a medic reached him the first thing Pittman asked was, "How many of my men were hurt?"

The tough little noncommissioned officer lived to receive his Medal of Honor at the White House.

Near the middle of the Eighth Army's line the U.S. 25th Infantry Division formed a special task force to advance along the east side of the Kuryong River, a major tributary of the Chongchon. Named for its commander, Lt. Col. Weldon G. Dolvin, the task force consisted of three handpicked rifle companies from three different battalions, supported by tanks, artillery, and engineers. Task Force Dolvin's mission was to spearhead the 25th Infantry Division's drive to the Yalu.

The first sign of trouble came on the afternoon of November 25 when the task force's ranger company attacked a hill north of Ipsok. That was as far north as Task Force Dolvin advanced. They took the hill but defending Chinese badly hurt the rangers; less than eighty-five were left to hold the hill through the night. The Chinese counterattacked at 10:00 P.M. By morning only twenty-one men remained in the ranger company.

Just a short distance away another Task Force Dolvin unit had a relatively easy time. Company E, 2d Battalion, 27th Infantry Regiment, occupied a hill about a mile west of the rangers the night they were chewed up, but passed a quiet night themselves. The next afternoon Colonel Dolvin pulled Company E back from its leading position and had it take up a reserve position behind his headquarters. The infantrymen were to get a full night's rest before resuming the attack the next morning.

REGINALD B. DESIDERIO

The commander of Company E, Capt. Reginald B. Desiderio, was one of the most professional and experienced company commanders in all of Korea. Born in Clairton, Pennsylvania, on September 12, 1918, he grew up in Gilroy, California. An adventurous youngster, Desiderio left high school at age seventeen to enlist in the army. He served a three-year hitch with a field artillery battalion in Hawaii from 1935 to 1938. Back in Gilroy Desiderio finished high school and kept his hand in the army by enlisting in the Howitzer Company, 184th Infantry Regiment, California National Guard.

When Desiderio's unit was called into federal service in March 1941 he was selected from the ranks to attend Officer Candidate School. After commissioning he joined the 70th Infantry Division as an infantry platoon leader. Lieutenant Desiderio fought through southern France and Germany, earning a Silver Star and four Bronze Stars for his courage.

After the war Desiderio acknowledged he'd found a home in the army by requesting, and receiving, a Regular Army commission. He was on recruiting duty in Los Angeles when the Korean War erupted. Immediately he requested a transfer to a line outfit. He was an infantry officer and he felt he belonged where the fighting was. He joined Company E in the Pusan Perimeter.

When Desiderio bedded down his company behind the task force CP on the evening of November 26 he anticipated passing a quiet night. But the Chinese had other ideas. About 11:30 P.M. they started hitting Task Force Dolvin at all its positions, including the artillery in the rear. At 12:30 A.M., November 27, Colonel Dolvin ordered Desiderio to have Company E at his command post in fifteen minutes. Desiderio instantly awoke his platoon leaders. Together, they roused the men, loaded them aboard five tanks, and reached Dolvin on time.

Dolvin ordered Desiderio to emplace his company on a 185-meter-high hill about two hundred yards north of Dolvin's CP. There was no action there now but with the sound of battle carrying in from the front and rear it probably wouldn't be long before fighting in front of the CP erupted.

Company E started forward in the cold darkness. The first platoon had barely made five steps up the slope when the enemy opened fire on them from nearby hills. With one platoon bounding upward while the others counterfired, Desiderio leapfrogged his company to the top of the hill. Once there he moved about in the open, oblivious to the heavy automatic-weapons fire pouring onto the hill from CCF positions to the west.

The heavy volume of enemy fire convinced Desiderio he would need the help of some armor if he was to hold his position. Since the hill's southern slope was relatively gentle he knew the tanks would have no difficulty making the climb. Alone, he made his way back to Dolvin's CP where he asked for the five tanks that had brought him forward. Dolvin agreed.

About the time Desiderio came up the hill riding the lead tank the Chinese launched their first ground assault. Wave upon wave of fanatical enemy soldiers spilled out of the dark, throwing grenades and firing rifles. Desiderio spaced the tanks about twenty-five yards apart. Riflemen took up positions between them.

The tanks fired their cannons at enemy machine guns emplaced on nearby hills; their machine guns swept the ground in front of them, cutting into the enemy's ranks.

Desiderio busied himself moving from position to position, encouraging his men, pointing out targets, helping them brace against the onslaught.

Whenever it seemed the Chinese were about to break through his lines, Desiderio would appear at the troubled spot. Blazing away with his rifle, screaming orders to those around him, the captain rallied his embattled men. Together, they threw the enemy back. About 2:30 A.M. the Chinese loosed a tremendous mortar barrage on Company E. Desiderio instinctively knew it signaled another major ground assault.

Chinese grenadiers had crept to within fifteen yards of the GIs. They suddenly rose en masse, threw their grenades, and rushed forward. From the hills to the west six Chinese machine guns opened fire. Behind the grenadiers came a new wave of Chinese, firing burp guns.

Once again Desiderio moved to the most threatened area. Yelling at the top of his lungs, he exhorted his men to hang on. An instant later hot steel from an exploding mortar round ripped into Desiderio's shoulder. The impact flung him hard to the ground. But he was up almost at once.

Aware that his position was the key to the security of the task force's CP, Desiderio was determined not to yield. He staked his claim to the hill on which he stood and dared the enemy to take it, and his life, if necessary. Desiderio grabbed a discarded M-1, slapped a bayonet on its barrel, then jammed the weapon into the ground.

With eyes ablaze, Desiderio yelled to those around him, "We stay here! No pulling back. Hold 'til daylight! Hold 'til daylight and we've got it made."

The men picked up the phrase and made it a rallying cry.

Over the din of firing the blare of Chinese bugles coursed over the battlefield, signaling a recall. In the one-hour lull that followed, clerks from Dolvin's headquarters brought up a supply of ammo. Then they helped the wounded down the hill. Desiderio repositioned his troops, ensuring all avenues of approach were covered.

About five in the morning the Chinese came again. In a repeat of their earlier assaults a mortar barrage preceded the ground attack. This time the weakened American line gave under incredible pressure. An enemy bazooka team charged through the perimeter, making straight for the tanks. Their first round hit the tread of one tank, disabling it. Chinese grenadiers then swarmed around the tanks, tossing more than a dozen grenades on the armored decks. The explosions wounded a number of GIs. Seconds later a barrage of mortar fire fell on the tanks, which the Chinese had obviously decided were the primary obstacles to their success.

The fighting was now at close quarters all along the line. Suddenly someone yelled, "The line's cracked. Get the hell out!" A few of the soldiers started down the rear slope. Two of the tanks started to back out of position.

Desiderio yelled, "No!" Though wounded a second time by a bullet through the leg, he ran to the tanks. He took his rifle by its barrel and ran from one tank to another, hammering on their armored hulls. "Dammit, we're not quitting!" he screamed at the tankers.

One of his platoon leaders, Lt. Bill Otomo, joined him. Together the two kept the jittery tankers on line.

No sooner had that crisis ended when a runner reached Desiderio with word the Chinese were breaking through a ravine on the right flank.

Otomo saw his captain charge right at the enemy. Initially firing a carbine, which he eventually discarded for any other available weapon, Desiderio ended up throwing grenades at the enemy. Otomo later said, "The enemy was throwing grenades at him, but this did not deter him. He continued firing, killing nine and wounding five. Running out of ammo he discarded his carbine and picked up an M-1. He killed three more of the enemy. Once again he discarded his weapon and then resorted to throwing hand grenades. I saw him throw two grenades directly at an advancing enemy group, killing three and wounding seven others."

There was no doubt in Otomo's mind that Captain Desiderio's bold actions were singularly responsible for disrupting the enemy's attack at this point on the line.

Back near the tanks, Desiderio saw the enemy forming for yet another attack. He picked up a discarded carbine and told Otomo, "They're coming on us now. You take one side and I'll take the other and we'll stop 'em."

Those were Desiderio's last words. He'd just turned from Otomo when a Chinese burp gunner stepped from the darkness. His burst of fire tore into Desiderio's side, killing him instantly.

For a few minutes it seemed as if the spirit of the defense might die with Desiderio. But reinforcements arrived under a sergeant. These fresh troops helped blunt the attack. A short while later the sun peaked over the eastern mountains. The Chinese soon broke off the attack, disappearing into the underbrush.

Company E had held until daylight and they made it. But sixty of their number were wounded and a dozen killed, including the intrepid Desiderio. His widow, Patricia J., and his two young sons accepted his posthumous Medal of Honor on June 21, 1951.

Regrettably, Desiderio's gallant actions had little effect on Task Force Dolvin completing its assigned mission. By 9:00 A.M. the 25th Infantry Division's commanding general had authorized the dissolution of the task force and its withdrawal below Ipsok.

In fact, CCF attacks on Eighth Army during the night of November 26–27 stopped Walker's offensive dead in its tracks. All day November 27 the U.N. forces adjusted their lines rearward. It didn't help.

By the next morning the storm which had blown away the ROK II Corps was beating against the Eighth Army's open right flank. Tremendous numbers of Chinese were cutting behind the Eighth Army, seriously threatening its supply and communications lines. General Walker called the U.S. 1st Cavalry Division out of reserve and tried to use it and the U.S. 2d Infantry Division to shore up his exposed flank. His efforts only succeeded in delaying the inevitable.

CCF soldiers seemed to be everywhere. They struck Eighth Army units head-on, from the flanks, and from the rear. On November 28, General Walker ordered his army to pull back to the Chongchon River. By that evening that retrograde movement had been accomplished. Rather than hold there, though, the Eighth Army began withdrawing back to Pyongyang. The general retreat began on November 30 under heavy pressure from the Chinese. The U.S. 2d Infantry Division, in particular, suffered heavily in its withdrawal. Moving south from Kunu-ri on that date the division had to run a six-mile gauntlet of enfilading Chinese fire. Out of approximately seven thousand division members at Kunu-ri, over four thousand became casualties during this movement.

Once in Pyongyang the Eighth Army did not stop. Panicked soldiers fled farther south; despite the fact the CCF had stopped along the Chongchon River and were not actively pursuing the Eighth Army.

Rather than halt the rout Walker instead ordered the evacuation of Pyongyang on December 3. He did not have confidence that his forces could battle the CCF and win a battle near Pyongyang. Evacuation of the North Korean capital began on December 4. By the end of the next day the city was devoid of U.N. troops.

Not until they neared Seoul did the U.N. soldiers halt their flight. Even then most members of the Eighth Army expected to withdraw all the way to Pusan. Once there they were convinced they would be evacuated to Japan, leaving Korea to the Communist Chinese. But that was simply wishful thinking.

By December 10 most major units of the Eighth Army were south of the Thirty-eighth Parallel. There the "bug-out" finally halted. After retreating 120 miles, the Eighth Army assumed defensive positions along the Imjin River, north of Seoul, and from there the U.N. line continued eastward across the waist of Korea to the east coast town of Kansong.

The Eighth Army, while rebuilding and reorganizing, waited to see what the Chinese would do next.

Meanwhile, in northeast Korea, General Almond's X Corps was generally oblivious to the debacle plaguing Eighth Army. Almond was anxious for the 1st Marine Division to proceed with its advance west from Yudam-ni. In contrast, Maj. Gen. Oliver P. Smith, commander of the marines, was reluctant to move into the unknown fifty-five miles separating him from the Eighth Army. He made up his mind to proceed slowly and cautiously.

At 9:35 A.M., November 27, two companies of the 5th Marines started down the road leading west out of Yudam-ni. Within five hundred yards they were stopped cold by a Chinese roadblock. Though they destroyed it, a sudden eruption of heavy fire from Chinese emplaced in the rugged hills on both sides of the road again brought the column to a halt. Three divisions of CCF were in the hills surrounding Yudam-ni, determined to destroy the marines. The marines fought the Chinese west of Yudam-ni through the early afternoon but made no gains. At 2:30 P.M. the attack was called off. The marines dug in, anticipating a night of combat.

The high ground around Yudam-ni was garrisoned by a number of companies from both the 5th and 7th Marines. The bitterly cold night prevented the marines from digging deep foxholes. Instead, they built walls of rocks around the meager scrapings they'd been able to make in the frozen ground. It wasn't much protection, but it was the best they could do.

The first probings against the marines' hilltop positions came about three hours before midnight, November 27. Then bugle calls filled the night. Seconds later clusters of hand grenades fell from the sky. Massed Chinese infantry advanced up the various hills, covered by heavy machine guns on rearward hills. Marines reacting to the onrush of enemy soldiers were caught in the open by a sustained mortar barrage. Within minutes the Chinese overwhelmed several key positions.

Sitting on top of Hill 1282, north and slightly east of Yudam-ni, was Staff Sgt. Robert S. Kennemore and the rest of Company E, 2d Battalion, 7th Marines. A thirty-year-old combat veteran of Guadalcanal, Kennemore was sleeping when the Chinese charged up the hill. Instantly awake, he fought his way to one of the two machine guns in his section. He arrived just in time to see the surviving machine gunner being pulled into the darkness by a horde of Chinese. He changed direction and made his way to his one remaining gun.

By that time the Chinese grenadiers and burp gunners were within yards of the vital position. Kennemore scrambled about, gathering up every grenade he could find, throwing them into the night. But they still weren't enough. The Chinese pressed in. Enemy grenades were landing in the deep snow around the gun. Kennemore groped for them, threw them back into the knots of enemy soldiers.

Then a grenade plopped into the snow in front of him. It was too far to reach. Kennemore put his left foot on it, pushing it into the snow bank. Another grenade landed alongside him. He dropped his right knee on it. The two grenades exploded.

Company E fought the Chinese all night. When dawn came the enemy pulled back, leaving hundreds of their dead and wounded dotting the hillside. The marines had been badly hurt, but they'd held. Medics tended to the many wounded, among them Sergeant Kennemore. They found him in the snow, huge cakes of red ice where his legs had once been. He lived to wear his Medal of Honor.

The dominant terrain feature on the route between Hagaru-ri and Yudam-ni was Toktong Pass. Overlooked by a forty-seven-hundred-foot peak, Toktong Pass was vital to the marines in Yudam-ni. The MSR twisted its way upward to Toktong Pass from Hagaru-ri for eight miles, narrowing to a single lane before dropping into the valley of Yudam-ni seven miles farther along. If the enemy held Toktong Pass the marines at Yudam-ni would be completely isolated from the rest of the 1st Marine Division farther south. It had to be held at all costs. Company F, 2d Battalion, 7th Marines, drew the assignment to hold the pass.

WILLIAM E. BARBER
RAYMOND G. DAVIS

Capt. William E. Barber had been commander of Company F for less than a week when he received orders to proceed to Toktong Pass. Just three weeks earlier he'd been attending a career school at the Marine Barracks in Philadelphia. When he finished the course in early October 1950 he received his orders to Korea. His long journey halfway around the world ended in the icy cold mountains of North Korea near Hagaru-ri. There he gathered the 240 men of his company around him.

Though composed mostly of reservists, Company F had fought well and hard at Inchon and Seoul. Barber celebrated his new assignment by telling his men to shave, clean their weapons, and knock off the talk about being home by Christmas. There was a lot of war left to fight and they'd see their share of it. After dismissing his company, Barber grinned when he heard them grumble about the new "old man" for he knew gum-beating marines were hard to beat. He knew, because he used to grumble quite a bit when he wore stripes on his sleeves.

Born on November 30, 1919, in Dehart, Kentucky, Barber played both baseball and basketball while at Morehead State Teacher's College in Kentucky. After graduation he worked for awhile in Ohio as a salesman. Then, looking for adventure, he joined the marines in March 1940.

Barber liked the marines from the very beginning. After boot camp at Parris Island, South Carolina, he volunteered for a new marine venture: parachute training. He did so well at the course at Lakehurst, New Jersey, he stayed on as an instructor.

In June 1943 Barber entered OCS, earning his gold bar that August. In January 1944 he joined the 26th Marines, 5th Marine Division, in San Diego. A year later he was crossing the ankle-deep volcanic ash on Iwo Jima. During the heavy fighting there Barber earned a Silver Star for rescuing two marines under fire. He also earned a Purple Heart.

And now, more than five years later, he was back at war.

As soon as Barber received the assignment to defend Toktong Pass he and his battalion commander drove there in a jeep to select a site for the company. They settled on a hill just north of the roadway. It took most of the rest of the day to get Company F loaded on trucks and transported to the hill position. Not until 9:00 P.M. were they finally settled in hastily dug foxholes and gun emplacements. Below them the last truck convoy from Yudam-ni passed by on the MSR. A bright full moon illuminated the hilltop, but a piercing wind added to the discomfort of the men on watch. The night was quiet, with any sound from the Company F marines amplified by the crisp air. Those men not on watch burrowed deeply into their sleeping bags, desperately seeking some warmth. None of them had any reason to know that they were now completely cut off by CCF regiments that had snuck down from the heights to sever the MSR to the north and south.

The Chinese hit Company F just before 2:30 A.M., November 28. An outpost from the platoon, covering a wide, steep-sided saddle leading to the forty-seven-hundred-foot peak called Toktong-san, yelled "Here they come!" and opened fire. A full company of Chinese was less than a hundred yards away. Fifteen of the thirty-five marines manning the outposts were killed as they stood to meet the onslaught; another nine were wounded. The others fought as valiantly as they could but three more soon fell. The eight survivors pulled back to their platoon's positions.

At Barber's CP a column of Chinese marched toward him right from the road. Soon a shower of grenades crashed down on the little command group. Barber called in his clerks and technicians and led them to a position behind a nearby earthen bank. From there they drove the Chinese column off.

Barber then raced across the bullet-swept open ground to his platoons. He moved fearlessly among them, encouraging them, repositioning them as the Chinese pressed their attack.

On the company's right flank twenty-one-year-old Pvt. Hector Cafferata of Montville, New Jersey, found himself the last man from his squad still on his feet. When the Chinese first attacked, Cafferata had been in his sleeping bag, his boots off for the first time in days. He instantly leaped from its warmth and joined the fight. Although silhouetted against the white snow, he boldly held his ground, emptying his rifle into the attackers. Then he started tossing grenades. While he did so, his wounded foxhole buddy loaded magazines, then tossed him a fresh rifle. Cafferata used it with deadly effectiveness, picking off the enemy soldiers, one for each of the eight .30-caliber rounds in the weapon's magazine.

When the Chinese attack shifted to the left Cafferata and his buddy raced there to meet the enemy. There the big youngster, a former semipro football player, continued firing the rifles loaded by his buddy.

Then a grenade landed at his feet. The big man scooped it from the snow and threw it back into the enemy's ranks. Six Chinese soldiers fell in the blast. He threw back a second one, killing more Chinese. A third went off just as it left his hand, blowing off one finger and wounding him in the arm.

But that never stopped Cafferata. He continued blazing away at the Chinese, keeping them from overwhelming that part of the line.

The fight on the newly named Fox Hill raged until dawn. Through it all Barber roamed the front lines, firing his carbine, killing the enemy, stopping them from overrunning his company. Bugles blared just before dawn and the Chinese tide began to recede. By daylight it was over.

Over four hundred frozen Chinese corpses lay around the company's positions. Barber's company suffered twenty dead, fifty-four wounded, and three missing.

One of the wounded was Hector Cafferata. Just after dawn a burst of enemy machine gun fire tore into his right arm. Fellow marines pulled him to an aid station. A medic noticed Cafferata's blue feet. Only then did the big man realize he had fought for five hours in his bare feet.

With daylight came fighter planes to provide air support for Barber's company. An airdrop provided much-needed rifle ammo and mortar shells. A radio message from battalion advised Barber he could pull out, linking up with another company a few miles north. Barber declined. He not only knew the value of Toktong Pass, but he also knew he couldn't leave carrying over fifty wounded. No, he told the battalion commander, he'd hold the hill.

Barber spent the daylight hours of November 28 strengthening his positions. His marines needed little encouragement to dig their foxholes deeper. Then, as night came, they waited for the Chinese.

The CCF came at Company F again at 2:00 A.M., November 29. This ground attack was preceded by a brief mortar barrage. Then the hordes of enemy soldiers came forward. The marines were ready, slaying dozens with their fire. But the Chinese broke through the line.

Barber quickly rushed to the breach. Using all his leadership skills he rallied the marines in throwing back the frenzied foe.

At the center of the line the platoon there was being pressed hard. Barber went there to help stabilize the line. He was moving forward when a searing pain erupted in his left leg. An enemy machine gun bullet had ripped into him. Refusing evacuation, he plugged the hole with a handkerchief and continued to hobble about, encouraging his men with his cheerful advice.

Company F held again on the second night. Over two hundred more Chinese died trying to force the valiant marines from their position. Five more marines were killed, another twenty-nine wounded. Barber would continue to hold his position, but he knew there was no hope of survival unless he was reinforced or relieved.

At the headquarters of the 5th and 7th Marines in Yudam-ni both regimental commanders realized their advance to link up with Eighth Army was at a stalemate. Chinese forces had attacked the marines' hilltop positions around the town each of the previous two nights. Casualties were high. The surviving marines were weakening from the near-constant fighting and bitter cold.

In addition, the marines knew they were cut off from Hagaru-ri. Unless the MSR linking the two towns could be reopened there was no hope of continuing the advance. And, if elements from Yudam-ni were sent south to open the MSR, their absence would dangerously weaken the forces holding that town. There was no doubt the CCF could then destroy the marines.

Further, Captain Barber's Company F had to be rescued. He was facing his third night isolated at Toktong Pass. With his high casualty rate he could not possibly hold out much longer.

A bold plan to reach Barber was developed on the afternoon of November 29. The following night the entire 1st Battalion, 7th Marines, would go south on the MSR for about three miles, then move east overland to attack the rear of the CCF hitting Company F. If all went well the rescued and rescuers would be back in Yudam-ni on December 1st.

Barber's third night at Toktong Pass was a repeat of the previous two. A few hours after midnight on November 30, the CCF came storming up the hill. Company F's marines fought back, using their mortars to lower a curtain of red-hot steel before the Chinese. Marine artillery at Hagaru-ri added its power to the fight.

Determined to inspire his remaining marines (there were now less than ninety left), Barber continued to roam the front line. Wherever the Chinese seemed about to break through his position, Barber would appear, hobbling on his wounded leg and leading a reinforcing squad of marines. Then an enemy round plowed into his other leg. Barber went down, hard.

Medics patched him up. Barber ordered a stretcher brought forward. Carried to the forward position, the gallant officer continued leading his men. Somehow, they held on through the night, repulsing everything the Chinese threw at them. Barber breathed a massive sigh of relief as dawn arrived. The Chinese withdrew, fearful of the fighters that would soon appear overhead.

While Barber had been preparing his dwindling company to face its third night at Toktong Pass, General Almond had flown into Hagaru-ri on November 30 to confer with General Smith. Almond told Smith of the disaster overtaking the Eighth Army. Based on that and the overwhelming odds against the marines, he authorized Smith to abandon Yudam-ni and withdraw its garrison back to Hagaru-ri. From there they were to move as rapidly as possible all the way back to Hungnam. Once there the 1st Marine Division and 7th Infantry Division, also pulling back, would be evacuated. Their evacuation would be covered by the newly arrived U.S. 3d Infantry Division, currently garrisoning Hungnam and Hamhung.

Preparations for the withdrawal from Yudam-ni began immediately. One battalion would lead the way down the MSR, clearing the route for the balance of the two regiments. At the same time, the battalions to the rear would disengage from the enemy at the hilltop positions around Yudam-ni. They would then fight a rear guard action, protecting the column of marines on the MSR from the ever-present Chinese. The relief of Barber's Company F would proceed as planned, though delayed for twenty-four hours.

The breakout from Yudam-ni began at 3:00 P.M., December 1. The lead battalion made nearly fourteen hundred yards without drawing enemy fire. Then the Chinese, in the first of many roadblocks, unleashed a fury of mortars and small-arms fire that brought the column to a halt. From well-prepared positions on hilltops on both sides of the road CCF infantrymen forced the marines into snow-filled ditches. A company was dispatched against each hill. The hill on the left fell after a brief firefight. The company on the right found itself in deep trouble.

As Company I, 3d Battalion, 5th Marines, moved into a draw it was cut apart by a cross fire from high ground on both sides. Before the company commander could deploy his men, the Chinese attacked. The rattled marines threw off the attackers. Then a heavy barrage of mortars erupted among them. For nearly ten minutes the lethal rounds dropped among the men, erupting in geysers of snow, dirt, and rocks. Then they stopped. An instant later the Chinese infantry returned.

Staff Sgt. William G. Windrich led his squad from the first platoon forward to plug a gap in the line. They met a Chinese assault force head-on. In the ensuing swirling battle seven of Windrich's eleven men fell wounded. An exploding Chinese grenade severely wounded Windrich in the head. Ignoring the intense pain, he raced back to the company CP to round up volunteers who could help him evacuate his wounded.

Windrich, a World War II veteran who had been among the first contingent of marines to reach Pusan in August, was hit by rifle fire in his legs as he took the volunteers forward. Again he declined aid. Instead, the East Chicago, Indiana, resident continued forward. He provided covering fire while the casualties were removed. For another hour Windrich stayed in the fight. He moved from position to position, keeping his small band together. Finally, the loss of blood and cold got to him. Windrich collapsed, dying behind his rifle. His young daughter would receive his posthumous Medal of Honor.

While the lead battalion fought to break through the Chinese on the MSR, Lt. Col. Raymond G. Davis maneuvered his 1st Battalion, 7th Marines, into position for his cross-country rescue of Barber. During the day of December 1, Davis put his battalion into the exact condition he wanted for his relief mission.

First, he stripped his battalion of all heavy weapons except two mortars and six .30-caliber machine guns. Each man carried one mortar round in addition to his own personal ammo. Extra mortar rounds were carried on stretchers. Personal gear, except for a sleeping bag, was loaded on company trucks. Four meals of rations were distributed to each marine. Extra batteries for the radios were passed out. After he culled sick and weak men from his battalion, Davis was ready.

A marine since 1938, Davis had been born in Fitzgerald, Georgia, on January 13, 1915. After high school in Atlanta he attended the Georgia School of Technology, graduating in 1938 with a degree in chemical engineering. Soon after graduation he resigned the commission he'd earned in the army's ROTC program to accept an appointment as a marine corps second lieutenant. By August 1942 he was commanding an antiaircraft machine gun battery ashore at Guadalcanal. Further combat followed in eastern New Guinea and on New Britain.

Davis's exceptional skill as a combat leader brought promotion and greater responsibility. As a major he took command of the 1st Battalion, 1st Marines, 1st Marine Division, in April 1944. Five months later he led them into the hell of Peleliu. Although wounded in the first hour of the attack on the coral island, Davis refused to leave his men. Later, when a Japanese banzai charge shattered his battalion's defensive lines, he personally rallied and led his men in fighting to reestablish the line. Davis's exceptional bravery brought him the Navy Cross.

And now, six years later, Davis was again commanding a marine battalion in a tight spot. His first objective was a hill on the east side of the MSR about a mile south of Yudam-ni. The men called it "Turkey Hill" in memory of the Thanksgiving dinner they'd enjoyed there just a few days before.

Davis expected a tough fight. Instead, Turkey Hill fell after a short firefight. He radioed his regimental commander. "I've taken Turkey Hill already," he said. "I'd like to press on. My marines are sweating from the climb. I don't want them to freeze in the night."

Though it was just about 9:00 P.M., the temperature already stood at minus twenty degrees. Davis wasted no time. He organized his battalion into a column of companies. He moved to the lead company's CO, a young lieutenant. Pointing to a bright star in the eastern sky Davis told the lieutenant, "Guide on that star." The marines started off.

In front of them lay a trackless waste, teeming with Chinese. Except for a few rounds of friendly artillery Davis's battalion was completely on its own.

After the troops started down the first slope they lost sight of the bright star. The column began drifting toward the right, or to the MSR. When Davis realized this he left his position toward the rear of the column and headed toward the point. Struggling through the knee-deep snow he made his way forward. When he passed marines lacking alertness Davis violated his own rule against noise to bark at them to keep awake. The marines, not knowing whom they were admonishing, responded with, "Shut up, marine!" Davis chuckled to himself.

Davis got his battalion back on course, then stayed up front. A little later Chinese riflemen began firing on the battalion as it crossed a wide meadow between two ridge lines. While the enemy fire increased in intensity Davis organized his battalion into two attack columns. The mortars and machine guns were deployed to provide supporting fire. Each marine who passed the mortars dropped off his shell. Soon they were dropping among the Chinese on the hilltop with deadly precision. Davis led his marines up the hill, firing his carbine as he ran. The marines' attack was so swift some of the Chinese were caught in their sleeping bags. It was very satisfying for many of the marines to avenge their dead buddies.

Now under fire from Chinese on more distant hills, Davis moved his battalion into a protected area to treat his casualties. Under his horrified gaze the battalion collapsed in the snow, exhausted from too much fighting, marching, cold, and not enough food.

Davis, his officers and NCOs moved among the parka-clad humps, cursing, screaming, kicking at the men. "Get up! Dammit, get up," they shouted.

Soon the column was shuffling forward through the frozen night, nearly oblivious to sporadic enemy fire. Around 2:00 A.M. the column's lead elements clashed with another Chinese strong point. Davis again demonstrated his exceptional courage by leading a group of marines into the fight. These Chinese were quickly overcome.

By 3:00 A.M. Davis knew his marines were nearly beat. He ordered them to dig in. Ordering every fourth man to stand guard, and under roving perimeter patrols, Davis allowed the marines to crawl into their sleeping bags, though unzipped.

Less than fourteen hundred yards to the southeast Captain Barber's remaining eighty-five effective marines remained alert for another night of CCF attacks. Surprisingly, only light, long-range sniper fire disturbed the marines. As Barber was carried around on his stretcher he was a little disappointed the Chinese weren't attacking. He was confident his marines could lick them again.

While his marines rested Davis personally reconnoitered the terrain ahead. Until he linked up with Barber he would not rest. Already the strain was starting to tell on Davis. At times he'd be in the middle of issuing orders to his company commanders when he'd stop talking. He'd forgotten what he was saying. He'd have to force his mouth to push out the words his brain was forming. When he was done issuing his commands he'd ask his officers if what he'd said made sense. Truth was, they were so cold and tired they weren't sure either.

Finally, everyone understood what was expected of him. The battalion was awakened and made ready to move. At first light, Davis sent one company to seize a hilltop dominating the route of the other two companies. That move went off without a hitch.

Both assault companies crossed nearly one thousand yards of hilly ground without hearing one shot fired in anger. Then Company B got hit hard. As they ground forward Davis was approached by his radioman. "I've got Barber on the radio, sir!"

Barber was in good spirits. He even offered to send a patrol out to help Davis battle the last line of Chinese. Davis declined. But he did ask Barber to direct some of the marine Corsairs overhead in an airstrike on the enemy. Davis's radios couldn't reach the pilots.

Assisted by the marine air and his own mortars Davis's battalion broke through the last barrier of Chinese. The first of his riflemen entered Barber's perimeter at 11:25 A.M., December 2. The relief had been completed. Barber was quickly moved to the aid tent while an officer from Davis's battalion assumed command of what was left of Company F.

Davis's 1st Battalion spent the rest of the day securing and patrolling the area around Fox Hill. By the next morning the rest of the Yudam-ni garrison had battled to within a few hundred yards of Toktong Pass. As soon as he heard that, Davis fashioned a plan to facilitate the breakout. He'd lead two of his companies against Chinese forces holding the road in the direction of Hagaru-ri. In the meantime, the remaining two companies would attack the rear of the Chinese facing the marines coming down from Yudam-ni.

The plan went off without any major problems. By noon on December 3 the lead elements of the Yudam-ni column had contacted the marines on Fox Hill. Davis, in the meantime, smashed into the CCF roadblocks, destroying them and clearing the way to Hagaru-ri.

At 7:00 P.M., December 3, Davis's forward units made contact with a tank force dispatched from Hagaru-ri. While they established an outpost to protect the rest of the Yudam-ni garrison, Davis ordered his men to dress ranks. They were tired, disheveled, dirty, wounded, and cold, but they marched the final six hundred yards into Hagaru-ri in formation, counting cadence. It was a magnificent sight.

Over the next twenty-four hours the balance of the Yudam-ni garrison made its way into Hagaru-ri. The able-bodied marines were pushed into warming tents and fed, while the wounded were treated. Next, the depleted rifle companies were fed into Hagaru-ri's line.

Captain Barber was evacuated from Hagaru-ri to Japan on December 5. He remained hospitalized until March 1951. From there he went to San Diego to serve at the recruit depot. While there he received a promotion to major and a summons to the White House where he received his Medal of Honor on August 26, 1952. He remained in the Marine Corps, retiring as a full colonel in 1970. Barber then worked in the aerospace industry as an operations analyst.

Lieutenant Colonel Davis became the executive officer of the 7th Marines on December 7. He remained in that position until he rotated out of Korea in June 1951. He spent the next two years at Headquarters, U.S. Marine Corps.

Soon after the Chosin Reservoir adventure, Davis was told by his regimental commander a recommendation for the Medal of Honor had been prepared for him. Davis didn't think he deserved the high award and put the matter out of his mind. Unknown to him, he almost didn't receive his decoration. First, a fire at 1st Marine Division headquarters destroyed all the documents relating to Davis's recommendation. Only the personal intervention of famed marine Gen. Victor Krulak resurrected the paperwork.

Then, once the recommendation reached Washington, it encountered opposition. A certain faction of senior marine officers felt Davis's actions had been only what should be expected of a Marine Corps battalion commander, a routine demonstration of command leadership.

More enlightened minds, however, recalled the case of marine Gen. Alexander A. Vandergrift who received the Medal of Honor for commanding the marines at Guadalcanal. The recommendation was approved. Davis would receive his well-justified Medal of Honor, along with Private Cafferata and Sergeant Kennemore, on November 24, 1952.

In July 1962 Davis received the star of a brigadier general. Six years later, wearing three stars, he assumed command of the 3d Marine Division in Vietnam. Davis's thirty-four-year Marine Corps career reached its apex in 1971 when he received his fourth star and the coveted appointment to assistant commandant of the U.S. Marine Corps. General Davis retired in April

1972. He then became executive vice-president of the Georgia Chamber of Commerce. Later, he organized a land development company. In 1988 he received a presidential appointment to the National Korean War Veterans Memorial Commission.

Even with the 5th and 7th Marine Regiments safely at Hagaru-ri, the marines' ordeal was only partially over. They were still sixty-four miles from the sea and safety. Over one hundred thousand Chinese were still intent on crushing the Americans. But before the marines could begin their march to Hungnam, they had to solidify their base at Hagaru-ri to prevent the Chinese from overrunning them.

Chapter Six
Retreat from North Korea

H

agaru-ri was a small mountain town located at the southern edge of the Chosin Reservoir. The significance of Hagaru-ri stemmed from the fact it sat astride an important road junction. The MSR connecting Koto-ri and Yudam-ni ran right through the town. Another important road ran from Hagaru-ri around the eastern edge of the now frozen Chosin Reservoir. Whoever held Hagaru-ri controlled access to the reservoir and movement throughout the area.

Hagaru-ri itself was a typical nondescript village of North Korea. Clusters of buildings, most concrete block with some thatched structures, ran along the roads. Only a few hundred people called the hamlet home. Several hill masses erupt from the otherwise flat terrain lying between the village and the surrounding mountains. The most significant of these, a high distorted mass of ridges, overlooked the town from the east, and was promptly dubbed East Hill by the marines.

The first Americans had arrived in Hagaru-ri on November 15. They were the vanguard of two marine regiments who would pass through the town before encircling the reservoir: the 5th Marines to the east and the 7th Marines to the west via Yudam-ni. The forward command post of the 1st Marine Division was established on the north side of the town. By the end of the first week Maj. Gen. Oliver P. Smith had moved his division headquarters there.

In the week after the first marines arrived there, Hagaru-ri was rapidly transformed into a vital headquarters and supply base necessary to support two full combat divisions. Somewhere around three thousand men garrisoned the little town. By far the majority of them were engineers and service/support personnel. A conglomeration of marine and army units set up positions throughout the area. No one had any idea exactly which units were in and around Hagaru-ri, but it was obvious few of them were combat-ready. The 11th Marines, an artillery regiment, had several batteries in the area, as well as its fire support center. Two companies from the 3d Battalion, 1st Marines, Companies H and I, had arrived during the night of November 26. They replaced two companies of the 7th Marines that had proceeded to Yudam-ni early that morning. The battalion's third company, Company G, was stuck in Koto-ri because of a lack of transportation. It was hoped they'd arrive on November 28.

Like their brothers-in-arms at Yudam-ni, the troops at Hagaru-ri had no idea over one hundred thousand Chinese lurked in the hills around them.

Initially, the 5th Marines had been sent up the east side of the Chosin Reservoir. From there they were supposed to link up with the 7th Marines coming around the west side of the reservoir. The combined force would then drive north to the Yalu. However, this mission was changed on November 25. The 5th Marines would now remove to the south through Hagaru-ri and move to Yudam-ni. Once there they would pass through the 7th Marines, leading the new attack westward to link up with the Eighth Army.

The 5th Marines turned over the east side of the Chosin Reservoir to the 1st Battalion, 32d Infantry Regiment, U.S. 7th Infantry Division, on November 26. The choice of this army unit to relieve the marines was based solely on chance. The 1st Battalion, 32d Infantry, had been the rearmost 7th Division unit on the road to the nearby Fusen Reservoir. Hence, it became the easiest unit to turn around and dispatch to the Chosin Reservoir.

About nine hundred soldiers comprised the 1st Battalion, 32d Infantry; two hundred of these were South Korean conscripts. The unit had come ashore at Inchon in September and acquitted itself rather well in the fighting for Seoul. Although the battalion commander was initially skeptical about his nine-hundred-man unit taking over from a thirty-five-hundred-man regiment, he was secure in the knowledge he would be reinforced over the next two days.

Indeed, the very next day the 3d Battalion, 31st Infantry, two batteries of the 57th Field Artillery Battalion, and a self-propelled antiaircraft battery joined the 1st Battalion, 32d Infantry. The balance of the two infantry regiments was scheduled to arrive on November 28 and 29. In the meantime, the mixed force on the east side of the Chosin Reservoir was dubbed Task Force Faith, named for the commander of the 1st Battalion, 32d Infantry.

DON C. FAITH

Born in Washington, Indiana, on August 26, 1918, Don C. Faith grew up in a military family. His father was a career army officer who retired as a brigadier general. Don Faith attended school at a variety of army bases around the world before entering Georgetown University in 1938. After graduating in June 1941 he immediately enlisted in the army. Eight months later, following Officer Candidate School, he received his commission as a second lieutenant. Parachute training at Fort Benning, Georgia, came next. Then he was assigned to the 82d Airborne Division.

Faith saw service with the paratroopers during the fighting in North Africa, Italy, France, and Germany. By the time World War II ended Faith was a lieutenant colonel on the staff of Gen. Maxwell Taylor with the XVIII Airborne Corps. Considered one of the army's most promising officers, Faith received several plush postwar assignments. In 1946, for example, he was tapped to be army secretary to the Military Staff Committee of the United Nations. In February 1948 he went to China as a member of the Joint United States Military Advisory Group, serving there for a year before being ordered to Japan.

In Japan he took command of the 1st Battalion, 32d Infantry. After the Korean War broke out Faith watched his unit deteriorate as his troops were transferred piecemeal to Korea as replacements for the decimated combat battalions holding the Pusan Perimeter.

Once MacArthur's plan for an amphibious landing at Inchon received approval, Faith's battalion was brought back to full strength. Unfortunately, few of the replacements were combat veterans. Many were transferred to the infantry battalion from service units in Japan. Others came direct from training camps in the United States. In addition, his battalion received several hundred conscripted South Koreans.

Faced with a raw battalion, Faith trained his men hard in the few weeks he had left. By the time Faith's battalion crossed the Inchon beaches he was justifiably proud of his men. They performed bravely during the fighting to liberate Seoul. When the 1st Battalion, 32d Infantry, landed in eastern North Korea, Faith envisioned a relatively quick dash to the Yalu River and a return to garrison duty in Japan by Christmas.

Then came the orders to proceed to the eastern shore of the Chosin Reservoir. On November 26 Faith took over the positions of the 5th Marines. He placed his three companies on commanding ground about twenty road miles north of Hagaru-ri. They passed the night of November 26 peacefully.

During the next day the rest of Task Force Faith arrived. The 3d Battalion, 31st Infantry, took up positions some five road miles south of Faith's battalion. They were widely dispersed along the narrow dirt road, on the south side of a long, eastward jutting finger of the Chosin Reservoir.

Farther south the headquarters of the 31st Infantry Regiment took up positions in and around a schoolhouse. Besides the headquarters personnel, a tank company, a heavy mortar company, and a variety of support and service personnel occupied the position.

Altogether, nearly three thousand army personnel had moved through Hagaru-ri and on up the eastern side of the frozen Chosin Reservoir.

On the afternoon of November 27, Faith and his regimental commander had reconnoitered the route Faith's battalion would take the next morning as it began its advance to the Yalu. Later, Faith met with his company commanders to discuss their missions. Then the battalion crawled into its sleeping bags for a cold night's sleep. In the hills to their east several CCF divisions crept silently toward the unsuspecting Americans.

The Chinese hit Faith's position with a numbing fury. Shortly after midnight, November 28, hordes of CCF swept down from the high ground east of Faith's battalion. Moving noiselessly over freshly fallen snow, they were on the outposts before the GIs realized it. Those men died in a quick flurry of hand grenades. The Chinese bore in on Company A. By the time the trip flares went off the Chinese were already within Company A's lines. Vicious fighting broke out everywhere. More Chinese fell on Company C, to the right of Company A.

Though disorganized, the GIs fought back bravely. In small groups they set up bases of fire, stopping the Chinese. Other men hunted down infiltrators. Only the stubborn strength of a few determined officers and men prevented the Chinese from overrunning the companies.

At his battalion command group, Faith directed the defense of his unit. He shuffled squads and platoons back and forth through the night, plugging holes in his lines. He was able to strengthen his lines with battalion personnel and slow the enemy attack.

With dawn the Chinese withdrew into the hills. Marine Corsairs appeared overhead and delivered air strikes on Chinese positions near the American lines. Small patrols left the battalion perimeter to throw Chinese off key positions. Wounded were moved to collection stations. The lines were reorganized, strengthened wherever possible.

After that first night's attack Colonel Faith postponed his advance to the Yalu. In fact, he was somewhat concerned about his ability to hold even his present position.

At 2:00 P.M. November 28, General Almond helicoptered into Faith's compound. Faith reported he had been attacked by elements of two Chinese divisions. Almond scoffed. "There aren't two Chinese divisions in the whole of North Korea," he said.

Faith was stunned at Almond's disbelief. He had dozens of dead and wounded from the Chinese. "Stragglers," Almond assured Faith. The two spoke privately for awhile. Then, as Almond prepared to depart, he reached in his parka pocket and withdrew a Silver Star medal. He pinned the medal to Faith's field jacket. Then he announced to Faith and those nearby, "The enemy who is delaying you are nothing more than remnants of Chinese divisions fleeing north. We're still attacking and going all the way to the Yalu. Don't let a bunch of laundrymen stop you!"

With that Almond boarded his helicopter and departed. As the little aircraft flew away Faith ripped the medal from his jacket and threw it into a snowbank.

The night of November 28–29 passed more quietly than the previous evening, but there were still Chinese attacks. Faith spent a good deal of the night with his companies, braving enemy mortar, small-arms, and automatic-weapons fire, to direct counterattacks against penetrations of his lines.

During the day Faith learned that the marines at Hagaru-ri had no forces to spare to effect a relief force. He was on his own.

The Chinese came again at 10:30 P.M., November 29. Several columns of CCF forces hit along the weakened perimeter at the same time.

While the fighting still raged Faith concluded he could no longer adequately hold his position. At about 2:00 A.M. on November 30 he ordered his battalion to withdraw south and join up with the 3d Battalion, 31st Infantry, on the far side of the inlet.

As many men as could be spared were pulled from the front line to unload the company's vehicles. Then the more than one hundred wounded soldiers were placed aboard them. As soon as a vehicle was loaded it moved into position on the road.

Faith planned to have two of his companies advance south on ridges along either side of the road while his third company fought a rearguard action. As soon as the first combat units were pulled from the line, though, the plan fell apart; everyone rushed to join the convoy on the road.

With a full snowstorm blowing, the convoy started south in the predawn darkness under sporadic enemy fire. As soon as it became light, however, the enemy fire picked up in intensity. Men fought as best they could but they were anxious to keep moving. The Chinese pressed in.

The mountain road ran south for about one mile before turning east to parallel the northern shore of the inlet. Then, after less than half a mile, it turned south to cross over a small bridge spanning the inlet, before turning back west along the inlet's south shore. The Chinese had set up a tough roadblock at the north end of the bridge. Faith took a small party to reconnoiter the position. Though exposed to heavy enemy fire, he evolved a plan to reduce the roadblock and free his column. He personally directed several platoons in attacking the Chinese stronghold.

Once the roadblock was cleared Faith took the first infantry squads across the bridge, placing them in positions to best cover the trucks as they crossed. Faith next directed each truck in crossing the small bridge, constantly exposing himself to enemy fire. Only when the last truckload of wounded passed into friendly hands did Faith cross to safety himself.

If Colonel Faith expected to improve his force by joining with the other battalion he was mistaken. The 3d Battalion, 31st Infantry, had been hit as hard the previous three nights as Faith had. Chinese and American bodies lay sprawled in death's grotesque grip throughout the area.

Faith quickly went about reorganizing the two units. He called for an airdrop of supplies. He called again for a relief column from Hagaru-ri but again was told no help was available. An army tank company did set out from Hagaru-ri but was turned back only a few miles north of the town by at least two battalions of CCF occupying the high ground along the dirt road.

Late on the afternoon of November 30, Faith's division commander helicoptered into the perimeter. He brought no good news. He confirmed the marines at Hagaru-ri were completely unable to mount a relief. If Faith wanted to see his task force reach safety, Maj. Gen. David W. Barr told him, he'd have to handle it himself. Barr then departed, tears in his eyes.

Colonel Faith quickly assembled his key officers. If they survived the night, he said, the task force would break out for Hagaru-ri the next day.

Task Force Faith barely survived the night of November 30–December 1. The Chinese launched their most determined attack to date. Anticipating a clear victory, they attacked continuously throughout the dark night. Half-frozen GIs, reluctantly accepting their fate, battled the enemy from shallow foxholes. A literal hail of enemy small-arms fire descended on the shrinking perimeter. Anyone who ventured above ground risked certain injury or death.

Five times before dawn the CCF penetrated the American lines. Five times Don Faith organized reaction forces and led them across the bullet-swept ground. Firing his .45-caliber pistol and yelling instructions to his men, the resolute officer helped kill the infiltrators. A thick morning mist delayed the arrival of American air support, emboldening the Chinese. So desperate was Faith for men, he gathered walking wounded from the aid station and led them to the front lines to plug holes.

When the mist finally cleared, a single marine Corsair appeared overhead. It dropped its bombs with telling effect before withdrawing to rearm.

Don Faith knew he had reached the end of his rope. He was nearly out of ammo. Rations were low. His casualties were mounting and his medical supplies were nearly exhausted. The bitter cold was causing nearly as many casualties as the enemy. Many of his troops had been in nearly constant combat for over eighty hours. Some men were so tired they actually fell asleep in the middle of the battle.

Faith ordered his task force to prepare to break out. The wounded were once again loaded aboard trucks. Equipment and supplies that could not be removed were destroyed. Faith called for more air support to clear the Chinese from the heights dominating the road. The column was finally ready about 1:00 P.M. Faith ordered an air strike against an enemy roadblock less than fifty yards from the first truck. Unfortunately, the napalm canisters fell among the leading elements of the column. Burning men shrieked horribly as they ran back along the waiting vehicles.

Realizing he was on the verge of a mass panic, Faith raced to the head of the column. Quickly organizing a reaction force, he led them in an assault on the enemy position. His bold attack shattered it. The column started forward.

Though Faith destroyed the Chinese roadblock, the disastrous napalm drop destroyed the cohesiveness of the column. The seventy-two vehicles and hundreds of walking troops broke into small groups, each individually fighting its way forward. Faith tried to restore order but the situation had deteriorated too far. He sent small bands of men up the slopes to wipe out enemy pockets but more times than not the attacks petered out.

For two miles the column fought its way south. Chinese troops on the heights rained a continuous barrage of fire on the column, killing and wounding men by the score. Wounded aboard the trucks were particularly vulnerable as enemy rounds tore through the canvas covers, slaughtering them.

A blown bridge two miles south of the starting point halted the ragged column. Strangely, the area was relatively free of Chinese. Faith organized the men in the area to clear a path through the dry stream bed. Then a half-track slowly pulled each truck across the gully. Several hours later all the wheeled vehicles were across and started down the road again.

A short distance later the road took a sharp, hairpin turn around the eastern side of a large hill. A roadblock sat at the curve's bend. Under Don Faith the infantry at the point moved against the roadblock. Just as it looked as though they might clear the position, enemy machine guns on a nearby hillside broke up the attack. Faith stormed back to his jeep where he climbed into the rear and grasped the handles on the .50-caliber machine gun mounted there. He sent short deadly bursts of fire into the Chinese positions, knocking out at least one machine gun.

By now night had fallen. Chinese pressed hard against the strung-out train, sometimes actually penetrating the column where they moved among the trucks, slaying the wounded huddled inside. American and South Korean soldiers began drifting away from the column in droves, heading into the hills and across the ice-covered reservoir to make their way individually into Hagaru-ri.

Still at the head of his troops, Faith assembled a group of officers and men to tackle the roadblock one more time. The momentum of the attack carried it through the roadblock, but with heavy losses. One of those wounded was Don Faith.

He staggered back toward his jeep, a gaping hole torn in his side by an exploding grenade. He collapsed before he reached his vehicle and had to be helped aboard. There, beside his driver, Don Faith, battered for five days, weak from the cold, and exhausted from his heroic efforts to save his beleaguered command, slowly bled to death.

Around him those still able to fight continued punching forward. Farther back Task Force Faith continued to disintegrate. More and more men abandoned the road to head cross-country for Hagaru-ri. By midnight the column no longer existed. Small groups of men fought on through the night but were killed or captured soon after dawn. Hundreds of wounded were left for the Chinese; most were never heard from again.

For days afterwards soldiers continued to stagger into the marines' line. But they were a pitifully small group. Despite Don Faith's valiant efforts to save his task force, only about five hundred men of the original three thousand survived the ordeal east of Chosin.

For his "outstanding gallantry and noble self-sacrifice" Lt. Col. Don Faith was posthumously awarded the Medal of Honor. In a ceremony at the Pentagon on June 21, 1951, Faith's widow and four-year-old daughter accepted the award from Gen. Omar Bradley.

Hagaru-ri had suffered heavily from November 27 onward. Each night the Chinese attacked the base. Most of the town's perimeter was held by army and marine service troops pressed into roles as infantrymen. The only trained infantry units at Hagaru-ri, Companies H and I of the 3d Battalion, 1st Marines, held the south and southwestern edges of the town. Night after night the Chinese came to do battle, suffering terrible casualties, but causing many among the defenders of the base.

Until the marines arrived from Yudam-ni, the key to holding Hagaru-ri was East Hill. A jumbled mass of sharp ridge lines and steep slopes, the hill mass overlooked the town from across the frozen Changjin River, which ran north-south along Hagaru-ri's eastern edge. Strapped for manpower, the man in charge of Hagaru-ri's defense, Lt. Col. Thomas Ridge, CO of the 3d Battalion, had been forced to assign the defense of East Hill to about 250 noncombatant army signal corps men. They lasted exactly one night.

The army communicators dug in on East Hill on the evening of November 28. At 12:30 A.M., November 29, the Chinese hit them. The thin army line collapsed even before most of the men could fire their weapons. Within an hour the survivors were streaming down the hill. A battalion of Chinese now occupied East Hill.

Colonel Ridge knew he couldn't leave the Chinese on East Hill. From there they could direct their mountain howitzers directly into the crowded base. Everything in Hagaru-ri, from the main ammo dump to the two crowded hospitals, was in clear view of East Hill.

Ridge's mobile reserve, assembled the previous evening with men from sixty separate army and marine service units, was down to twenty men; the rest had been fed into the lines during the night battles along Hagaru-ri's perimeter. They would have to do. Ridge summoned his executive officer several hours before dawn. Ridge told him to take the twenty men up East Hill and attack the Chinese. As he could round up more men, Ridge said, he'd send them up the hill.

REGINALD R. MYERS
CARL L. SITTER

Ridge's executive officer, Maj. Reginald R. Myers, had been a marine for nearly ten years. Born in Boise, Idaho, on November 26, 1919, he'd graduated from high school in Salt Lake City, then attended the University of Idaho. After graduating in June 1941 with a degree in mechanical engineering and an army ROTC commission, he transferred to the Marine Corps in September 1941.

Myers spent most of World War II as a seagoing marine. Aboard the cruisers *New Orleans* and *Minneapolis* he participated in the invasions of Guadalcanal, the Gilbert Islands, and the Marshall Islands. After a brief tour of duty in the United States, Myers received his promotion to major and a transfer to the 1st Marine Division. As executive officer of the 5th Marines, Myers fought on Okinawa and later served with the occupation forces in northern China.

Routine assignments followed in the States until Myers joined the 3d Battalion, 1st Marines, as its executive officer in July 1950. He earned two Bronze Stars during the fighting in and around Seoul, then participated in the movement to Hagaru-ri.

After receiving his assignment from Colonel Ridge, Myers led his small force through the crowded base. A steady snowfall added to the misery of a minus-twenty-degree night. At the base of the hill Myers found much confusion. Many of the hill's original defenders were milling around, unwilling to return to the fight. By cajolery, bullying, threats, and physical force, Myers organized his ragtag group, including reinforcements sent as promised by Ridge, into a skirmish line. He now had some three hundred men at hand, as mixed an assortment as could be imagined. With himself in the center of the line, he gave the order to start up the hill.

The first part of the climb was the toughest. East Hill rose nearly straight up from the road. With new snow falling on the ice-covered ground the route upward was extremely difficult. Still, Myers moved among his men, forcing them to find new sources of strength. It took nearly an hour for the force to reach its line of departure.

Once there, Myers got the group in the best attack formation he could, then ordered, "Let's go!"

Upward they went, slipping and sliding, wiping snow and ice from tired eyes, dodging bullets and mortar bursts. The broken terrain forced the attackers into narrow columns, easy targets for Chinese machine gunners. Casualties mounted. Reluctantly, Myers ordered the casualties left on the slopes. He couldn't spare the manpower to carry them downhill.

As daylight broke, outlining the attackers, the Chinese increased their fire. More men fell in the snow. Moving forward in short bursts, a determined core of men moved toward the hill's crest. At their head was Myers, braving the heavy enemy fire to urge his men forward.

Nearing the military crest Myers had but seventy-five men left. Still determined to throw the Chinese off the hill, Myers led them toward the enemy. A heavy tattoo of machine-gun fire drove them to ground. Myers got his men up and moving forward again. A barrage of hand grenades suddenly erupted around them, again forcing them down. Myers realized a further attack was suicidal. He pulled his men back, forming a thin defensive line just below the military crest of the hill.

At 9:30 A.M. Corsairs appeared overhead. Myers directed them in strikes against the Chinese positions. Smoky bursts of napalm erupted on top of the hill. Rockets whooshed downward from the sky, sending huge clouds of dirt, snow, and rocks into the air. The Corsairs then strafed the enemy with their six wing-mounted .50-caliber machine guns.

When the air attack was over Myers ordered his men forward. The Chinese met them with a wall of fire. Myers pulled his attack force back again.

Myers held his position throughout the long day. Occasional groups of reinforcements reached him, but rarely more than five or six men at a time. He called artillery in on the enemy, but they had gone to ground. Every time Myers tried to move forward a flood of hand grenades flowed down the hill. The two forces stood toe-to-toe atop the hill, neither side giving an inch. Though Myers could not conquer East Hill, he had prevented the Chinese from dominating Hagaru-ri.

As the sun lowered on the western horizon, Myers became more worried. He doubted he could hold through the night against a determined enemy thrust. He looked desperately southward along the MSR from Koto-ri. Repeatedly throughout the day he had been told his battalion's third company was coming up from Koto-ri. But the assurances he'd received came to naught.

Myers decided to hold his position. It was a nearly impossible challenge, but he knew he would have to accept it.

What he didn't know was that just five miles south of East Hill the expected reinforcements from Koto-ri were desperately fighting for their lives.

In response to General Smith's request for reinforcements to help hold Hagaru-ri until the marines from Yudam-ni arrived, Col. Lewis "Chesty" Puller at Koto-ri assembled a nine-hundred-man force to fight its way through the blocking Chinese. Two hundred fifty of the men belonged to the British 41st Royal Marine Commando under Lt. Col. Donald Drysdale. They would lead the advance. Behind them would be Colonel Ridge's third rifle company, Company G, under the command of Capt. Carl L. Sitter. These two units would alternate the lead—41st Commando to take the first enemy position, Company G to move through them and on to the next, and so on, to leapfrog up the MSR.

Following Sitter was Company B, 1st Battalion, 31st Infantry. Behind them came a hodgepodge of service and support personnel, most of them transients eager to rejoin their units in Hagaru-ri. A motor column brought up the rear. Tanks took up positions at each end of the column and at various spots within the convoy. In all, about 150 vehicles and thirty tanks added to the bulk of the column.

Task Force Drysdale departed Koto-ri just after dawn, November 29. Its first objective was a series of heights just north of town. The British commandos moved out first and quickly took their ridge. Behind them, Captain Sitter started his company forward to tackle the second ridge.

A native of Syracuse, Missouri, where he was born on December 2, 1921, Sitter enlisted in the marines in June 1940 after graduating from high school in Pueblo, Colorado. A year later he went with the 1st Provisional Marine Brigade to Iceland. After eight months on that frosty island he received orders to the Pacific war zone. In December 1942 he received a field promotion to second lieutenant.

Sitter saw action as a platoon leader at Eniwetok, where he was wounded on February 20, 1944. Five months later, during the fighting to retake Guam, he was wounded a second time. Evacuated to the States, he remained there until the war ended. He applied for a regular commission soon afterwards and was accepted. In August 1950 he received orders to Korea.

Sitter hadn't expected his move to Hagaru-ri to be easy but it started off far worse than he could have imagined. He started his company up its assigned ridge after marine artillery peppered the hill for thirty minutes. As they reached the crest of the ridge a heavy barrage of enemy automatic-weapons fire tore into the company. Fourteen men fell. Undaunted, Sitter rallied his marines. They fought against stubborn resistance, killing over forty of the enemy. The last enemy machine gun nest had to be destroyed by bazooka. Only then was the ridge secure.

By now it was noon. Sitter had fought as hard as he could and was just barely two miles from Koto-ri. In the meantime, Drysdale had led his men against the next ridge. Sitter caught up with him and suggested a change in tactics.

Both Drysdale and Sitter realized the enemy defense was far deeper than they had imagined. They concluded the column would never reach Hagaru-ri on foot. The only solution was to mount the infantry on trucks and run the gauntlet of Chinese.

The tanks would lead. The army infantry would follow, then Sitter's marines followed by the commandos. In their wake would come the rest of the trucks.

Sitter moved his company behind the tanks and directed the armor in placing suppressive fire on visible targets. In this way they fought their way forward nearly three miles in the next two hours.

But it was not an easy two hours. Time and again Chinese fire halted the convoy. Men would spill from their trucks, charge up the hill, knock out the enemy positions, trudge back downhill to reboard the trucks, and move forward again.

By the time the bulk of the column reached the halfway point to Hagaru-ri some of the lead tanks had driven all the way into the town. They returned to Drysdale to report they didn't think the truck convoy would survive the final five miles to Hagaru-ri. Drysdale radioed ahead for instructions.

General Smith responded: "Get through at all costs."

Task Force Drysdale continued its desperate journey. Intense enemy fire fell on the column. Stopping every few hundred yards to fight destroyed the cohesiveness of the column. Trucks ruined by enemy fire fragmented the column. Soon it was stretched out for several miles, each little group alone and battling furiously for its life.

In the lead fragment Sitter's company entered a narrow defile. Enemy mortars dropped on the trucks. Machine-gun fire tore into them, killing and wounding many. A burst of fire riddled Sitter's jeep, killing his driver and knocking out the engine. Sitter went to find Drysdale.

By this time Drysdale was badly wounded. He turned command of his task force over to Sitter. Sitter returned to his company, got the tanks rolling, and his men loaded aboard trucks. With the tanks blazing a path through the enemy, Sitter's rapidly dwindling company fought on.

Finally, Sitter could see the lights of Hagaru-ri in the distance. He urged his men onward for the final push into the town. A last Chinese roadblock barred the way. Sitter exposed himself to enemy fire to batter on a tank until he got it to unbutton long enough to spray the roadblock with machine-gun fire.

When the roadblock was destroyed Sitter's company lurched forward. At 9:00 P.M., twelve hours after he started the eleven-mile journey, Sitter entered Hagaru-ri. Of his original 270-man company only 160 remained.

Behind him 41st Commando was still fighting. Though wounded, Colonel Drysdale fought through one roadblock after another. At 1:30 A.M. Drysdale reached Hagaru-ri. With him were about 125 of his men, half of what he'd started with.

On the MSR the surviving 450-odd men were slowly being hacked up by the Chinese. All through the night and into the next day the CCF whittled away at the remnants of Task Force Drysdale. Finally, it was no longer worth fighting. There were too many wounded and not enough ammo. With no hope of reaching either Hagaru-ri or Koto-ri, the survivors surrendered.

Though some men managed to slip away and reach safety after days of wandering the hills, most became prisoners. Of the nine hundred men that left Koto-ri, 169 died, 159 were wounded, and 321 captured. Less than three hundred reached Hagaru-ri. But they were enough to help the beleaguered bastion.

Company G was tired and disorganized after its series of running fights on the MSR and it took Capt. Sitter until past 1:00 A.M., November 30, to get his people reorganized and bedded down. Then he turned in. A few hours later his radio operator summoned him. It was the regimental operations officer.

"Look outside your tent to your front," he told Sitter. "See that hill? Take it."

Sitter surveyed the hill mass. He knew Myers was up there, hanging on through sheer guts. Sitter would relieve him.

Sitter roused his men from their warming tents at dawn. The arctic-like wind quickly cut through their bulky parkas. At 9:00 A.M. they were at the base of East Hill. They started up. The way was made more difficult by the men who had preceded them. The snow had been pounded to an icy hardness by hundreds of boots. Several hours of difficult climbing brought Company G to the line to which Myers had pulled back.

Sitter divided his company into two assault elements. His first platoon was on the left, the second on the right; the third platoon would follow in reserve. They went after the Chinese.

Fighting every step of the way, taking heavy fire from the Chinese on the commanding terrain, Company G blasted its way up the ridge. Halfway there Sitter realized the futility of his attack. To continue farther meant additional casualties. Sitter's marines were getting weaker from the incredible exertion combined with the freezing cold. They couldn't go on much longer.

Sitter radioed Colonel Ridge. He said he felt he held enough of the hill to deny the Chinese the approach to Hagaru-ri. He requested permission to dig in for the night where he was. At 5:00 P.M. Ridge radioed his okay.

Under Sitter's direction Company G set up defensive positions, his second platoon in the center, the first to its right, and the third on the left. For three hours the hill enjoyed a quiet night. Then the bray of bugles echoed in the cold night air. Green flares exploded in the sky. The second platoon leader yelled, "Here they come!"

Out of the night the Chinese attackers came. Sitter's machine guns opened fire, mowing the enemy down on the frozen rocks. Sitter got his mortars working, dropping them back and forth across the front of the second platoon. Under this concentrated barrage of death the enemy attack broke.

Company G's ammo supply was by now critically low. Sitter hastily organized a carrying party to go to the bottom of the hill and bring up more. They returned just minutes before the Chinese came again.

Sitter moved from position to position helping his men fight the enemy. It seemed impossible to Sitter that there could be so many Chinese. The hillside seemed to be covered with them. Back at his CP Sitter was on the radio to Colonel Ridge when an enemy mortar exploded nearby. Shrapnel tore into Sitter, painfully ripping his chest and face. Regardless, he stayed on the job. For a while it didn't appear Sitter would have a job for long. Chinese broke through where his second and third platoons joined, closing rapidly on the CP.

Rushing forward at the head of his headquarters troops, Sitter engaged the infiltrators with his rifle. One of the enemy approached close enough to throw grenades into the CP. Sitter went after him. Another grenade erupted. Splinters of hot steel tore through his heavy winter clothing, but Sitter again refused to leave his company.

At 4:00 A.M. the Chinese came again. Though weak from blood loss and in pain from his many wounds, Sitter continued leading his men, urging them to keep fighting. At dawn the CCF finally pulled back, leaving more than half their number on the slopes, dead and dying.

Company G remained on East Hill for three more days. The Chinese came each night, attacking the thin line. As they became available, reinforcements were sent to Sitter. He took the noncombatants and skillfully integrated them into his company, forming a strong, cohesive defensive line. As had Major Myers, Sitter's determination denied the CCF a key point in the Hagaru-ri perimeter. Marines on East Hill prevented a slaughter of the marines in the town.

On the morning of December 5, Captain Sitter was relieved by elements of the 5th Marines, recently arrived from Yudam-ni. Only ninety-six men were left to march down to the road with him.

Both Myers and Sitter survived the subsequent march to the sea that added another page of glory to marine corps history. For their sustained gallantry and remarkable leadership the two received the Medal of Honor in a double ceremony at the White House on October 29, 1951. They remained in the Marine Corps, each attaining the rank of colonel before retirement.

A major factor in the marines' success in holding back the hordes of CCF soldiers around the Chosin Reservoir was the near-constant air support they received from navy and marine corps aircraft. Weather permitting, the tireless pilots flew all day long, providing the vital firepower needed to hold the superior enemy forces at bay. With their skillful flying ability and the knowledge that the lives of thousands of American men depended upon them, the pilots of the World War II-vintage Corsairs and P-51 Mustangs were able to lay their ordnance within yards of friendly positions.

The concept of close-air support had been pioneered by the Marine Corps. First developed during the campaigns in Central America before World War II, the practice was fine-tuned on dozens of islands as the marines island-hopped across the Pacific toward Japan.

In the years before the Korean War, navy and marine pilots received intensive training in close-air support. The marines also began the practice of placing a highly trained pilot with the ground forces. By being able to speak the language of his fellow pilots the forward air controller was able to exercise a tremendous amount of precision in calling in airstrikes.

From aircraft carriers off the east coast of Korea as well as from airstrips at Yonpo, near Hungnam, the planes provided a near-constant umbrella of protection for their comrades on the ground. When not flying directly in support of ground units, the pilots crisscrossed the Chosin Reservoir area seeking targets of opportunity. Though the Chinese were adept at concealing themselves during the daylight hours, the pilots sometimes were able to surprise Chinese formations. Then their destructive napalm, bombs, and .50-caliber machine guns created havoc among the enemy.

But sometimes, the enemy surprised the pilots.

THOMAS J. HUDNER

Early on the afternoon of December 4, 1950, eight Corsairs from Fighter Squadron 32, off the aircraft carrier U.S.S. *Leyte*, flew in loose formation about ten miles north of the Chosin Reservoir. They were on a general support mission, looking for targets of opportunity for their heavy .50-caliber machine guns and the air-to-ground rockets slung under each wing. At an altitude of less than one thousand feet above ground level, the gull-winged fighters skimmed across the snow-covered, mountainous terrain, the pilots' eyes anxiously scanning the ground for any sign of the Chinese.

Suddenly, Ens. Jesse Brown, a native of Hattiesburg, Mississippi, radioed to the other pilots, "I'm losing power!"

For some reason, perhaps due to a lucky enemy round, Brown's engine was slowing. As the other Corsairs circled anxiously, Brown's plane glided toward the ground. Unable to help, the other seven pilots watched in horrified fascination as Brown rode his powerless Corsair down. Brown, the navy's first black pilot, nursed his plane toward the most level spot he could find. With its landing gear up, the plane touched down, bounced once, twice, then skidded to a halt. The engine was torn from its mountings, coming to a rest a hundred yards from the plane. The impact bent the fuselage sharply just forward of the canopy.

As the other pilots watched, Brown slid the plane's canopy open, then waved feebly to his buddies overhead.

The flight's leader, Lt. Comdr. Richard Cevoli, immediately radioed for a rescue helicopter. With any kind of luck Brown would be safely in American hands within an hour. In the meantime, Brown's buddies would fly protectively overhead, keeping a sharp eye open for any Chinese intent on capturing an American pilot.

While Cevoli radioed for a helicopter, Brown's wingman, Lt. (jg) Thomas J. Hudner, noticed smoke drifting backward from the cowling of Brown's plane. He feared a fire was raging just forward of the cockpit. He mentally urged Brown to climb out. After he'd circled two more times and Brown made no effort to evacuate the plane, Hudner realized his wingman was either trapped in the wreckage or too badly injured to move.

In that instant, Hudner made a momentous decision.

"I'm going in," Hudner radioed Cevoli.

With that, Hudner chopped power, dropped flaps, and set himself up for an emergency landing.

Hudner, a native of Fall River, Massachusetts, was born on August 31, 1924, and was a 1946 graduate of Annapolis. After graduation he served aboard the cruiser *Helena* before reporting for aviation training. Hudner completed his training and received the coveted wings of a naval aviator in August 1949. In November he joined Fighter Squadron 32.

In August 1950 the *Leyte* was in Cannes, France, when word came for them to sail to Korea. The carrier arrived off North Korea on October 10, after a brief stop in Newport News, Virginia.

Though he was senior in rank to Brown, Hudner was assigned as his wingman because Brown had more experience in Corsairs. The two quickly became friends.

But that wasn't why Hudner went down after him. As he said later, "We were a team. One of us was in trouble. Somebody had to help. I decided to be that one."

Hudner's plane hit the mountainside hard but it was a good landing. He came to rest about a hundred yards from Brown's plane.

He jumped out of the plane and ran to Brown. The snow was deeper than he'd expected; nearly a foot of wet snow covered the ground. It clung heavily to the soles of Hudner's boots. As a result, he found it very difficult to climb up the Corsair's slanted wing root in order to get up to the cockpit. Finally, he got a purchase on the handholds in the plane's side and hoisted himself up to the cockpit.

As he feared, Brown's legs were trapped under the instrument panel by the twisted and bent hydraulic lines and frame members. Brown was already suffering badly from the subzero temperatures though he'd been on the ground less than twenty minutes. In his efforts to free himself, Brown had removed his helmet, then taken off his gloves to unbuckle his safety harness. In his anxiety he dropped the gloves out of reach. When Hudner reached him his hands were already stiff with the cold.

Hudner worked to free Brown. While he did so he was acutely conscious of the smoke still wafting up from in front of the firewall. He spoke reassuringly to Brown, offering words of encouragement.

"I could tell he had severe internal injuries," Hudner said. "He spoke very slowly, as if he were tired. I felt I didn't have much time if I was to save his life."

Hudner left Brown and ran back to his own plane. He radioed Cevoli to have the helicopter bring a fire extinguisher and an axe. Then he grabbed a wool scarf and hat he kept in his cockpit for emergencies. Back at Brown's plane, he pulled the hat over his friend's head and wrapped the scarf around his hands. Then he jumped off the wing. He gathered armsful of snow to pack around the still smoking nose.

Once he'd done all he could there he scrambled back up the wing to Brown. He struggled to free Brown but had no luck. Brown was just too badly trapped. Moreover, Hudner's awkward position, hanging over the fuselage into the cockpit, made it hard for him to get the proper leverage.

"Brown was pretty calm during all this," Hudner said. "Although groggy, he was alert. We talked a bit, but we didn't have much to say. At no time, though, did Jesse utter one word of complaint. He must have been in a lot of pain, and it was bitterly cold, but he never complained."

Finally, Hudner heard the faint beat from the rotors of an approaching helicopter. A few minutes later marine Lt. Charles Ward put his craft down adjacent to Brown's Corsair. He brought the axe and fire extinguisher to Hudner.

Together, the two worked to free Brown. But their efforts proved futile. The axe simply bounced off the metal plate trapping Brown's legs. The fire extinguisher did nothing to the smoldering fire. Brown was growing weaker. He spoke less often, his words fainter.

Finally, Ward called Hudner aside. It was growing dark, he told Hudner. Since his helicopter was not equipped to fly at night, flying among the mountains in the dark could prove fatal. To stay would only mean disaster for all three. Their only hope lay in returning to the base camp and coming back the next day with better equipment.

Hudner knew Brown would not survive the night. Already he was lapsing in and out of consciousness. "Jesse must have known it was hopeless," Hudner recalled sadly. "He couldn't move at all. Ward and I weren't accomplishing anything. But just by being there we let him know he wasn't alone.

"I told Jesse we were going for help. He gave me a message for his wife. Then he fell unconscious."

Reluctantly, Hudner and Ward left.

The helicopter reached Hagaru-ri at nightfall. Hudner spent three days there before catching a flight back to the coast. When he returned to the *Leyte* the captain ordered him to report to the bridge immediately. He expected to be reprimanded for crash-landing his plane. Instead, after hearing Hudner's story, the skipper told him he was recommending him for the Medal of Honor.

President Truman presented the medal to Hudner on April 13, 1951. Jesse Brown's widow attended the ceremony.

Hudner continued his naval aviation career, transitioning to jet aircraft in 1955. He retired in 1973 as a captain. He then worked as a private consultant before accepting an appointment as the deputy commissioner for veterans services for Massachusetts.

Once the marines from Yudam-ni were all safely into Hagaru-ri the next step was to move the garrison to Koto-ri, eleven miles farther south on the MSR. First, though, there were casualties to treat. From the small airstrip hacked from the frozen ground outside Hagaru-ri, over forty-three hundred wounded and frostbitten men were evacuated. Those not too badly wounded remained with their units.

Though General Smith was given the opportunity to evacuate North Korea by air, he declined. His division would leave on foot, as marines, or not at all. Smith's plan called for the 1st Marine Division to move as a unit. Infantry would lead the column down the MSR, and protect the flanks and the rear. The rest of the division would proceed south in a prearranged order, with tanks spaced throughout the line. Except for air support, the marines would be a completely self-contained entity in their trek down the frozen one-lane dirt road.

The first units began leaving Hagaru-ri early on the morning of December 6. As other units got into place they, and the lead companies, came under fire from Chinese emplaced on hills overlooking the MSR. It was tough fighting all the way. Marines wiped out one stronghold, pushed forward a few thousand yards, fought again, then went forward once again.

By dawn on December 7, the first marines from Hagaru-ri reached Koto-ri. Behind them a near solid column of men and vehicles reached all the way back to Hagaru-ri, where the final, rear guard units were not scheduled to depart until noon on December 7. Around the former marine base, engineers busied themselves destroying all equipment and supplies not to be carried out. Nothing was to be left to the Chinese.

The last marines from the north entered Koto-ri just before midnight, December 7. Nearly twenty-five thousand men jammed into the little North Korean town. The next phase would be the fifty-three miles to Hungnam where navy transports would carry the marines to Pusan for recuperation and rebuilding.

Koto-ri had not suffered the heavy CCF attacks that had plagued Hagaru-ri and Yudam-ni. Nonetheless, Koto-ri had been subjected to a nightly dose of enemy action. Chinese forces had not only cut the road north to Hagaru-ri when it destroyed Task Force Drysdale on November 29, but had gained control of the MSR south of Koto-ri the next day. The army's 2d Battalion, 31st Infantry, had fought its way into Koto-ri on November 30, hoping to link up with its sister battalions on the east side of the Chosin Reservoir. Though no one yet knew of Colonel Faith's demise, the soldiers were advised they could go no farther north. They were, instead, fed into the line protecting Koto-ri.

Though the retreat from the Chosin Reservoir is normally viewed as a marine corps operation, a large number of soldiers participated in the fighting on the frozen Korean plateau. Besides the organized infantry units from the 7th Infantry Division around the Chosin Reservoir, there were a large number of X Corps units scattered among the marines.

Most of the soldiers acquitted themselves rather well as they fought shoulder-to-shoulder with marines against their common enemy. One soldier in particular, a staff officer from X Corps who stayed at Koto-ri as a volunteer, performed repeated acts of bravery. His exceptional conduct during the withdrawal from Koto-ri to Hungnam wrote a new, illustrious page in the history of the U.S. Army.

JOHN U. D. PAGE

John Upshur Dennis Page had wanted to be a soldier ever since he could remember. The son of a regular army officer, Page was born in the Philippine Islands on February 8, 1904. Young Page longed for an appointment to West Point but weak eyes kept him from passing the academy's rigorous physical. Instead, Page entered Princeton University as an engineering student.

When he graduated in 1926 Page also received an ROTC commission as a second lieutenant of artillery. Over the next sixteen years Page not only built his own very successful plastic molding business, but also served as a dedicated reservist. He faithfully attended every meeting and every summer camp. He took one military career course after another. He became a crack shot. He even learned to fly.

Called to active duty in 1942, Page was assigned to the artillery school at Fort Sill, Oklahoma, as an instructor. He did such a fine job his outstanding performance nearly cost him the opportunity to serve overseas. He had to fight his superiors for an assignment in Europe. But at last he had his way. He fulfilled his lifelong ambition by commanding an artillery battalion in combat.

When World War II ended Page requested a regular army commission. Rather than return to his lucrative prewar plastics business, Page became a major in the army. When the Korean War erupted, Page, newly promoted to lieutenant colonel, was in New Orleans as an instructor to the Louisiana National Guard. He was on orders to the prestigious Command and General Staff College at Fort Leavenworth, Kansas, so he had to pull a lot of strings, but he got those orders changed. He was on his way to Korea.

Lieutenant Colonel Page arrived in Hamhung on November 27. When he reported to X Corps Headquarters the officer's assignment chief told Page he would receive the first available command vacancy with a X Corps artillery battalion. In the meantime, they had need of an officer for a special assignment.

With the Chinese infiltrating down from the high ridges and flowing into the countryside where they attacked truck convoys moving along the MSR, some method had to be found for regulating, controlling, and reporting on the many convoys headed north from Hamhung. Page was attached to the 52d Transportation Battalion to see that this job was done. He would establish checkpoints along sixty miles of the MSR and check them twice a day—120 miles round-trip on the icy, narrow, corkscrew mountain roads between Hamhung and Hagaru-ri.

Page made his first foray north from Hamhung at 5:00 A.M., November 29. His party, in seven jeeps, made good progress into the mountains. At prearranged points a team of officers and men left the column to set up their checkpoints. A short distance south of Koto-ri, Page and his jeep driver could see marine Corsairs making runs on the Chinese battling Task Force Drysdale north of town.

The driver, Cpl. David Klepsig, commented to Page, "You know, sir, I'm a fatalist. If I'm going to get it, I'm going to get it."

"By golly, corporal," Page exclaimed, "I like you. I'm a fatalist, too. We'll get along."

In Koto-ri Page quickly learned of the battering TF Drysdale had taken. He issued his first order: No more convoys north of Koto-ri until the road could be opened.

Page and Klepsig headed back to Hamhung around 3:00 P.M. Less than a mile south of Koto-ri they encountered two MPs who were talking to some local civilians. The North Koreans said six Chinese had forced them from their house down the valley.

"Well, let's go," Page announced. "Four of us ought to be a match for six Chinese."

The four climbed into the jeep. Klepsig parked in the middle of a field a short distance from the house. The four advanced in a thin line toward the structure. Halfway up an incline Klepsig spotted a group of about forty Chinese on a nearby hill. He pointed them out to Page. Page immediately ordered his little band to open fire. Vastly outnumbered, the four men pulled back to the jeep. However, instead of heading back to Koto-ri, Page directed Klepsig to drive south to the top of a nearby pass. There they came upon a field artillery radio relay station. Page advised the lieutenant in charge of the nearby Chinese. Fearing he might be attacked after dark, the lieutenant told Page his men were low on ammo.

Page immediately said he'd go to Koto-ri for help. Leaving the two MPs at the relay station, Klepsig and Page headed up the MSR. Their jeep was fired on as it drove around a damaged bridge. Both men leaped from the jeep. They took cover behind a nearby embankment. The enemy machine gun continued spraying the area.

As it grew darker Page addressed Klepsig. "We can't stay here. Corporal, go get the jeep. I'll cover you and meet you where you turn back on the road."

Klepsig took off running, slogging his way through a creek two feet deep and nine feet wide. He jumped into the jeep, then looked behind him. He expected to see Page firing from behind the embankment. Instead, he later recalled, "There he was standing in the middle of the road, firing at the enemy machine gun with his carbine on full automatic. He was drawing attention away from me and it took the Chinese by surprise."

Klepsig roared up to Page, missing him by inches. The officer climbed aboard. Klepsig tore down the icy road. "Good God, corporal," Page admonished. "Slow down. Do you want to kill us?"

At Koto-ri Page rapidly went about preparing a small convoy to reinforce the relay station. Before they could depart, however, he learned the artillerymen had escaped from being cut off from the Chinese. They had made it safely into the American lines at Chinhung-ni.

The next day, November 30, Page met with Colonel Puller. He learned the Koto-ri plateau was completely surrounded by Chinese. Puller authorized Page to form a reserve force from the myriad army units scattered about Koto-ri. Equipping and organizing these troops took the rest of the day. By the time the sun set Page had a full company, with three rifle and one weapons platoon, at his disposal.

There was little heavy action around Koto-ri during the first week of December. The Chinese did attack at night, but these seemed to be half-hearted attempts meant more to harass than destroy. The daytime hours were filled with sniper fire and random mortar bursts. Men died and were wounded. Helicopters shuttled in from the coast to evacuate the casualties, but they were too few and were easy targets for snipers.

Colonel Page came up with the idea for an airstrip to evacuate wounded and bring in supplies. Puller approved. Under Page's direction an army combat engineer battalion began carving the strip from the frozen ground at the town's northern edge. His provisional rifle company provided security for the engineers. Within twenty hours the strip was large enough to accommodate light planes. The wounded were soon on their way to safety. By the end of the fourth day the strip measured a hundred feet by two thousand feet. Air force C-47s were able to land and evacuate up to forty wounded in one load. In all, nearly eight hundred casualties would depart from Page's Koto-ri strip.

The airstrip did not escape Chinese attention. Sniper fire grew more frequent, hampering the work of the engineers. When one bulldozer driver died from a sniper's bullet, Page quickly organized a response team from his provisional company. After getting them on line, Page rushed across open ground to a nearby tank. He pounded on the turret until it opened.

"Fire there!" Page ordered as he pointed into the hills.

After the tank's 90mm cannon blasted the hillside Page manned the behemoth's .50-caliber machine gun. He was still firing away when the tank slid on the ice into a ditch.

The very next day Page went after the snipers again. This time he used an airplane. When Lt. Charles Kieffer landed his unarmed Aeronca L-19 artillery spotter plane at the airstrip Colonel Page hustled over to him. He wanted to make a quick recon of the nearby hills. Would Kieffer take him up?

Within fifteen minutes they were airborne. Kieffer had been a little startled when Page boarded the plane carrying a carbine, several full magazines, and grenades stuffed in his pockets and dangling from his web gear.

In the air Page directed Kieffer to fly over a tent the Chinese had erected at the top of a pass. After surveying the area Page asked Kieffer to fly back over the tent. Kieffer was astounded when Page pulled the pins on three grenades and dropped them right on the tent.

Next, Page had Kieffer fly over a ridge line dotted with enemy fighting holes. Page yelled for Kieffer to swoop down low. Again, Page "bombed" the enemy, using up all his grenades. Then he had Kieffer make another low pass while he fired his carbine out the window. Kieffer estimated Page's grenades cut down at least three CCF soldiers and the colonel drilled at least one enemy soldier with his carbine. Kieffer was somewhat relieved to deposit Page back on the ground.

On another day Page calmly watched a small group of Chinese approach his position near the airstrip. "Those characters want to surrender," he announced. He formed a patrol and moved boldly out of the perimeter to meet the enemy. A short while later he returned with ten prisoners.

The exodus from Koto-ri began on the morning of December 8, 1950. Every combat unit, both marine and army, was assigned a series of objectives as the long column of vehicles and men began the movement down the MSR. Few combat units would be down on the road, for the high ground all the way to Chinhung-ni had to be held by U.N. forces if they were to reach safety. A critical factor in the security of the marchers was the availability of artillery. Barrages of heavy shells could destroy enemy positions emplaced on rugged hillsides much easier than tired men storming up icy slopes.

To ensure sufficient artillery would be available and accurate, Page hitched a ride on a C-47 to Hungnam on December 9. Corporal Klepsig assumed he had seen the last of the feisty colonel. Certainly he had done all, and much more, than a staff officer could be expected to do. Page had every right to remain in Hungnam. But that wasn't his style.

Klepsig was loading wounded aboard an airplane at the airstrip when an L-19 bounced into a landing. One passenger deplaned.

It was Page.

Klepsig was amazed. Years later he would recall, "I figured a man who could get out of something like that ought to stay out. All the fellows felt the same. We all figured that no one with common sense would come back."

The young corporal rushed over to greet Page. "Why didn't you stay back there where you had a good thing?" he asked.

Page grinned. "You didn't think I was going to leave the men, did you?" was his response.

About noon on December 10 Page climbed into his jeep for the final leg of the withdrawal. Klepsig had driven only five hundred yards from Koto-ri when the column halted due to enemy fire ahead. Page instantly sprang from the vehicle. "I'll go see what this delay is about," he announced before disappearing into the crowd of men and vehicles.

Klepsig waited patiently, but Page did not reappear. When the column moved forward again Klepsig eased the clutch out and began inching ahead. As he passed abeam a broad side valley he saw a tank sitting on a flat stretch of ground. Atop the tank a lone figure manned the .50-caliber machine gun. Its tracers cut a path to an enemy machine gun nest up the valley.

Klepsig moved on. At the top of the next pass Page finally caught up with him. Laughing, he boarded the jeep. Between laughs he told Klepsig how invigorating his little duel with the Chinese gunner had been.

Later that day the jeep carrying Page and Klepsig arrived at a deep chasm cut by a mountain stream. The Chinese had blown away the original bridge. In its place marine engineers had erected a temporary treadway bridge. Cautiously, Klepsig crept across the two narrow steel beams. On the other side Page left the jeep. He'd catch up with Klepsig, he said.

Klepsig made it into Chinhung-ni late on the night of December 10. He stayed there, looking for his colonel, through the next day. Klepsig vainly eyed every passing vehicle and foot soldier but saw no sign of Page. Certain that he had missed him in the clutter of parka-encased men, Klepsig drove farther south to Sudong-ni. There he finally turned in.

The next day Klepsig drove to the X Corps artillery headquarters to see if anyone had heard from Page. No one had. He received the same story at the 52d Transportation Battalion. Not until later that day did Klepsig learn his beloved colonel had been killed the night before.

According to witnesses, Page had trudged back along the column of men to a point where Chinese machine gunners had stopped the column with heavy fire. He happened upon Capt. George Petro's Antitank Company, 1st Marines. Under Petro's direction the marines were laying down a base of fire around the enemy position.

After observing the firefight for a few minutes Page motioned to a nearby marine, Pfc. Marvin Wasson. "Let's go ahead and see what's holding up the convoy," Page said.

As they approached a stalled truck a band of Chinese looters walked around the vehicle, their arms filled with foodstuffs. Before either Page or Wasson could fire the Chinese scurried to cover. Leading Wasson, Page gave pursuit. They surprised more than a score of Chinese who turned and fled toward some houses across the road.

The two Americans charged after them, firing their rifles into the dark. A grenade hurtled from one of the houses and erupted near Wasson. He fell, wounded in the head and arm. Page pulled him behind some rocks.

"I'll draw their attention while you run for it," Page told his young companion.

Wasson tumbled down the hillside, landing beside an ammo carrier filled with wounded. He yelled for them to clear out before the Chinese charged down from the houses.

Above the road the dark figure of John Page could be seen, firing his rifle at the swarming Chinese. As Wasson watched in horror a burst of enemy machine-gun fire caught Page full in the chest, lifting him up and slamming him into the nearby rocks. Page crumpled in a lifeless heap. Later, Page's body was carried down to a truck to be taken to Hungnam.

The Marine Corps awarded Lt. Col. John U. D. Page the Navy Cross for his self-sacrifice on the night of December 10. It took until 1956 for the army to reward Page. Then, it took an act of Congress to waive the normal three-year time limit for a Medal of Honor award. Page's widow accepted her husband's posthumous Medal of Honor on April 2, 1957. It was the last award made for Korean service.

On December 9, 1950, the advance elements of the 1st Marine Division moving south down the MSR linked up with elements of the army's 3d Infantry Division moving north from Hamhung. For three more days the marines and soldiers continued coming down from the frozen plateau of Koto-ri. They came down bringing their wounded, dead, and prisoners. They brought out nearly all their guns and vehicles.

The Chinese would continue to harass the column until it was well south of Chinhung-ni. The column would lose more men and some vehicles, but most would survive.

Down to the level ground abutting the Sea of Japan came the men of the 1st Marine Division, along with the survivors of Task Force Faith. The rest of the 7th Infantry Division departed the Yalu River and hurried south. The ROK I Corps scurried back from the frozen fringes of Siberia.

Around the port of Hungnam, X Corps artillery covered the western hills with blankets of steel. United Nations airplanes strafed and bombed the Chinese. But the CCF made no effort to push the U.N. forces into the sea. Well beyond their supply lines, the Chinese were content to sit while the Hungnam perimeter shrank day by day.

Dozens of ships carried the marines and soldiers south to Pusan where the units would be rebuilt before going back on the line. Finally, the covering artillery pieces were firing from Hungnam's wharfs. On Christmas Eve they were trundled aboard ship. The last to leave Hungnam were the engineers. Behind them they left a towering conflagration. Huge columns of dark smoke attested to the destruction of mounds of abandoned equipment and supplies.

One of the worst debacles in American military history had at last ended. American casualties exceeded seventy-five hundred, of which more than fifteen hundred were dead or missing. The North Koreans, assisted by the Chinese Communists, once again controlled their country. But the war, just six months old, was far from over.

Chapter Seven
First U.N. Counteroffensive

The Eighth Army received a new commander on the day after Christmas 1950. Gen. Walton H. Walker, who had twice in less than six months seen his command decimated by enemy forces, was killed on December 23 when his jeep collided with a ROK truck while he was on his way to visit one of his corps headquarters. An armored leader of some note in World War II, Walker had done his absolute best, against great odds, in Korea, but, given the state of his army, and with MacArthur effectively controlling the war from Tokyo, it is doubtful any leader could have performed more satisfactorily.

The man selected to replace Walker was Lieut. Gen. Matthew B. Ridgway, then serving as commander of U.S. forces in the Panama Canal Zone. Ridgway, a well-built, balding man, was just exactly the kind of leader the Eighth Army needed. As the commander of the 82d Airborne Division he had jumped into Normandy on D-Day. He further distinguished himself during the Battle of the Bulge and the allied crossing of the Rhine River into Germany. By the time World War II ended he was commanding the XVIII Airborne Corps.

When General Ridgway arrived in Korea he assumed control of about 365,000 men. Most were ROKs, but he also commanded seven U.S. divisions, two British brigades, a Turkish brigade, and various units from nine other U.N. members. Against them were arrayed an estimated 486,000 enemy troops in twenty-one Chinese and twelve North Korean divisions. His intelligence officers estimated there were close to one million more Chinese poised near the Yalu River in Manchuria.

Ridgway quickly learned all was not well with his command. His army was roadbound, wasteful of supplies, careless in cold weather, and badly demoralized. He set about correcting the situation in various ways. First, he insisted that commanders at all levels exercise their functions in the combat zone rather than at their rear command posts. Second, he demanded aggressive patrol action with the intention of restoring confidence through small tactical successes. Third, he instituted a policy of tactics he called the "Meatgrinder." This acknowledged that taking and holding ground was less important than destroying the enemy's major asset, manpower. Accordingly, every available source of firepower, including aircraft, artillery, and armor, was to be used in killing the enemy.

A flamboyant commander, Ridgway made himself highly visible to his troops. He appeared as often as possible at the front lines, hand grenades suspended from his web gear. He made it a point to answer the questions of his men about why they were in Korea and why they were going to stay there. "The issue now joined here," he said, "is whether Communism or individual freedom shall prevail. You will have my utmost support. I shall expect yours."

It was fortunate that Ridgway arrived in Korea during a lull in the fighting; the Chinese had once again advanced to the end of their supply line. The interlude provided him the opportunity to solidify his defensive line more or less along the Thirty-eighth Parallel. General Ridgway concentrated the bulk of his Eighth Army in the relatively flat central and western sectors, more or less along the Imjin River. It was here that the Chinese were concentrating the bulk of their forces preparatory for another drive on Seoul.

On the far left of the U.N. line Ridgway placed his I Corps, composed of the U.S. 25th Infantry Division, the ROK 1st Infantry Division, the Turkish Brigade, and the 29th British Brigade. To its right sat the IX Corps consisting of the U.S. 1st Cavalry Division, U.S. 24th Infantry Division, ROK 6th Infantry Division, the 27th British Brigade, and other U.N. units. Extending across the mountainous land in the center of the peninsula and on to the Sea of Japan he placed the ROK III Corps, the ROK I Corps, and then the ROK II Corps.

Still refitting to the south near Pusan was Ned Almond's X Corps consisting of the U.S. 2d, 3d, and 7th Infantry Divisions; the 1st Marine Division had been released to the Eighth Army and sat in reserve. The independent X Corps had finally been placed under the Eighth Army soon after Ridgway assumed command.

Though Ridgway desired to launch an offensive as soon as possible it was recognized his forces were not up to it. In fact, on December 30, General MacArthur advised the Joint Chiefs of Staff that the CCF could well drive the U.N. completely out of Korea. The JCS ordered MacArthur to defend his position but, if necessary, retire under pressure through a series of defense lines as far back as the old Pusan Perimeter. Further, he was authorized to completely evacuate Korea if that drastic measure proved necessary to avoid massive losses.

Generals MacArthur and Ridgway executed the first part of these orders sooner than either anticipated.

The New Year's Eve quiet along the Eighth Army's lines was shattered by a tremendous barrage of Chinese artillery and mortar fire. The bombardment continued without letup until dawn. Then, with bugles blowing and whistles shrilling, the CCF infantry hit the U.N. lines in massed formations.

The CCF main effort was directed against the U.S. I and IX Corps. As they had done before, the Chinese hit the unreliable ROK-held positions as hard as they could. Both the ROK 1st Division in I Corps and the ROK 6th Division in IX Corps broke, quickly abandoning their positions, fleeing weaponless to the south. Unable to stem the panic, Ridgway reluctantly ordered his westernmost forces to pull back to a line which ran along the south bank of the frozen Han River to Yangpyong, thence to the Sea of Japan through Hongchon and Chumunjin. The new line included a northward-pointing bulge around Seoul which was intended to delay the enemy and deny them the bridges over the Han.

In the center of the line the situation looked even worse. The Chinese struck a gap between the ROK I and III Corps and sent them reeling. To bolster the sagging line Ridgway rushed forward the U.S. X Corps. The barely restructured U.S. 2d Infantry Division again found itself holding an open shoulder while ROK forces fled past it to the rear.

CCF forces infiltrated behind the ROK I Corps and established a strongly defended roadblock astride a main escape route to the south near the hamlet of Changbong-ni. As long as the roadblock existed the ROKs could neither be reinforced nor withdrawn. The 2d Battalion, 23d Infantry Regiment, 2d Infantry Division, was ordered to eliminate the roadblock.

JUNIOR D. EDWARDS

As a youngster growing up in the small Iowa town of Indianola, Junior D. Edwards did well in school and played a good game of football. He received his induction notice in January 1945, three months after he turned eighteen. The United States was entering its fourth year of world war and its leaders called young Edwards to its defense, just as it had already called millions of others. Like them, Edwards willingly donned his country's uniform.

Edwards was trained as a combat infantryman and was scheduled for deployment to the European Theater of Operations. Before his division boarded ship, though, Germany surrendered. He was next slated for duty in the Pacific and for the impending invasion of Japan, but the atomic explosions at Hiroshima and Nagasaki ended Edwards's division's departure for the Pacific. Instead, he remained in the army stateside until his discharge in August 1946.

Back in Indianola, Edwards sought work but there was little available. The hordes of discharged WWII veterans made competition for available jobs fierce. After nearly a year of part-time jobs Edwards reenlisted in June 1947.

Eventually assigned to the 2d Infantry Division, Edwards went with it to Korea in August 1950. He saw extensive combat with Company E, 23d Infantry in the perimeter battles that summer and as the division fought its way toward the Yalu that fall. Edwards survived the bitter fighting around Kunu-ri and, because of his experience, his company commander appointed him a platoon leader with the rank of sergeant first class. Edwards worked the replacements that filled his platoon as hard as he could, but he had precious little time. He wasn't sure they were ready for combat when the order to move up to the line came, but he had no choice.

Late on the night of January 1, Company E dug in on a hill near Changbong-ni. Their position was vital because it was the commanding terrain feature in the area. From it the entire 2d Battalion could be observed and brought under fire, thus threatening its mission.

At 3:15 A.M., January 2, a bitterly cold night, the CCF launched a furious attack against Company E. Under extremely heavy fire the rookies of the company gave ground. The Chinese quickly occupied the GIs' abandoned foxholes. Soon their automatic weapons fire peppered the battalion's bivouac.

At the base of the hill Edwards quickly reorganized his platoon. It had suffered heavy casualties and many of the men were missing. Edwards urged his few men forward but they were reluctant to move up the hill under the heavy fire. Edwards knew he had to take direct action to get his men going. He asked for volunteers. Four men scooted forward. One at a time Edwards led them back up the hill. Completely exposed to Chinese fire, he personally placed each man in a fighting hole.

Once they were in position Edwards told them where he wanted them to fire.

About this time Edwards realized that the enemy's most effective machine gun was firing from a hole dug earlier by his platoon. It was set up in such a way that none of the usual flat trajectory weapons the platoon carried would be of any use. He also couldn't call in his mortars. Some of his men were so close to the Chinese positions they could be hit by the incoming shells.

Along the fire-swept hillside Edwards moved from man to man, gathering grenades. When he had an armful he spurted up the hill. His one-man charge carried him right into the Chinese lines. Heaving grenades as he ran, Edwards forced the enemy riflemen to pull back. As he neared the machine-gun nest he ran out of grenades. Edwards headed back downhill.

While he collected more grenades the Chinese reoccupied the positions they'd just abandoned. Again armed with a load of grenades, Edwards went back up the hill.

This time he used his grenades more frugally. He had one left as he neared the enemy machine gun. It sailed through the cold night air to land with a dull thud in the bottom of the nest. Its explosion destroyed the gun and its crew.

By the time Edwards rejoined his platoon the Chinese had already rushed forward a replacement machine gun. Its fire pinned down another platoon that had started to maneuver up the hill.

So Edwards again loaded up—for the third time that early morning. Just as he had twice before, he charged singlehandedly up the hill. He closed on the emplacement for a third time. This time the Chinese easily spotted him in the dawn light. They pumped lead at him from point-blank range, hitting him several times.

Edwards staggered under the hits, falling to one knee. He had the strength to throw one grenade. He had to make it good.

He pulled the pin, cocked his arm.

The Chinese machine gun barked again. Edwards took several more hits.

Summoning his last remaining reserve of strength, Edwards heaved the missile. The grenade flew true. It destroyed the enemy gun and killed its crew.

A few feet away Edwards slumped forward, dead.

Below him there were shouts and curses as Edwards's platoon members charged after him. Inspired by his gallantry they attacked the Chinese. By the time the sun crested the horizon they'd pushed the Chinese off the hill.

During the day the rest of the battalion cleared the roadblock. The ROK corps that had been cut off was able to withdraw through them to safety. Edwards's willingness to give his own life made their retreat to safety possible.

Edwards's parents accepted his posthumous Medal of Honor in a Pentagon ceremony on January 16, 1952.

The CCF continued their strong attacks against the U.N. lines. With the ROK units falling back everywhere Ridgway tried to strengthen his badly weakened lines by ordering the barely recovered U.S. 1st Marine Division to take positions alongside the U.S. 2d Infantry Division. Their firepower helped, but with exposed flanks they, too, were soon in danger of being surrounded.

The Chinese and North Koreans, believing they would not be seriously opposed, followed up their local successes much faster than they had two months earlier. The Eighth Army fought hard but could not check the enemy's advance.

Ridgway quickly saw that holding his present line invited destruction of his forces. Withdrawing south meant preserving his army and forcing the CCF to extend their supply lines. The enemy's logistical capabilities did not match his tactical abilities, a fact noted in previous clashes. When the enemy's advance faltered, Ridgway planned to hit him, hard, before his supplies and replacements caught up.

General Ridgway ordered the Eighth Army to pull back to a new line in the vicinity of the Thirty-seventh Parallel, about thirty-five miles below Seoul. His new front line began at Pyongtaek on Korea's west coast, ran east through Ansong, northeast to Wonju, then continued in a curving, irregular fashion to the east coast town of Samchok.

The withdrawal began on January 3. By the end of the next day Seoul and Inchon had been abandoned for the second time in seven months. Massive quantities of supplies were destroyed to prevent them from falling into enemy hands. Throngs of refugees clogged the roads leading south out of Seoul. They created such a massive traffic jam on the vital roads that control points were established to shunt them to trains which then carried them to Pusan.

By January 7 the I and IX Corps on the west end of the line reported a slackening in the enemy's offensive. Local patrols met only scattered enemy detachments. Heavy fighting continued in the central and eastern fronts, however. The X Corps stood virtually alone in the center. Around it four ROK divisions had either been destroyed or had fled. Enemy units flowed out of Seoul to the southeast toward Wonju, an important rail center. If they captured the town they would be in an excellent position to drive southwest behind the I and IX Corps.

Elements of the much-bloodied U.S. 2d Infantry Division held positions just south of Wonju. They fought off any number of enemy assaults, but the adverse weather greatly reduced their air support. Thus, when the ROKs on their right collapsed, the 2d was again forced to pull back. By January 12 the enemy controlled Wonju.

Once again the enemy's advance slowed. Only limited contact was made along the front line. Aerial reconnaissance revealed that the enemy was building up reserves and stockpiling supplies for his next push. To learn more about his foe Ridgway organized Task Force Wolfhound from the 27th Infantry

Regiment, U.S. 25th Infantry Division. On January 15 the task force moved north on the Seoul highway to Osan. Not a single enemy soldier was encountered. The next day they moved north again, almost reaching Suwon before drawing fire. The task force was ordered to withdraw. General Ridgway had all the information he needed.

Over the next ten days Ridgway mounted more recons toward the enemy. These confirmed that the enemy did not occupy in depth any positions close to the front lines. Therefore, Ridgway scheduled Operation *Thunderbolt* for January 25. The operation was to be a methodical, coordinated advance by the I and IX Corps designed to push through the area south of the Han River and find the enemy. Ridgway would then employ his "Meatgrinder" tactics to chew them up.

Seven columns of U.S. infantry, solidly supported by armor and air, moved north that cold morning. They generally met only scattered resistance. Slowly, systematically, *Thunderbolt* ground ahead. Ridge line by ridge line the U.S. troops cleared out each pocket of resistance. Whenever possible, enemy positions were pounded by air strikes and artillery before the infantry moved in. During the first few days of *Thunderbolt* the enemy launched a few small night counterattacks but in general fought only outpost actions. By the end of the month, though, their resistance stiffened.

In the IX Corps area Company E, 5th Infantry Regiment, U.S. 24th Infantry Division, was assigned the mission of attacking and occupying a key hill position on the afternoon of January 30. Because nightfall was rapidly approaching, the company was told to take the hill as soon as possible. They had to occupy the high ground before the enemy could launch a counterattack.

Halfway up the hill the Chinese defenders began throwing grenades by the handful. Previously unseen automatic weapons chattered their deadly rounds on the infantrymen. One squad leader in the third platoon yelled for his men to take cover.

The platoon leader stopped dead in his tracks. "Take cover, hell!" snorted 2d Lt. Carl H. Dodd. "Use marching fire and follow me!"

With that, the twenty-six-year-old coal miner from Harlan County, Kentucky, started upward. Behind him his platoon spread out and followed. Two or three fell wounded almost at once but Dodd continued urging his platoon forward. Throwing grenades as fast as he could pull their pins, Dodd wiped out one Chinese position after another. In all, Dodd destroyed seven enemy strong points. He then took on a mortar position, causing casualties among the attackers. He boldly dashed right up to the mortar pit and destroyed it with his last grenade.

By now well ahead of the rest of the company and subjected to a murderous onslaught of enemy fire, Dodd halted his men just 150 yards from the top of the hill. They spent the night there, fighting off repeated enemy probes.

In the morning Dodd, a former enlisted man who'd received a battlefield commission in October 1950, again led his platoon against the enemy. In bitter hand-to-hand fighting they rousted the Chinese from the hill, clearing the way for his battalion to continue its advance. Dodd survived the war to wear his Medal of Honor.

Also on January 30, another IX Corps division, the U.S. 1st Cavalry, encountered stubborn resistance near Kamyangjan-ni, a hamlet east of Suwon.

ROBERT M. McGOVERN

Company A, 5th Cavalry Regiment, faced yet one more hill on its advance north. The cavalrymen had seen relatively little action since the beginning of *Thunderbolt*. What they had seen was one rocky hill after another. Each had to be climbed, the enemy holding it wiped out. It was an exhausting task, made more difficult by cold winds and deep snow.

First Lt. Robert M. McGovern was as tired as his platoon members. The strain of the physical exertion was beginning to show on the twenty-three-year-old. Combat was far more physically demanding than his training had prepared him for.

The hill before them looked no different than any of the others they'd attacked in recent days. McGovern deployed his thin platoon in a skirmish line. At his signal they started up. The climb grew more difficult as they progressed. The only noise was the grunt of tired infantrymen as they slipped and slid on loose rocks.

Seventy-five yards from the top it happened. Without warning the Chinese opened fire. From more than a dozen foxholes rifle fire tore into the ranks of U.S. soldiers. A machine gun raked the advancing infantrymen before they could seek cover. One round slammed into McGovern's side, tearing a gaping hole. He crawled behind a boulder where he applied a field dressing to the bloody wound.

McGovern's platoon sergeant crawled up to him. "Looks like you'd better head downhill, sir," he suggested.

McGovern refused. "I'll be okay," he assured the NCO. "Get the men ready. Next time there's a break in the fire, we're going up."

A few minutes later the enemy fire slackened. McGovern stood and started uphill. By dodging from one boulder to another he closed to within a few yards of the machine-gun nest. Behind him, the surviving platoon members took cover and laid down a covering base of fire. Before the young officer could launch his final attack, the Chinese threw and rolled a vicious barrage of hand grenades on the group, halting their advance.

At the same time enemy rifle fire increased in volume and intensity. Men cried in pain as hot lead found flesh. One of McGovern's men broke from cover, headed downhill. The Chinese shot him dead before he'd covered ten yards. Other GIs appeared on the verge of panic, too. Something had to be done.

Without warning, McGovern burst from cover. Alone, he raced toward the Chinese machine-gun nest. Triggering his carbine as he ran across the rocky ground, McGovern headed straight for the enemy automatic weapon. Enemy rounds tracked him, tore the carbine from his hands. Undaunted, the brave young lieutenant pulled his .45-caliber automatic pistol from its holster.

Firing his pistol and throwing grenades, McGovern closed on the nest. He killed seven protecting Chinese riflemen before one got him. Just as his last grenade exploded in the machine-gun nest, killing its three gunners, enemy fire caught him full in the chest. McGovern died on the lip of the enemy position.

Behind him, his platoon, enraged and emboldened by the lieutenant's death, went after the rest of the enemy. Some fixed bayonets, others braved direct fire to charge headlong into the enemy's position. Within a few more minutes it was over. All the Chinese were dead. The Americans stood victorious on the high ground.

The recommendation for the country's highest award, prepared for McGovern at his men's insistence, slowly wound its way through bureaucratic channels. In the meantime, public support for the conflict in Korea waned. President Truman became the target for increasing criticism over the conduct of the war. The once-well-liked chief executive saw his popularity drop drastically.

When Lieutenant McGovern's Medal of Honor was announced in January 1952, his father, J. Halsey McGovern of Washington, D.C., created a stir when he refused to accept the award. He also refused to accept the Silver Star posthumously awarded to his second son, Jerome, a member of the 187th Airborne Regiment, killed in action on February 10, 1951.

The senior McGovern's refusal was based on his belief that medals were superfluous. He felt they did not do justice to all the heroes of the war. And, as he told reporters, he did not feel Truman "was fit to confer medals on anybody's sons."

Several members of Congress offered to make the presentation to the hero's father, but he still refused. He stated he did not want to turn his refusal into a "political thing."

There the matter ended. No presentation ceremony was ever held. Nonetheless, the name of 1st Lt. Robert M. McGovern was entered on the rolls of America's greatest heroes.

The story of Halsey McGovern and his two gallant sons faded from the papers after just a few weeks. Then, about a month later, the media reported that the Selective Service standing of the third McGovern son, Charles, age nineteen, had been reevaluated. He was now found fit for induction.

General Ridgway's Operation *Thunderbolt* continued its strong gains. Eighth Army troops were not only finding and destroying the enemy but were taking ground and holding it. Spearheaded by massed artillery, bombing and napalm attacks, as well as naval gunfire from offshore ships, the U.N. forces drove aggressively toward the Han River.

In return, the enemy increased the size and strength of his counterattacks. Columns of U.N. tanks and other vehicles found roads heavily mined. All along the front the Chinese and North Koreans vigorously resisted the U.N. advance.

In the X Corps zone of action the U.S. 2d Infantry Division started the drive to retake Wonju. Company I, 23d Infantry Regiment, held a hilltop near Ipo-ri on the night of January 31. Just before dawn the next day the Chinese attacked, throwing the company off the hill. Master Sgt. Hubert L. Lee, of Leland, Mississippi, took over his platoon after his lieutenant was severely wounded.

Regrouping the remnants of the platoon, Lee, thirty-six years old and a veteran of thirteen years' military service with extensive combat experience in World War II, led his outnumbered group in repeated attacks against the enemy. Wounded three times in the legs and back, Lee was thrown off the hill five times. Each time he rallied the remaining members of his platoon, leading them in attacks against the enemy. Lee repeatedly ignored the enemy's heavy small-arms and mortar fire to retake his former position. Each time he did the Chinese counterattacked, forcing him to order a withdrawal.

On the sixth charge Lee had only twelve men left. He told them they had to take the hill because if they lost it everything would be lost. He led the final charge, yelling for his men to follow. Even when an enemy rifle bullet tore through his back, incapacitating him, Lee urged his men onward. When the position was retaken for good, Lee crawled about, placing his few remaining men in position. Not until they were reinforced did Lee consent to evacuation. He lived to wear his Medal of Honor and complete his army career.

Two days after Lee's action Company A, 19th Infantry, 24th Infantry Division, set up defensive positions near Sesim-ri for the night, preparing to continue their attack the next morning, February 4. A platoon led by Sfc. Stanley T. Adams, a twenty-nine-year-old from Olathe, Kansas, held an outpost on the nose of a ridge about two hundred yards in front of the rest of the company.

At 11:00 P.M., February 3, the CCF hit two adjacent companies of Adams's battalion, driving a deep wedge between them. While those two units battled their foe in the icy cold night air, about 250 more Chinese poured out of the night directly at the outpost held by Adams's platoon. A murderous barrage of small-arms, machine-gun, and mortar fire hit the platoon from three sides. For forty-five minutes they held on, but finally were pushed back about fifty yards.

Unwilling to concede the ground to the enemy, Adams suddenly leaped to his feet, slammed his bayonet on his rifle, and called for his platoon to follow him with fixed bayonets. He was so intent on his mission he did not notice that only thirteen men obeyed him.

Knocked to the ground when an enemy slug tore into his leg, Adams regained his feet and continued forward. Four more times, while closing with the enemy, he was knocked down by the concussion of exploding grenades as they bounced off his body. Each time he arose and, shouting orders to his men, charged on.

Finally closing with the enemy formation as his thirteen men fanned out on each side of him, Adams plunged directly into them so savagely with bayonet and rifle butt that the Chinese in the front tried to recoil from his attack but were hampered by the masses behind them. Undaunted by the odds against him, Sergeant Adams continued his furious attack. Chinese after Chinese fell under slashing bayonet and smashing rifle butt.

After nearly an hour of vicious hand-to-hand fighting in the darkness the Chinese finally fled from the position. Only then did Adams fire his rifle, cutting down the retreating enemy. Sprawled on the scrub-covered ground around Adams and his men were the bodies of at least fifty enemy, dead of bayonet wounds or shattered skulls.

Adams's gutsy charge had prevented the Chinese from exploiting their earlier successes and wreaking havoc on his battalion. As did Sergeant Lee, Sergeant Adams survived to wear proudly his well-earned award.

The tenacity of the Chinese and North Korean soldiers forced the men of the Eighth Army to battle them at close quarters reminiscent of the Civil War. The only way to remove the enemy from their hilltop positions was to dig them out. Men like Sergeant Adams knew this and effectively used the almost obsolete bayonet to accomplish their missions. Not many soldiers were willing to engage in close combat with the Chinese. But a few were.

LEWIS L. MILLETT

It is said lightning never strikes twice in the same place. That maxim did not hold true for Company E, 2d Battalion, 27th Infantry Regiment, 25th

Infantry Division. Within two weeks after the death of its gallant commander, Capt. Reginald Desiderio, Company E received a second commander who would write another heroic page to that unit's glorious history.

For the first two weeks of the general retreat from the Yalu River, Company E headed south without a commander. Besides the confusion of the time, no experienced captain wanted to try to fill the shoes of the idolized Desiderio. Not until the company went into bivouac just north of the Thirty-eighth Parallel was the slot filled.

On a bitterly cold day in mid-December 1950, Capt. Lewis L. Millett jumped from a jeep in Company E's bivouac area and announced himself as the new company commander. A lean six-footer at 170 pounds, Millett's close-cropped light hair was offset by the reddish tint of his magnificent handlebar mustache. Though this was his first command, Millett was no stranger to Company E. During their desperate fight along the Chongchon River, Millett had battled at their side as their forward observer from the 8th Field Artillery.

But that was not his first combat experience. A veteran of nearly ten years' army service, Millett held a reputation as a near fearless fighter.

Born in Mechanic Falls, Maine, on December 15, 1920, Millett graduated from high school in South Dartmouth, Massachusetts, in 1940. His yearbook denoted him as the class member "most likely to become a soldier of fortune." He fulfilled that prophecy by enlisting in the U.S. Army Air Corps that September.

With the world on the verge of another global conflict, Millett expected to be in the thick of things soon after he joined up. That was not to be. The United States preferred to remain out of what most of its people viewed as a European conflict. That pacifism did not suit Millett. He wanted to be where there was action.

After a year in the army Millett decided he could wait no longer for the U.S. to go to war. He went AWOL, traveled to Canada, and joined the Canadian Army. His army air corps unit carried him on its rolls as a deserter.

Within a few months Millett was in England, a member of an antiaircraft battery shooting at the German bombers that filled London's night skies.

When U.S. troops began arriving in England in late summer 1942, Millett turned himself in to the American embassy in London. He was told to return to his Canadian unit to await orders. They came in September 1942, assigning him to the U.S. 1st Armored Division.

Millett fought with that unit's 27th Armored Field Artillery Battalion in North Africa, Italy, France, and Germany. It was in North Africa that Millett shot down a strafing German plane with his half-track's .50-caliber machine gun. For that he received Pfc.'s stripes. A few weeks later he drove a loaded ammo truck to safety during an artillery barrage. For that he received a Silver Star.

While in Italy Millett's desertion charge from his original USAAC unit caught up with him. One day, while in reserve near Naples, Millett's company commander called him in to inform him that the previous day a summary court-martial had found him guilty of desertion. The sentence was thirty days' hard labor and a $52 fine. Since Millett was wearing sergeant's stripes at that time the labor sentence was suspended. Millett protested he should have at least been present at the court-martial but paid the fine when his CO convinced him it was easiest just to pay up and shut up. Millett did both.

Less than a year later, in France, Millett received a battlefield promotion to second lieutenant. He later earned a Bronze Star in Germany for calling an artillery barrage down on his own position in order to break up a German infantry attack.

Relieved from active duty in August 1945 as a first lieutenant, Millett enrolled at Bates College in Lewiston, Maine. He did well in college but yearned to return to the army. In his junior year he requested a return to active duty. His request was approved and he received orders to report to Japan in January 1949.

Soon after hostilities began in Korea, Millett and the 25th Infantry Division were ordered to the fighting. Just as he had done in World War II, Millett went to war as a forward observer, working at the front lines where the fighting was hottest.

On August 5, 1950, Millett repeated his heroism of World War II. When North Korean T-34 tanks threatened to overrun his strategic position on the Pusan Perimeter, Millett called down an artillery barrage directly on his post. When the barrage ended the NKPA tanks had been stopped cold. Millett added an oak leaf cluster to both his Bronze Star and Purple Heart.

On the same night Desiderio died Millett's artillery post came under a heavy mortar barrage. Fascinated, Millett watched a shell burst just fifteen feet away. "I knew I was going to get it," he later said, "but I just had to see."

Millett got it, all right. Hot steel shards tore into his leg. He was treated and placed aboard an ambulance headed to Pyongyang. Along the way Chinese infiltrators shot up his convoy. Millett gathered up a group of walking wounded and led them in an attack on the enemy, blasting a path to safety.

Following treatment at the aid station, Millett was assigned duty as an aerial observer. Flying over enemy positions in a light plane, he called down artillery concentrations on them. During one mission he rescued a South African P-51 pilot shot down behind enemy lines. He ordered his pilot to land on a nearby road, surrendered his seat to the injured pilot, then waited patiently until the pilot returned to pick him up. For that deed he received a much-appreciated bottle of scotch from the pilot.

Flying recon patrols was useful, Millett knew, but he felt it was too tame. He volunteered to transfer to the 27th Infantry.

The regimental commander was not too encouraging. "The only job I have open right now is commander of Company E," he said.

"I'll take it, sir," Millett said at once.

For the first few days of his command Millett had his hands full overseeing his company's retreat to the Thirty-seventh Parallel. Once there the company went into reserve and began receiving replacements. Millett immediately began an intensive training schedule. Whenever he had a day or two off the line Millett trained his men. With Millett in the lead, they spent most of their mornings running up and down nearby hills with full field packs. "By the time we go back up front, you'll be part mountain goat," Millett told his new charges.

In the afternoons Millett gave modified courses on the commando tactics he'd picked up in a British course he'd taken while in the Canadian Army. He taught his company close-in fighting, grappling with them to demonstrate hand-to-hand fighting. To prove one could survive the blast of an exploding grenade Millett used personal example. He explained that grenade fragments tend to fly upward and outward, like an inverted cone. If you were close to a grenade, and low to the ground when it went off, you could live. Then he'd pull the pin on a grenade, drop it five feet away, and hit the dirt. After the explosion Millett would rise unharmed, dust himself off, and continue his lecture.

Company E spent its evenings behind the lines practicing bayonet moves. To many soldiers, the bayonet was an obsolete weapon, useful only as a can opener. Not to Lew Millett. To him it was a fear-inspiring weapon, designed for close-quarters fighting with the enemy. He had to scrounge to round up enough bayonets to equip his 135-man company, but every man soon had one. He paid Korean women to hone them to a keen edge before beginning the training.

For a week, every evening for several hours, Company E practiced using the bayonet. While others watched in amusement, Millett's men danced around, his shouted commands echoing across the campground. They parried, thrust, and butt stroked until their arms ached. He told his men, "From now on bayonets will be fixed any time we attack. You're gonna use them to kill Commies."

Millett had hoped to have more time to train his company, but it wasn't available. With the launching of Operation *Thunderbolt* the entire 25th Infantry Division started pushing north. Millett hoped the intensity of his training would compensate for its brevity.

Company E boarded tanks and started forward. On February 5, 1951, it was moving through a frozen rice paddy west of the road running south out of Osan. Suddenly, the crackle of enemy machine-gun fire broke the morning air. The first platoon found itself pinned down. Chinese were emplaced on two hills straddling the road. Their fire picked up. The bullets whistled through the air, slapping into the ice.

"Second platoon!" Millett hollered. "Fix bayonets—move to the left of the first."

Then Millett was off, shouting, "C'mon with me!"

He bounded to the base of the hill. There he waited for his platoons to form up.

"We'll get 'em with the bayonet! Let's go!" he yelled when they were ready.

Up the hill the two platoons went, all the GIs yelling at the top of their voices. Above them, Millett appeared on the skyline, rifle in one hand, waving his men upward with the other. Even as he did so, Chinese soldiers scurried from their foxholes, skittering down the reverse slope helter-skelter. By the time the two platoons joined Millett on the crest only a few enemy stragglers remained. They were quickly dispatched.

To the rear, the rest of Millett's battalion observed the audacious charge. The colonel quickly came forward to shake Millett's hand and congratulate him for his courage. That night the colonel began the paperwork that would bring Millett the DSC. Little did he know that Millett's charge was but a rehearsal for what would come just forty-eight hours later.

At midday on February 7, Company E had the point for the battalion. Near the smoke-blackened village of Soam-ni, just west and north of Osan, they approached a ridge line. On military maps it was designated Hill 180. To the men of Company E it would forever be Bayonet Hill.

Accompanied by two of his platoons astride tanks, Millett approached Hill 180, fully expecting to bypass it completely. Then one of his men noticed movement among the thick foliage near the top of the hill. It was crawling with Chinese. And Company E sat almost directly under their guns.

Once apprised of the situation, Millett quickly ordered the tanks off the road. He got his two platoons deployed along a paddy dike. By now the Chinese had opened fire. A number of Millett's men fell, cut down by vicious machine-gun fire. Leaping aboard the nearest tank, Millett grabbed its .50-caliber machine gun. He sent a stream of tracers flying toward the enemy position.

"Keep it going there," he told the gunner. Then he jumped off the tank and moved on.

He knew from here on it was all a matter of timing. He had to get an attack under way quickly. He didn't want these Chinese to get away like the others had two days earlier.

Millett called to one of his platoon leaders to get ready to move out. Seconds later, enfilading fire from a previously quiet Chinese machine gun tore into the first platoon. Casualties mounted. Then the .50-caliber machine gun supporting first platoon went silent—jammed with a ruptured cartridge.

Millett swore under his breath. His attack was crumbling even before it started. He scrambled from his position and raced across the bullet-swept ground to the first platoon. Spotting the platoon sergeant as he barrelled into the position Millett just hollered at the men, "Get ready to move out! We're going up the hill. Fix bayonets! Charge! Everyone goes with me!"

He raised his rifle and took out across the open fields. Bounding from the small rises and hurdling the ditches, Millett kept his feet across the ice-covered ground. Behind him the platoon sergeant and a dozen men ran after Millett. Those who hadn't followed were cut down minutes later as enemy machine-gun fire from Hill 180 zeroed in on them.

When he reached the base of the hill, Millett flung himself down under a rocky outcropping while he waited for the others to catch up. After they did Millett motioned upward. "Let's go," he said.

Dashing from rock to rock, Millett made the first of three small knobs that comprised Hill 180. The center and far knob rose some twenty meters higher. Millett spotted a Chinese machine gun to his left. He ordered a BAR to fire on it. Another soldier spotted eight Chinese squatting in a hole just ten yards from Millett. The captain ran to it, firing his carbine and throwing grenades. The enemy died.

Millett now radioed for his third platoon to come forward. After he had them in position Millett told them, "Attack straight up the hill!"

With their bayonet-tipped rifles carried at high port, screaming Chinese phrases as they ran, Millett and his assembled men raced toward the two higher knobs.

Lunging into the first line of enemy foxholes, the GIs ripped into the Chinese, bayonets first. The terror-filled shrieks of the bayoneted enemy rose above the din of battle.

Millett was so far in front of his men he had to dodge grenades thrown by both sides. Ignoring the thundering explosions, he charged headlong at an antitank gun firing point-blank at him. A few well-tossed grenades took care of that weapon.

A cluster of grenades flew down from a Chinese position farther uphill. Millett danced and dodged around, avoiding the detonations of eight grenades. A ninth got him, sending hot steel shards into his back and legs. He could feel the blood coursing down his skin, drenching his fatigues beneath his parka.

Unmindful of the intense pain, Millett continued his charge. He urged his men forward. "Let's go," he screamed. "Use grenades and cold steel! Kill 'em with the bayonet!"

At the crest of the highest knob he jumped into one arm of a V-shaped slit trench. With a savage thrust of his bayonet he impaled one enemy soldier. He had to fire a round to dislodge his weapon. A second enemy soldier rushed at Millett. The emboldened captain met him like a frenzied tiger, jamming his sharp steel blade into the man's throat, ripping it wide open.

A third Chinese, in the far arm of the V, raised his rifle. Before he could fire Millett was on him, slamming his blood-stained bayonet into the enemy soldier's chest.

While Millett dispatched the soldier, the rest of his men rushed past. Millett leaped after them. Together they went on, screaming and yelling, firing from the hip, ripping and stabbing enemy flesh with their bayonets, throwing grenades into bunkers and foxholes until they had completely eliminated the enemy from the hill.

When it was all over Millett stood atop the saw-toothed ridge and pumped his bloody rifle up and down, signaling to those below he had conquered Bayonet Hill.

After the battle forty-seven enemy dead were counted on the forward slope of the hill; thirty had died as a result of bayonet wounds. On the reverse slope lay another fifty enemy, dead of either bayonet or gunshot wounds. Witnesses estimated another hundred Chinese escaped.

Evacuated due to the seriousness of his wounds, Millett spent several months in the hospital recuperating. His Medal of Honor was presented to him at the White House on July 5, 1951.

Lewis Millett remained in the army after the Korean War. He became one of the country's leading experts on paratroop, commando, and guerrilla fighting. In 1960 he first went to South Vietnam where he helped develop that country's ranger program. He served in Laos between 1968 and 1970, then returned to South Vietnam for three more years, staying until the American withdrawal.

The much-decorated warrior retired from the army in July 1973 as a full colonel, with over thirty years' service. Today, he lives in the peaceful mountains of southern California where he enjoys the company of his grandchildren.

Two days after Millett's magnificent charge the CCF in front of the I Corps abruptly gave way. Nightfall of February 10 found most of the corps closed up on the south bank of the Han River, looking across at the scarred capital city. Both Inchon and Kimpo Field fell to the U.N. the next day without any resistance.

On the central front, the X Corps recaptured Wonju and pushed north against light resistance to Hoengsong. On February 5, the X Corps continued north in Operation *Roundup* with the objective of Hongchon, north of Hoengsong. Enemy pressure increased steadily as the X Corps advanced north. Reports of large enemy forces in their path preceded a strong counterattack by Chinese and North Koreans on the night of February 11. As they had previously, the ROK divisions of the X Corps quickly gave ground and headed south. Hoengsong was abandoned on February 13 as the rest of the X Corps moved south back toward Wonju.

At nightfall on February 13 the enemy attacked in strength at Chipyong-ni, which sat on the left border of the X Corps northwest of Wonju. This key road junction hamlet had to be held or the entire Eighth Army line might be endangered. The 23d Infantry Regiment, U.S. 2d Infantry Division, and a French battalion held the town and its surrounding hills. By the end of February 14 the Chinese had completely surrounded the little cluster of ramshackle huts

For three days the beleaguered garrison staved off repeated enemy assaults. Only constant air support and air resupply allowed the defenders to hold out. At night U.N. planes dropped flares, lighting the battlefield.

On the night of February 14 Company M, 23d Infantry, had one of its machine guns placed along a strategic draw leading right into Chipyong-ni. When the Chinese came up the draw, accompanied by the blare of bugles, Sfc. William S. Sitman directed his weapon's fire into the enemy's ranks. Though the machine-gun fire cut heavily into the Chinese, they kept coming. Soon they were close enough to lob grenades at Sitman's position. One fell into the machine-gun pit.

Sergeant Sitman never hesitated. He knew the importance of his gun. If it were silenced the Chinese would have an unobstructed path right into Chipyong-ni. Without a word he vaulted over another man directly onto the grenade. The deep explosion instantly killed the thirty-six-year-old native of Bellwood, Pennsylvania. But the gun crew lived. They were able to fend off the attacking Chinese, preventing them from overrunning Chipyong-ni.

A unit of the U.S. 1st Cavalry Division finally broke through the ring of Chinese to relieve the 23d Infantry. The battle for Chipyong-ni turned out to be the major effort of the current Chinese offensive. By blunting it, the U.N. had halted their advance and disrupted their plans for the immediate future. The U.N. forces continued to hold the initiative.

They pressed that advantage wherever they could. In the I Corps's zone of operations the U.S. 3d Infantry Division worked to destroy pockets of enemy soldiers left behind in the U.N. advance. It proved to be extremely difficult work. Cut off from their comrades, the CCF remnants fought bitterly. Only close-in fighting could eliminate their strongholds.

DARWIN K. KYLE

At thirty-two, Darwin K. Kyle was old for a second lieutenant. But then the combat veteran of World War II had only received his battlefield promotion in January 1951.

Kyle was born in Jenkins, Kentucky, on June 1, 1918. He grew up in Charleston, West Virginia, where he enlisted in the army in 1939. He saw extensive combat in France and Germany during World War II. His personal valor brought him both a Silver and Bronze Star.

Kyle returned to West Virginia after taking his discharge in August 1945, but, like thousands of other veterans, he decided to make the army a career. He reenlisted in July 1947. Two months later he went to Korea where he served for more than a year on occupation duty with the 6th Infantry Division.

In the summer of 1950 Kyle was a master sergeant stationed at Fort Devens, Massachusetts. From there, in September 1950, Kyle accompanied his unit, Company K, 7th Infantry Regiment, 3d Infantry Division, to Korea. His first taste of combat in Korea came during the evacuation of the marines and soldiers from North Korea after the Chosin Reservoir retreat. He frequently volunteered to lead patrols into the hills around Hungnam to seek out and destroy infiltrating Chinese.

It was during the evacuation of Hungnam that Kyle earned the Soldier's Medal, the army's highest noncombat award for personal heroism. When an ammunition dump suddenly exploded with a tremendous roar, Kyle braved the flames and scattered unexploded shells to carry several injured men to safety. When a landing craft at a dock adjacent to the ammo dump could not be started, Kyle found the necessary tools to make the needed repairs. Once the landing craft was running, Kyle used it to carry a large number of men to safety.

For this and other repeated acts of heroism, as well as his demonstrated leadership abilities, Kyle received his direct promotion to second lieutenant. He took over a platoon in the same company with which he'd come to Korea.

On February 16 Company K had orders to clear the Chinese from a commanding position overlooking Kamil-ni, northeast of Suwon. Adverse weather nearly canceled the attack. A blizzard, whipped by forty mph winds, not only drastically reduced visibility but dropped the temperature to far below zero. But the enemy position threatened a key road along which U.N. truck columns had to move. It had to be taken.

Trucks carried the company to the departure line. Once the men were assembled they started toward the hill. Despite the raging weather the enemy quickly spotted the Americans. In a few minutes several Chinese machine guns reached out to fell the attackers. Men fell into three-foot drifts, their blood staining the fresh snow.

Sgt. James D. Yeomans, a squad leader in Kyle's platoon, provided an eyewitness account to what happened next: "We were confused by the sudden enemy fire but Lieutenant Kyle came down the line, slapping us on the back and giving his instructions for the attack.

"We began deploying forward but a machine gun opened fire, wounding six men and further holding up the advance of the entire company.

"Lieutenant Kyle personally charged the emplacement. Why he wasn't hit I'll never know. The enemy was firing everything he had and it all seemed to be directed at Lieutenant Kyle. He threw a grenade into the position and then killed the occupants, three Chinese, when they came out of the hole.

"He then waved us forward and we killed six Chinese who were defending the gun. We began to move toward the objective but only had fifteen men left. The Chinese allowed us to pass through and then opened up on us from the rear."

The swirling snow made it difficult to spot the enemy. Deep drifts of snow impeded the Americans' movement. The biting cold sapped the men's strength, making every step harder than the one before. Totally oblivious to the hazards, Kyle ranged ahead of his platoon until he'd pinpointed the Chinese.

"Lieutenant Kyle closed in among the enemy and led us in a savage bayonet attack," Sergeant Yeomans continued. "He was still tired from his previous fighting but he killed four more Chinese in hand-to-hand combat. It was after this that a Chinese killed Lieutenant Kyle with point-blank submachine-gun fire from about ten yards.

"Lieutenant Kyle's leadership and bravery were an inspiration to us all. He was the bravest man I ever saw."

The army agreed with Sergeant Yeomans. It awarded his posthumous Medal of Honor to Kyle's widow and his two young daughters on January 16, 1952.

Determined to keep the enemy off balance, General Ridgway launched Operation *Killer* on February 21. *Killer* was a general advance by both the U.S. IX and X Corps designed to deny the enemy important terrain positions and kill as many Chinese as possible before they could retreat across the Han. *Killer*'s main objective was a line which ran generally eastward from Yangpyong on the Han River east of Seoul through points north of Chipyong-ni to the boundary of the X Corps and the ROK Army near Pagnim-ni, northeast of Wonju.

Initially, both corps made good progress—up to ten miles per day. Then the inhospitable Korean winter created havoc. An early thaw swelled streams which overflowed their banks. The resultant mud greatly hampered military operations. The extremely rugged mountainous terrain, coupled with the mud, made each day's effort a supreme physical endurance test. Heavy rains turned the numerous rice paddies into treacherous brown slime holes through which men stumbled and slithered. At night temperatures dropped back below freezing, greatly adding to the troops' overall misery.

As *Killer* progressed, opposition in front of the two corps stiffened, with NKPA and Chinese forces contesting the U.N. every step of the way. But it was obvious to the U.N. commanders that the enemy was using strictly delaying tactics. One such delay took place near Malta-ri in the X Corps's zone on February 26, 1951. Company E, 17th Infantry Regiment, U.S. 7th Infantry Division, stirred up a hornet's nest when they stumbled into a band of stubborn Chinese determined not to yield.

EINAR H. INGMAN

First Lt. Charles B. Wagner deployed his platoon of Company E along the base of a high ridge just south of Malta-ri. Confident there was no enemy on the hill, Wagner's platoon members relaxed their guard as they crossed onto the crest.

Suddenly, two enemy machine guns opened fire. Green tracers ricocheted off the rocks into the afternoon sky. GIs frantically dived for cover. Some didn't make it. The squad leader in the right-hand squad died instantly. The leader of the next squad to the left moaned quietly from the pain of several bullet wounds. Isolated from the rest of the platoon, the squad members faltered, reluctant to advance into the face of the heavy fire. Casualties mounted at a fearful rate.

Before the two leaderless squads could disintegrate into a rabble, Cpl. Einar Ingman, assistant squad leader of the right-hand squad, took charge. He formed the survivors of the two squads into one, then moved among the scared soldiers, distributing ammo, pointing out targets, and offering calming words of encouragement. For a youngster who'd joined the army to learn mechanics, Ingman was doing a pretty good job as a combat infantryman.

Ingman was born October 6, 1929, in Milwaukee, Wisconsin. The son of a Swedish mechanic father and a German mother, Ingman grew up on the family farm near Tomahawk, in north central Wisconsin. He attended the local country school until he completed the eighth grade. Classroom work bored Ingman. Mechanics fascinated him. He liked working with his hands, tinkering with stalled tractor engines, hanging around the local garages talking cars with mechanics. Since there was little opportunity to learn his chosen trade around Tomahawk, Ingman succumbed to the promises of the local army recruiter. He'd be sent to a first-class school, the recruiter promised. This would be an excellent chance to gain valuable experience that would lead to a good civilian job. Just sign here. Ingman did. It was November 2, 1948.

Instead of mechanic's training, though, Ingman learned the trade of an infantryman before being sent to Japan. In September 1950 Ingman and the 7th Infantry Division hit the beaches at Inchon. He wore corporal's stripes by then and was second in command of a rifle squad. Two weeks later, in the fighting north of Seoul, Ingman stopped an enemy round. He spent several weeks in a hospital in Japan before rejoining his squad in time to take part in the exodus from North Korea.

After Ingman whipped his squads into shape on the hill outside of Malta-ri he moved out ahead of the men, calling for them to advance. A few of the GIs tried, but the heavy beat of the two enemy machine guns held them back.

Ingman knew he sat at a crossroads. He could lay there hugging the damp earth, waiting for someone else to do something, or he could do something himself. He made a decision.

Scrambling to his feet, Ingman raced straight toward the first enemy machine gun. Bullets buzzed by his head as he tore right at it. As he neared the nest he drew a grenade from his web gear. He pulled the pin, tossed the missile, hit the dirt. After the explosion he jumped atop the machine gun emplacement, pumping bullets into the enemy soldiers.

Before Ingman could savor his victory, the second machine gun loosed a barrage of fire at him. Perhaps buoyed by the success of his first attack, he turned his attention to this new threat. Dodging from one rock outcropping to another, he made his way to within fifteen yards of this weapon. Only open ground lay in front of him. He swallowed deeply and charged forward.

Halfway across the open stretch an enemy grenade exploded alongside Ingman's head. The blast tore off his left ear, splattered his head with steel fragments, and knocked him to the ground.

Adrenaline and training took over. Ingman staggered upright. He moved toward the gun. It fired.

A .30-caliber bullet slammed full into Ingman's face. It hit him on the left side of the nose, smashed through his upper teeth, then exited behind the missing left ear. It destroyed his ear drum.

On his knees in front of the nest, Ingman slowly shook his head, splattering blood all around him. He was in a daze. "I don't remember much about what happened after I got hit," Ingman later admitted. "That bullet through my head kind of made me quit thinking . . ."

Exhibiting tremendous strength, Ingman pulled himself to his feet. Before the Chinese could fire again, he was on them. He fired a full clip from his M-1 into the gun crew, then finished them off with his bayonet. Ten enemy soldiers died. Ingman stumbled to the sandbagged wall of the bunker, then collapsed.

Below him the two squads, rallied by Ingman's remarkable charge, stormed forward. In front of them more than a hundred Chinese broke from cover and fled down the reverse slope. Squad members took up firing positions along the ridge and dropped more than half the enemy before they disappeared out of range.

In the meantime, the platoon medics worked frantically to stabilize Ingman. There was so much blood, so much damage. They didn't think he'd survive the arduous journey down the hill. But the Wisconsinite was tough. He not only survived the trip to the battalion aid station but the trip to the hospital farther behind the lines and to Japan as well. By May 1 he was a patient at Percy Jones Army Hospital, Battle Creek, Michigan.

Skillful army plastic surgeons went to work rebuilding Ingman's face. Using a lot of silver wire and numerous skin grafts, they repaired the damage done by the enemy slug. Ingman went under the knife more than a dozen times. Frequently, he felt the cure was worse than the disease. But finally, after nearly a year of hospitalization, Ingman's new face was completed. The doctors even made him a new left ear. It had only one drawback—he couldn't hear out of it.

Ingman's hospital stay was interrupted by a trip to the White House on July 5, 1951, to receive his Medal of Honor. After his discharge Ingman returned to Tomahawk and the family farm.

The next phase of General Ridgway's drive back to the Thirty-eighth Parallel was Operation *Ripper*, beginning on March 7, 1951. Again, the U.S. IX and X Corps in the center of Korea were to advance north through successive phase lines to Line IDAHO. While the ROKs on the east held fast and with the U.S. I Corps on the west making only diversionary attacks, success in the center would create a northward pointing bulge in the U.N. line centered on Chunchon, northeast of Seoul. From here U.N. forces would be in position to envelop the capital city.

Ripper commenced with a tremendous artillery barrage at dawn. Following it the U.S. 25th Infantry Division crossed the Han River near its confluence with the Pukhan, about twenty-five air miles east of Seoul. While they established a bridgehead, other I Corps units made diversionary attacks around Seoul.

The CCF and NKPA fought delaying actions before the IX and X Corps, but the determined GIs ground forward. Wherever the terrain was least favorable to attack, wherever slopes were steep, where roads were lacking, and natural approaches few, there the enemy held most stubbornly.

Such was the case when the 1st Battalion, 17th Infantry Regiment, U.S. 7th Infantry Division of the X Corps, approached Hill 1232, known locally as Taemi-dong, just before noon on March 9, 1951.

RAYMOND HARVEY

As the three rifle companies of the 1st Battalion neared Hill 1232, the day's objective, the battalion commander radioed Capt. Raymond Harvey, CO of Company C.

"I want you in the lead, ahead of Companies A and B," the lieutenant colonel said.

Harvey begged off. "Sir, we've been leading the advance for seven straight days. We're worn out. Let one of the other companies take the lead."

The colonel agreed, but only reluctantly. Harvey was his best company commander and he liked him out in front.

Companies A and B started up Hill 1232. Company A followed a ridge line which led to a series of ridges running to the left of the objective. As a result, they drifted farther from Company B. Harvey brought his company up to fill in the gap. North Korean soldiers peppered Company C with small-arms fire.

Harvey, a World War II combat veteran, knew the value of closing on the enemy. He urged his platoons forward. On the radio, the colonel kept ordering Harvey closer to the enemy. "Get up there," he ordered. "Move closer!"

"Yes, sir," Harvey responded.

The colonel kept pushing Harvey forward. Harvey kept saying "Yes, sir." Finally, Harvey saw where he stood.

"Sir, I'm the lead company now," Harvey radioed.

"Good, that's just where I want you," the colonel answered. "Take over the advance."

Infuriated at how he'd been pushed into the lead, Harvey smashed his radio down on the snow-dusted rocks. A curse passed his lips. His platoons were weak, short of men. Those he had were nearly worn out from over a week's steady combat. While he calmed down, a plan of attack formed in Harvey's mind.

Raymond Harvey was no stranger to combat. A native of Ford City, Pennsylvania, where he was born on March 1, 1920, he grew up in Inglewood, California. After high school and a succession of part-time jobs as he traveled about the country Harvey enlisted in the army in August 1939.

The army sent Harvey to Fort Sill, Oklahoma, where he eventually became part of the cadre charged with training the flood of new artillery officers entering the expanding military. Once World War II began for the United

States, 1st Sgt. Harvey decided he didn't want to be stuck in the States as a trainer. He applied for infantry OCS and was accepted.

Upon graduation in June 1942 as an infantry second lieutenant, Harvey joined the 79th Infantry Division. He served with them through the campaigns in Normandy, Northern France, in the Rhineland, the Ardennes-Alsace Campaign, and across Germany. Harvey started out as a platoon leader and ended up the war as a company commander.

Harvey excelled as a combatant. He earned the DSC for singlehandedly destroying a Panzer. He also earned two Silver Stars and two Purple Hearts.

Discharged as a captain in late 1945, Harvey returned to Los Angeles. There he found employment as a public relations man working with the major film studios. Though extremely good at what he did, Harvey found he missed the military. He joined the army reserves, but he wasn't happy with his reserve assignment.

Harvey had charge of a collection of miscellaneous quartermaster troops. He was an infantry officer and he wanted an infantry company. He took his problem to the regular army officer assigned to the reserve unit, Capt. Reginald Desiderio.

Harvey presented his case to Desiderio. "I have just the solution," Desiderio assured him. "Come back next weekend."

When Harvey returned, Desiderio handed him a sheaf of papers. "Sign here," he said. Harvey did, barely glancing at them. He did remember seeing the phrase "voluntary recall to active duty."

Harvey put the incident out of his mind. Then, a couple of months later, he received orders to report to Camp Lee, Virginia. His request had been approved! It was August 1948.

By early 1950 Harvey was in Japan, working with the Japanese civilian employees of the U.S. Army. When the North Koreans plunged the U.S. into war, Harvey volunteered for combat duty. Instead of a rifle company, though, as he'd requested, Harvey was assigned as battalion adjutant in the 1st Battalion, 17th Infantry Regiment. He made the landing at Inchon and the east coast landings that preceded the drive to the Yalu River, still itching to do what he did best—command a rifle company.

His chance finally came as the Chinese forced the X Corps out of North Korea. Just before Thanksgiving 1950 he took over Company C. He brought them out of North Korea and rebuilt his command in a rest camp near Pusan. When the Eighth Army went back on the offensive, Capt. Raymond Harvey and his Company C were ready. His aggressiveness in closing with the enemy made him the battalion commander's favorite. He could depend on Harvey to get the job done.

On March 9, as he hugged the ground just below the crest of Hill 1232, Harvey was about to prove the wisdom of his CO's judgment.

Harvey ordered his third platoon to lay down a base of suppressive fire. Then he crawled up to the first platoon leader. "Let's go," he said calmly.

Under his guidance the first platoon started forward. Sudden enemy gunfire drove the men to cover. Harvey moved among them, urging them forward. About this time a previously unseen enemy machine gun opened fire. Two GIs volunteered to wipe it out. They barely made ten yards before the enemy machine gun dropped them.

"Cover me!" Harvey shouted above the gunfire.

Under a protective umbrella of rifle and BAR fire from the first platoon, Harvey inched his way to within grenade range of the enemy nest. He unpinned two grenades, held them for a few seconds, then hurled the missiles toward the nest.

Because he was ducking down, Harvey didn't see the grenades land. When he looked up after they went off, though, the feathers floating in the air from the North Koreans' down-filled jackets told him his aim had been accurate.

Convinced he had opened the way for his men to take the hill, he rose to his feet shouting, "Follow me!"

Nobody did.

Alone, but committed, Harvey plunged forward, armed only with his carbine. Just on the backside of the hill he stumbled on a two-man machine-gun nest. Harvey snapped off two quick rounds. The two North Koreans died.

Continuing forward, Harvey became the target for all the nearby NKPA. Hoping to escape their fire, he jumped into a nearby hole. Five North Koreans greeted him. Harvey reacted before they did, pulling the trigger of his carbine five times in rapid succession. All five North Koreans died.

Still alone, Harvey left the foxhole. He took another enemy position under fire, wiping it out. About now he started back up the slope, calling for his first platoon leader. As he reached the top of the hill an enemy rifleman got him. The rifle bullet slammed into Harvey's left side, tearing a hole through his lung.

Scarcely able to breathe and bleeding profusely, Harvey refused his executive officer's efforts to have him evacuated. Instead, he relayed what he knew of the enemy's positions. With that information, the XO took two platoons forward and destroyed the remaining North Koreans. He later counted twenty-five dead enemy soldiers on the hill. He figured Harvey had accounted for at least ten. Only when he'd reported back to Harvey that the enemy had been eliminated did Harvey consent to evacuation.

The trip back to the battalion aid station nearly succeeded where the North Koreans had failed. The aid station lay more than seven miles away, down the twisting, winding road. Two men carried him back on a stretcher. On the way it started snowing. The bearers continually slipped and slid on the snow, dumping Harvey onto the ground several times. Fully conscious, Harvey frequently wondered if he'd make it to the doctors.

He did. At the aid station Harvey was startled to be greeted by General Ridgway and his division commander, General Quinn. The two had come forward to present Harvey with the Silver Star he'd earned five months earlier in North Korea. While he was being prepped for surgery Quinn made the presentation, placing the medal on Harvey's bare chest.

Four months of hospitalization followed for Harvey. He was still not completely healed when he appeared at the White House on July 5, 1951, to receive his Medal of Honor.

Soon afterwards Harvey was recruited by the Central Intelligence Agency. He served with them for nearly a year until a plan to deliver him clandestinely into Communist-dominated mainland China was halted because his wounds still had not completely healed. Harvey returned to the army.

Ten more years of active duty service followed before Harvey retired in 1962 as a lieutenant colonel. He pursued a career as an investment banker, then accepted a position as Director of Indian Affairs for the Arizona Division of Emergency Service in 1979. He retired from that position in 1982.

As intended, the advance in the center of the line to Line IDAHO threatened the enemy's control of Seoul. Ridgway began feeding patrols across the Han. When they encountered minimal resistance, larger forces crossed. By March 15 Seoul was again in U.N. hands.

Once Seoul fell, Ridgway included I Corps in Operation *Ripper*, authorizing them to move north and west to the Imjin River. Preceded by an airborne assault by the 187th Airborne Regiment, the new attack began March 23. The enemy collapsed. I Corps quickly reached the Imjin in a nearly bloodless advance.

By March 31 the U.N. forward line sat nearly on the Thirty-eighth Parallel. A major crossing of the parallel was not an undertaking to be entered into lightly. The enemy had withdrawn north of the Thirty-eighth Parallel to defensive positions which had apparently been constructed prior to June 1950. The most stalwart portion of the line lay at its center, where a series of fortifications, built in solid rock and reinforced by logs and concrete, protected the enemy positions. This area, bounded by Chorwon, Kumhwa, and Pyonggang, became known as "The Iron Triangle." It would prove to be a troublesome area for the U.N. until the war ended.

United Nations intelligence reported the Chinese and North Koreans were building up their forces in the Iron Triangle. In light of this Ridgway decided it was better to continue the advance. He activated Operation *Rugged* on April 5. *Rugged* had as its objective a new phase line dubbed KANSAS. KANSAS ran along commanding ground just north of the Thirty-eighth Parallel.

By April 9 all U.N. units had battled their way forward to KANSAS. The U.S. I Corps and the western divisions of the IX Corps continued pressing forward toward Chorwon, the southwest corner of the Iron Triangle. Their objective was designated UTAH, a northward bulge of the KANSAS line.

During this phase of the fighting a major command change occurred. Infuriated over General MacArthur's repeated public utterances concerning U.S. foreign policy, after he had been advised several times to refrain from such announcements, President Truman relieved General MacArthur of command on April 11. A public uproar ensued but MacArthur was indeed through. General Ridgway moved to Japan to replace MacArthur. Lt. Gen. James A. Van Fleet, a brilliant corps commander in Europe in World War II, rushed from Washington to take command of the Eighth Army on April 14.

The change in command had little or no effect on the front line troops. By April 17 nearly all U.N. units sat along the UTAH line. Though progress was virtually unopposed, intelligence continued to reach Eighth Army headquarters of enemy preparation for a major counteroffensive. Van Fleet did not ignore the warnings. But he reasoned that to anticipate an enemy offensive did not mean he had to sit and wait for it.

By April 19 the U.S. I and IX Corps were preparing to move northeastward from the UTAH bulge to Line WYOMING, essentially an extension of UTAH. If this attack proved successful, U.N. forces would hold the high ground overlooking Chorwon. But over the next two nights the Chinese began probing the U.N. lines with unexpected aggressiveness. These clashes were the first rumblings of a major attack that would soon break over the Eighth Army with a violent fury.

While he was still reported missing in action, Gen. William F. Dean's wife accepted his Medal of Honor on January 9, 1951.

Marine S. Sgt. Archie Van Winkle.

Cpl. Lee H. Phillips, USMC.

Marine Corps S. Sgt. Robert S. Kennemore.

Capt. Carl L. Sitter, USMC.

Maj. Reginald R. Myers, USMC.

Navy Lt. Thomas J. Hudner with President Truman, April 13, 1951.

Left to right: army M. Sgt. Ernest R. Kouma, 1st Lt. Carl H. Dodd, and S. Sgt. John A. Pittman prior to receiving their Medals of Honor on May 19, 1951.

Pvt. Hector A. Cafferata, USMC.

Marine Corps Lt. Col. Raymond
G. Davis.

Evie Coursen and Samuel S. Coursen, Jr., accept from Gen. Omar Bradley the post-humous Medal of Honor earned by 1st Lt. Samuel S. Coursen on October 12, 1951.

Darwin K. Kyle receives the gold bars of a second lieutentant from Gen. Matthew Ridgway in January 1951, less than one month before he was killed earning a Medal of Honor.

Pfc. Charles L. Gilliland, just seventeen years old when he sacrificed his life on April 25, 1951, to save his comrades. (Courtesy B. Gilliland)

Marine M. Sgt. Harold E. Wilson.

Navy helicopter pilot Lt. John K. Koelsch.

M. Sgt. Hubert L. Lee, *left*, and Sfc. Joseph C. Rodriguez receive congratulations from President Truman after he presented them their Medals of Honor on January 29, 1952.

Left to right: Cpl. Rodolfo Hernandez, army secretary Frank Pace, and 1st Lt. Lloyd L. Burke prior to the Medal of Honor ceremony on April 11, 1952.

Cpl. Jerry Crump, *left*, and Cpl. Ronald E. Rosser with President Truman after receiving their Medals of Honor from him on June 27, 1952.

Cpl. Jerry Crump.

Capt. William E. Barber, USMC, congratulated by President Truman after White House Medal of Honor ceremony on August 20, 1952.

Capt. William E. Barber, USMC, shares a moment with his son after August 20, 1952, White House Medal of Honor ceremony.

Cpl. Duane E. Dewey, USMC.

Marine Pfc. Alford L. McLaughlin.

Marine Pfc. Jack W. Kelso receives the Silver Star from Col. Thomas C. Moore, Jr., on September 24, 1952. Kelso was killed ten days later earning the Medal of Honor.

1st Lt. Raymond G. Murphy, USMC.

Left to right: the fathers of Donn F. Porter, Clifton T. Speicher, and Lester Hammond accept their sons' posthumous Medals of Honor from under secretary of the army Earl D. Johnson, *far right*, on August 5, 1953.

Army S. Sgt. Hiroshi H. Miyamura receives his Medal of Honor from President Eisenhower on October 27, 1953.

1st Lt. James L. Stone, *behind microphones*, at the press conference held at Freedom Village, Panmunjom, to announce the award of the Medal of Honor on September 2, 1953.

1st Lt. James L. Stone receives the Medal of Honor from President Eisenhower on October 27, 1953.

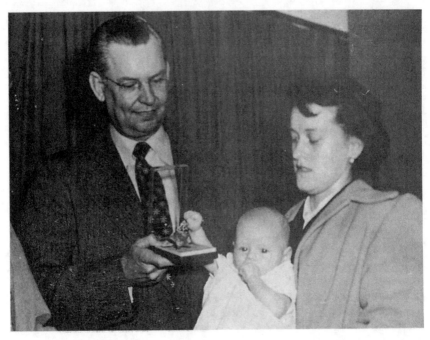

Phyllis Hammond holds her son, Francis C. Hammond, Jr., who holds the Medal of Honor posthumously awarded his father, Corpsman Francis C. Hammond, USN, by navy secretary Robert B. Anderson on December 29, 1953.

Corpsman William R. Charette, USN.

Chapter Eight
CCF Spring Offensive

Though a CCF offensive had been anticipated for some time, the viciousness of the enemy's initial attack still stunned the U.N. forces. Beginning early on the evening of April 22, 1951, Chinese and North Korean artillery began bombarding nearly every sector of the WYOMING line. For four hours the shells fell without a lull. The men of the Eighth Army huddled protectively, deep in their bunkers and foxholes.

Just before midnight three full Chinese armies, about 350,000 men, poured out of the crisp night. Their tactics—assaults by a "human sea" of massed infantry—were the same as before, again accompanied by tactical bugle calls and whistles.

The initial attacks came against the IX Corps in central Korea. Here the ROK 6th Division held the middle position with the U.S. 24th Infantry Division on the left and the U.S. 1st Marine Division on the right. The ROKs gave ground almost immediately, exposing the flanks of both U.S. divisions. The attackers moved quickly to exploit the opportunity.

A marine observation post north of Chunchon was manned by leathernecks of Company C, 1st Battalion, 7th Marines. Pfc. Herbert A. Littleton, a radio operator with the artillery forward observation team, was on watch when the Chinese hit. He quickly gave the alarm, then moved from his bunker into the open to get into a better position to call down artillery fire on the attacking Chinese. Despite the artillery fire the enemy closed on the OP. A firefight began in earnest. Forced to withdraw to the bunker, Littleton and his teammates battled the Chinese at close range. Heavy machine-gun fire blasted through the night. Grenades crashed around the bunker. One flew through the black-out curtain. Death seemed a certainty for the group of marines. Then Littleton acted. The twenty-year-old from Nampa, Idaho, moved swiftly. Before the others realized what was happening, Littleton hurled himself on the grenade. He died so that the other marines could live.

With his line breached, General Van Fleet authorized both the I and IX Corps to pull back step-by-step to the KANSAS line. Artillery and air support would help hold the enemy at bay while the infantry units withdrew. This was giving up hard won ground but Van Fleet reasoned that a pullback would stretch the Chinese supply lines, weakening his front line troops.

The 1st Marine Division drew back from the Hwachon area to take up new positions before Chunchon. During daylight hours the CCF broke contact and, using camouflage as well as natural and man-made features, sought cover from American air. The marines were able to take up their new positions but, as soon as the sun set, the CCF came again.

HAROLD E. WILSON

Technical Sgt. Harold E. Wilson spent twenty-seven months on Midway Island during World War II. When the war ended he returned to his native Birmingham, Alabama. There he worked as a gas station attendant and held a job at the local railroad yard. Wilson also attended weekly drills and summer camp as a member of the local marine corps reserve unit.

When the shooting began in Korea, Wilson was called up. He joined Company G, 3d Battalion, 1st Marines, after Inchon but in time to make the landing on Korea's east coast. He proved himself to be one of Capt. Carl Sitter's key NCOs during the road fight from Koto-ri to Hagaru-ri and the later defense of East Hill. Wilson was wounded during the march out of North Korea but quickly returned to duty.

Wilson's combat experience and coolness under fire brought him the opportunity to command his own platoon during the drive back to the Thirty-eighth Parallel. For his outstanding leadership qualities during this period he earned the Bronze Star. It was merely a prelude to what was to come.

On the evening of April 23, 1951, Wilson sent one of his squads to outpost a prominent knob forward of Company G's position.

All was quiet until about 10:00 P.M. Suddenly, multiple grenade explosions erupted around the OP. Seconds later the characteristic ripping sounds of Chinese burp guns followed. Tracers from enemy machine guns crisscrossed the dark sky. Radio contact was lost with the OP. Wilson tried repeatedly to reach his men but had no success.

Though the OP defenders fought valiantly, they had been quickly overwhelmed. At about the same time, the Chinese poured out of the night to slam directly into Wilson's platoon. While mortars crashed around him, Wilson moved among his men, calming them, directing their fire.

In the light of an explosion Wilson spotted several survivors from his OP trying to make their way across the "no-man's land" to his lines. Oblivious to the hail of fire directed at him, he went to their rescue. Doggedly, he made his way into the open area, gathered together the disoriented men, and brought them safely into the marines' lines. After he saw them to the aid station he hastened back to his platoon.

No sooner had he reached there then he caught the blast of an artillery shell. Jagged fragments of metal ripped into his arm and leg. He went down. Medics reached him, hastily bandaged him, and pointed him to the rear. Wilson refused.

His platoon's firing line was still battling the rushing Chinese. They needed him.

Back into the melee he went. Shouting orders to his platoon, Wilson continuously ignored the enemy fire to move from man to man. His valiant disregard for his personal safety greatly inspired his marines.

Just as the Chinese attack intensified, Wilson was hit twice more, in the head and the shoulder. Again he refused to be evacuated.

The twenty-nine-year-old couldn't use either arm to fire his carbine, but he could still move about. He ranged the line, loading magazines for his men, unjamming rifles, and pulling ammo from the dead for the living.

The weight of the Chinese attack threatened to burst through Wilson's platoon. Barely able to walk, nearly doubled over in pain, he staggered back to the company CP.

"I gotta have more men," he begged.

The skipper gave him a squad, all he could spare; his company was being pressed from all sides. Wilson led the squad back to his platoon. Once they were in place he continued on his rounds. He'd barely made five feet when an enemy mortar round landed right in front of him.

The blast flipped Wilson backward onto the hard, rocky ground. More hot metal tore into his face. Dazed, ripped, and with blood streaming from a dozen new holes in his body, Wilson groggily rose to his feet. Still refusing medical evacuation, he elected to stay with his badly worn platoon.

Time and again through the long night the Chinese attacked. There was barely a quiet minute as one assault after another was thrown against Company G's staggering, but unwavering, line. And in the midst of the line, limping back and forth through the smoke and grit, was the indestructible Sergeant Wilson.

If any marine thought about quitting that night he was undoubtedly inspired to continue fighting by the imposing figure of Wilson. His uniform tattered and covered with blood, he crawled painfully from man to man, assuring they were supplied with ammo and weapons.

Finally, at dawn, the Chinese broke off their attack. Weakened beyond description, hobbling so painfully that every step brought a wince to his lips, Wilson still had one task to perform. Up and down the line he moved, taking roll call. Once satisfied he had a complete roster, Wilson turned the list in to his skipper. Then he walked, unassisted, the half mile to the aid station.

Following a long period of hospitalization, Wilson returned to active duty. After receiving his Medal of Honor on April 11, 1952, he stayed on active duty, retiring as a chief warrant officer in 1974.

With the center of the U.N. line still reeling under the initial Chinese blows, two more enemy attacks were launched. A push developed on the eastern flank, focused on Inje along the border between the Eighth Army and the ROK Army. The CCF made some progress but were not able to exploit their successes due to the rugged mountainous terrain.

The main enemy thrust, however, was aimed at I Corps units above Seoul. Three Chinese divisions of the 63d Army forded the icy Imjin River about midnight, April 22. They took up positions on the south bank between Korangpo-ri and Majon-ni. Other Chinese troops attacked south along the Chorwon-Seoul highway. I Corps slowed the attackers as it retired to the KANSAS line but then, on April 23, the CCF forced the ROK 1st Division, holding the line westward to the sea, south of the KANSAS line. This setback exposed the left flank of the 1st Battalion, Gloucestershire Regiment, 29th British Brigade. Over the next several days the Britishers gallantly held their isolated position until surrounded and destroyed. Only a handful of the "Gloster" men ever made their way back to U.N. lines.

With the ROKs and Britishers out of the way, the CCF put all their weight into a strong attack directed against Seoul. Attempting to utilize the traditional invasion route via Uijongbu, the Chinese ran smack into the U.S. 3d Infantry Division.

Forced to withdraw from its positions ten miles south of Chorwon during the initial attacks, the "Rock of the Marne" division occupied a series of hilltop positions along the northern outskirts of Uijongbu. They had barely finished digging in on the evening of April 24 when the Chinese hit.

Company B, 1st Battalion, 7th Infantry Regiment, was among the first to be hit by the fanatical Chinese attackers. A few hours before midnight a withering barrage of mortar and artillery shells crashed down on the company's positions. As they always did, the CCF followed up the barrage with a vigorous ground assault. Furious fighting soon raged all along the company's perimeter. A key factor in the defense of the company was a light machine gun from Company D attached to it.

Finally, at about 1:00 A.M., the company's positions were being overrun by the crush of attackers. The GIs became disorganized and panicky. The company commander ordered a pullback to more tenable positions. Realizing that his .30-caliber weapon was the only one capable of slowing the Chinese, Corp. Clair Goodblood, a twenty-one-year-old from Burnam, Maine, volunteered to remain in place and cover the withdrawal.

Although he quickly became the focal point for the enemy, Goodblood refused to budge. When his assistant gunner and ammo bearer were wounded by grenade fragments he sent them to the rear. Alone, Goodblood operated and fed the weapon without assistance. Ordered to withdraw, Goodblood told the runner, "They'll take this gun over my dead body!" Then he loosed another burst into the massing Chinese.

Until about 3:00 A.M. Goodblood's machine gun could be heard firing away. Then the Chinese launched another human wave attack. The machine gun fell silent. When the ground was retaken by the GIs later that morning they found the courageous corporal's lifeless body surrounded by eleven empty ammo boxes—he'd fired over twenty-seven hundred rounds before he died. Scattered around his position were more than two dozen enemy dead.

A short distance away from where Corporal Goodblood made his stand, Company I, 3d Battalion, 7th Infantry, faced a similar onslaught. Manning a BAR at the top of a vital defile leading to the center of the company's perimeter was Pfc. Charles L. Gilliland of Yellville, Arkansas. Although only seventeen years old, Gilliland had already served nearly a year in the army.

Right from the start the Chinese attack seemed directed at Gilliland's position. As fast as his loader could feed him fresh clips for his weapon, the husky youngster slammed them into his BAR and fired into the Chinese attempting to reach him. Despite his accurate firing, two enemy soldiers slipped past him. Gilliland chased after them, armed only with a .45-caliber pistol. In a violent hand-to-hand battle the youngster killed both the infiltrators.

On the way back to his BAR Gilliland was shot in the head. He refused medical attention, asking only that he be allowed to return to his BAR. He did so, remaining there even when the rest of his unit pulled out. The last anyone saw of young Gilliland he was on his knees, BAR at his side, firing into a cluster of Chinese rushing at him.

A third outpost of the 7th Infantry Regiment also fell to the Chinese hordes that night. The fate of the soldier who led the outpost defenders through that terrible night remained a mystery for over two years.

HIROSHI H. MIYAMURA

Hiroshi H. Miyamura was born in Gallup, New Mexico, on October 6, 1925. A Nisei (second generation Japanese-American), he graduated from the local high school in 1943 after learning the trade of auto mechanics from an older brother during his summer vacation.

When World War II began the U.S. government issued its infamous order to round up and intern all Japanese and Japanese-Americans as potential security threats. In nearly every community in the United States, Japanese, whether citizens or not, were deprived of their personal freedom and their personal property. One of the few communities to refuse to obey the round-up order was Gallup. Perhaps it was because the town sat in the middle of the country's largest Indian reservation. Long accustomed to racial harmony, the town leaders simply refused to abide by the order. Gallup's small community of Japanese-Americans remained free.

By the time young Miyamura turned eighteen the attitude of the U.S. government toward youthful Nisei had radically changed. They were being accepted into segregated combat units. Miyamura received his induction notice in January 1944. Trained as a heavy weapons specialist, he was on his way to join the famed 100th Infantry Battalion, 442d Infantry Regiment, in Italy when the war ended.

Upon receiving his discharge in the fall of 1945, Miyamura enlisted in the army reserve. Then he returned to Gallop and a job as an auto mechanic. The life of a mechanic had lost its appeal by the time the Korean War began. When it came time for him to reenlist in the reserves, Miyamura did so with the understanding he would be called to active duty. He was, in September 1950.

After a brief period of refresher training, Miyamura headed to Japan and the 3d Infantry Division stationed at Sasebo. Once there he joined Company H, the heavy weapons company, 2d Battalion, 7th Infantry Regiment. Their first assignment upon arrival in Korea was to screen the X Corps advance to the Chosin Reservoir and the Yalu River. During the Chinese attack Miyamura's machine-gun squad served with a variety of infantry units, providing the firepower needed to blunt the steady attacks. He boarded the last ship to depart Hungnam, watching in fascination as Chinese soldiers infiltrated the burning town from the surrounding hills.

The 3d Infantry Division next participated in the drive to retake Seoul. They then went farther north, ending up south of the Iron Triangle. Miyamura's machine-gun squad continued to be parceled out to support different infantry units. Like most front line soldiers, he had little idea of where he was and what role he and his unit played in the war. All he knew was what he was told by his platoon leaders. Mostly, they told Miyamura to take his guns and fire at any Chinese who came within range.

When the Chinese hit the night of April 22–23, Miyamura's squad killed a lot of Chinese. At dawn came the order to pull back. Miyamura didn't know where his outfit was going, he just marched along. When they forded a river someone told Miyamura it was the Imjin.

A few hundred yards south of the Imjin, Miyamura's platoon sergeant pulled him out of the column. Pointing to a nearby hill, the sergeant said, "Take your squad and set up there. I'll send some riflemen to cover you. Hold the position as long as you can. See ya."

Miyamura never saw his platoon sergeant again.

For the next few hours Miyamura directed his men in setting up their positions. The area had been fought over four times in the previous ten months so it was littered with the debris of war. The hill itself was spotted with foxholes, bunkers, and trenches. Miyamura picked positions overlooking the road, giving him the best field of fire.

When he went up the hill Miyamura had about fifteen men. Five of these were riflemen. The rest were machine-gun squad members. About half of these were conscripted South Korean ammo bearers. They fled south as soon as it grew dark.

Miyamura and his remaining squad members waited anxiously for the enemy. Soon they could hear the chattering of Chinese voices at the base of the hill. Bugle calls and blowing whistles signaled the start of the attack.

"Here they come," someone announced.

As soon as the waves of Chinese came into view Miyamura opened fire with his .30-caliber water-cooled machine gun. The Chinese began to fall. Others rushed to take their place, firing burp guns from the hip. To Miyamura's left the other machine gun, a .30-caliber air-cooled, also tore into the Chinese. Still they came. Grenades crashed around the embattled group, wounding many of the GIs.

Soon the sheer number of attackers overwhelmed the position. A group of them threatened to overrun the Nisei from the flank. He boldly charged from his bunker, bayoneted rifle at the ready. Dodging, slashing, stabbing, Miyamura hacked his way through the enemy. Ten fell under his blade.

Back at his machine gun, Miyamura found his men all wounded. He took the time to bandage them, then ordered them to leave. He manned the weapon himself. Pouring fire into the enemy's ranks, Miyamura kept up his one-man stand until a fouled cartridge jammed the weapon.

About this time the other machine gun also fell silent. Outraged, the slightly built soldier made his way to the position through the swarming Chinese, using his bayonet and rifle to cut them down. He found a number of wounded GIs huddled in the position. After quickly patching them up he sent them rearward, then turned to the machine gun. Sighting on the figures darting about in the night, Miyamura blazed away at them.

On into the night Miyamura fought. Successive waves of enemy soldiers were forced back by his machine-gun fire. Finally, his ammo was nearly gone. He'd held out as long as he could. It was time to get out.

He gave the handful of men still fighting with him directions down the back of the hill. "Take off," said the reticent sergeant. "I'll cover you."

As the riflemen slipped into the night, Miyamura returned to his machine gun. His firing diverted the enemy from the retreating GIs. When one of them turned back, he could see Miyamura hunched behind the weapon, firing at the Chinese closing in on him. As the soldier made his way down the back slope, the machine gun firing stopped. The escaping GIs made it safely back to their own lines.

Back on the hill, Miyamura sought refuge in a covered bunker. He hoped to wait until dawn before making his way back to U.S. lines, but then white phosphorous artillery shells began falling on the hill. It was time for him to leave.

Miyamura dropped into a trench. He moved down it until he bumped right into a Chinese soldier coming around a blind bend. Miyamura slammed his bayonet into the middle of the man's chest, then pulled the trigger of his M-1. The recoil of the shot knocked him down. At the same time an armed grenade fell from the dying Chinese's fingers. From his supine position Miyamura saw the grenade alongside his leg. He kicked at it. It went off.

Shrapnel filled the sergeant's legs but he barely felt it. He was just intent on getting out of there. He jumped out of the trench and started downhill. He hadn't gone very far when he fell into an unseen barbed wire fence. The harder he struggled to free himself the more entangled he became. The sharp barbs punctured his skin, leaving dozens of holes.

Finally freeing himself from the wire, Miyamura reached a dirt lane at the base of the hill. In the distance he could just make out the silhouette of an American tank. He started for it. As he grew closer the tank suddenly came to life. It began moving. Miyamura ran after it. Weak from loss of blood and now feeling for the first time the pain in his legs, he lost the race. In frustration he watched the tank disappear into the night.

Utterly exhausted from his ordeal, Miyamura crawled into a roadside ditch and lost consciousness. When he came to it was to the sound of hundreds of Chinese filing past in the gray dawn. He played dead until they marched by. Then he heard a Chinese officer, in perfect English, ordering him to his feet. "Get up," said the man. "Don't worry. We won't harm you. We have a lenient policy toward prisoners."

Miyamura was marched off to a POW camp. He spent twenty-eight months as a captive, resisting the intense, near-constant brainwashing efforts of the Chinese. He watched men die by the score because the Chinese denied the prisoners adequate food and medicine. Miyamura suffered horribly from dysentery, dropping fifty pounds from his already lean frame.

Finally, on August 23, 1953, Miyamura was repatriated. As he made his way through the processing line at Freedom Village near Panmunjom, an American brigadier general suddenly appeared at his elbow.

"Are you Sergeant Hiroshi H. Miyamura?" the general asked.

Miyamura swallowed hard. During his long months of internment he'd often worried he'd be court-martialed for losing so many of his men. Now it looked like his past had caught up to him. He acknowledged his identity. The general stuck out his hand. "Congratulations! You've been awarded the Medal of Honor."

Miyamura gaped in astonishment.

The general went on to explain that approval of the award had been kept secret. If the award had become known to the enemy, the general said, "You might not be here, alive, today."

The formal presentation occurred at the White House on October 27, 1953, when President Eisenhower placed the blue ribbon around Miyamura's neck.

Miyamura returned to Gallup where he and his wife raised their family. He bought a service station which he ran for twenty-five years before retiring in 1984.

While Miyamura fought his delaying action, the rest of the U.S. 3d Infantry Division established a defensive line about four miles north of Seoul. Van Fleet rushed forward all available reinforcements. He had to hold the enemy north of the Han. With the help of U.S. Air Force planes, which slaughtered masses of Chinese moving south, the U.N. forces held. As a result, the CCF survivors never offered a serious threat to Seoul from the northwest.

The enemy also attempted to outflank Seoul to the east via the V-shaped area formed by the confluence of the Han and Pukhan Rivers. In their path sat the U.S. 24th Infantry Division.

RAY E. DUKE

The platoon sergeant of the first platoon of Company C, 21st Infantry Regiment, 24th Infantry Division, was Sfc. Ray E. Duke. A husky, square-jawed veteran of World War II, Duke had been in Korea since the start. He fought at Pusan, to the Yalu, and in the seesaw battles around Seoul. His coolness and repeated courage under fire earned for him the respect of everyone in his unit.

Born May 9, 1923, in Whitwell, Tennessee, Duke was the youngest of three children of a Spanish-American War veteran. Duke's father instilled in his offspring a deep sense of loyalty and patriotism. He carried that with him when he enlisted in the army at age nineteen. After fighting across Europe Duke realized he'd found a home in the army. He reenlisted when World War II ended.

On April 25, 1951, Duke's company was dug in on a hilltop near Mugok.

All was quiet during the afternoon and early evening. Then, just past sundown, the GIs could hear bugles blaring from beyond the next hill. They waited. Nothing happened. Quiet again descended across the area.

At about three o'clock the next morning, the Chinese hit with a sudden fury. They had snuck up the hill in absolute silence. One minute the hill was quiet, the next it erupted in a cacophony of gunfire. As one survivor later said, "It was as if they appeared out of nowhere."

The suddenness of the attack quickly overwhelmed the thin company. Duke, bedded down at the platoon's CP, immediately raced to the forward foxholes to be with his men. While moving among them, an enemy round hit Duke in the head. Bleeding profusely, he shrugged off the ministrations of the medic.

Within thirty minutes it became apparent the company could not hold its positions. With casualties mounting under the hail of enemy fire, the CO ordered a withdrawal. At the new positions on higher ground, Duke finally allowed the platoon medic to bandage his head. Then word reached him that several wounded members of his platoon had been left behind at the old positions.

Duke had no intentions of leaving those men to the Chinese. He hastily organized a counterattack. He had no difficulty rounding up volunteers. As one man said, "Following Duke back to that area even against those odds didn't seem difficult because he was a leader of men, capable of doing any job well."

Under Duke's intrepid guidance the band went back. They stormed the beleaguered positions, using bayonets and rifle butts to rout the Chinese. The isolated casualties were rescued and sent back to the company's new position.

In the meantime, Duke placed his men into their old foxholes. Now that he was back he didn't see any reason to abandon the area again.

Before he'd finished his task, though, the Chinese roared out of the night. Dropping into a foxhole, Duke fired his M-1 into the packed enemy ranks.

This Chinese assault was even more intense than the first one. Supported by mortars, they pressed in close, killing the men manning the forward foxholes. Duke leaped from his position to go to their aid but fragments from an exploding mortar hit him in the head and back. He crawled back into his hole, firing at the Chinese soldiers running by him.

Again the positions became untenable. Duke passed the word to pull back to the main company positions. At great risk to his own life Duke crawled to each man and gave him the word to move out. He had no intention of leaving anyone behind this time.

At his signal the men started pulling back. While one fire team laid down a base of rifle fire, another raced for cover higher up the hill. In this manner they worked their way toward the company.

Duke was the last man to pull out. Once assured everyone else was moving, he scrambled from his hole. Just a short distance from his men a Chinese soldier spotted Duke running in the dark. He fired. The bullet plowed through Duke's legs, breaking bones in both limbs.

Two of his men dashed from behind a boulder and pulled Duke to safety. On his knees, blood pouring from the holes in his body, Duke ordered his men to pull out. "I'll hold 'em off," he said.

Most of the men started moving again. The two GIs who'd first pulled Duke to safety refused to leave their sergeant behind. Against his protests, they grabbed Duke under the arms and started carrying him uphill. While the others raced ahead, the two GIs struggled with Duke. One of them fell, hit in the side.

Duke wouldn't allow any of the other men to endanger themselves by carrying him. "Get outta here!" he ordered. "I'll be okay. Now go."

Reluctantly, the others left him behind.

Duke propped himself against a rock, his rifle at his shoulder. As the Chinese advanced on him he shot them down. Finally, he ran out of ammo.

Word reached Duke's family in Tennessee that he was missing in action. For months they waited nervously, hoping he was alive, a prisoner. Then, late in 1951, the army told them he had indeed been captured that night. Unfortunately, he had died in a North Korean POW camp on November 11, 1951.

When the Korean War ended, Ray Duke's mother received a visit from a former POW who had known her son in the prison camp. He told her how the North Korean guards singled out Duke for special treatment because he was a senior NCO. They refused him all but the most rudimentary medical care for his wounds. Convinced he held vital military intelligence, they tortured him to reveal what he knew. Duke refused to yield. As a final punishment the North Koreans withheld Duke's food, telling him he would be fed only when he talked. But he never said a word.

"If he had opened up, he would have lived," said the former POW. "He was very brave."

The army thought so, too. They awarded him a posthumous Medal of Honor on March 10, 1954.

The massive enemy offensive continued for three more days. Unlike previous Chinese offensives, however, this one slowly ground to a halt in the face of stubborn resistance by the U.N. forces. At least fifteen thousand Chinese and North Koreans died in this latest attempt to drive the U.N. out of Korea. Though Van Fleet conceded terrain, he did it primarily to ensure that none of his units would be exposed.

On April 29, 1951, General Van Fleet established a new defensive line. He called it the NO NAME Line. It ran from just north of Inchon, passed north of Seoul to Sabangu, then northeast across the Thirty-eighth Parallel to Taepo-ri on the east coast. Because the major weight of the enemy's attack had struck in the west, Van Fleet reshuffled his units to put more American divisions there.

Van Fleet spent the first week of May capitalizing on a lull on the battlefield while the Chinese brought forward supplies. He established regimental patrol bases eight to ten miles north of NO NAME Line and sent armored recon patrols even farther north to harass CCF withdrawing from NO NAME. By May 10 half the distance to the KANSAS Line had been recaptured. General Van Fleet planned a general offensive designed to carry all the way to the KANSAS line, but mounting evidence that the enemy was preparing to resume his offensive forced the Eighth Army commander to postpone his plans.

After May 10 enemy resistance in front of the U.N. grew stiffer. Airborne reconnaissance reported a buildup of men and supplies behind the Chinese lines. NO NAME Line was strengthened with men and matériel. Mines were sown, artillery registered, and fire lines for automatic weapons established. This time Van Fleet resolved not to yield ground, but to hold with all the weapons and power at his disposal.

On the night of May 15–16, 1951, the enemy hit. Twenty-one Chinese and nine North Korean divisions struck the U.N. line, with the primary thrust directed at the U.S. X Corps and the ROK III Corps. The latter was routed, as it had been on every previous occasion when attacked, and the enemy made a penetration of nearly thirty miles. The collapse of two more ROK divisions again threatened the flank of the U.S. 2d Infantry Division. The men of the "Indianhead" division held fast, suffering over nine hundred casualties while inflicting an estimated thirty-five thousand on the Chinese.

To bolster the X Corps, Van Fleet sent part of the U.S. 3d Infantry Division and the 187th Airborne Regiment eastward from Seoul. A series of counterattacks against the western edge of the Chinese salient began pushing the enemy back.

Once again, the CCF did not have the logistical strength to maintain or exploit their breakthrough. By May 20 they had overrun their already overextended supply lines. Their drive weakened. The resoluteness of the U.N. defenders cost the enemy a staggering ninety thousand casualties in less than one week. The units of the X Corps began counterattacking to regain lost territory.

To the left of the X Corps, the U.S. 7th Infantry Division held the right flank of the IX Corps. On May 21, Company F, 2d Battalion, 17th Infantry Regiment, was committed to taking the high ground north of the village of Munye-ri. After obtaining a toehold on the ridge, the third platoon pushed on to attack a small peak dominating the ridge line. The platoon made it to within a hundred yards of the peak before the enemy opened up. They tried three times to take the peak, each time being driven back. Casualties mounted.

The second platoon pushed through the battered third. The enemy unleashed such a heavy volume of rifle and automatic-weapons fire that three squads of this platoon were used to lay down a base of fire while its second squad maneuvered forward.

Sixty yards from their objective the second squad was brought to a halt by the heavy enemy fire. At this point one of the squad members, twenty-two-year-old Pfc. Joseph C. Rodriguez of San Bernardino, California, began making his way to the left side of the enemy's positions. Unaided, completely exposed, but determined to destroy the enemy, Rodriguez dashed across sixty yards of open terrain.

He dropped several grenades into the first enemy foxhole he reached, then ran around to the left where he wiped out an automatic weapon. He next dashed across the top of the peak, dropping grenades into two more enemy holes as he passed them. Reaching the right flank, he rolled it up from the rear, using his grenades and his rifle to knock out the remaining enemy position.

In all, Rodriguez, who had less than seven months' service, accounted for fifteen enemy soldiers and five enemy positions. A week later Rodriguez was badly wounded and evacuated from Korea. He was in good shape on January 28, 1952, when he received his Medal of Honor. He later accepted a regular army commission and eventually retired as a full colonel.

A week later, on May 29, a few miles to the east and across several mountain ranges, the 5th Marines closed in on North Korean soldiers emplaced along the approaches to the Hwachon Reservoir. On May 29, Company C moved in on a strongly held enemy position. As twenty-one-year-old Pfc. Whitt L. Moreland, an intelligence scout from Austin, Texas, took the point, Chinese further up the hill started heaving grenades downhill on the marines. Moreland danced around, kicking the grenades away to explode harmlessly. Then he slipped in the loose soil, landing near one of the grenades. Knowing he didn't have time to dispose of it before it exploded and killed, or wounded, a group of nearby marines, Moreland rolled over on the deadly missile. He didn't survive the explosion.

The paratroopers of the 187th Airborne Regiment fought alongside the marines on the road to Inje. Near Wontong-ni at 2:00 A.M. on May 31, the enemy counterattacked the sector held by Company G. Grimly waiting in their path was Cpl. Rodolfo P. Hernandez, a twenty-year-old from Fowler, California, and his foxhole buddy, Pfc. Carl M. Hamrick. When they sighted the North Koreans on this moonless night, the pair opened fire with their BARs. Within minutes both men were wounded by enemy fire.

GIs on either side of the two pulled back, but Hernandez and Hamrick continued fighting. Hernandez's rifle jammed with a ruptured cartridge. Without a word, he jumped out of the fighting hole and, armed only with grenades, plunged headlong into the charging enemy. Hamrick pulled back to a nearby position where he continued fighting until the North Koreans pulled back at dawn.

Hamrick found Hernandez at daybreak the next morning. Severely wounded, he lay about twenty-five yards in front of their hole, head-to-head with an enemy soldier. Around him lay six more dead North Koreans, killed by grenade explosions or Hernandez's bayonet. According to Hamrick, "Hernandez stopped the attack with his courageous action."

Although Hernandez survived his severe wounds to wear his Medal of Honor, they left him permanently disabled.

By the end of May, Eighth Army had scored a significant advance which brought it nearly back to the KANSAS Line. Except on the west where the line slanted southward to take tactical advantage of the Imjin River, the new line lay north of the Thirty-eighth Parallel. South Korea was virtually free of the enemy.

May had not been an easy month for the Eighth Army. Its casualties exceeded 33,700. American battle casualties alone were 745 dead, 4,218 wounded, and 572 missing. Enemy casualties for just the last two weeks of May included seventeen thousand counted dead and seventeen thousand captured.

What to do next? Political considerations, as well as military realities, precluded any major advances north of the Thirty-eighth Parallel. All General Ridgway authorized Van Fleet to do was make local advances to gain better ground.

Consequently, on June 1, Van Fleet decided on two courses of action. He would strengthen the KANSAS Line, hoping to make it impregnable. At the same time, elements of the I and IX Corps would continue their advance toward the WYOMING Line, the bulge north of KANSAS. This operation, dubbed *Piledriver*, was carried out with relative ease, except as the GIs approached the Iron Triangle. Increased enemy resistance, coupled with driving rains, limited the advances made by the infantrymen. On the right flank of I Corps, the U.S. 25th Infantry Division ran into some particularly tough enemy positions.

One of the 25th Infantry Division's regiments, the 24th, was the last remaining segregated army unit. Since the Civil War black soldiers had served in all-black units commanded by white officers. Accustomed to gross discrimination, the black regiments nontheless served valiantly on America's frontiers after the Civil War. Generally denied the chance to fight for their country in both world wars, the men of the 24th Infantry Regiment resented having to fight and die for another country's freedom as members of a segregated unit.

President Truman desegregated the military in 1947. None of the services was quick to respond; the Marine Corps, for example, resisted integration into the early 1960s. Not until July 26, 1951, did Matthew Ridgway drop the 24th Infantry Regiment from the army's rolls, ending segregation in the army. The black soldiers were transferred to other units throughout the Eighth Army.

But, before that happened, the 24th Infantry Regiment would add another one of its members to the army's honor roll.

CORNELIUS H. CHARLTON

Cornelius H. Charlton was born in East Gulf, West Virginia, on July 24, 1929. The eighth of seventeen children born to Van and Esther Charlton, he was also the largest, weighing fifteen pounds at birth. When he arrived in Korea in 1950, Charlton stood just over six feet tall and weighed a husky, muscular two hundred pounds.

Charlton's father spent thirty-eight years working in the Appalachian coal mines. Finally, in 1944, he moved his family to the Bronx, New York, where he worked as an apartment building superintendent. Cornelius, nicknamed "Connie," entered James Madison High School. He was a bright youngster who made good grades and stayed out of trouble. His prospects for the future looked good, which made his interest in quitting school to join the army all the more puzzling.

His parents refused to give their permission to allow him to enlist until he'd earned his diploma. When he did so in 1946, they signed the papers. Connie Charlton entered the army in November of that year.

After basic training Charlton went to Germany and occupation duty. He finished his first enlistment there, then re-upped. He drew an assignment to an engineering battalion at the Aberdeen Proving Grounds, Maryland. Early in 1950 he was transferred to Okinawa.

By then Charlton wore the three chevrons of a buck sergeant. He was a quiet young man, confident in his role as a leader of others. His company commander quickly recognized Charlton's potential. "You keep performing at this pace and you'll be a master sergeant within a year," he promised.

The captain would not be able to keep his promise.

Once the Eighth Army broke out of the Pusan Perimeter, Charlton's unit was sent from Okinawa to Korea. Assigned primarily administrative tasks, Charlton grew impatient with his work. While others fought he stayed in the rear, doing his paperwork. Finally, he knew he had to make the choice. He requested a transfer to a line outfit.

His CO reluctantly signed the papers. "I hope you know what you're doing, Sergeant," the captain said. "You can get killed up there."

"I just don't feel right sitting back here while the others are doing the fighting up north," Charlton responded.

The transfer came through in March 1951. Instead of being integrated into a previously all-white regiment, as other blacks were at the time, Charlton headed to Company C, 24th Infantry Regiment.

Morale was at an all-time low in the 24th when Charlton arrived. The regiment had an unwarranted reputation for "bugging-out" in the face of the enemy. So pervasive was the reputation that the black GIs had created the self-deprecating song "Bug-out Blues" as their unofficial regimental song.

Company C's commander, Capt. Gordon E. Gullikson, was instantly suspicious of any man who would leave a cushy job in the rear for line company. Something had to be wrong. He kept an eye on Charlton. Soon, Charlton's competence as a squad leader dispelled his fears.

Gullikson watched with growing admiration as Charlton turned his squad into a first-class fighting outfit. Whenever they had spare time off the lines, Charlton trained his men incessantly, honing their combat skills. On the line the sergeant repeatedly demonstrated his fearlessness and natural leadership abilities. By the time Charlton had spent two months in his company, Gullikson had advanced him over more senior NCOs to be platoon sergeant of the third platoon and had recommended him for a battlefield commission. Gullikson hoped to personally pin the gold bars on Charlton's shoulders as soon as *Piledriver* ended.

For the first day of *Piledriver* Charlton's battalion was held in reserve. The 3d Battalion took the first objective, Hill 1147, with relative ease, but they really caught it when they stormed Hill 543. Chinese forces showered the attacking GIs with artillery and mortar fire. All that day, June 1, the 3d Battalion attacked the deadly hill. They were hurled back repeatedly. After spending a rainy night huddled at the base of Hill 543, they tried again. Once again the Chinese threw them back. At noon the 1st Battalion got the word they'd be taking over the assault. Charlton's platoon would lead the way.

A devastating air strike rocked the boulder-strewn hill with napalm and bombs. As the last plane dropped its load Company C started its attack.

Halfway up the hill the Chinese mortars started falling. Men screamed in pain as steel shards tore their flesh. The platoon leader, in command for just a week, fell, badly wounded. Before the leaderless platoon could become immobilized for want of an officer, Charlton jumped into the breach, rallying those around him.

The hillside above Charlton erupted in an intense hail of rifle and machine gun fire. Most of the platoon dived for cover. Not Charlton. He stayed on his feet, firing his rifle from the hip as he charged forward. His movement brought him abreast of two Chinese positions. With grenades and rifle fire he destroyed both, killing six enemy defenders.

With these two positions gone, Charlton took a few minutes to regroup and calm his jittery platoon. He sent the casualties downhill, then prepped his twenty or so remaining able-bodied soldiers for the continued assault. As he led them toward the crest, a barrage of concussion and fragmentation grenades sailed down on them.

He felt several grenades kick by him. Then he was slammed to the ground where he lay, stunned. Blood poured from a gaping wound in his chest. Suffering intense pain and groggy from the shock, Charlton shrugged off a medic's attempt to help him. He wasn't interested in saving himself. He just lay there, studying the hill.

He called out instructions to his men, now less than twenty. He gave the signal. They moved out but were almost immediately halted by another barrage of grenades.

Charlton saw to it that the new casualties were evacuated. Then he laid out the new attack for the remaining dozen or so GIs.

Inspired by his indomitable courage and personal strength, the small band started forward again. Shouting, "Let's go! C'mon! Let's Go!" Charlton led the way. Somehow, despite the tremendous enemy fire, he and not more than eight other brave men reached the summit.

Charlton quickly determined that the key defensive position lay just over the top and down the reverse slope. He flattened himself alongside a rock and looked for a way to get the emplacement. Blood from his wound soaked the ground under him. He saw there was no other way.

"Cover me!" he yelled, then jumped to his feet.

Pumping rounds from his rifle as fast as he could pull the trigger, Charlton charged straight at the Chinese position. A grenade blew him off his feet. Bleeding from a dozen new wounds, he staggered upright. Knowing he had no chance of survival, the husky sergeant continued forward. Somehow, he fired off a few more rounds, felling the remaining Chinese. The position fell silent. Charlton collapsed in front of it.

Enraged by their sergeant's death, the handful of remaining GIs stormed the other positions, wiping them out and taking the hill. Medics rushed to Charlton's side. They worked frantically to save him, but it was too late. He'd lost too much blood. Charlton died quietly on the rocky hillside.

Van and Esther Charlton accepted their son's posthumous award on March 12, 1952. Later that year, army ferryboat No. 84, used in New York Harbor as a ferry to Governor's Island, was christened the *Sgt. Cornelius Charlton.*

In the IX Corps zone of action in central Korea a week of heavy rain slowed the advance toward Hwachon, located at an important road just north of the KANSAS Line and about midway to the WYOMING Line. Until Hwachon fell, the Chinese-held Iron Triangle would pose a serious threat to the stability of Van Fleet's WYOMING Line. Except for a range of hills, the

Iron Triangle was a low-lying area surrounded by saw-toothed mountains. It was the terminus of a main highway from Manchuria and was crisscrossed by numerous dirt roads and two railroad tracks. The Iron Triangle served the CCF as both a supply and communications center. As elements of the IX Corps fought their way back to the WYOMING Line, the enemy fought back hard from positions arranged in depth.

The attack of the U.S. 7th Infantry Division not only captured Hwachon, but resulted in one of its members earning his country's two highest awards in just four days.

BENJAMIN F. WILSON

The route M. Sgt. Benjamin F. Wilson took to Company I, 31st Infantry Regiment, 7th Infantry Division, was a long, circuitous one. Born June 2, 1922, in Vashon, Washington, Wilson graduated from Vashon High School in June 1939. Uncertain as to which direction to take after school, he enlisted in the army in January 1940.

By December 7, 1941, Wilson was a corporal stationed at Schofield Barracks, Hawaii. He saw the Japanese bombers spreading their destruction around the base that infamous Sunday morning but took no part in the action. A few months later Wilson was swept up by the army's near insatiable need for junior officers and was sent to Officer Candidate School. Although he volunteered for overseas duty several times, Wilson remained in the States as a training officer. In late 1945 he was discharged as a first lieutenant.

After nine months of uncertainty as a civilian, Wilson reenlisted as a private. A year later, still seeking some excitement and challenge, Wilson volunteered for airborne training. When the Korean War broke out he requested, and received, an immediate transfer to the combat zone.

As a member of the 7th Infantry Division, Wilson made the landing at Inchon, the advance to the Yalu, the retreat out of North Korea, and the hard months of fighting back to the Thirty-eighth Parallel. Along the way his combat savvy and leadership skills earned him successive promotions until by June 5, 1951, he wore the stripes of a master sergeant, the top NCO in Company I.

Three days after Wilson's twenty-ninth birthday, Company I was committed to a daylight attack against heavily fortified enemy positions near Hwachon. Within minutes of the attack's start the lead elements were pinned down by heavy enemy fire.

As company master sergeant, Wilson's position was with the command group, at the rear of the company. From this vantage point he could see the two enemy positions holding up the company. Without a word he left the command group and started forward alone.

Artfully dodging from cover to cover, he closed in on the two enemy machine-gun nests. When he'd moved to a flanking position he hurled a grenade into the closest nest. Its explosion killed one gunner. He shot the other with his rifle. He wiped out the second position the same way.

With these obstacles out of the way, the day's objective came within sight. The company laid down a base of fire, pinning down the enemy for the next phase of the attack. Sensing the need for decisive action, Wilson passed among the men, giving an order. "Fix bayonets," he said. "We're taking this place by storm."

Wilson led a platoon in a direct charge on the enemy's position. Braving a hail of fire, the GIs, screaming and yelling, followed Wilson right into the enemy's main position. Slashing cold steel left and right, firing into the Chinese at point blank range, the platoon quickly overran the enemy.

When the dust settled, twenty-seven enemy dead littered the area; the survivors fled northward. The rest of the company came forward and set about consolidating their newly won position. Before they could finish clearing the area of enemy dead and wounded, the Chinese counterattacked.

In a blizzard of enemy fire the attack nearly overran the tired GIs. Quick to act, Wilson sprang from his hole. Kneeling in the open, he fired into the enemy's ranks, disrupting their attack. His fire killed seven Chinese, wounded two more, who were taken prisoner, and routed the remainder, who pulled back into a defensive perimeter.

After overseeing the evacuation of his own wounded, Wilson volunteered to lead an attack on the remaining enemy. He took a platoon forward, advancing to within fifteen yards of the enemy position before their fire forced him to halt. Realizing his force was too small to carry the attack, Wilson ordered his men to pull back. He'd cover them.

Popping up and down from behind a rock, Wilson kept the enemy pinned down while the others slipped away. While he concentrated his fire on the enemy positions, a Chinese grenade landed behind him. He heard it hit. He ducked. It exploded. A jagged piece of metal tore into his shoulder, lodging near bone.

In great pain he rolled back behind the boulder and resumed his fire, staying in position until he was sure all the others had withdrawn safely. Only then did he pull back to the company.

A medic patched up the hole in Wilson's shoulder and tagged him for evacuation. He threw the tag away. As far as he was concerned the day wasn't over.

Just before nightfall, after the company had dug in, the Chinese came again, in force, covered by a blistering mortar barrage. While moving to the area of heaviest activity, both the company commander and one of his platoon leaders went down in a mortar blast. Sensing the overwhelming superiority of the attackers, the senior surviving officer authorized a withdrawal.

While the others pulled back, Wilson spotted a knot of enemy soldiers advancing on him. Determined to stop them, he charged singlehandedly right into their midst. Fighting like a madman, firing his rifle directly into the enemy's faces, trading punches, Wilson killed three Chinese before his rifle was clubbed from his hands.

Groping around in the failing light while the Chinese pummeled him, Wilson grabbed an abandoned entrenching tool. He swung it, hard. It thudded dully, heavily against a Chinese skull. Whirling around, dancing about like a prize fighter, Wilson clubbed three more Chinese to death, crushing their skulls with the tool. The rest ran away.

By this time most of the company had pulled back to a more defensible position several hundred yards away. With a few other stragglers, Wilson made his way in the darkness to the company.

At the new position Wilson busied himself by helping the more seriously wounded. While he did so, a stray enemy round tore into the fleshy part of his right thigh. Again refusing evacuation, he continued helping the others until all had been removed. He then took up a position on the firing line, holding it through the night.

When dawn broke it was obvious the enemy had abandoned their positions. Only then did Wilson consent to evacuation. While lying on the ground at the rear aid station waiting for evacuation, the indestructible NCO grew impatient. He hoisted himself off the stretcher and headed back to his company. In the hustle and bustle of the busy aid station no one noticed his departure.

Wilson spent three more days limping along with his company. On June 9, in another series of singlehanded attacks on enemy positions, Wilson killed another thirty-three Chinese. His vigorous activities reopened his wounds. This time the new company commander insisted Wilson be evacuated. The gutsy master sergeant reluctantly agreed. He headed for Japan and a hospital aboard a medical transport plane.

While Wilson was recovering in an army hospital, his regimental adjutant was in a quandary. Wilson's heroic activities certainly merited recognition, but of what nature? It was against military practice to award more than one Medal of Honor to one man, no matter how gallant his conduct. The adjutant did not know which of Wilson's courageous days merited the ultimate decoration. In the end, he wrote them both up for the Medal of Honor, suggesting the decorations board make the final decision.

The review board had no easier task. They studied the documentation for three years, asking for more eyewitness statements before finally making a decision. In the end they awarded Wilson the Medal of Honor for his actions on June 5 and the DSC for June 9.

By that time Wilson was a first lieutenant, having been recommissioned in November 1951 while stationed at the Redstone Arsenal, Huntsville, Alabama. In a ceremony at the summer White House in Denver, Colorado, on September 7, 1954, President Eisenhower draped the Medal of Honor around Wilson's neck. Wilson was the last living recipient from the Korean War to receive his medal.

Wilson remained in the army, retiring in 1960 as a major. He then worked for the Selective Service System and the VA before retiring again in 1975. He died in Hawaii on March 1, 1988.

While Wilson's company fought the determined Chinese, another 31st Infantry Regiment company a few miles away at Pachi-dong also found itself besieged by the enemy. Company F, 2d Battalion, was hit by a surprise attack at 3:00 A.M., June 7, 1951. The security of the command post and weapons platoon was seriously threatened, so the company commander ordered a withdrawal.

A twenty-year-old machine gunner from Escatawpa, Mississippi, Pfc. Jack G. Hanson, declined to yield his position. In spite of repeated orders to pull out, Hanson refused. He knew his gun provided the only covering fire for the rest of the company. Reluctantly, his lieutenant left him at his weapon.

In the morning, when the ground was retaken, Hanson was found slumped behind his machine gun. Twenty-two dead Chinese lay around him. The ferocity of the fight was evidenced by the empty pistol in Hanson's right hand and the bloody machete clenched in his left. His willful self-sacrifice had saved his company from sure destruction.

Heavy combat erupted in the area known as the Punchbowl, in east central Korea north of Inje, where the fanatical foe slowed the U.S. 1st Marine Division to daily advances measured in mere yards. The frustrations of the incessant combat sometimes drove men to heroic actions that are difficult to comprehend. Such was the case of Cpl. Charles G. Abrell, a nineteen-year-old member of Company E, 2d Battalion, 1st Marines.

A native of Terre Haute, Indiana, Abrell had enlisted in the marines in 1948 just after he turned seventeen. He made the landing at Inchon, then fought with his unit at Seoul, Wonsan, the Chosin Reservoir, and in the drive back to the Thirty-eighth Parallel. He'd witnessed more death and experienced more fighting in his nine months in Korea than any nineteen-year-old should.

Early on June 10, 1951, the lead assaulting squad of Abrell's platoon was pinned down by vicious fire from a well-fortified enemy bunker. Although previously wounded by a Chinese grenade, Abrell left his place near the rear of the platoon and ran right through the pinned-down squad, firing his M-1 at the enemy bunker. Hit twice, he staggered to the edge of the bunker, pulled the pin from a grenade, popped its spoon, then, clutching the armed bomb, threw himself bodily into the Chinese bunker. Abrell and the Chinese gun crew were killed in the explosion.

As the end of June neared, the Eighth Army had largely attained the principal terrain objectives of *Piledriver*. Combat continued nearly all along the front line but, except for the marines engaged around the Punchbowl, few of the actions materially affected the dispositions of either side.

With almost exactly twelve months of bloody, bitter fighting behind them, the adversaries stood nearly at the same positions they had held when the war began. The U.N. forces could look back on their accomplishments with considerable satisfaction. After losing Seoul twice and being nearly driven from South Korea, they had pushed back north of the Thirty-eighth Parallel and successfully executed the missions that were within their power to accomplish.

It was also apparent to the Chinese and North Koreans that the badly battered and bleeding Chinese Army was unable to defeat the United Nations forces. The war was also placing an unacceptable burden on the Chinese economy, which was primarily financed by the Soviet Union. As a result, the financial consequences for the entire Communist bloc became serious. The time had come when further pursuit of the Korean adventure was viewed as counterproductive.

Thus, when on Sunday, June 23, 1951, the Soviet delegate to the U.N., Jacob Malik, proposed cease-fire discussions among the participants in the Korean War, his proposal was accepted by both sides as a fortuitous turn. Neither adversary could foresee that the offer would drastically change the complexion and dimension of the war. Or that the fighting would drag on for two more years.

Chapter Nine
U.N. Summer Offensive

Two days after Jacob Malik made his proposal for discussions among the belligerents in Korea, a Chinese newspaper, *People's Daily*, endorsed the proposal. Through a series of delicate diplomatic machinations over the next several weeks it was agreed by the adversaries that cease-fire negotiations would commence at Kaesong, located northwest of Seoul and the site of bitter fighting during the Eighth Army's drive to the Yalu River in October 1950.

Far from being an acceptable neutral site for the negotiations, Kaesong was firmly in Chinese hands. This allowed the Chinese Communists to score a number of propaganda points during the first cease-fire session held on July 10, 1951. For example, when the U.N. negotiators arrived at Kaesong by helicopter, the Chinese drove them to the conference site in captured American jeeps sporting white flags. Throughout the early days of the talks the Chinese displayed a condescending attitude toward the U.N. delegation to the effect they were there to negotiate a surrender rather than discuss a mutually beneficial cease-fire.

To the Americans on the U.N. negotiating team the Chinese were totally unrealistic in their demands and appeared far more interested in achieving a propaganda coup than reaching any significant agreement. This opinion was reinforced when the Chinese abruptly broke off the talks on August 22, 1951, after alleging the U.N. had tried to murder their delegation by an air attack.

In the meantime the war went on. Men on both sides died as they jockeyed for tactically superior positions. Casualties were lighter than they had been in recent weeks, but the Eighth Army aid stations were still kept busy tending to the wounded and dying. A wounded U.N. soldier in Korea had a far better chance for survival than had his comrades in earlier wars thanks to the extensive use of a relatively recent innovation.

The concept of an aircraft using rotary blades to provide lift had been developed prior to World War II. Such a craft would be able to become airborne vertically, hover in a fixed position, and maneuver across the ground at slow speed. The helicopter had only limited use during World War II. Advancement in technology after the war greatly enhanced the chopper's acceptance among the military. The outbreak of war in Korea provided a unique testing ground for the new machine. It quickly became obvious the helicopter exceeded all expectations.

Among its primary functions was the evacuation of casualties. In the rugged, mountainous terrain of Korea it could take hours to carry a wounded man to an aid station—hours that often meant the difference between life and death. A helicopter, however, could have a wounded man at a mobile army surgical hospital (MASH) unit in a matter of minutes.

Another major job for the helicopter was the rescue of U.N. pilots shot down behind enemy lines. Under a protective umbrella of fighter aircraft a helicopter could dart in, pick up a downed pilot, and have him back in friendly hands in relatively short time. Dozens of U.N. airplane pilots owed their lives to the intrepidity of this fearless new breed of helicopter pilots.

JOHN K. KOELSCH

It was approaching dusk when the rescue call hit the ready room of Navy Helicopter Squadron 2 aboard the USS *Princeton*. Sailing off the coast of North Korea, the *Princeton* had launched a flight of Corsairs earlier that day, July 3, 1951, on a reconnaissance mission. After making several passes over a suspected enemy supply area about twenty miles south of Wonsan and fifteen miles inland, the flight leader had failed to detect any targets of opportunity.

Satisfied that nothing unusual was going on, he ordered his flight to return to the ship. As the planes made a final low pass over the area, marine Capt. James V. Wilkins suddenly felt his plane buck heavily three times. Reacting instinctively, he punched the ejection button. He flew from the cockpit, barely feeling the flames licking his legs. On the ground Wilkins discovered his calves were badly burned.

Wilkins had landed on the inland side of a small bowl-shaped area surrounded by higher hills. While he scrambled for cover, the Corsairs above him strafed North Korean riflemen firing at him from the high ground to the west.

The standby rescue pilot aboard the *Princeton* was Lt.(jg) John K. Koelsch. A twenty-six-year-old resident of Los Angeles, California, the Princeton University graduate had earned his commission through the ROTC program. Trained as a fighter pilot during the final days of World War II, Koelsch had leaped at the chance to fly helicopters. It was exactly the type of challenge he relished.

By July 1951 Koelsch had already served a full, rugged tour of duty in Korea. He had taken part in many rescues and had earned a well-deserved reputation as a past master of the art. He had even invented a new type of rescue sling that came to be widely used in Korea and also developed several safety devices that made helicopter operation in the cold climate of Korea possible.

Koelsch had received orders rotating him back to the United States but had volunteered for another tour. He explained to a fellow chopper pilot that he could not stand to be living in safety while his experience as a rescue pilot could be used to save lives in Korea.

Within minutes of receiving the rescue call on the evening of July 3, Koelsch and his crewman, Aviation Machinist's Mate George M. Neal, were airborne.

On the ground Wilkins had moved farther uphill after a solid overcast blew in from the sea to blanket the area. Sporadic enemy rifle fire whistled through the air as he painfully made his way upward.

No sooner had Wilkins reached a hiding spot than he heard the distinctive *whoop-whoop* of a helicopter. He was saved! He hurried back down the mountain trail, bearing on the sound of the chopper.

When he reached his abandoned parachute, Wilkins saw the helicopter turning back after having made its first pass over the bowl. Koelsch had skillfully lowered himself through the treacherous cloud bank to search for Wilkins. Now he was flying just fifty feet over the ground, ignoring the enemy fire directed at his ship.

From the ground Wilkins could see the helicopter shudder as it took hits. He could only marvel at the courage necessary to continue the mission. "It was the greatest display of guts I ever saw," Wilkins later said.

As Koelsch turned his ship about he spotted Wilkins. He hovered above him while Neal lowered the winch-operated rescue sling. Wilkins watched in fascination as Koelsch held his ship stationary, oblivious to the fusillade of enemy fire zeroing in on the big target.

Once the sling reached him, Wilkins quickly slipped his arms into the canvas harness. He signaled he was ready. Seconds later he rose off the ground.

Above the roar of the rotor blades Wilkins suddenly heard a grinding sound, then the tearing of metal. The next thing he knew he was facedown on the ground, a heavy weight pressing on his back. He twisted around. He found himself looking directly into the helicopter's cockpit, where Koelsch and Neal hung upside down in their seat belts.

"Are you all right?" Wilkins shouted.

"Never mind us, are you all right?" Koelsch responded.

In minutes Koelsch and Neal were free. They pulled Wilkins out of the wreckage, collected two carbines from the helicopter, and then all three hobbled into the mountains, chased by enemy fire.

Once out of range, Koelsch called a halt, taking command in his quiet self-confident manner which Wilkins, the senior officer, had no inclination to question. "Let's take stock of what we've got," Koelsch said.

In minutes they had an inventory: two carbines with ammo, a loaded .38-caliber pistol, two half canteens of water, a small flask of brandy, a signaling mirror, six flares, and one candy bar.

"Not much," Koelsch admitted, "but we can make it." Then he laughed. "Why don't we introduce ourselves."

Koelsch then offered a plan of escape. "We'll head for the sea where we can look for a boat. Once we get to sea we'll be picked up by a rescue boat," he said optimistically.

Under Koelsch's guidance the three began their trek to the coast. In their way lay several mountain ranges and a whole lot of North Korean soldiers and civilians. Traveling only at night, hiding frequently from enemy patrols and possible civilian informers, the trio wandered in a general eastward direction for nine days. They collected water from mountain pools; their only food came from potatoes dug surreptitiously from peasant fields. Wilkins's burns festered and became infected. Koelsch tended them by using the brandy to wash the wounds and his own clothing to make bandages. When the brandy ran out, Koelsch used rainwater to bathe the burns.

On the ninth day they topped a wooded crest and came face-to-face with the sea. They moved to cover and studied the area. A two-lane dirt road ran north and south a few hundred yards inland. A string of peasant huts was scattered along both sides of it. The three discussed what to do. It didn't take long to reach a decision; they were in the midst of the third day of a driving rainstorm. They wanted to find shelter until they could steal a boat and head out to sea.

As soon as darkness fell they dashed down the hill and into the nearest hut. Once inside, they posted a one-man guard while the others slept, stripped of their wet clothes.

While Koelsch stood watch early the next morning, a North Korean patrol stumbled upon the trio. The Americans tried to escape but a burst of submachine-gun fire from one of the Koreans, and their weak condition, quickly brought them to a halt.

Tied together with commo (communications) wire, the three were marched north through several villages where the peasants taunted them. Finally, they arrived at a local police headquarters. They received a bowl of rice and some tea, their first decent meal in ten days.

A high-ranking North Korean officer appeared and began interrogating the captives in Korean. Koelsch ignored his chattering and walked to the large desk where the officer had seated himself. He pounded his fist on the desktop three or four times and shouted, "Look!" Turning, he walked to Wilkins and pulled up his pant leg, revealing the maggot-infested burns. "Medicine!" Koelsch yelled. "He needs medicine."

The enemy officer glared at Koelsch for a minute, then shouted a series of orders to the guards in the room. Within minutes Wilkins was being escorted away. He said to the navy pilot as he was led off, "See you in the morning, Jack."

"Right," said Koelsch. "They'll put us on a truck in the morning and take us north."

Both were wrong. Wilkins never saw Koelsch again. Then a few days later Koelsch and Neal were separated.

Wilkins, who never did receive medical attention, and Neal both survived the horrible ordeal of the North Korean POW camp. Koelsch did not. He died on October 16, 1951, of malnutrition.

After the war, when the facts of Koelsch's heroic rescue attempt of Wilkins and his stubborn resistance to his captors became known, the secretary of the navy announced that his conduct in prison camp had set an inspiring example for other POWs. Koelsch repeatedly shared his meager rations with those sicker than him. He constantly defied the North Korean guards by demanding proper treatment for the prisoners under the accords of the Geneva Convention. He stubbornly refused to provide any information beyond his name, rank, and serial number and resisted the daily propaganda sessions.

Not only did John Koelsch's heroism on July 3, 1951, result in his being posthumously awarded the Medal of Honor on August 3, 1955, but his resistance in the POW camp served as the basis for the Code of Conduct, the set of standards adopted by the military in 1955 to guide all Americans captured by an enemy.

Throughout the summer of 1951 there was continuous, though localized, fighting for limited objectives, and no day passed without casualties. To resist the enemy and reduce casualties, the Eighth Army built massive fortifications across its hilltop positions. The log and sandbag bunkers and deep, narrow trenches along the KANSAS line resembled World War I entrenchments.

The bunkers, usually joining the lateral trenches, housed automatic weapons. Most were dug into hillsides or saddles on the military crests of hills, with the larger ones on the higher hills serving as forward command and observation posts. The bunkers were constructed with solid overhead covers and separate living quarters behind the battle stations. They often reflected the ingenuity of the occupants. Some even sported cots, floors, and makeshift furniture.

Along the trenches, in their forward walls, the rifle and bazookamen dug revetted bays for their weapons. Slightly behind them recoilless rifle emplacements were dug in and revetted. On the hill's reverse slopes, protected mortar positions were constructed. Roads were sometimes cut into the hillsides to allow tanks to move forward and fire from parapeted positions.

Camouflaged nets and shrubbery were used to conceal the bunkers. Barbed wire fences were built in front of the trench lines. Minefields were laid in such a pattern as to funnel attackers into the heaviest defense zones.

Late in August, after the truce talks had been suspended, General Van Fleet determined to resume the offensive. The biggest thorn in his side was the presence of enemy troops in the vicinity of Hwachon Reservoir (Seoul's primary source of water and electrical power). Twenty miles northeast of the reservoir lay the circular valley known to the Americans as the Punchbowl. North Koreans held the high ground to the north, east, and west of the Punchbowl. From there they could observe the U.N. defenses and bring artillery fire down on the KANSAS line.

Seizure of the enemy-held high ground would lessen the threat of attacks aimed at splitting the X Corps and the ROK I Corps along their boundary, which ran just to the east of the Punchbowl. ROK troops had begun limited offensives in the jagged ridges west of the Punchbowl on August 18. Their objective was an east-west ridge with three peaks.

The ROKs fought for five days before taking the ridge, which correspondents quickly dubbed Bloody Ridge. That same night, August 23, the North Koreans counterattacked and threw the ROKs off. Elements of the U.S. 2d Infantry Division were called in to support the ROKs, but the NKPA still refused to budge. U.N. casualties mounted. Panic spread. Only the resoluteness of a few prevented a complete rout.

LEE R. HARTELL

Korea was 1st Lt. Lee R. Hartell's second war. Born in Philadelphia on August 23, 1923, Hartell grew up in Danbury, Connecticut. In 1940, while still a senior in high school, Hartell enlisted in the Connecticut National Guard's Battery D, 192d Field Artillery. A slightly built youth, he stood just five feet eight inches tall and weighed only 135 pounds. Hartell broke family tradition by joining the army. His father, Andy Hartell, had pulled a hitch in the navy during World War I. Two of Lee's three brothers served in the navy during World War II, as did his father who reenlisted and served aboard a destroyer in the Pacific.

Lee's outfit was called to federal service in March 1941 as part of the 43d Infantry Division. He saw action as an artillery surveyor and forward observer on Guadalcanal, Rendova Island, New Guinea, and in the Philippines. He picked up a Purple Heart for wounds received in action in the Philippines.

Back home in Danbury after the war, Hartell bought a couple of surplus army trucks and went into the trucking business. The local unions proved too strong for an independent trucker, though, and Hartell soon found himself out of business. He took a job with a surveying firm but found he lacked the formal education necessary to become a licensed surveyor.

He needed a permanent career. In 1947 he reenlisted as a full-time member of the National Guard. Within a few months he'd passed the tests for a commission as a second lieutenant of artillery. He then enlisted in the regular army as a sergeant. Less than a year later he was called to duty as a reserve officer. He married his girl and spent the next two years as a training officer at Fort Dix, New Jersey.

Late in 1950 Hartell received orders to the Far East. As an experienced artillery forward observer, Hartell's transfer to Korea was expedited by events beyond his control. The battered 2d Infantry Division, fresh from its disaster at Kunu-ri, had a crying need for FOs. Hartell was snapped up by the 15th Field Artillery Battalion. Within days of arriving at Seoul, Hartell was leading a three-man FO team working with Company B, 1st Battalion, 9th Infantry.

Hartell proved his worth as an FO on January 14, 1951, when Company B was fighting in subzero weather near Wonju. After taking a hill, the cold GIs watched in awe as Hartell calmly called in an artillery barrage that effectively trapped the fleeing Chinese in the mountain gap through which they were retreating. Hartell picked up the nickname "Colonel Hilltop" for his steely manner in slaughtering the Chinese.

Beginning in February Hartell began a six-month tour as an aerial forward observer. He flew over two hundred missions, earning seven Air Medals for his effective work.

Then, in late August, an FO up front was killed. The line company in need of an FO was Company B, 9th Infantry; Hartell instantly volunteered. "Colonel Hilltop" was back.

Hartell rejoined Company B on the afternoon of August 26. The 1st Battalion, 9th Infantry, had been ordered to support ROK units trying to retake lost ground at Bloody Ridge. Company B was assigned Hill 700.

The company easily took its objective, the North Koreans falling back with only minimal resistance. Hartell, right up front with the lead platoon, adjusted artillery fire on the retreating enemy. Then he dug in for the night.

At 4:00 A.M., August 27, North Korean troops surprised Korean civilians bringing supplies up to Company B from the rear. Within seconds, firing broke out on the company's right. In rapid succession, attacks erupted all around the company's perimeter. They were surrounded!

Hartell immediately moved from his foxhole to an exposed knoll. Ignoring the screaming, yelling North Koreans, Hartell called for artillery flares. Their light revealed masses of NKPA soldiers swarming up the hill.

Hartell held his exposed position, relaying to his artillery battery the requests of platoon leader 1st Lt. Joseph Burkett. Hartell's combat experience allowed him to anticipate many of Burkett's requests. "I asked for defensive fire," Burkett said, "and Hartell told me they were already on the way. A few moments later they started to fall right where I needed them."

The fight raged for over two and one-half hours. Throughout it all Hartell remained in his exposed position atop the small knoll. He expertly maneuvered the artillery fire to do the most harm to the determined foe. Despite his best efforts, the NKPA continued their fanatical attack.

One particularly determined group of North Koreans closed to within ten yards of Hartell's position. An enemy machine-gun bullet exploded in Hartell's right hand, destroying it. Rather than seek aid, he simply picked up his radio's microphone in his good hand and continued talking to his battery. He brought a wall of artillery shells down right in front of the hill, temporarily dispersing the attackers.

They stormed back in a few minutes, closing in on Hartell's position. Amidst the yelling and shouting he stuck grimly to his radio, ignoring the chaos around him, ringing the area with a steel curtain of artillery fire. Suddenly, a bullet crashed into his chest. Hartell collapsed on the ground, still clutching his phone. In a husky but weak voice, he relayed his final instructions to the battery: "Keep firing. I think they've got us."

Burkett said, "When daylight arrived the area surrounding Hartell's position was strewn with enemy casualties. Our casualties were heavy, but would have been much heavier if it had not been for the accurate adjustments of artillery fire by Lieutenant Hartell."

On January 16, 1952, Secretary of Defense Robert Lovett presented the Medal of Honor earned by Lee Hartell to his widow and three small children. At her side, Andy Hartell sobbed silently as his son's citation was read.

Company B was thrown off Hill 700 the next night, taking heavy casualties. Among the wounded was the CO, Capt. Edward C. Krzyzowski of Cicero, Illinois. Born in Chicago on January 16, 1914, Krzyzowski first enlisted in 1935. He went to OCS in 1942, then fought his way across Europe, earning a Bronze Star. He took command of Company B in April 1951.

Refusing medical evacuation, Krzyzowski led repeated attacks over the next seventy-two hours against Hill 700. Well-emplaced North Koreans threw them back each time. On September 1, Krzyzowski wiped out two enemy bunkers holding up his company's advance. Then he personally took the lead, making it almost to the top before murderous enemy fire forced him back. When a second attack the next day again proved unsuccessful, the captain ordered his men to recover their dead and wounded and pull back. He remained behind alone, hiding beneath the debris of a destroyed bunker from where he sniped at the North Koreans for more than an hour. Only when he sustained a third wound from an enemy grenade did he leave his advanced position.

Although his multiple wounds more than justified evacuation, Krzyzowski continually refused to leave his battered company. Instead, he chose to lead his few remaining men in yet another attack on Hill 700. Progressing slowly under devastating fire, the small company again became immobilized by intense, accurate small-arms fire. Realizing that only mortars could pulverize the enemy, Krzyzowski moved forward of his company, stood in a shallow foxhole, and adjusted mortar fire on enemy emplacements less than fifty yards away.

While thus exposed, the valiant officer was cut down by an enemy sniper. Enraged by the death of their leader, the thirty or so men left in Company B assaulted the hill, overran the enemy, and took Hill 700.

On September 5, 1950, after having lost over fifteen thousand men, four thousand of them dead, the NKPA relinquished Bloody Ridge. But they did not flee. They merely pulled back to positions on the next prominent ridge, one that ran perpendicular to Bloody Ridge and sat about fifteen hundred yards north. It soon became known as Heartbreak Ridge.

In preparation for the U.N. attack on Heartbreak Ridge, the U.S. 1st Marine Division drove into the heights along the northern portion of the Punchbowl on September 11. Like their army brethren a few miles west, the marines faced a resolute foe who defended each ridge top from mutually supporting positions. Like the soldiers, the marines, often burdened by having to carry 60mm mortar or 75mm recoilless rifle rounds, in addition to their own ammo and equipment, crawled hand over hand up towering, knife-crested ridges to assault the hard-fighting enemy. Yielding only under the most direct pressure, the North Koreans always came back in a vigorous counterattack. Sometimes the same crest changed hands several times in less than twelve hours.

Company B, 1st Battalion, 7th Marines, was going up Hill 673 on September 12, 1951, when it was stopped cold by a vicious blast of mortar and machine gun fire. Casualties lay everywhere. From his position with the reserve platoon, Sgt. Frederick W. Mausert, a twenty-one-year-old from Dresher, Pennsylvania, worked his way forward through a mine field and rescued two wounded marines. Though painfully wounded in the head during this daring mission, Mausert next took his squad forward in a bayonet charge.

Struck again in the head and knocked down, Mausert regained his feet and continued his attack. He wiped out one enemy machine-gun nest singlehandedly, then took his squad forward to eliminate several more. Mausert later deliberately exposed himself to enemy machine-gun fire so members of his squad could slip past an enemy bunker and attack it from the rear. Wounded yet a third time, Mausert continued his whirlwind attack, destroying a third North Korean machine-gun nest with grenades before he died in a hail of enemy fire.

In conjunction with a French infantry battalion and several ROK infantry units, the U.S. 2d Infantry Division's 23d and 38th Infantry Regiments prepared to attack Heartbreak Ridge beginning on September 13. Beginning at 5:30 that morning, and lasting for a full thirty minutes, five battalions of U.N. artillery pounded Heartbreak Ridge. Then the rifle companies moved out.

As the GIs approached the southern reaches of the various hills making up Heartbreak, the NKPA loosed a retaliatory artillery barrage. The GIs were caught in the open. Casualties piled up. Despite their losses the companies pushed on. Before they'd covered much ground enemy machine-gun fire poured down on them from the heights. More men fell, dead or wounded. The prospects for a swift penetration of the enemy's lines quickly evaporated. It was apparent that taking Heartbreak Ridge would mean another bloody slugfest for the Indianhead division.

The battle raged furiously over the next four days. Tanks of the 72d Tank Battalion were brought forward but even their massive cannons could not dislodge the North Koreans. The enemy's firepower kept the assault forces pinned down on the ridge's lower slopes.

The 9th Infantry Regiment, barely recovered from its fight at Bloody Ridge, was fed into the fight. They conquered Hill 894, the southernmost of the three major hill masses making up Heartbreak, on September 15, but just managed to hold on against repeated enemy counterattacks. The two main hills to the north, 931 and 851, still resisted the GIs' attempts to take them from the east. To attempt to relieve the pressure on those 2d Division units driving west, the 1st Battalion, 23d Infantry Regiment, passed through the positions of the 9th Infantry Regiment on Hill 894 and tried to take Hill 931 from the south.

The attack on Hill 931 began on September 16. Artillery and air support flashed across the ridge, further denuding it of vegetation. Secure in their deep bunkers, the North Koreans simply waited patiently until the bombardment ended, then crept back into their fighting positions. As the GIs of the 1st Battalion, 23d Infantry Regiment, closed on the crest, the North Koreans opened fire. The ensuing battle seesawed for several hours, but late in the day the 1st Battalion finally ousted the NKPA from Hill 931. The weary GIs quickly assumed defensive positions in anticipation of a counterattack. It came at three o'clock the next morning.

HERBERT K. PILILAAU

Pfc. Herbert K. Pililaau arrived in Korea in July 1951. A full-blooded Hawaiian, he was born at Waianae, Oahu, on October 10, 1928. A quiet, soft-spoken youth, Pililaau turned to religion at an early age to guide him through life. He was so religious he considered applying for conscientious objector status when his draft notice arrived in March 1951. But he finally decided he had civic responsibilities as well as spiritual ones. He reported for induction. A nondrinker and nonsmoker, he preferred to read his Bible while the other trainees engaged in traditional barracks bull sessions.

Because of his introverted manner, Pililaau was the butt of more than a few jokes from the rougher members of his basic training company. At least until the tests for physical endurance began. Here, the six-foot Hawaiian surprised everyone by scoring the highest number of points of anyone in his entire training battalion. He further proved his endurance and strength when, on long, hot road marches, he was the one who carried the packs of the weaker men. Still, he remained a loner, preferring the solitude of Bible study to the company of men. He sought no recognition, no leadership position. He bothered no one and, eventually, the others stopped bothering him.

When Pililaau joined Company C, 23d Infantry, those who came with him from basic were surprised when he volunteered to man the BAR. Everyone knew that automatic weapons were among the first sought out by enemy attackers. Nevertheless, Pililaau's response was typical of him. "Someone has to do it," he said.

Pililaau barely had time to get acclimated to Korea and his new outfit before being thrown into the chaos of Bloody Ridge and Heartbreak Ridge. His squad leader, another Hawaiian who'd gone through basic with Pililaau, remembered him years later: "We all thought he was kind of a mama's boy. Then he turned out to be the strongest of us all in basic. In Korea, Herb proved he had a lot of guts."

Pililaau was on guard duty in the early morning hours of September 17 when the North Koreans sent two battalions to retake Hill 931. He raised the alarm by firing a long burst of deadly .30-caliber rounds from his BAR into their ranks. Almost immediately the rest of the company was up and firing.

The GIs fought valiantly but the weight of the massed attackers threatened to overrun them. Pililaau's platoon leader passed the word to pull back down the hill. The men started withdrawing. All except Pililaau.

Thinking only of the others, Pililaau knelt directly in the path of the on-rushing NKPA, his BAR at his shoulder. While the others scrambled down-hill, he kept up his fire until he ran out of ammo. Then he threw grenades. When those ran out he pulled out his knife and charged the enemy.

His squad leader saw what happened. "There was Herb standing up fighting a lot of the enemy. It was hand-to-hand and just Herb against all of them. We all wanted to go back up to help him but the captain said 'No.' We tried to help Herb by firing a few shots but they didn't do any good. All of a sudden, they shot him and when he went down they bayoneted him. That was it."

A half hour later, after an ammo resupply, the remnants of Company C went back up the hill. They succeeded in taking the ridge. They found Pililaau's body. Around him lay forty dead North Koreans.

For sacrificing his life to cover his company's retreat, devout, quiet Herbert K. Pililaau received a posthumous Medal of Honor on May 26, 1952.

Hill 931 changed hands several more times in the next few days. The U.S. 2d Infantry Division launched diversionary attacks against NKPA positions to the south and west to draw away North Korean units from the main objective. The plan worked, but it did not help the GIs take Heart-break. The North Koreans simply brought up fresh units to fill the voids.

On September 27 division headquarters called a halt to the attacks on Heartbreak Ridge. They realized their major mistake had been in feeding their units into the battle piecemeal. The new plan called for all three of the division's regiments to attack simultaneously, supported by air and artillery fire.

On October 4, forty-nine fighter-bombers worked over the various hill masses of Heartbreak Ridge all afternoon. Throughout the day on October 5, land artillery and naval gunfire from cruisers sitting offshore pummeled the targets. That same night the infantry attacks began. With the help of tanks they quickly overran several key objectives, easily defeating the dazed defenders.

Over the next several days the three regiments fought hard, taking one hill after another. The NKPA rushed reinforcements into the fight, but many of them were caught in the open during daylight and slaughtered by marine Corsairs. The GIs at last began taking the upper hand.

Attacking up the Mundung-ni valley west of Heartbreak Ridge in one diversionary attack was the 3d Battalion, 38th Infantry Regiment, 2d Infan-try Division. Supported by heavy tanks, the battalion conquered several key enemy hill positions before running into heavy opposition on October 8.

Sfc. Tony K. Burris, a veteran of just one year's military service, called for a BAR team from his platoon in Company L to cover him, then boldly charged the main enemy emplacement. Oblivious to the fire directed at him, Burris, who already held one Silver Star and two Purple Hearts, hugged the ground until he reached the side of the bunker. Sneaking along its side, he tossed four grenades through its apertures, killing the fifteen occupants. With this obstacle removed, the company secured the hill and dug in for the night.

The next day Burris sustained two wounds leading the attack on the next ridge north. Spotting several enemy machine-gun nests, Burris jumped to his feet, yelled "Banzai!", and charged the nearest nest. He dropped a grenade into it, destroying the emplacement. Just after he tossed a grenade into a second bunker, the twenty-two-year-old Oklahoman was killed by a burst of enemy fire. He didn't live long enough to see his grenade explode in the enemy bunker and destroy it.

Heartbreak Ridge finally fell to the U.S. 2d Infantry Division on October 13, after thirty days of incessant combat. The cost of the long battle had been very high. The 2d Infantry Division suffered over thirty-seven hundred casualties in that thirty-day period. Enemy losses were estimated at twenty-five thousand.

But the successful conclusion of the operation had removed a bulge in the X Corps line, shortened it, and brought the X Corps into phase with the IX Corps to its west.

The rest of the Eighth Army had not been idle during the 2d Infantry Division's fight around the Punchbowl. Action along the front lines was characterized by local attacks, counterattacks, and patrolling. Neither the CCF nor the NKPA was content to allow the U.N. forces to occupy their positions unmolested. Employing tactics similar to those they had used when attacking advanced U.N. formations in North Korea in November 1950, the Chinese would sweep silently out of the night to strike unsuspecting, isolated U.N. outfits. Such was the case on the night of September 6, 1951, when they fell on several units of the U.S. 3d Infantry Division.

JERRY K. CRUMP

Alert in his foxhole just inside the innermost band of barbed wire surrounding the hilltop position of Company L, 7th Infantry Regiment, near Chorwon, Corp. Jerry K. Crump heard the sound of a foot sliding on the rocky ground below him. He eased the safety pin from a fragmentation grenade, waited until he heard the noise again, then tossed the missile at it. Seconds later the flash of the explosion silhouetted several Chinese soldiers just outside the wire. Crump fired at the shadowy figures. Around him other GIs also opened fire. It was over in seconds. Quiet once again descended on the hilltop.

Although only eighteen years old, Crump was already a combat-wise soldier with nearly a year on the front lines. Born in Charlotte, North Carolina, on February 18, 1933, Crump grew up in nearby Forest City. He attended high school through the eleventh grade and then, with his parents' permission, enlisted in the army in June 1950. He was still in basic training when the NKPA stormed into South Korea. Assigned to the 3d Infantry Division, he landed with them at Wonsan in October 1950. For the next eleven months he fought in every one of his regiment's battles.

On the hill outside Chorwon, the next few hours after Crump scared off the Chinese passed uneventfully. Then, at 2:30 A.M., the night suddenly exploded in a roar of rifle and automatic-weapons fire. Red and green flares arched into the sky, adding an eerie cast to the moonlight. Whistles and bugles echoed across the hill. The sly Chinese had crept unnoticed to the outer line of wire and were now crashing through it.

Company L fought well, beating off the first attack after a wild two-hour firefight. Crump held his exposed position throughout the fight, adding his deadly rifle fire to the outgoing volleys.

After a brief lull the Chinese, estimated at a full battalion, made a desperate, last-ditch charge. They made it through the final barricade, swarming over the hill. Twice Crump left his foxhole to bayonet Chinese. Four more times he went after wounded comrades, pulling them to a shell hole, bandaging their wounds, and protecting them with his rifle fire.

Then an unseen Chinese soldier dropped a grenade into the shell hole. One of the wounded screamed in horror. Crump turned. He saw it there, sputtering. "I got it!" he yelled.

He dropped on the grenade, curling around it. The explosion threw him three feet in the air, tore a hole in his stomach, and drove shrapnel into his arms. He was badly hurt but he'd saved four men from sure death.

When the fight was over, the enemy finally repulsed, medics found Crump and the four soldiers he'd saved. Crump refused to be evacuated until assured all the others had received attention. Only then did he permit the medics to put him on a stretcher.

After several months' hospitalization Crump recovered from his wounds and returned to active duty with no serious disability. He received his Medal of Honor on June 27, 1952. Crump elected to remain in the army, making it his career.

In 1958 Crump was selected to be a pallbearer for the Korean War Unknown Soldier. He later said it was "the proudest and most humble experience of my life."

Crump retired from the army in 1975 as a master sergeant, settling in Cornelius, North Carolina. On January 11, 1977, while driving near his home, a patch of icy road succeeded where a Chinese grenade had failed; Jerry Crump died when he lost control of his car and crashed into a ditch.

Enemy activity was particularly strong in front of the U.S. 25th Infantry Division in mid-September. A part of the IX Corps, the 25th held the corps' left flank, adjacent to the U.S. 3d Infantry Division in the neighboring I Corps. While attempting to throw the enemy off Hill 520, north of Kumhwa, Company A, 1st Battalion, 27th Infantry Regiment, ran into a well-emplaced Chinese force. After fighting for eight hours to take the hill, Company A was bled nearly dry. On September 12, Company B was ordered to move up and continue the slugfest.

Leading Company B's first platoon was 2d Lt. Jerome A. Sudut. A thirty-three-year-old from Wausau, Wisconsin, Sudut had served five years in the enlisted ranks before receiving a battlefield commission in July 1951.

Almost immediately upon assuming the lead, Sudut's platoon took heavy casualties from a strongly defended enemy machine gun. Ordering his men to cover him, Sudut went after the gun alone. Firing a tommy gun from the hip, he killed three of the enemy in silencing the gun, but was hit himself.

Sudut returned to his scattered platoon and started issuing orders for the final push. A few minutes later the enemy bunker blazed anew with machine-gun fire. Unknown to the Americans, a concealed tunnel network had allowed Chinese to move back undetected into the position.

Determined to silence the bunker once and for all, Sudut charged back up the hill, accompanied by a BAR man. When his companion was cut down in a hail of enemy fire, Sudut picked up the BAR and continued his charge.

He was hit a second time before he reached the bunker, but went on. When only a few yards from the bunker he ran out of ammo. He dropped the BAR. Pulling his trench knife from its scabbard, he plunged into the bunker.

When the platoon caught up with its leader, they found two Chinese machine gunners dead behind their gun, cut down by Sudut's fire. The lieutenant lay fatally wounded, partially across a third enemy soldier. The trench knife was still clenched in his hand, its blade buried deep in the Chinese throat.

Although the bulk of the fighting in Korea in the late summer of 1951 was carried out by the ground forces, the Far East Air Force materially contributed to the successes on the ground. Through close-air support tactical missions U.N. fighter-bombers destroyed thousands of enemy soldiers and saved thousands of U.N. lives.

The Fifth Air Force, based in Japan, concentrated the bulk of its medium bomber sorties on the interdiction of enemy supply lines. Railroads, bridges, highways, marshaling yards, and supply depots were hit repeatedly to impede the southward movement of troops and equipment. In August the Fifth Air Force inaugurated a rail-cutting program called *Strangle*. By destroying enemy supply trains they hoped to weaken the forward supply chain and reduce the enemy's capability to resist the Eighth Army's ground attacks. Because the Chinese moved most of their supplies at night, the majority of *Strangle* missions were conducted under cover of darkness. The major instrument in the "night intruders" sorties was a World War II-vintage bomber, the B-26 Marauder.

JOHN S. WALMSLEY

One of the "night intruders" was Capt. John S. Walmsley, Jr., a native of Baltimore, Maryland, where he was born January 7, 1920. At age twenty-two he enlisted in the army air force. After successfully completing flight training, he was commissioned in 1943. Though he itched to test his considerable flying skills in actual combat, that would not happen in World War II. Instead, he spent the war as a flight instructor at Turner Army Air Field, Georgia.

Between 1946 and 1949 Walmsley served in Japan as a pilot in a bombardment squadron. When the air force was established as a separate service branch in 1947, Walmsley switched to it, retaining his rank and mission. Stationed back in the States when the Korean War started, Walmsley returned to Japan in June 1951. He drew an assignment as a B-26 bomber pilot in the 8th Bombardment Squadron, 3d Bomb Group. On August 18, 1951, his squadron was tapped to take part in *Strangle*.

Walmsley's twenty-sixth night intruder mission began normally on September 14, 1951. The target area was a north-south rail line near Yangdok, North Korea, in the center of the peninsula west of Wonsan. Flying low over the valley through which the railroad ran, Walmsley spotted a supply-laden train emerging from a mountain tunnel. Setting up a bombing run, Walmsley flew toward the train as slowly as he dared. At precisely the right moment he triggered his bombs.

An ammo car on the train disintegrated in a huge red explosion, breaking the train in two and halting both sections. Banking in a sharp turn, Walmsley flew back over the train, strafing it with the 20mm cannon in his plane's nose. As he pulled out of the run he cursed. His guns were either out of ammo or jammed. Climbing to altitude, he radioed for another B-26 in the area. The train was burning but not destroyed. Walmsley wanted to finish the job.

"Where's the target?" the other pilot asked. There were several other fires in the area, making it difficult for him to identify the train.

"Follow me," radioed Walmsley. "I'll lead you down."

When the second B-26 was in position for the run, Walmsley radioed, "Watch for the target." Then he turned to begin his run.

With the other bomber following, Walmsley closed on the burning train. As he drew closer, Walmsley dramatically pointed to the target by turning on the powerful searchlight newly installed in the nose of his plane. Through intense antiaircraft fire he led the way down the valley, illuminating the train.

The other B-26, taking advantage of the full visibility, fired into the train, causing more damage. Walmsley, though, would not be satisfied until he'd destroyed the locomotive. He turned for another pass.

Aligning himself with the target, he swooped down, his searchlight stabbing at the train like a long, pointing finger. "My God," warned the other pilot, "they'll blow you out of the sky with that thing on!"

Intent only on highlighting the target, Walmsley flew right through the ground fire, clearing a path for his companion. With all the fire aimed at the lit-up B-26, the second plane came in low, guns blazing. The locomotive blew up.

But, as Walmsley tried to fly out of the valley, his bomber suddenly yawed violently to the right. Enemy machine-gun rounds had severed the fuel line to the right engine. Walmsley immediately ordered his crew to bail out; only one man, the flight engineer, made it.

Seconds later a brilliant explosion cut the night. The engineer thought Walmsley's plane had flown into a mountain. When the engineer was released from a POW camp in 1953 he confirmed the other B-26 pilot's story of John Walmsley's heroism. His posthumous Medal of Honor was awarded on June 12, 1954.

In the I Corps area of operations, on the far west of the Eighth Army's line, a modest advance of about eight miles to a new defensive line named JAMESTOWN was proposed by the corps commander in late September. According to the plan, JAMESTOWN would begin on the west bank of the Imjin River northeast of Munsan-ni, then arch northeastward to about five miles north of Chorwon.

Seizure of the key terrain features along this new line would protect vital communications routes, permit development of the Seoul-Chorwon railroad, and allow the main line of resistance (MLR) to be advanced. Also, the offensive would keep the enemy off balance and prevent I Corps troops from getting stale.

All four divisions of I Corps would be used. On the far left stood the ROK 1st Division, followed by the 1st British Commonwealth Division, the U.S. 1st Cavalry Division, and the U.S. 3d Infantry on the corps' right boundary with the IX Corps. United Nations intelligence identified four Chinese armies—42d, 47th, 64th, and 65th—facing the attackers.

The move to JAMESTOWN, dubbed Operation *Commando*, began on October 3, 1951. Unusually dry, cool, clear weather permitted full utilization of air power. Only moderate enemy resistance met every attacking unit except for the 1st Cavalry Division. The dismounted troopers had to battle for every foot of ground. Strong bunkers supporting each other with interlocking fields of fire dotted every ridge line and hillside in the cavalry's path. The CCF also made good use of artillery and mortars to slow the division.

Slowly, steadily, though, the I Corps pushed the Chinese back. The dogged enemy defense took a particularly heavy toll on 1st Cavalry Division line companies. With some companies reduced to but a few dozen men, they frequently lacked the strength needed to hold hard-won objectives against Chinese counterattacks.

Not until October 19 were the final objectives of *Commando* secured. In the course of the operation I Corps suffered over four thousand casualties, with the 1st Cavalry Division alone suffering twenty-nine hundred dead and wounded. Chinese losses were estimated at twenty-one thousand, with the battered 1st Cavalry Division accounting for nearly sixteen thousand of that total.

Attainment of the JAMESTOWN line did not mean relief for the battle-weary cavalrymen. Every attempt the division made over the next few weeks to cross the Yokkok-chon River near Sangnyong-ni, an important supply base for the CCF, was met with strong resistance. The 2d Battalion, 5th Cavalry Regiment, fought for several days near the end of October to clear the Chinese off strategic Hill 200, overlooking the Yokkok-chon. They had only limited success until a gutsy little lieutenant took it upon himself to remove the Chinese.

LLOYD L. BURKE

While the 2d Battalion bled itself against the Chinese Hill, 1st Lt. Lloyd L. Burke, who'd served with Company G, 2d Battalion, 5th Cavalry Regiment, for just over a year, was at the regimental rear. His tour of duty in Korea was up and he was going home; he even had his ticket in his pocket.

There was no doubt in anyone's mind that Burke deserved to go home. Since his arrival he'd fought with his company in North Korea, facing the hordes of Red Chinese pouring across the Yalu. When other men turned tail and fled, Burke stood strong, guiding his platoon through the enveloping enemy. For skillfully taking his outfit through a Chinese roadblock near Samsori on November 28, 1950, Burke received the DSC.

A lot of men would have used the decoration as a reason to avoid further combat—after all, he'd surely proven his worth—but not Burke. He desired no cushy staff job. His place was at the front, leading the war-weary enlisted soldiers by personal example.

Burke understood perhaps better than most other officers the need for strong leadership. Born in Tichnor, Arkansas, on September 29, 1924, Burke attended Henderson State College in Arkadelphia, Arkansas, for a short while before enlisting in the army in April 1943. He spent nearly two years in Italy as an enlisted member of a combat engineer outfit. Though he saw some good officers during his tour, most did not impress him. He vowed if he ever sported gold braid on his hat he'd be the best officer he could be.

After his discharge in January 1946, Burke returned to Henderson State. He studied hard, working toward his degree, and actively participating in the school's ROTC program. Twice he served as president of his fraternity and was president of his junior and senior classes. Though too short in stature to play college football, Burke loved the game and played on his fraternity's intramural team. It was during one such game that Burke picked up a nickname that stuck with him for life. After dodging through the opposing line for a touchdown a teammate shouted, "Did you see how he scooted through that line? Just like a scooter!" Burke became "Scooter" from that moment forward.

Burke married while at Henderson State and started a family. When he graduated on May 28, 1950, he was named the ROTC's Distinguished Military Graduate. That honor carried with it the opportunity for a commission in the Regular Army. Burke leaped at the chance. Five months later he was in Korea.

In addition to the DSC, Burke had also earned two Purple Hearts for wounds received in action during his tour. When his orders arrived sending him home, Burke was anxious to be on his way. His wife and eighteen-month-old son were waiting for him in Stuttgart, Arkansas.

Then the 2d Battalion started throwing itself against Hill 200. For several days the companies of Burke's battalion had been trying without success to dislodge the Chinese. Time after time they moved against Hill 200 only to be met by showers of grenades, mortar fire, small-arms, and automatic-weapons fire. From his bivouac in the rear Burke followed the progress of the fight. Finally, he couldn't stand it anymore. "I couldn't see leaving my guys up there without trying to do something," he said.

The first thing Burke did was load eight to ten Korean porters with supplies, ammo, rifles, and grenades. Then he led them on the two-mile trek to the front.

What Burke found there shocked him. Never before had he seen such demoralized men. The heavy casualties (there were only thirty-five men left in the whole company), the incessant boom of exploding mortars, and the slim prospect for survival had totally whipped the GIs. "These men were completely beat," he remembered years later. "They lay huddled in foxholes, unable to move. They all had the thousand-yard stare of men who'd seen too much fighting, too much death."

He knew something had to be done. Only positive action could revitalize these men.

Burke hauled up an abandoned 57mm recoilless rifle and fired three rounds point-blank at the first enemy bunker uphill. Nothing happened. The bunker, and nearly all the others, was a wooden-fronted structure covering a cave carved right into the hill. Grenades continued to fly out of the Chinese trench onto the Americans.

Grabbing an M-1 from an abandoned foxhole, Burke positioned himself in a spot that gave him a clear shot at the Chinese trench line. Next time a Chinese popped up to throw a grenade, Burke drew a bead on his head and fired. He thought he saw the man's head jerk, but within minutes another grenade flew from the trench. Burke kept firing at every target, but the grenades kept coming.

"I used to consider myself a pretty fair shot, but this was getting ridiculous," Burke said. "I had to do something."

He handed his rifle to a nearby soldier, armed a grenade, and, catapulting from the trench, dashed for the base of the enemy trench, about thirty yards away. He careened into the base, grateful for the two-foot dirt wall which now protected him from the Chinese.

During a brief lull in the firing, Burke jumped up and over the wall into the trench. What he saw surprised him. Four or five dead Chinese lay sprawled on the bottom of the trench, each killed by a single rifle shot to the head. He hadn't missed after all. He tossed his grenade down the trench and jumped out.

By now the Chinese knew where Burke lay. They started dropping grenades on him from directly overhead. Most rolled further downhill to explode harmlessly. Some went off within yards of Burke's prone form. Burke snatched three grenades right out of the air and tossed them back at the Chinese. Finally, he said to himself, "You dummy. This isn't very smart, you'd better get out of here." He sprinted downhill.

Back in his own trench Burke commandeered the one remaining workable machine gun, a .30-caliber air-cooled weapon, and two boxes of ammo.

His foray into the enemy's lines had shown him a way to flank the Chinese trenches. If he could sneak up on the enemy's flanks, that move might galvanize the still-reluctant GIs into action.

All alone, laden with the gun and its ammo, Burke worked his way to the right of the American positions. After he crawled up a small draw, he came upon a Korean grave. Like all Korean graves, this one was mounded high with dirt. Burke crawled up on top of the grave for a look.

What he saw astounded him. Below him, not more than one hundred yards away, sat the main Chinese trench. It ran as far as he could see, disappearing out of sight around the far side of the hill. All along its length were Chinese soldiers. Some fired mortars, others threw grenades. Most, though, seemed complacent as they laughed and chatted away.

Burke's blood raged.

Quickly setting up the light machine gun, Burke fed in a belt of ammo. He held his breath, then pulled the trigger.

He started at the forward part of the trench and sprayed lead into it. His main targets were the mortars which had caused so much trouble for his men. He hosed those positions repeatedly until he was sure the Chinese were dead.

Next, he turned his attention to an enemy machine gun. He pressed the trigger a few times. His deadly accurate fire killed those gunners, too.

Through all this the Chinese were too shocked by Burke's audacious attack to respond. They just milled about, jabbering away. Burke couldn't believe his luck. "It was just like shooting ducks sitting on a pond," Burke recalled.

For several more minutes Burke played his machine-gun fire up and down the enemy trench, killing them left and right. Finally, the stunned Chinese reacted. A mass exodus began, with the Chinese climbing over one another to flee from the killing ground.

About this time Burke's machine gun jammed. While he worked frantically to clear it, a bold Chinese soldier snuck up and started lobbing grenades at Burke. Shrapnel from one tore into the back of Burke's hand but he barely noticed. When he'd cleared the jam, Burke shot and killed the grenadier.

A small group of Americans led by Sgt. Arthur L. Foster now joined Burke and added its rifle fire to the carnage. Below them enemy soldiers continued their retreat. Burke wasn't about to let them escape. He pulled off his field jacket, wrapped it around the machine gun's hot barrel, lifted the weapon from its tripod, and, trailing a full belt of ammo draped over his shoulder, started toward the enemy trench.

Firing as he walked, he cut down a number of Chinese stragglers. With Sergeant Foster at his side, Burke moved along the enemy trench line, spraying machine-gun fire before him. It was quite a feat for a 120-pounder standing just five feet eight inches tall.

When he ran out of machine-gun ammo, Burke used grenades and his pistol to flush out remaining Chinese from their bunkers. In a few more minutes it was over. The hill was cleared of Chinese. Burke and the soldier who had followed him returned to their own trench line. Later that night another unit of the 1st Cavalry Division relieved them. For a while their fighting was over. And for Lloyd L. Burke, he could continue his journey home.

The relieving unit had the unpleasant task of policing up the Chinese dead from Burke's attack. They counted no less than 250 bodies scattered around the hill; about 120 lay crumpled in the trench.

Less than six months later, while stationed at The Infantry School at Fort Benning, Georgia, where he taught small-unit tactics to OCS students, Lieutenant Burke received word he would join the ranks of America's bravest of the brave. The White House ceremony was held on April 11, 1952.

Burke remained in the army, serving in a variety of command and staff positions. In 1965 Burke took his battalion, the 2d Battalion, 16th Infantry Regiment, 1st Infantry Division, to Vietnam. His tour in that war zone lasted a mere eight days. The helicopter he was riding in was shot down in a Viet Cong ambush. Burke was evacuated back to the States where he remained hospitalized for nine months. "Scooter" Burke finished his thirty-five years of service to his country as a full colonel and the army's liaison officer to Congress.

General Van Fleet's efforts in the August-October period had inflicted great casualties on the Chinese and North Koreans. Undoubtedly, their capacity for offensive action had been severely damaged. As a result, the war of movement ended in Korea. From November 1951 onward, the war in Korea became one of local battles for dominating terrain features along the foe's respective defense lines. Efforts similar to those of the U.N. command at Heartbreak Ridge and in reaching the JAMESTOWN Line would be repeated endlessly in grim monotony in the months ahead.

No doubt the improved military position of the United Nations Command contributed to the Chinese offer in late October to return to the negotiating table.

Chapter Ten
Second Korean Winter

Negotiations among the opposing forces recommenced on October 25, 1951. This time the U.N. negotiators insisted on a site less favorable to Communist propaganda exploitation. Selected for the new round of negotiations was the small village of Panmunjom, on the north side of the Imjin River about midway between Communist-held Kaesong and U.N.-held Munsan-ni. A neutral zone around the conference site and the road leading to it from both sides was one of the first points agreed upon. From there the negotiations bogged down and would drag on for twenty-one more months.

Once the two sides began meeting, a lull settled over the battlefield. This resulted primarily from General Ridgway's decision to halt general offensive ground operations in Korea. His decision was based on two major factors: the cost of further major assaults on the enemy's defenses would be more than the results would justify; and, since peace might result at any time from the reopened armistice talks, costly large-scale offensives were ruled out. According to orders issued by Ridgway on November 12, Eighth Army was to cease offensive operations and begin an active defense all along the front. Any attacks were to be limited to those necessary to strengthen the MLR and to establish an outpost line three thousand to five thousand yards forward of the main line.

Although Ridgway's orders changed the Eighth Army's mission to one of defense, he did not mean that all actions should cease. Indeed, patrols went forward from the MLR nightly. Their mission was to feel out the enemy, capture prisoners, and locate enemy positions. From an intelligence point of view the patrols often proved futile. Few prisoners were taken and, more often than not, contact with the enemy was not effected. But the patrolling kept the frontline troops alert and gave them valuable experience and training under combat conditions. This type of patrol formed the majority of activity for the balance of the war.

Most of the patrols began at the outposts forward of the MLR. Rarely garrisoned by more than a platoon, these isolated outposts provided an early warning to the MLR of enemy attacks, as well as acting as observation posts to report on enemy activity.

Because of their forward location, the outposts also had an effect on the peace negotiations. A key point of the discussions centered on establishment of a demilitarized zone. In the initial armistice meetings a compromise had been reached establishing a DMZ not less than four miles wide with the line of contact as the median. The capture of hostile terrain by either side, then, improved its position relative to the future DMZ.

At times over the remaining months of the war both sides went to great lengths to capture barren hilltops that advanced their positions a few thousand yards. The clashes were violent, with heavy casualties for defenders and attackers alike. The mission of defending these outposts often demanded extraordinary heroism.

JAMES L. STONE

The third platoon of Company F, 8th Cavalry Regiment, 1st Cavalry Division, held a hilltop outpost above the Imjin River, west of Yonchon. Sitting some two thousand yards in front of the MLR, the outpost overlooked a broad valley fronting the CCF defensive positions. From here the GIs could observe any Chinese movement across their front. Whenever targets presented themselves, the GIs called down an artillery barrage. Their nightly patrols probed deeply into the Chinese lines, taking prisoners, causing casualties, and generally making life miserable for the enemy.

The GIs knew they were hurting the enemy because the Chinese not only frequently pummelled the hilltop with artillery and mortar barrages, but had several times sent reinforced platoons to attack the outpost at night. All had been repulsed. But everyone knew the CCF wouldn't give up.

Commanding the forty-nine men of the third platoon was 1st Lt. James L. Stone, a twenty-eight-year-old from Pine Bluff, Arkansas. After graduating from the University of Arkansas in 1947, Stone was commissioned an army second lieutenant through the ROTC. One year later he was called to active duty.

Following several years of routine stateside assignments, Stone received orders to Korea in March 1951. He joined the 2d Battalion, 8th Cavalry, as an infantry replacement officer. Over the next nine months Stone alternated between Companies F and G as a platoon leader. The attrition rate for frontline junior officers was so high the survivors were frequently shuttled between officerless platoons in different companies to provide needed leadership.

Most of Stone's time, though, was spent with the third platoon of Company F. He knew most of the men, trusted them, and was proud of them. His bond with them showed clearly in October during Operation *Commando*. During an attack on a numberless hill, his platoon had several men shot down within close range of an enemy machine gun. Disregarding its deadly fire, Stone made two trips in front of his lines to pull the men to safety. For this he received a Silver Star.

Soon after dusk on November 21, 1951, Stone's listening posts—two- and three-man teams placed several hundred yards downhill from the platoon's main positions—reported movement about them.

At his CP Stone radioed instructions to his LPs. Sit tight, he told them, it's probably just another routine Chinese probe. On the cold, moonless night the GIs couldn't see more than a few yards. But they could hear the scrape of cloth against rock, the occasional clang of equipment knocking together.

Just as Stone prepared to order his LPs to throw grenades at the sounds, the night exploded in a violent prism of color. One instant there was silence, the next the roar and crash of incoming artillery shells.

Everyone pulled himself deep into the bunkers. Stone worried about his LPs, but it was too late: the men were probably already dead or captured.

The enemy barrage ended within five minutes. The more experienced GIs knew what was coming next. Stone radioed his supporting artillery battery for flares. When they burst overhead their million-candlepower light revealed a chilling sight: several hundred CCF soldiers swarming up the hillside. At least two full companies of Chinese infantrymen were bent on throwing the GIs off the hill.

Stone's third platoon was just as determined not to yield.

With bugles and whistles guiding their deployment, the Chinese charged upward. Stone ordered his two 60mm mortars into action. That was the strongest support he'd receive all night. United Nations artillery batteries couldn't drop their shells on Stone's side of the hill.

Stone crawled through the trench to the point of heaviest contact. Repeatedly exposing himself to the blistering volume of enemy fire, he moved about the area, giving orders and offering encouragement.

"Here they come. Fire slow. Make every shot count. Pick your targets."

His presence calmed the GIs.

Several times Stone boosted himself above the trench line to fire at the attackers. On occasion he actually stood atop the sandbagged lip of the trench to fire on the Chinese.

One of Stone's most effective weapons that night was the platoon's flamethrower. Its operator would send sheets of roaring flames into knots of Chinese closing on the platoon's positions. The screams of its victims and the smell of burned flesh testified to the flamethrower's effectiveness. Then it malfunctioned. The operator worked frantically to repair it but was unsuccessful before he was felled.

"Flamethrower out!" The call came down the trench.

Unwilling to concede the loss of this important weapon, Stone scurried along the trench until he reached the dead operator. Stone pulled the bulky, clumsy tanks from the corpse. He tried to find the source of the malfunction but it was too dark at the bottom of the trench.

Unmindful of the lethal danger from the mortar and artillery shell fragments whistling through the air, Stone hefted the tanks atop the sandbags, then pulled himself out of the trench. Straddling the sandbags, he used the light of flares to find and repair the problem. Even when enemy bullets tore into the sandbags just inches from him, Stone refused to budge until he had the flamethrower working. Only then did he drop from his exposed position.

"Put it to good use," he said as he passed the tanks to a new operator.

Back at his CP Stone quickly assessed the battle reports from his squads. He moved a few men to weak spots but couldn't do much more. He just didn't have the men. He gave his troops all the encouragement he could, urging them to "Hold on! We gotta make it 'til morning!"

Despite the heavy resistance put up by Stone's men, the enemy broke through. "Chinese in the wire!" came the cry. Stone wasted no time in responding. He rushed to the scene of the breach. He could just make out three Chinese inching their way through a hole blasted in the encircling barbed wire.

Without a word he bounded out of the trench, making straight for the intruders. Swinging his carbine like a club and brandishing his trench knife, Stone brained the closest Chinese and knifed the other two before they knew what hit them.

On his way back to the safety of the trench, he was hit in the right leg. He stumbled. One of his GIs started for him. "Get back," Stone yelled. He didn't want anyone hurt because of him. He dragged himself into the trench, collapsing in a heap on its bottom. He let a medic bind the wound, then, hobbling along, returned to his CP.

Somehow, the gallant band of GIs fought off the Chinese. With a blare of bugles the Chinese firing slowed until it had all but stopped. Shadowy figures could be seen slinking downhill past boulders and shell-torn tree stumps.

"They'll be back," Stone warned. "Get ready for them."

In the lull Stone kept himself busy, moving among the wounded, helping dress their wounds, and carrying them back to the aid station. He took a head count. More than a dozen of his platoon were dead; more than half the survivors were wounded, some more than once.

When Stone's company commander radioed him and volunteered to send reinforcements, Stone declined. He felt his remaining platoon members could hold out and he didn't want to risk any more lives. It was now past midnight and the impending dawn would see the Chinese abandon their attack.

Stone moved among his men, offering encouragement. "Only a few more hours until dawn," he assured them. "You can make it until then. Only a few more hours."

Around 1:00 A.M. the Chinese came again. As before, the silence was suddenly broken by bugle calls. Seconds later, mortar shells dropped from the sky, then the Chinese infantry opened fire.

For more than an hour Stone heroically directed his platoon in holding off the attackers. Constantly on the move, he seemed to show up wherever the going was roughest. He'd magically appear, adding his fire to the battle and urging his soldiers to hang on.

The fighting was so tough two of the platoon's three machine guns burned out their barrels firing so much ammo. Stone took charge of the remaining gun. He carried it to the point of the perimeter where the Chinese threatened another breakthrough. His deadly accurate fire broke up that attack.

While Stone was moving the automatic weapon to yet another vantage point, a Chinese rifle bullet tore a chunk of flesh from his neck. Blood gushed from the deep wound, but Stone ignored the pain. Instead, he fought his way down the trench, firing quick bursts over the sandbags.

Finally, the loss of blood weakened Stone. He slipped to the bottom of the trench. Faint and in great pain, Stone still refused to give up the fight. At his request, others passed empty magazines to him. He loaded the magazines, then handed them back to those still on their feet. Stone even cleaned a few carbines for the others before a medic patched him up.

Stone took stock of his platoon. Less than twenty men were still on their feet. Every man in his platoon was dead, or wounded at least once. The Chinese had already overwhelmed the flanks of his line. From a firing position in the trench, Stone could see the enemy massing for another attack. Around him small knots of Chinese and Americans grappled in desperate fights to the death.

Stone was as proud of his men's bravery and ability to stand and fight as any combat commander has ever been, yet he knew that courage alone was sometimes not enough. The Chinese wanted the hill and were willing to absorb great casualties to take it.

He had no idea exactly how many of his men were still alive, but to those around him Stone spread the word, "Pull out. Get out of here. Get back to the company as best you can. I'll cover you."

Slowly, as quickly as the fighting permitted, the survivors of the third platoon withdrew from the fight. The Chinese attackers sensed the reduction of fire-power and rushed forward. GIs pulling out could hear Lieutenant Stone's voice above the sharp crack of his carbine, still encouraging the others to leave.

Then it was over. The Chinese had the hill. And they had Lieutenant Stone and a half dozen of his men who were too badly wounded to escape.

Stone was unconscious by the time the Chinese got to him. They hastily applied crude bandages, loaded him on a stretcher, and sent him off on a journey that ended at Officers Camp No. 2 on the Yalu River. His stay there lasted twenty-two months. Life in the camp was cruel and harsh. Food was scarce, medical care nonexistent, and disease rampant. One-third of all Americans captured during the Korean War died in captivity. There would have been more except the Chinese finally realized they couldn't use the POWs as a bargaining chip at Panmunjom if they all died. While conditions were never good, they did improve after that second winter.

When Lieutenant Stone was finally exchanged during the processing at Freedom Village on September 2, 1953, he was quite surprised when he was called out of line by a general officer. He thought he had been selected at random to be interviewed by the press. He was to be interviewed, for sure, but his selection had not been at random.

Brig. Gen. Ralph Osborne announced to the assembled reporters that Lt. James Stone was to receive the Medal of Honor. As had been the award for Hiroshi Miyamura, Stone's citation was classified "Secret" to prevent any retaliation from his captors.

Stone was stunned at the announcement. He tried to tell the general it was surely a mistake, but the general assured him it was no mistake. The survivors of the third platoon had wholeheartedly recommended Stone for the prestigious award.

President Eisenhower hung the Medal of Honor around Stone's neck on October 27, 1953. Still not convinced he had merited the medal, Stone accepted it on behalf of every man of the third platoon that fought alongside him that terrible night.

Stone continued his career in the army, retiring as a full colonel in December 1976. His service included twelve months in Vietnam as the senior advisor to the Army of the Republic of Vietnam Noncommissioned Officers Academy at Nha Trang in 1969–70. Today he is a general contractor of custom homes.

The night after Lieutenant Stone was captured the Chinese struck in strength at the U.S. 3d Infantry Division's positions to the north of the U.S. 1st Cavalry Division. Company F, 2d Battalion, 7th Infantry Regiment, held a key knoll right in the center of their push. Wounded early in the attack, Pfc. Noah O. Knight of Jefferson, South Carolina, refused to be evacuated and, in the day and night that followed, continually maneuvered through the cold and mud to keep laying fire on the ever-attacking CCF. When he finally ran out of ammo, the twenty-two-year-old veteran of three years' service charged a three-man Chinese demolition team, swinging his empty rifle like a club. He smashed two of the Chinese to the ground but the third set off the charge. The three Chinese and Knight died in the explosion.

The U.N. attacks during the late summer and fall of 1951 had undoubtedly improved their military stance and deeply hurt the enemy, thus encouraging the latter's resumption of armistice negotiations. However, U.N. casualties continued to climb. With negotiations resumed and the end of the war apparently in sight, the flood of telegrams to American homes created considerable concern. It was one thing to fight and die for one's country and its system of government, quite another to fight and die for a barren, rocky hillside halfway around the world. While protests against America's involvement in Korea would never reach the level of the Vietnam War, there was a growing concern about the war's lack of progress.

Politicians put pressure on the Pentagon to end the war, and the Pentagon, in turn, put pressure on General Ridgway. Consequently, when the Chinese Communists announced at Panmunjom on November 6 that they would accept the actual current line of contact as the permanent demarcation line, the U.N. readily agreed. On November 27, 1951, both sides initialed an agreement to that effect, provided the final armistice was signed within thirty days.

Essentially, the CCF received a thirty-day reprieve. They apparently had no intention of honoring their commitment. Instead, they used the time to reinforce their defensive positions in depth until they were almost impervious to attack. With both their flanks firmly anchored on the sea, the CCF held a solid line that would require an effort worthy of the campaign before Verdun in 1916 to dislodge them. No Western power had the desire for such a slaughter.

Ever mindful of international political considerations and still smarting from the heavy losses it suffered in the spring and fall campaigns of 1951, the U.N. never again undertook any large-scale offensive actions in Korea.

The week before the expiration of the thirty-day waiting period saw major troop disposition changes on both sides. The U.S. 45th Infantry Division, the first National Guard division to arrive from the States, landed in Korea and replaced the U.S. 1st Cavalry Division in its positions north of Seoul in the I Corps sector; the 1st Cavalry Division rotated to Japan. While some of its units returned to Korea, it never fought there again as a unit.

The North Korean I Corps left its positions on the western end of the line to move opposite the ROK II Corps on the far eastern end of the MLR. As a result, the CCF now held the entire western and central portions of the line. The NKPA had its forces in the rugged eastern sector, where there was little likelihood of a major U.N. thrust. This shift spoke not only of the apparent weakness of the NKPA, but of the mistrust the Chinese had for their comrades' ability.

The December 27 deadline passed with no agreement. The major stumbling block was the prisoners held by each side. The Chinese and North Koreans held about 11,500 POWs. Of these some 3,200 were Americans— out of 11,224 officially reported as missing in action. The U.N. held over 132,000 POWs, of whom some 95,500 were North Koreans, 20,700 were Chinese, and the balance were pro-Communist South Koreans who had joined the NKPA. A large number of the North Koreans and Chinese (many of whom were former Nationalist soldiers impressed into the CCF after the 1949 Communist takeover of China) had no desire to return to Communist rule. They had indicated to their captors they would refuse repatriation. Because of the harsh treatment received by former Soviet prisoners of the Germans when they returned to their homeland at the end of World War II, the U.N. felt it had no choice but to honor the desires of the prisoners in its care. Besides, the U.N. command had no intention of returning what amounted to an entire army to the Communists.

On January 2, 1952, the U.N. announced at Panmunjom its decision regarding the POWs. Only those prisoners who expressly stated a wish to return home would be repatriated.

The Chinese were livid, but not because they were concerned with the welfare of their men. Rather, if a large percentage of Chinese and North Koreans refused repatriation, the West would score a major propaganda coup with a corresponding loss of face for the Chinese. They adamantly refused to accept the American position.

The U.N. delegates also refused to yield. As a result, the war in Korea would continue for another year and a half. The U.S. would suffer another thirty-seven thousand casualties while the talks dragged on.

At the front lines few of the U.N. infantrymen were aware of the daily negotiations at Panmunjom. For them the war was the nightly probes by enemy patrols, harassing enemy artillery, their own patrols into enemy territory, cold, damp bunkers, the dead, and the wounded. While the opposing sides argued at Panmunjom the daily grind of the war went on.

RONALD E. ROSSER

As the oldest of seventeen children, Ron Rosser often found himself protecting his younger siblings from schoolyard bullies around their hometown of Crooksville, Ohio. He gave more than one bloody nose to those foolish enough to pick on his brothers and sisters.

When Ron Rosser entered the army right after his seventeenth birthday on October 24, 1946, he passed the mantle of protectorship on to his next youngest brother, Richard. Ron Rosser spent nearly three years in the army, all of it as a paratrooper with the 82d Airborne Division.

When Ron received his discharge in July 1949, Richard then entered the army. Ron went to work in the coal mines near Crooksville.

It was a cold day in February 1951 when Ron Rosser came home from work. He knew something was wrong as soon as he entered the house. He found his mother sobbing in a corner of the living room. In her hand was the telegram advising of Richard's death in Korea on February 10.

After the funeral a few weeks later Ron Rosser pulled his parents aside. "I'm going to get even with the Commies for what they did to Dick," he told them. "I'm going back in the army and going to Korea. I'm going to kill as many of them as I can."

True to his vow, Rosser reenlisted in May 1951. After a short refresher course at Fort Breckenridge, Kentucky, he was sent to the 187th Airborne Regiment in Japan. That was not to his liking. He told his CO he'd enlisted to fight in Korea. Japan was not Korea. He wanted to go to Korea. The CO started the paperwork. Rosser finally arrived in Korea in August 1951. He was assigned to the Heavy Mortar Company, 38th Infantry Regiment, 2d Infantry Division, as a forward observer.

Rosser got his first taste of combat at Bloody Ridge in late August and early September. He called in a lot of mortar fire on the enemy, killing scores. Whenever possible he'd join the line companies as a rifleman, frequently volunteering for patrols and raids. He experienced a considerable amount of combat throughout the fall and winter months of 1951 as the 38th Infantry fought to maintain their positions near Kumhwa, at the base of the Iron Triangle.

On January 12, 1952, Rosser and his buddy, Cpl. Stanley W. "Smitty" Smith, were attached as an FO team to Company L, 38th Infantry. Company L, about 170 men in strength, was to conduct a daylight raid on Hill 472, about one and one-half miles forward of the MLR. Intelligence reported the hill lightly defended. The GIs were to snatch a few prisoners, destroy the enemy's bunkers, and kill as many of them as they could.

The company commander, Captain Davies, led his men forward just before daybreak. The temperature stood at minus twenty. About a foot of crusty snow covered the ground. Halfway across the broad valley leading to Hill 472 at the edge of the Kumhwa Valley, Company L came under fire. The Chinese on the hill could plainly see the Americans against the snow. They loosed a barrage of mortars and machine gun fire on Company L.

Rosser could see hundreds of Chinese swarming on the hill. More than a dozen trench lines encircled Hill 472, each standing out like a black ribbon against the snow. He radioed back to his mortars, calling in fire on the hill.

"Drop it in anywhere," he radioed. "There's so many Chinamen up there you can't help but hit something."

In seconds, explosions from the heavy mortars blackened the hill.

Company L suffered about a dozen casualties in moving across the valley. Those wounded GIs who could still walk carried the dead and more seriously wounded back to their own lines.

Through the near-continuous battering, the company continued toward its objective. Every time he surveyed the hill through his binoculars, Rosser could see Chinese moving about the trenches, carrying mortars and machine guns.

Once in position at the base of the hill, Captain Davies sent one platoon up its front to create a diversion. He led the rest of his company around to the right to attack what he hoped would be the softer flank.

It was not. Over the next several hours the company fought its way uphill through several trenches filled with Chinese. The fighting was brutal. By the time the company reached a point a hundred yards below the hill's crest only about thirty-five men were still on their feet. Captain Davies had been wounded, the artillery FO, a lieutenant, was wounded, and many of the thirty-five men had been hit. The only radio still working was Rosser's. He used it to call both mortar and artillery fire on the Chinese with telling effect.

About mid-afternoon Captain Davies crawled to where Rosser was sheltered behind a large rock. With blood dripping down his face from a bad head wound, Davies called a situation report back to battalion using Rosser's radio.

"I'm down to about three dozen effectives, we're low on ammo, and there's still one trench full of Chinese in front of us," Davies reported. "What are my orders?"

Davies listened intently for several minutes, then handed the phone back to Rosser. His face was blank. "They want us to take the hill," he said in a monotone.

Rosser looked at the man. It was obvious he was in no shape to lead a charge on the next trench and its fortified bunkers. But they couldn't just stay there; enemy mortar rounds were dropping on them with increasing intensity. The Chinese were moving up more men. The hillside below them was covered with dead and wounded Americans. If the attack failed, they would all fall into Chinese hands.

Rosser couldn't let that happen.

"I'll take 'em up for you, Cap'n," he said.

Davies nodded wearily. Rosser turned his radio over to Smitty, then busied himself putting the men on line. He placed the wounded on the flanks so they could provide covering fire; the able-bodied were arrayed around Rosser so they could attack as one force. When he was satisfied, he gave the order. "Let's go," he said.

Rising to his feet, Rosser took off at a trot, pumping his carbine in the air while he yelled words of encouragement to the others. Oblivious to the enemy's fire, he made it to the base of the earthen berm fronting the enemy trench. He flopped down and turned around. What he saw filled his stomach with ice-cold fear.

He was all alone.

Not one man had followed him. Once the Chinese had started firing at them they had hit the ground, scrambling for available cover. Now Rosser was by himself, a good fifty yards from the remnants of the company. On the other side of the berm, just three feet away, he could hear what sounded like three or four Chinese jabbering away.

"My first thought was to run like a rabbit," Rosser said. "I was scared to death. Then I said to myself, 'This is what you wanted, why you're over here,' so I decided to make the best of it. I figured I was going to die and I'd just try to take as many of them with me as I could. I'd try to make them pay for Dick's death."

He jumped up and straddled the enemy trench. Instead of three or four Chinese, he found eight squatting in the bottom of the trench, seven in front of him and one behind, all armed with burp guns. Rosser leaned down, stuck the barrel of his carbine in the ear of the closest one and pulled the trigger. The Chinese soldier behind him stuck his burp gun in Rosser's back, apparently trying to take him prisoner. Rosser whirled and fired, shooting the man in the neck. The Chinese grabbed Rosser's leg. Rosser next shot him in the heart.

The gutsy Ohioan then spun back around, put his carbine on automatic, and fired into the crouched Chinese on full automatic. He killed five more and wounded two. While he reloaded, the two wounded fled down the trench to a bunker. They disappeared inside.

Rosser followed them. He pumped a few rounds into the bunker entrance. When no one came out he tossed in a grenade. Two Chinese crawled out. Rosser shot them both in the head. He then turned and called downhill to the rest of the company, "Come on! Let's go! I got them on the run!"

Not waiting for a reply, Rosser continued moving down the enemy trench. Ahead of him he could see "a whole bunch more of them" coming toward him, their heads bobbing above the trench line as they trotted along. Rosser met them at a turn in the trench. As soon as the first Chinese saw Rosser standing there, unmovable, his carbine at the ready, he turned and tried to flee. He was still trying to crawl over those behind him when Rosser drilled him. Screaming at the top of his lungs, Rosser shot a few more before the rest managed to get untangled and retreat down the trench.

Rosser now jumped out of the trench, cutting the corner on the retreating Chinese. He moved across the exposed ground where the trenches met at a right angle, all the while firing at the fleeing Chinese. Totally oblivious to the virtual hail of enemy fire directed at him, Rosser chased the Chinese as they sought refuge in a pair of bunkers. His fire killed another dozen Chinese.

Suddenly, Rosser realized he was nearly out of ammo. He threw his last two grenades, then started back down the trench. Near where he'd started his one-man assault he came across a wounded GI, the only man who had followed him into the trench. Rosser picked him up, slung him over his shoulder, and carried him back down the hill.

As he passed the wounded artillery FO, the officer accosted him. "What's your name, soldier?" the lieutenant demanded.

Rosser told him.

"Do you know what the hell you're doing?"

Rosser assured him he did.

"I'd be proud to shake your hand, Rosser," the lieutenant offered to Rosser's astonishment. Rosser then turned the wounded man over to the medics.

Anxious to return to the fight, Rosser rushed over to Smitty. "Give me some ammo," he demanded.

Smitty did, but pleaded with Rosser not to go back uphill. "Hell, they didn't get me last time," Rosser told him. "I can get back up there and get some more of them." Rosser then moved among the U.S. casualties, stripping the dead of their rifle magazines, stuffing their grenades down the front of his field jacket. When he was loaded down, he started back to the enemy trench.

As Rosser neared the trench, he realized the Chinese had moved back into it and were waiting for him. He readied a grenade. From about fifty feet he threw it.

"It was about the most perfect throw I ever made," Rosser said later. "It landed smack in the center of the trench."

Five seconds after it went off, killing at least a half dozen Chinese, Rosser leaped over the trench, dropping in another grenade to take care of any survivors.

For the next fifteen to twenty minutes Rosser roamed over that section of the trench line, firing his carbine, throwing grenades. Whenever he saw an enemy soldier Rosser unhesitatingly went after him. Several times, as he moved across the open ground, grenades or mortars went off near him, their explosions knocking him down. One time he was blown at least twenty feet into the air. Bits of shrapnel tore into him, but nothing could stop Rosser. Each time he rose back to his feet and continued after the enemy.

He ran out of ammo a second time, returning once more to the company for more ammo. Again laden with grenades, he tried to get someone to go back with him, but no one budged. For the third time Rosser returned to the trenches alone. This time the Chinese had brought up a machine gun. When it opened fire on him, he ducked for cover, rolling down a slight ledge that offered protection. "Enough is enough," he admitted to himself.

Convinced his luck was nearly gone, Rosser returned to the cluster of Americans. There he learned a reinforcement platoon from the battalion was trying to reach them but were slowed by Chinese who had reoccupied the previously cleared trenches. Rosser also saw that six American tanks had moved into the valley to provide covering fire.

Rosser volunteered to reach the tanks and give them precise firing instructions, but first stopped to pick up a wounded man. Carrying the man across his shoulder, Rosser made his way back downhill, never stopping. When he reached the tanks, Rosser hoisted the casualty up on one tank, then pointed out targets to the others.

While five tanks brought their cannons and machine guns to bear on the Chinese positions, Rosser helped load more casualties onto the sixth vehicle. Then he accompanied it back to the American positions on the MLR.

Rather than stay there in safety, Rosser went to his bunker, loaded himself down with ammo and grenades, then ran the mile and a half back to the scene of the fight. As the remnants of Company L made their way downhill toward the protective tanks, Rosser boldly provided covering fire, keeping the pursuing Chinese at bay.

It was well after dark by the time the survivors of Company L made their way back to the American lines. Of the 170 men who started out, only eighty were still on their feet.

While Rosser was having his wounds dressed, Captain Davies, swathed in bandages, paid him a visit. He invited Rosser to join his company.

"No thanks," Rosser replied. "I'd get killed for sure if I spent much time with you."

Within a few weeks Captain Davies and the artillery FO had initiated the paperwork for Rosser to receive the Medal of Honor for his actions on Hill 472. Consequently, the commander of the 38th Infantry ordered Rosser off the front lines. Rosser refused. He'd come to Korea to kill the enemy and he wasn't through yet.

Not until June 1952 did Rosser rotate from Korea. At home he told his mother, "I got even for Dick, Ma."

President Truman presented Rosser the Medal of Honor on June 27, 1952. At that time Rosser decided to make the army a career. He figured if his experiences could be used to help somebody else stay alive in combat he'd be satisfied.

Rosser served as an instructor at airborne school and as an operations NCO for several years before entering recruiting duty. He headed the recruiting office in West Palm Beach, Florida, for five years.

Then Rosser received some more bad news. His youngest brother, Gary, only 19, was killed in action in South Vietnam on September 20, 1966, while serving with the 1st Marine Division. At the funeral his dying mother asked Ron Rosser not to go to Vietnam to avenge Gary's death. He agreed not to.

Two years later Rosser retired from the army as a master sergeant to accept a position as the chief of police in Haverhill, Florida. He held that job for several years before going to work for the VA. He later entered college, earning a degree in history. Rosser taught junior high school in West Palm Beach for a number of years before becoming a general contractor of luxury homes in Boca Raton, Florida.

In 1982 he retired to Ohio. Today Rosser devotes his time to helping his fellow veterans.

The Fifth Air Force's Operation *Strangle* was proving less effective than conceived as the CCF and NKPA learned to repair rail cuts and damaged roads faster than they could be bombed. A new tactic was developed to meet the situation. Fighter-bombers would attempt to blast smaller, but more numerous, holes in the tracks. Forced to fly low and slow to attain their objectives, the fighter-bombers were easy pickings for the Soviet-built MiG fighters flown by Chinese pilots from air bases just north of the Yalu River.

To combat the MiGs the air force rushed to Korea its newest jet fighter, the F-86 Sabre. On paper the MiG-15 rated as a better plane than the F-86. The skill and bravery of the U.S. Air Force pilots, however, allowed the F-86 to best consistently the MiG-15. The Chinese Air Force lost about seven hundred MiGs to the U.N. air forces during the Korean War. The U.N. lost around 250 jets to MiGs, for a superiority ratio of nearly three to one.

Most of the enemy jets were downed in the infamous "MiG Alley." Located just south of the Yalu River in the far northwestern corner of North Korea, MiG Alley was more than two hundred miles away from the nearest U.N. air base. Once on station in the alley, the U.N. pilots could see the MiG-15s lined up at four big airfields just north of the river. Most of the time the Chinese pilots rose to the challenge and a high-speed, high-altitude dogfight ensued.

Generally, because of flying all that distance to MiG Alley, the U.N. pilots had less than fifteen minutes, fighting fuel left. Then they would have to streak for home, more often than not pursued by the MiGs.

If there was any glamour in the war in Korea it belonged to the jet-fighter pilots. A new breed of warrior, zipping across the sky at speeds in excess of five hundred mph, the jet-jockeys caught the imagination of the American public. They were pursued by correspondents, eager to file exciting stories in an otherwise monotonous and routine war. One fighter pilot whose exploits were regularly reported on was a quiet Texan.

GEORGE A. DAVIS

Born December 1, 1920, on a farm near Lubbock, Texas, George A. Davis plopped down $2.50 for an airplane ride in an old World War I Jenny at the local county fair when he was just thirteen. The thrill of that fifteen-minute ride aloft decided his future right then and there. After spending a year at Searcy College in Arkansas, Davis enlisted in the Army Air Force's Aviation Cadet program in 1942. A year later he was sporting the gold bars of a second lieutenant and riding in P-47 Thunderbolts and P-51 Mustangs.

Assigned to the Fifth Air Force in the Pacific, Davis flew 266 combat missions. His aggressive spirit resulted in his downing seven enemy planes in the skies over New Guinea and the Philippines.

In the post–World War II years Davis decided to make the military a career. He made the transition to the newly created air force and jets in 1947. Davis loved to fly and was often heard to remark that flying jets for the air force was "the best profession in the whole world."

Davis was a family man, having married Doris Forgason, a local Texas girl, while on leave in 1943. When he received his orders to Korea in September 1951, he had a daughter age seven, a nineteen-month-old son, and a third child due in April 1952.

When Major Davis arrived in Korea in October 1951 he went to the 4th Fighter Group. He flew ten missions as a wingman, then took over the 334th Fighter Squadron in November.

Though Davis was a quiet, meek-appearing man, he possessed nearly every attribute necessary for an outstanding fighter pilot. His reflexes were instantaneous and he had especially sharp eyesight. He had a natural gift for shooting, honed by hours of practice. He also had a very practical attitude toward flying a fighter. To him an airplane was nothing more than a flying gun platform. Move the platform into position, pull the trigger, and blast the enemy out of the sky. It was that simple.

As a squadron commander Davis put his aggressive spirit to work almost immediately. Beginning on November 27, 1951, he destroyed nine MiGs and three twin-engine bombers in seventeen incredible days that fighter pilots talked about for years.

Davis bagged two MiGs on November 27; for that deed he would be awarded the DSC. Two days later he downed four enemy planes, three bombers and a MiG, in less than four minutes. On December 5, he got two MiGs, and on December 13 he added four more to his score, two in the morning and two that afternoon. The U.S. newspapers and magazines were filled with stories of his victories. "He's a natural," one fellow pilot told reporters. *Newsweek* magazine on December 24, 1951, characterized Davis as "calm, quiet, iceberg-cool under fire, and deadly efficient." It noted he did not live up to the popular image of a jet fighter pilot as a "hotrock" and irresponsible "fly-boy." He was, instead, "an old married man of thirty-one."

That same week *Time* magazine quoted a jet mechanic who called Davis "the hottest pilot since they invented jets—and so help me, he looks about as aggressive as Bugs Bunny." According to the article, back home in Texas Davis liked to putter in the kitchen, cooking steaks and pot roasts. As for his incredible skill in the air, Davis simply said "it's just my job, my business."

Davis's sharpshooting feats led his wife to express her fear that her husband would become "a marked man." Her concern led her to petition the air force to recall Davis to the United States, based on earlier jet pilots being returned after having shot down just five enemy planes. Since her husband had twelve to his credit in Korea, she felt he had done enough.

The air force did not bring Davis back from Korea. He was too valuable a leader. As one man in his squadron said, "He inspires his squadron with confidence and certainly sets an example for courage." Davis and two other squadron leaders had all become aces at about the same time. None could be spared. Instead, the Fifth Air Force commander ordered Davis to fly just one mission per day. Reluctantly, Davis complied.

For nearly two months after he'd downed four enemy planes on December 13, the missions for Davis and his squadron were relatively routine. They saw few enemy planes and most of those fled across the Yalu before the U.S. pilots could engage them. Then, on February 10, 1952, Davis led a flight of four F-86s to a patrol along the southern edge of MiG Alley. Halfway there one of the other pilots radioed Davis that his oxygen system was malfunctioning. Davis ordered him and his wingman to return to the base near Seoul. Davis and his wingman flew on north, continuing the mission.

No sooner had they taken up their station at thirty-five thousand feet altitude than Davis spotted a flight of twelve MiG-15s heading south toward an area where U.S. fighter-bombers were preparing to carry out a low-level mission against a CCF communications center.

Though outnumbered, Davis unhesitatingly headed down to the enemy. From their higher altitude the two Sabres streaked earthward, attacking the MiG formation from the rear. Davis pulled out of his dive behind the rearmost MiG-15, lined it up in his electronic sights, and squeezed the trigger. The MiG visibly staggered under the impact of the heavy bullets, then rolled over and plunged downward.

By now several MiGs had peeled off, looped up and over, and were on Davis's tail. Disregarding their bullets zinging past his cockpit, Davis pressed his attack on another MiG. He maneuvered his gun platform into position, fired off a burst, watched the MiG explode, then turned violently to miss the wreckage.

By all rules of logic Davis should now have poured on the coals, dived, and used his superior speed to outrun his pursuers. Instead, he reduced power and pulled behind a third MiG. Before he could squeeze the trigger, his Sabre took a direct hit.

Davis's wingman, trying to elude an attacker of his own, turned in time to see Davis plunging earthward. "It was all over in seconds," he said. Davis crashed on a mountain about thirty miles south of the Yalu.

For his incredible airmanship and remarkable personal heroism, Davis was posthumously awarded the Medal of Honor. The presentation ceremony was held at Reese Air Force Base outside Lubbock on May 14, 1954. Mrs. Davis and her three children, the youngest born two months after his father died in Korea, accepted the award from Air Force Chief of Staff Gen. Nathan F. Twining. Though justifiably proud of her husband, she was still bitter at his death. "If I could feel that he lost his life for some good reason, I could feel better about it," she said.

The spring of 1952 brought heavy rains to Korea that cloaked the numerous valleys in heavy mists. Air and ground operations were severely limited, yet patrols went out as often as they could. In the X Corps zone in east central Korea a small patrol from Company G, 14th Infantry, U.S. 25th Infantry Division, set out on the night of March 12, 1952, to capture some prisoners from the Chinese positions on Hill 871, in the vicinity of the Punchbowl.

The patrol went well until it approached to within about fifty yards of the first Chinese outpost. Then suddenly the clouds parted to expose a bright moon. A Chinese machine gun opened fire on the silhouetted figures. A sergeant fell, riddled with bullets.

Farther up the hill a Chinese mortar started dropping shells on the patrol. More machine guns fired. Then burp guns opened up. Grenades flew through the night air. Several GIs cried out in pain as enemy metal cut their flesh. One mortar round blew Pvt. Francis Ray off his feet, seriously wounding him.

From a slight depression where he was treating another casualty, Pfc. Bryant H. Womack, a twenty-one-year-old medic from Rutherfordton, North Carolina, instantly went to Ray's aid. Through the blistering fire he ran. He'd covered about half the twenty-five yards when a machine-gun bullet slammed into his shoulder, spinning him to the ground. He crawled the rest of the way, reaching Ray and patching him up as best he could. Then, as Womack started crawling back to get help to evacuate Ray, a mortar round went off just feet away from him, blowing off his right arm below the elbow.

Without stopping to treat his grievous wound, Womack continued his quest to seek aid for Ray. A sergeant spotted him and ordered Womack off the hill, but he refused. There were too many wounded and he was the only medic.

While two others went to pull Ray to safety, Womack started telling able-bodied GIs how to treat the casualties they brought to him. As the battle raged all around him, Womack calmly directed the lifesaving efforts his wounded buddies needed.

Womack kept up his endeavor until the patrol began to withdraw. Then, though he'd already lost a tremendous amount of blood, he stayed behind making sure all the patrol members were accounted for. Only when convinced all the others were safe did he start down the hill, holding his shattered arm at his side. A few minutes after reaching safety, he collapsed and never regained consciousness.

The armistice negotiations continued without significant progress throughout the winter and spring of 1952. The impasse centered on two main issues: the construction and/or rehabilitation of airfields in North Korea and the POW issue. Of the two, the repatriation of POWs produced the most aggravation. The U.N.'s hard stand against forced repatriation infuriated the Communists. The issue was so volatile the sessions at Panmunjom frequently broke down before they began; on April 14, for example, only fifteen seconds elapsed between the opening and closing of the meeting.

In order to clear the impasse the U.N. command decided to screen the POWs in their control to determine exactly how many of them would actually refuse repatriation. Of the more than 132,000 prisoners held by U.N. forces, it was estimated around sixteen thousand would resist repatriation. When the screening was completed on April 15, the U.N. learned that only seventy thousand wanted to return to Communist control. When that information was relayed at Panmunjom on April 19, the Communist negotiators reacted with stunned silence.

The Communists had previously been heartened in their negotiations by riots that had taken place at POW compounds on Koji-do, an island prison compound off Pusan. (So serious were the riots, culminating in the capture of an American brigadier general on May 6, that the entire 38th Infantry Regiment was pulled off the line to put them down.) This new information shattered any hopes the Communists had for parlaying the riots on Koji-do into a massive propaganda campaign.

The U.N. hoped to finalize the negotiations by presenting a complete armistice proposal to the Communists. This they did on April 28, 1952. The proposal created about as much stir as a pebble dropped in the ocean. The Communists reacted by calling for an indefinite recess. The U.N. had fallen back on its final and irrevocable position. The debate was over. Patience and firmness were to be its chief weapons in future negotiations. In the meantime, the war at the front continued, essentially as a defensive war for both sides. Fought within carefully defined boundaries and under tacit rules, the war of active defense continued unabated and took its daily toll of casualties.

Beginning in March, General Van Fleet began shifting his units along the MLR in order to give the ROKs a greater share of responsibility for defending the front line and to concentrate American firepower in the more vulnerable western sector above Seoul. The biggest change involved the movement of the U.S. 1st Marine Division from the Punchbowl area in the X Corps zone to the I Corps zone on the Eighth Army's western flank. Here the marines took up positions north of Munsan-ni overlooking the Panmunjom area where their presence added a great psychological factor to the armistice negotiations.

When the shifting was completed, the I Corps had the U.S. 1st Marine Division on its left flank, the 1st British Commonwealth brigade in the center, and the ROK 1st Infantry Division on the right. To the east the IX Corps had the ROK 9th Division, the U.S. 7th Infantry Division, and the U.S. 40th Infantry Division arranged west to east across its front. Next was the ROK II Corps composed of the ROK 6th, the ROK Capital, and ROK 3d Infantry Divisions. The X Corps held the east central zone with the ROK 7th Infantry Division, the U.S. 25th Infantry Division, and the ROK 8th Infantry Division holding its sector west to east. On the far eastern zone, the ROK I Corps had the ROK 11th Infantry Division on its left half and the ROK 5th Infantry Division on the right, adjacent to the Sea of Japan.

Ground action had been limited in March primarily to patrol actions, but the enemy became bolder as the weather improved during April. The Communists increased their patrols and probing attacks, intensified their artillery barrages, and aggressively laid ambushes to intercept U.N. patrols. Enemy activity was particularly intense in the I Corps sector where the Chinese executed particularly violent attacks against isolated U.N. outposts. One such assault fell against a marine hilltop position about a mile east of Panmunjom on the night of April 16, 1952.

DUANE E. DEWEY

On that day a reinforced platoon of Company E, 2d Battalion, 5th Marines, was concluding its tenth day on outpost duty. The platoon's reinforcements consisted of two .30-caliber machine-gun squads. One of them was commanded by Cpl. Duane E. Dewey, a twenty-year-old from Muskegon, Michigan. He'd enlisted in the marines in March 1951. At home on leave after boot camp he'd married his sweetheart. Then more training as a machine gunner followed. In October 1951 Dewey arrived in Korea.

Since taking over the outpost the marines had enjoyed a quiet time. They spent their days improving their positions and looking for Chinese activity. The biggest event on the hill was the arrival of a letter from Dewey's wife announcing the birth of their baby daughter. Intensely proud, the husky youngster promised everyone cigars once they returned to the MLR.

Sunset came on April 16 and a hushed atmosphere fell over the hilltop as eighty marines bedded down for what they prayed would be another uneventful night. Unknown to them, more than five hundred Chinese had silently snuck into position at the bottom of the hill. Their commander carried an order to "take the hill at all costs."

They proceeded quietly. Then suddenly, at 11:00 P.M., they announced their presence with the crazy blare of bugles and horns. Intense small-arms and automatic-weapons fire erupted all around the marines. They were surrounded.

The first rush of Chinese soldiers carried right through the marine's outlying positions. Many Chinese broke into the center of the perimeter where savage close quarters fighting erupted. Surrounded and cut off from their main line by more than a mile, the outnumbered marines fought a vicious battle in an eerie blackness punctuated by the fiery flash of grenades, burp gun chatter, and the staccato bursts of machine-gun fire.

For nearly an hour Dewey fought his gun valiantly, pouring well-aimed, measured bursts of fire into the ranks of the Chinese. Just before midnight Dewey's gun ran low on ammo. He sprinted across the bullet-swept perimeter to the other gun, about fifty yards' distance. As he darted back, lugging a can of ammo, an enemy grenade went off behind him. A red-hot piece of jagged metal ripped open his left calf. He sprawled headfirst on the ground, grimacing against the intense, burning pain in his leg.

In minutes a navy corpsman crawled up, medical bag in hand. It was his first time in combat. What a way to start, Dewey thought. As the medic ripped apart his pant leg, Dewey's face was sprayed with dirt as a hard object hit the ground beside his head and rolled to his waist. Instinct told him what it was.

Grenade!

Faster than it can be told Dewey made a decision. "My first thought was to roll away from it," he later told officers. "It's hard to explain. There were three other wounded guys stretched out near me on the ground. There was the medic—he didn't even know what was happening. It's training, I guess."

Straining for his last reserve of strength, Dewey shoved the sailor aside and rolled over on the missile. Its muffled explosion lifted him a foot off the ground. The corpsman plunged back to Dewey's side. Gasping and choking on the smoke and fumes, Dewey told him, "Get me outta here!"

After stuffing a field dressing into the gaping hole in Dewey's hip, the corpsman summoned another marine to help him carry the corporal to the aid station. They found it crowded with wounded so they laid Dewey on the ground outside, then returned to the fight.

Dewey lay there for five or ten minutes, his ears still ringing from the blast, the fury of the battle filling the background. He started feeling woozy. His memory of the medical training he received in boot camp told him he was about to go into shock. If he did he knew he'd die. He had to find a place where he could lie with his feet above his head.

Though nearly overcome with pain from his wound, Dewey struggled to his hands and knees. Then he crawled about twenty yards to a shallow crater. He rolled onto his back and slid into the hole, his feet resting on the lip of the crater.

He lay there for nearly an hour while marines and Chinese fought just yards away. Finally, another corpsman found him and pulled him into a bunker where he gave Dewey a shot of morphine. At last the pain eased.

The bunker was filled with wounded. Most were in worse shape than Dewey, filling the small enclosure with their painful moans and plaintive cries for water. Not until dawn did the Chinese pull back, leaving the hill stained with dead and dying, American and Chinese.

Dewey was grateful for the dawn. "It was the longest night I ever lived," he said.

Dewey spent nearly two months in the hospital recovering from his wounds. In August 1952 he received a medical discharge. On March 12, 1953, he became the first person to receive the Medal of Honor from newly inaugurated President Dwight D. Eisenhower. "You must have a body of steel," Eisenhower told Dewey.

In late May the commander of the 7th Marines determined the need to develop intelligence on the enemy facing his 1st Battalion. After meeting with his staff and the planners from the battalion, he ordered a two-platoon raid for the night of May 27–28, 1952. A platoon from Company A, 1st Battalion, would conduct the raid against the Chinese situated on Hill 104, about a thousand yards in front of the marines' main positions.

While the Company A marines tried to snatch prisoners, a platoon from Company C would take up defensive positions on a small rise about halfway to Hill 104. From there their machine guns could provide supporting fire for the assault marines and they'd be available if Company A ran into trouble.

DAVID B. CHAMPAGNE
JOHN D. KELLY

Soon after midnight the two columns of men slipped through the barbed wire fronting their positions. The platoons moved together across the no-man's land until the Company C platoon peeled off to take up its positions. The Company A platoon moved forward until it reached its jump-off spot. Once everything was set, the assault platoon started up the hill. Almost at once they came under heavy fire. Ignoring it, Cpl. David B. Champagne, a nineteen-year-old aspiring actor from Wakefield, Rhode Island, led his fire team through a gauntlet of automatic-weapons fire and grenades to drive the Chinese out of the nearest trench. Soon after he placed his men in defensive positions the Chinese counterattacked.

Champagne was hit almost at once by an enemy round but angrily refused to leave. He stayed on, pinpointing targets for his riflemen. Suddenly, an enemy grenade dropped among the fire team. Concerned only for the safety of his men, the teenager groped in the darkness for the bomb. His fingers finally closed around it. He tossed it back toward the enemy, but just as it left his hand it exploded, tearing off his hand, and blowing him out of the trench. An exploding mortar round killed him before he could scramble back to safety.

Champagne's actions saved his four men from certain death or injury and allowed them to continue battling the Chinese.

The fighting continued on Hill 104, threatening the marines pinned down there. To aid them, a reaction force was organized from the Company C supporting platoon. One of those who volunteered to reinforce the heavily pressed marines was twenty-three-year-old Pfc. John D. Kelly of Homestead, Pennsylvania.

Normally a radioman, Kelly turned his instrument over to a buddy, then hurried off to join the fight. Just after he reached the firing line an enemy machine gun took Kelly's group under fire. Yelling for the others to cover him, Kelly bounded out of his trench and headed straight for the enemy machine gun.

With Chinese bullets whistling by him, Kelly fired his own rifle, killing the two enemy gunners. He next turned his attention to a nearby enemy bunker. He closed on it, was hit by rifle fire, but kept going. Kelly wiped out the three Chinese in the bunker, destroying their machine gun with a grenade. He stormed on, attacking a third bunker. He continued this charge even while he was being riddled with machine-gun bullets. He got off one last grenade before he collapsed in front of the enemy position.

Champagne's and Kelly's heroism and self-sacrifice could not stem the Chinese counterattack. The fight raged on into the morning without letup.

At mid-morning another platoon reached Hill 104, adding their firepower to the fight. But the marines still could not extricate themselves. Not until close-air support laid five-hundred-pound bombs and napalm across the top of Hill 104 were the marines able to pull back. It was early afternoon before they returned to their own lines.

The younger brother of David Champagne received his sibling's posthumous Medal of Honor in a ceremony held in Wakefield in July 1953. Two months later, on September 9, John Kelly's parents accepted their son's posthumous award from Vice President Richard M. Nixon.

Chapter Eleven
Summer 1952

In mid-May 1952 Gen. Matthew B. Ridgway left the Far East Command to assume new responsibilities as Supreme Allied Commander, Europe. His successor as Commander in Chief, Far East and the United Nations Command was Gen. Mark W. Clark. General Clark came well qualified for his new job. As commanding general of the U.S. Fifth Army in Italy during World War II, he was intimately familiar with mountain warfare. The rugged terrain, brutal weather, and tenacious enemy he'd encountered in driving the Germans out of Italy gave him a keen appreciation for the difficulties faced by his troops in the stalemate in Korea.

Arrayed across the waist of the Korean peninsula, Clark had in the Eighth Army four U.S. Army divisions, the U.S. 1st Marine Division, the British Commonwealth Division, and nine ROK divisions, totaling 247,500 men. Facing them, the Chinese had an estimated 422,000 troops and the NKPA another 185,300. With support troops the Communists mustered just over 900,000 men, while the U.N. command totaled about 700,000.

In Panmunjom the U.N. and Communist negotiators were still deadlocked over the issue of POW repatriations. Clark recommended to Washington that the U.N. negotiators meet more infrequently with their counterparts until the process of rescreening the POWs had been completed. In order to appease the Communists, the U.N. had volunteered once again to question the POWs about their desire for repatriation; some POW compounds had not been screened during the initial process because of the threat of violence. When the rescreening ended in late June the new figures revealed eighty-three thousand out of 132,000 now wanted to be repatriated. It was hoped this increase would motivate the Communists to accept the package proposal. It didn't.

The major ground action in the early summer of 1952 occurred in the I Corps zone held by the U.S. 45th Infantry Division. In hard, close quarters fighting that raged from June 6 to June 14, the division drove the enemy off eleven hilltops dominating their MLR. Just west of Chorwon and fronting the Yokkok-chon, the eleven positions ran in a southwest-northeast arc with Old Baldy and Porkchop Hill on the south, through positions with names such as Eerie, Arsenal, and Alligator Jaws to White Horse Hill north of Chorwon.

In the IX Corps zone the U.S. 40th Infantry Division held the ground east of Kumhwa. They faced a situation similar to the 45th Infantry Division, their sister National Guard unit. The enemy held several dominant hill masses overlooking the division's positions. Division headquarters ordered a series of patrols to attack the most prominent hills.

DAVID B. BLEAK
CLIFTON T. SPEICHER

One such patrol left the line of departure at 2:45 A.M. on June 14, 1952. The evening before the ninety men from Company F, 223d Infantry, had been briefed on their mission. From their starting point the column would move several thousand yards until it reached the base of Hill 499. It would then form an assault line, move up the slope until it reached the top, destroying enemy positions, killing or capturing the enemy, and hold the hill.

All went well for the patrol as it snaked across several fingers of land that stretched into the valley separating the two forces. By the time the men had formed up at the base of Hill 499, the first faint rays of dawn were breaking across the eastern sky.

"How I hate to attack in the daylight," offered Cpl. Clifton T. Speicher, the commander of one of the attack squads. Born March 25, 1931, in Gray, Pennsylvania, the coal miner's son entered the army in January 1951. Six months later he was in Korea.

A devout student of the Bible, Speicher always carried a copy of the Good Book with him, reading it whenever he had a spare moment. He spoke wistfully to his buddies about how he planned to marry his girl as soon as he got home. He was due to rotate from Korea in just a few more weeks. The wedding was planned for soon after his arrival home.

The command came, "Let's go!"

Speicher turned to a buddy, Cpl. Rudy G. Polin, and said, "Let's kill a lot of them today."

The assault line started up the hill. Pulling themselves upward from rock to rock, the GIs had reached the halfway point before the first Chinese grenade blew up among them. A soldier collapsed in pain. More grenades exploded, their flashes casting an eerie glow across the barren landscape. One erupted just ten feet from Speicher. He barked in pain as its steel shards ripped into his side. He went to one knee.

Polin appeared next to him. "I'll be okay. Let's get going," Speicher told him.

Rising slowly to his feet, braced on his rifle, Speicher continued up the hill, now alive with enemy small-arms fire.

Meanwhile, a few yards from Speicher, an enemy grenade bounced off a soldier's helmet and rolled a few feet away.

One of the medics with the patrol, Sgt. David B. Bleak, the twenty-year-old son of an Idaho Falls, Idaho, potato farmer, saw the incident. Without hesitation, Bleak, a huge bear of a man, flung himself at the other soldier. His weight forced the man to the ground. The grenade went off. Neither man was hurt. The soldier mumbled his thanks and returned to the fight.

Bleak, a veteran of nearly eighteen months' service, busied himself caring for the many wounded. Unmindful of the blaze of enemy machine-gun fire sweeping down from the Chinese positions above, Bleak darted from one casualty to the next, applying field dressings, pulling men to cover, and offering words of encouragement.

Returning to the line of advancing GIs, Bleak saw a man fall just on the other side of an enemy trench. Bleak went for him. Three Chinese soldiers suddenly popped up from the trench, firing their burp guns at the big man, now just feet away.

Intent only on reaching the casualty, Bleak dived headfirst into the trench, tackling one of the enemy. In seconds the Chinese was dead, his neck broken. Bleak whirled on the other two. Towering over the terrified pair, he wrapped his massive hands around one man's throat, crushing it, then buried his trench knife in the third man's chest. Then he crawled out after the wounded man.

Speicher's squad, meanwhile, had advanced nearly to the top of the hill. There an enemy machine gun, firing from a heavily sandbagged bunker, drove them to cover. They huddled there for a few minutes before Speicher said to Polin, "Fire at the door. I'll get the gun."

While his squad members blazed away at the bunker's open door, Speicher fearlessly charged straight toward the bunker. An enemy rifle round suddenly slammed into him, spun him to the ground. He bounced back to his feet, firing his rifle. While his squad members watched, Speicher disappeared into the bunker.

Inside, Speicher, his eyes ablaze, confronted four enemy gunners. He shot two, firing his rifle from the hip. As the third enemy soldier leveled a pistol at Speicher, he lunged forward, bayoneting the man. Before he could pull the blade free, the last enemy soldier fired a burst from his burp gun directly into Speicher's stomach.

Just then one of Speicher's squad members burst through the doorway. He killed the remaining enemy soldier.

With this key bunker destroyed, the attack proceeded up the hill. As it did, Speicher staggered out of the emplacement, his hands gripped to his torn stomach, holding his intestines in place. Without a word to anyone, he started down the hill, dazed, stumbling along the rocky ground. He'd just reached the aid station when he collapsed. A few minutes later he died.

The last enemy soldiers were driven off the hill as the sun burned higher in the sky. As was expected, Chinese artillery and mortar rounds began falling among the GIs on the hilltop. Having accomplished its mission, the patrol began withdrawing. Suddenly, a previously undetected enemy machine gun opened fire. Three men fell wounded.

Medic Bleak immediately rushed to their aid. The machine gun chattered again. A bullet plowed into Bleak's leg. He wrapped a dressing around the wound, then continued treating the others.

Two of the wounded men were able to continue on their own. The third couldn't walk. Bleak hoisted him on to his broad shoulder and started down the hill.

Without warning, two Chinese soldiers charged Bleak, bayonets gleaming dully on the ends of their rifles. Hastily, Bleak lowered his burden to the ground and in a fury flew at the two enemy soldiers. He closed with them, dodging their thrusts, his hands and muscles working in feverish combination. Each broad hand closed around a Chinese head, then slammed them together with a resounding thunk, cracking their skulls. Bleak shoved the bodies off the path so he could continue his self-appointed mission of carrying the wounded American to safety.

Bleak survived his wound and the balance of his tour in Korea to return home to Idaho. In October 1953 he received word his actions on June 14 the previous year would be rewarded with the Medal of Honor. President Eisenhower made the presentation on October 27, 1953.

Two months earlier, on August 19, John Speicher had accepted his son's posthumous decoration.

Increased combat activity along the MLR and the lack of progress at Panmunjom in the summer of 1952 cast a discouraging tone over the war both in Korea and in the United States. Many Americans grumbled over the POW impasse; continuing the fighting and dying for the sake of Oriental POWs, who probably didn't have true control of their own minds anyway, made little sense to them. Why not just turn them over to the Communist Chinese and bring our boys home? The American public was not only tiring of the weekly casualty list but finding it more difficult to understand why the U.S. was fighting in a far-off land where total victory was not possible. If the U.N. wasn't able to reunite all of Korea, why not just get out and avoid further losses?

The U.N. military intelligence somewhat agreed. In their estimate, the enemy was firmly entrenched in depth and showed no desire to return to large-scale fighting. The CCF and NKPA seemed content to rest on their increased defensive strength, confident in their ability to wait out the U.N. Unless the U.N. launched a major offensive, driving into North Korea again, the intelligence corps did not believe that sufficient military might could be brought to bear on the enemy's current defensive positions to swiftly conclude the war. Since there was little likelihood of securing additional U.N. troops to mount such a massive offensive, the prospect of a dramatic shift in the course of the war appeared remote. With the U.N. unwilling to yield on the POW issue and the Communists making no attempt to alter the status quo, the future held only more of the same type of seemingly senseless hill warfare that had dominated the conflict in Korea for the past year.

Typical of this was a series of sharp clashes between the 1st Marine Division and the CCF in early August 1952. On August 9, the Chinese threw the marines off Hill 58, four miles east of Panmunjom. The marines immediately launched a counterattack. Over the next two days Hill 58 changed hands no less than five times. In the end, the Chinese prevailed; the marines conceded Hill 58 to them.

The marines then shifted their attention a thousand yards south to Hill 122, which overlooked Hill 58. This maneuver caught the Chinese by surprise. From August 12 to 14, Company H, 3d Battalion, 7th Marines, fought off repeated Chinese counterattacks of near-battalion strength. They held onto Hill 122—proudly nicknamed "Bunker Hill"—but suffered heavy casualties. The losses would have been worse but for the gallant self-sacrifice of a young navy corpsman.

JOHN E. KILMER

Heroic military service was no stranger to the family of Hospitalman 3d Class John E. Kilmer. He was a distant cousin of famed poet Joyce Kilmer who gave his life for his country during World War I. An uncle, Everett A. Kilmer, earned the DSC on October 3, 1918, when he pulled a wounded comrade from the 16th Infantry, 1st Infantry Division, to safety under a heavy enemy artillery barrage.

John E. Kilmer, known as "Jackie" to his family and friends, was born in Highland Park, Illinois, on August 15, 1930. When he was six the family relocated to San Antonio, Texas, where his father, John R., worked as an electrical engineer. Regrettably, John R. Kilmer died within a few months after moving his family to Texas. His widow went to work to provide for her two sons.

Jackie Kilmer attended high school until his seventeenth birthday. On that day, with his mother's permission, he enlisted in the navy. After boot camp in San Diego, Kilmer attended the Hospital Corps School at San Diego, graduating in April 1948.

When fighting started in Korea, Kilmer was assigned to the hospital ship *Repose*. The large number of casualties that passed through the mercy ship provided Kilmer with a tremendous amount of practical medical experience, more experience than many doctors and nurses receive in a lifetime of practice. Kilmer hoped to transfer that medical knowledge into a civilian career. However, during a leave in San Antonio, he found that his experience and training were not in large demand in the civilian job market. When his enlistment expired in August 1951, he reenlisted.

A fun-loving, mischievous young man, Kilmer was popular among his comrades aboard the *Repose*. He was always looking for a good time, living life to the fullest. He also excelled at his job, providing excellent care to his patients. He performed his duties so well he was being considered for an accelerated promotion when he ran afoul of a superior.

Rather than face a court-martial, Kilmer accepted a transfer to the Fleet Marine Force. He attended the Field Medical School at Camp Pendleton, California, took a leave at home, and then, in June 1952, reported to the Headquarters and Service Company, 3d Battalion, 7th Marines.

Kilmer quickly earned the respect of the marines. All his training and practical experience made it easy for him to deal with the aches, pains, and battle wounds that plagued the marines. Kilmer came to be known as a corpsman who could be depended on to do his best to provide care to his marines.

Kilmer took part in the initial attack on Bunker Hill on August 12. The assault went well. The Chinese were not expecting an attack, so resistance was light. So were the casualties. Only a few marines were hit. Kilmer patched them up and saw to their evacuation. He then joined the marines in digging in for the anticipated counterattack.

It came just after midnight, August 13. A heavy barrage of enemy artillery and mortar shells slammed into Bunker Hill. Kilmer and the marines crouched deep in their holes, praying the shells wouldn't find them. Soon, though, the cries of "Corpsman!" "Corpsman up!" rang loud over the crash of the heavy shells.

Leaving his place of safety, Jackie Kilmer dashed across the hilltop. Ignoring the carnage around him, he went from one casualty to another. All through the first CCF infantry assault, Kilmer dauntlessly administered lifesaving aid to the wounded. While rifle fire cut the air around him, he repeatedly exposed himself to reach wounded marines. He carried several men to safety, giving that extra effort that saved several lives.

The Chinese fell back, their ground assault beaten back by the tenacious marines. But they weren't giving up. They again loosed a barrage of artillery and mortar fire on the hill.

Within seconds a cry for help reached Kilmer; a marine had been caught in the open. Badly wounded, unable to move, his pain-filled calls for help continued.

Kilmer started for him. A sergeant grabbed him.

"You can't go out there," he shouted. "You'll die."

"So will he unless I do something," Kilmer stoically replied.

Hugging the fire-swept ground, Kilmer snaked his way toward the casualty, about twenty-five yards away. Halfway there a mortar shell erupted just feet from him. Metal fragments tore into his side, blood poured from a dozen holes. The pain was intense but Kilmer had a casualty to treat. He continued forward.

As shells hit all around him, Kilmer reached the man. He pulled battle dressings from his pouch and began first aid. He had almost completed his task when enemy shells shattered the immediate area. Intent only on saving the marine, Kilmer unhesitatingly threw himself over the man, shielding him from danger with his own body.

While covering the man, Kilmer was mortally wounded by flying shrapnel. The marine lived.

When she was notified her son was to receive America's highest award, Lois Kilmer was surprised. She had never heard of the Medal of Honor. "You mean they don't give out this medal often?" she asked. "Oh my! What did Jackie do? I've never heard."

At the ceremony in Washington on June 18, 1953, she learned of her son's unselfish sacrifice when Navy Secretary Robert B. Anderson read the Medal of Honor citation. Lois Kilmer told the secretary her son was "always interested in medicine and interested in helping others."

The day after Jackie Kilmer gave his life on Bunker Hill a six-man patrol from Company A, 187th Airborne Regimental Combat Team, headed into enemy territory near Kumhwa. By 11:30 A.M. the patrol had penetrated two miles into enemy land. While navigating through a narrow ravine cut by a fast-moving stream, the patrol was suddenly fired on by Chinese. The men were trapped!

Cpl. Lester Hammond, Jr., the patrol's twenty-one-year-old radio operator, was wounded in the first burst of fire. When the other five men withdrew farther up the ravine seeking better cover, Hammond refused to move.

The Quincy, Illinois, native instead crawled forward to an exposed position from where he could see the large enemy force and call in friendly artillery fire.

A patrol member crept forward to help Hammond to cover in a nearby ditch. Hammond refused. "Leave me here. I'm alright," he said.

While the others engaged the enemy with rifle fire from covered positions, Hammond stayed in the open, calling down artillery on the advancing Chinese. He remained in the exposed position, his back against a cliff, for over two hours, adjusting the artillery which held back the enemy and kept them from overrunning his five buddies.

When the Chinese finally gave up, the others rushed forward to Hammond. They were too late. Within twenty yards of his lifeless body lay twelve dead enemy soldiers, cut down by Hammond's rifle fire. Another twenty-five were killed by artillery fire. Hammond's actions had saved his patrol from destruction.

Beginning in late August heavy rains drenched nearly all of Korea. The torrential downpour turned the trenches on both sides of the MLR into morasses of thick, gooey mud. Nearly all ground operations came to a halt as the skies unleashed several inches of rain each day. Eighth Army GIs kept busy bailing out bunkers and repairing damage to their fortifications from mud slides.

September 1952 began with clearing skies and increased attacks by the Chinese. The enemy raids were accompanied by increased volumes of artillery and mortar fire. On one particular day in early September an all-time high of forty-five thousand enemy rounds crashed down on the Eighth Army's lines. Despite the courageous efforts of the Fifth Air Force and the naval air arm to sever the enemy's supply lines, the Chinese and North Koreans kept their frontline troops well supplied, even managing to build up a reserve stock of ammunition and supplies. The enemy moved his supplies solely at night, using his vast pool of manpower resources to defeat the umbrella of air cover thrown overhead by the U.N.

One area that continued to receive brutal attention from the Chinese was the marine position on Bunker Hill. Soon after they had taken Bunker Hill, the marines of the 3d Battalion, 7th Marines, were replaced by elements of the 3d Battalion, 5th Marines. The fresh troops reinforced the bunker positions and established a series of outposts along the hill's numerous spurs and ridges to provide early warning of any enemy probes.

Beginning at dusk on September 4, the Chinese began pounding Bunker Hill with a heavy artillery concentration. While the marines sought cover deep in their bunkers, the Chinese moved an entire battalion of infantry into assault position. They were determined to wrench Bunker Hill from the marines. The first word of the massed Chinese forces came from a tough marine machine gunner manning Outpost Bruce, a few hundred yards in front of Bunker Hill's main positions.

ALFORD L. McLAUGHLIN

Pfc. Alford L. McLaughlin had spent the entire previous week on outpost duty. When it came time for his relief he volunteered for another tour. He felt his experience as a machine gunner was greater than the man sent to relieve him and he could thus be more effective behind the trigger. His replacement accepted McLaughlin's decision without any argument; he was very willing to spend another week in the relative safety of the main positions.

McLaughlin was a pugnacious little Alabaman, born in Leeds on March 18, 1928. He enlisted in the Marine Corps shortly after his nineteenth birthday. Trained as a machine gunner, he arrived in Korea in the spring of 1952, joining Company L, 3d Battalion, 5th Marines. He quickly proved his worth with the automatic weapon. He possessed an uncanny sense of accuracy—some called him a natural shot. He'd have more than ample opportunity to demonstrate his talents on the night of September 4–5, 1952.

The spunky gunner knew from past experience the Chinese would be coming as soon as the artillery barrage lifted. No sooner had the last shell exploded on the hill than McLaughlin was out of his protective bunker. He dashed to his machine gun, cleaned off the dust and dirt, and fed a fresh belt of ammo into the chamber. With the bolt pulled back he stood ready. Off to his right the outpost's other machine gunner did the same. Around them the handful of riflemen took up firing positions. Grenades and spare ammo clips were placed within easy reach. The marines were as ready as they could be.

Shortly after 10:00 P.M. a red flare burst high in the sky. Seconds later the shrill notes of a bugle echoed across the hills.

"Here they come!" McLaughlin yelled.

Below Outpost Bruce row after row of Chinese soldiers raced up the rocky hill, firing rifles and burp guns. McLaughlin and the other marines held their fire until the Chinese came within range. Then someone yelled, "Let 'em have it!"

The little band of men opened fire. McLaughlin pressed the butterfly trigger on his .30-caliber air-cooled machine gun. The weapon bucked as its heavy slugs tore into the night. Under the eerie glare of the flares McLaughlin could see Chinese falling from his fire. But as soon as one fell, another rushed forward to take his place.

For over an hour McLaughlin kept up his fire, sending short measured bursts down the ridge. Around him the other marines fired their rifles and threw grenades. A few times the charging enemy faltered under the vicious fire, but not for long. They just kept coming.

By midnight several groups of Chinese had fought their way past the tenacious knot of marines, bringing them under fire from the flanks and the rear. Soon their rounds started hitting marines. Those that weren't killed fought on, valiantly ignoring their wounds in their desperate fight for survival.

About this time the other machine gun fell silent; its gunner had been cut down in a hail of enemy fire. Other marines were reluctant to take over the weapon—it was too good a target for the Chinese.

McLaughlin realized that without the second machine gun the outpost's defenses were greatly weakened. He had to get it back into action.

Bounding across the bullet-swept ground, he crawled behind the weapon. After quickly checking to be sure an ammo belt was in place, he opened fire. Less than fifty yards away a squad of Chinese screamed in pain as the weapon's bullets cut them down.

McLaughlin kept up his steady fire until the gun's barrel emitted a faint glow. He then moved back across the battleground to his original position. He crouched behind that machine gun, feeding ammo himself. He fired that gun until its barrel grew too hot, then crossed back to the other machine gun.

The Alabaman kept crisscrossing the killing ground, singlehandedly keeping both guns in action. Though the target of concentrated enemy fire, McLaughlin ignored it to keep up the fire, giving the enemy a false impression of the marines' strength.

Whenever any enemy soldiers crept close to McLaughlin's position, he stopped firing his machine gun long enough to throw grenades and fire his pistol or carbine.

McLaughlin's aggressive tactics forced the Chinese to pull back from their attempts to take Outpost Bruce. In the resulting lull he helped treat the many wounded. When they were tended to, he worked on his machine guns; they'd be needed if the dozen or so marines still on their feet were to survive the next CCF attack.

It came about 2:30 A.M. As before, the Chinese stormed out of the night, row after row of enemy soldiers intent on destroying this unyielding outpost.

Their biggest obstacle remained the indomitable Pfc. McLaughlin. Summoning all his strength and courage, he fearlessly manned his weapons, spraying deadly bullets down the hill, bowling over individual enemy soldiers. Eventually, though he alternated machine guns to prevent burning out a barrel, it happened: One of the machine guns could no longer fire. Its barrel was warped from the intense heat from the thousands of rounds fired through it.

Despite McLaughlin's heroics and the valiant efforts of the other marines, the Chinese seemed to be gaining the upper hand. They pressed in from three sides, advancing behind a wall of mortar blasts.

Emboldened by his past successes, and knowing decisive action had to be taken to prevent Outpost Bruce from being overrun, McLaughlin lifted his .30 caliber from its tripod. Cradling the weapon in his arms, he knelt on the rim of his emplacement, firing the weapon into the rapidly closing enemy.

Suddenly, a Chinese mortar erupted with a sharp roar just yards from McLaughlin. Shards of shrapnel peppered his side. He fell backwards into the trench. With blood pouring from the many holes in his body, McLaughlin clawed his way back to his gun. In the dark his practiced fingers told him the weapon was still in good shape. Again cradling the weapon in the crook of his left arm, McLaughlin first knelt, then stood upright, a perfect target, raking his fire into the massing enemy.

Within minutes the red-hot barrel burned through the cloth of McLaughlin's jacket, searing his flesh. Still determined to keep his gun in action, McLaughlin kept on firing, then switched the barrel to the crook of his right arm. Though the smell of burning flesh mixed pungently with blood and gunpowder, he kept shooting.

His firing had a telling effect on the Chinese attackers. They fell by the score, creating great gaps in their formations. This weakened the attack. Eventually, the survivors began pulling back. Whenever McLaughlin glimpsed a group of Chinese fleeing for safety, he'd trigger a burst in their direction. More Chinese died.

Finally it ended. The Chinese were gone. Behind them they left several hundred of their comrades, sprawled across Bunker Hill in their mustard yellow tunics. More than two hundred Chinese bodies lay around Outpost Bruce, at least 150 of them slain by McLaughlin's machine guns.

When the corpsmen finally reached McLaughlin they recoiled in horror. Not only did he have numerous holes in his body, but both his forearms were burned nearly to the bone, with long, white blisters snaking down his arms. They treated him as best they could, then hustled him to the rear for more sophisticated treatment. From there McLaughlin went to Japan, then to burn treatment centers in the States. He'd spend nearly a year in the hospital recovering from the effects of his burns. Though he would never have a complete recovery, McLaughlin returned to active duty late in the summer of 1953.

On October 27, 1953, newly promoted Cpl. Alford L. McLaughlin stood proudly at attention while President Eisenhower draped the Medal of Honor around his neck. He had joined the ranks of America's greatest war heroes.

McLaughlin remained in the Marine Corps, attaining the rank of master sergeant before retiring in 1972. He enjoyed his life as a civilian for just five years before dying on January 14, 1977.

While McLaughlin was waging his fierce battle at Outpost Bruce, the Chinese pressed heavily against every other marine position on Bunker Hill. Almost without letup that brutal night, the Chinese attacked again and again. The valor of all the marines prevented the Chinese from achieving their objective, but casualties were heavy. The navy corpsmen supporting the marine units made tremendous sacrifices to reach the wounded and save their lives. Some made extraordinary efforts.

One such man was Hospital Corpsman 3d Class Edward C. Benfold, a twenty-one-year-old from Philadelphia and a member of McLaughlin's Company L. He had a busy night, moving across the battleground, treating casualties, carrying them to a clearing station. He repeatedly exposed himself to heavy enemy fire, focusing on saving lives.

As he scurried toward the main trench line in search of more casualties, Benfold spotted two wounded marines in a shell hole, not more than twenty-five yards away. While he watched, two enemy soldiers appeared out of the darkness, bayonets on the ends of their rifles. Before they reached the shell hole, both Chinese tossed grenades into it.

Benfold moved like greased lightning. He charged forward from his place of concealment, jumped into the shell hole, and scooped up a grenade in each hand.

In a flash Benfold careened out of the shell hole, an armed grenade clenched tightly in each fist. The two Chinese soldiers saw Benfold, knew what he was to try. They started to backpedal, but couldn't get out of his way.

Benfold was on them in an instant. He shoved a grenade against the chest of each soldier. An instant later the grenades exploded. It was all over. The two Chinese and Benfold disappeared in the resounding blast. The two wounded marines in the shell hole lived. The entire action had taken less than ten seconds.

The NKPA was not idle in September. Where they faced U.N. forces they launched attacks against key terrain features. The U.S. 25th Infantry Division held the right flank of the X Corps, about thirty-five miles inland from the Sea of Japan. Their main positions on the MLR were along the ridge lines west of the Punchbowl, the area known as Heartbreak Ridge.

On the east side of Hill 851, overlooking Satae-ri, the men of Company A, 27th Infantry, held a position they called "Sandbag Castle." At 12:45 A.M., September 6, the North Koreans tried to take the Sandbag Castle. In their way stood a listening post manned by twenty-one-year-old Pfc. Benito Martinez of Fort Hancock, Texas, and two other men.

Martinez's two comrades were killed in the initial exchange of fire, leaving him all alone. Rather than return to the main positions, the youth elected to stay put, fighting the North Koreans singlehandedly. Effectively using his machine gun, Martinez poured a deadly fire into the ranks of enemy soldiers moving toward the Sandbag Castle.

Several times during the night the company commander made contact with Martinez over a sound-powered telephone. Each time he was told a reaction force was being sent to his aid, Martinez said no, don't send anymore. It was far too dangerous; NKPA were all over the hillside.

For nearly six hours Martinez held his position, fighting off the North Koreans. At 5:50 A.M. he radioed the alert bunker on the Sandbag Castle to report the North Koreans were digging their way into his bunker with pickaxes. As the operator listened, Martinez left the phone. Seconds later the operator heard three pistol shots. He called repeatedly for Martinez, but he never returned to the phone.

When U.S. troops retook Martinez's position three days later they found him dead in his bunker, an empty pistol in his right hand. Three dead North Koreans lay around him. In the words of his company commander, "Martinez's ability to hold the enemy off 'Castle' kept the rear positions from being overrun and gave us time to reorganize and prepare for the attack."

On the west side of Hill 851 Company G, 14th Infantry Regiment, 25th Infantry Division, manned outpost positions similar to Sandbag Castle. The night after the North Koreans hit Pfc. Martinez's position they struck Company G.

DONN F. PORTER

Love sent Sgt. Donn F. Porter to Korea. The twenty-one-year-old from Ruxton, Maryland, was madly in love with a girl from home and longed to return to her. Since he'd enlisted in the army in February 1951, Porter had written his girl just about every day. Even while attending airborne and ranger school after basic training, Porter kept up a steady stream of letters to her. Whenever he could he called her, planning for their wedding as soon after his discharge as possible.

In November 1951 Porter reported to the 187th Airborne Regimental Combat Team, then in garrison in Japan. Porter was well liked by the members of his platoon. They knew him as a tall and slender youngster, quiet, and very loyal. One former platoon mate said, "You couldn't ask for a better friend." He spent a good deal of his off-duty time helping Porter shop for fine Japanese porcelain and dishes to send back to his girl.

Normally, Porter would have spent eighteen months in Japan, the standard tour of duty, before rotating back to the States. In Korea, however, a GI with a front line outfit could complete a tour of duty in as little as nine months. Porter decided to expedite his return to Maryland. Just after 1952 began he volunteered to go to Korea as an infantry replacement. He figured with his airborne and ranger training he'd have no trouble surviving nine months. He was almost right.

September was Porter's seventh month in Korea. In just sixty days he'd be on his way home. But first his company had to pull a tour on outpost duty. Beginning on September 1, Company G went on the line. Each night a squad of men manned the various listening posts established in front of the MLR. On September 6, Porter's squad, consisting of just three other men, made its way down the rocky hillside to its assigned LP. The men they were relieving were happy to see them arrive. For the last several nights the North Koreans had been probing the American lines. Their forays meant sleepless nights and frazzled nerves.

Porter kept his men busy until nightfall preparing firing positions and setting up fields of fire. When night came he set up the watch schedule: two men awake at all times, two-hour shifts. Porter would be on the first watch, from 8:00 P.M. to 10:00 P.M.

During Porter's watch all was quiet. He woke his relief, Cpl. Raymond Schwab, at 10:00 P.M., then crawled into the sandbagged bunker for a few hours sleep.

The first mortar shell hit the LP a few hours later. Porter instantly awoke. He crawled out of the sleeping bunker and into the fighting trench. Up and down the ridge enemy mortar shells burst in a near continuous roar.

Schwab saw the first wave of attackers. He announced their presence by firing off a clip from his M-1. It was 12:15 A.M.

Under extremely heavy pressure from the attacking NKPA, the four GIs took up fighting positions in the LP's two bunkers. Through the bunker's firing ports Porter poured a steady barrage of rifle fire into the attacking North Koreans. His bunker mate, Corporal Schwab, estimated Porter's deadly accurate fire accounted for twelve to fifteen of the enemy.

The resolute determination of the four GIs drove off the attacking North Koreans. As they regrouped out of range, their supporting artillery and mortars renewed the bombardment. One shell landed directly on the bunker containing Cpl. Paul Matichek and Pfc. Jerry Bachelor, killing them instantly.

Minutes after their two companions died, Porter and Schwab saw the North Koreans coming back. "Let's get 'em," Porter said.

Together the two young soldiers took up firing positions outside the bunker. Their combined rifle fire slowed the attackers but did not stop them. A pair of North Koreans snuck up on the intrepid pair. Unseen, they opened fire. Both Porter and Schwab recoiled from the impact of the bullets. Recovering first, Porter cut down the attackers.

Below their firing position Porter spotted six North Korean soldiers advancing toward them in the dark. Determined to prevent the enemy from getting any closer, Porter shouted to Schwab, "Cover me!" as he scrambled out of the trench.

In the flashes of exploding mortar shells Schwab saw Porter wade into the enemy. Lunging, thrusting, stabbing, Porter slashed his way through the six North Koreans. Like a madman, the tall lanky soldier jabbed his bayoneted rifle into one enemy chest after the other. His attack was so furious and so close-in the enemy troops never had a chance to react. In less than a minute all six North Koreans lay dead of stab wounds.

Gasping heavily from the exertion of his attack, Porter turned to return to the trench but never made it. An enemy shell went off at his feet, killing him instantly.

After Porter's valiant singlehanded charge, the North Koreans broke off their attack. Corporal Schwab was convinced it was Porter's bayonet attack that drove them off.

At first light a relief force reached Schwab. All he could do was talk about the gallant actions of Sergeant Porter. Based on his testimony, Porter was posthumously awarded the Medal of Honor on August 5, 1953.

For the rest of September the Communist forces maintained the pressure on the U.N. lines. Night after night Chinese and North Korean soldiers clashed with U.N. forces. Serious attacks were launched against Outpost Kelly in the U.S. 3d Infantry Division's zone along the Imjin River, against White Horse Hill northwest of Chorwon in the ROK 9th Infantry Division's zone, and at Jackson Heights northeast of White Horse Hill where the U.S. 7th Infantry Division held the MLR.

The U.N. forces won some of these fights, lost others. But, as the Korean War approached the start of its third winter, there was still no significant change in the frontline positions.

Chapter Twelve
Third Korean Winter

As October 1952 began the United States and its U.N. allies faced a third bitterly cold winter of fighting in Korea with no end to the conflict in sight. At Panmunjom the U.N. negotiators still could not break the impasse on the POW issue. They kept reminding the Communists of the finality of the offer they had made in the spring, but also let it be known they were open to positive suggestions. The Communists, however, would not budge on their demand for the unequivocal return of all POWs. In an attempt to appease the Communists, the U.N. negotiating team advanced three separate proposals regarding the POWs, none of which required an unwilling POW to return home if he did not so desire. The Chinese rejected them all.

As the presidential campaign approached its climax in the United States, the war in Korea dominated the political arena. The problem was that the United States seemed unable to win a victory, secure an armistice, or get out of Korea. For a nation that had defeated the formidable Axis powers just seven years earlier this was an untenable position.

As would happen fifteen years later over U.S. involvement in South Vietnam, both hawks and doves combined in anger against the incumbent administration. Pacifists wanted America out of Korea. Warmongers wanted the U.S. to achieve a complete military victory at any price. The Truman administration found itself battered from all sides.

The campaign of Republican candidate Gen. Dwight D. Eisenhower, the hero of World War II, focused on the traditional American view toward war:

246 KOREAN WAR HEROES

Don't get involved if at all possible, but once in the fray, give 'em all you got. In its earlier forays into conflicts around the world, the American public had always believed, rightly or wrongly, that it was fighting for a higher moral purpose. They did not believe they sent their boys off to fight to retain a despot or to secure the interests of private enterprise. Instead, they went to war to stamp out evil, to right wrongs, or to free the oppressed. The Republican campaigners, by saying they would either end the war or end the evil underlying it, struck much closer to the hearts of the American people than had the framers of Truman's containment doctrine.

For the GI on the line in Korea, the realities of the political situation in America had little impact on his life. The war went on unabated. Neither side could advance; neither side would retreat. Each side held its hills and valleys in depth. As they had for nearly a year the enemy continued to be more aggressive than the U.N.

The Communists patrolled more often, launching limited attacks again and again. They took vital hill positions, destroying in the process the U.N. squads and platoons that had been on them. Then they killed more men when the U.N. counterattacked to retake its property. Most of the actions were minor in the overall scheme of the war, except, that is, to the men pounded by artillery falling at the rate of hundreds of shells per minute, or caught in the savage masses of swarming Chinese or North Koreans.

One such attack was launched in the early morning hours of October 2, 1952, against the marines of Company I, 3d Battalion, 7th Marines, holding Detroit Hill northeast of Panmunjom. While maneuvering among the trenches, both the platoon leader and the platoon sergeant were felled by an artillery shell. The only man to respond to the critical need for leadership was an eighteen-year-old private first class from Fresno, California.

Jack W. Kelso had less than one year's service but had already proven himself an indomitable fighter. Just one week earlier he had been presented the Silver Star he'd earned in the fighting at Bunker Hill on August 13. A few days after the award ceremony, his company took over defensive positions on Detroit Hill. Kelso's platoon received the assignment to man Outpost Warsaw.

When he saw his platoon leader fall, Kelso immediately rallied the men around him to repulse the attackers. Despite their efforts the Chinese prevailed, forcing Kelso and four other marines to take shelter in a bunker. Almost immediately, the enemy swarmed over the sandbagged structure. One tossed a grenade into the bunker. Unhesitatingly, Kelso scooped up the deadly missile, rushed outside, and hurled it back at the enemy. The grenade exploded just as it left his hand, painfully wounding him. Rather than return to the safety of the bunker, Kelso remained in his exposed position, returning the enemy's fire and allowing his four buddies to escape. While they fled down the trench line, Kelso remained behind, battling it out with the Chinese until he was cut down in a hail of rifle fire.

Despite the intrepid actions of Kelso and other marines, the Chinese succeeded in capturing Detroit Hill. But the marines would not relinquish it easily.

The fight for control of Detroit Hill raged over the next five days. The marines repeatedly fed in reinforcements but they sometimes ran into trouble before reaching the main fighting positions. One group of twelve marines was cut off and trapped by the Chinese for three days. In the morning darkness of October 7, a patrol led by Jack Kelso's platoon guide, twenty-seven-year-old S. Sgt. Lewis G. Watkins of Seneca, South Carolina, attempted a rescue.

Halfway up the slope leading to the trapped marines the enemy opened fire on the patrol. Watkins fell, badly hit. Disregarding the pain, Watkins stayed in command, leading his men into a trench. When one of his BAR men went down, Watkins picked up the weapon. He advanced toward an enemy machine gun, firing the bucking BAR from the hip. He wiped out the position.

With that obstacle out of the way, Watkins continued down the trench toward the bunker housing the trapped men. Suddenly, an enemy grenade plopped among Watkins's men. He pushed the nearest man aside, grabbed the grenade, and moved to throw it out of the trench. He was too late. The missile went off in his hand, killing him instantly. But he had saved those around him from death or certain injury.

Inspired by Watkins's courageous self-sacrifice, the patrol pushed forward. They broke through the cordon of Chinese, rescuing the twelve marines.

The Chinese kept up their attacks on Detroit Hill for another two days. After a hard bloody fight the marines finally relinquished the hill.

Gunfire still echoed among the hills overlooking Panmunjom when Lt. Gen. William K. Harrison, the head of the U.N. negotiating team, arrived at the conference site on the morning of October 8. At the previous meeting the Communists had agreed to a ten-day recess in order that, as they said, "The United Nations Command might reconsider its basic stand," regarding the POW issue.

At the outset of this meeting the Chinese negotiators repeated their demand for the return of all their prisoners, just as they had been doing for months. Then the chief Chinese negotiator launched into the same tirade of anti-U.S. rhetoric that had characterized nearly all of the previous meetings.

When the Communists were finished, General Harrison fixed his counterpart with an icy glare and then, with a decided edge to his voice, stated, "The United Nations Command has no further proposals to make. The proposals we made remain open. The U.N.C. delegation will not come here merely to listen to abuse and false propaganda. The U.N.C. is therefore calling a recess. We are willing to meet with you again at any time you are willing to accept one of our proposals . . . which could lead to an honorable armistice. I have nothing more to say."

With that, General Harrison and his entourage departed the building. They would not return until the following spring.

Chinese attacks during the early fall of 1952 were primarily political in nature. Balked on the POW issue, they adopted this policy to pressure the U.S. out of the war. Their assaults on hills all across the front—at Reno, Carson, and Vegas held by the marines; on Old Baldy, Arrowhead, and Pork Chop Hill in the U.S. 2d Infantry Division sector; on Triangle Hill and Sniper Ridge occupied by the ROKs in the IX Corps area near Kumhwa, and on dozens of other less famous hills—accomplished little of military value but did stir public emotion in the United States over the never-ending casualties.

The typical frontline GI knew little of the politics behind attacks on his position. All he knew was the Chinese or North Koreans would suddenly charge out of the night, intent on killing him and his buddies. For him the war went on, personal and deadly.

Fortunately for the frontline GI the Eighth Army maintained a fairly generous rotation policy. Few units spent more than thirty days at a stretch on the MLR. Then it was off to a reserve area for hot chow, hot showers, clean clothes, and several weeks of training before heading back to the stinking bunkers and trenches of the MLR.

The U.S. 25th Infantry Division had been holding a sector of the MLR near the Punchbowl and Heartbreak Ridge for several weeks. They were overdue for relief. Word finally came that they'd be pulled off the line October 14. Until then, though, it was business as usual.

Through Eighth Army intelligence the commander of the 3d Battalion, 14th Infantry Regiment, 25th Infantry Division, learned that the North Koreans had established a new outpost on a finger of land jutting off Heartbreak Ridge, north of the MLR. Because it posed a threat to U.N. positions overlooking Satae-ri and to U.N. patrols moving through the area, he decided to send a detachment to wipe it out.

The twelve-man patrol slipped out of its trench after dark on October 12. In single file the men proceeded down a well-used trail, planning on reaching their assembly point around 8:00 P.M. If the attack went according to plan they would hit the enemy bunkers, kill or capture the North Koreans occupying them, and be back in their bunkers by midnight.

About four hundred yards from the assembly point, the clear night suddenly erupted in a blaze of rifle fire and the crash of hand grenades—the North Koreans had executed a clever ambush. The patrol members scurried for cover behind nearby rocks, firing their rifles at the muzzle blasts flashing from the high ground around them. Some GIs began pulling back. Others would have, too, except for the crumpled forms of the patrol leader and two others lying in the middle of the trail. They had caught the full blast of one of the first grenades thrown by the enemy. The patrol leader writhed in pain, unable to make his way to safety. The two others had also received debilitating wounds.

A corporal tried to reach the casualties. He took a round through the shoulder. The enemy was using the casualties as bait. Any attempt to reach them bordered on suicide.

ERNEST E. WEST

One man wasn't going to leave the casualties to be killed or captured. Pfc. Ernest E. West, a twenty-one-year-old from Wurtland, Kentucky, who'd been in Korea since May, spoke to those around him, "You guys can pull out, but I'm not leaving."

With that, he ran down the trail toward the limp figures. As he scurried through the gauntlet of enemy fire, he realized he didn't even know the lieutenant's name. The man had just assumed command of the platoon a few days earlier and West hadn't even met him. Not that it mattered; they'd gone through more than half a dozen platoon leaders in the five months since West had joined Company L. He could only remember the names of two or three of them.

Once at the wounded officer's side, West fired a full clip from his M-1 into the darkness. He wanted to discourage any nearby North Koreans from getting any closer. Since the lieutenant was bigger than he, West knew he couldn't pick him up. Instead, he rolled the officer onto his back, grabbed him under the arms, and started dragging him backwards down the trail.

Enemy grenades and mortar rounds crashed on the trail, filling the night air with lethal shards of shrapnel. One grenade bounced off West's helmet and rolled down past the lieutenant's feet. Thinking only of the officer's safety, West unhesitatingly threw himself on the prostrate form, shielding him from the blast.

Huddled protectively over the officer, West kept him from further injury. But several jagged shards of shrapnel ripped into West's face, one tearing violently into his left eye. Blood streamed down his face while he continued his self-appointed task of saving this man's life.

When three North Koreans were spotted trying to work their way behind the embattled patrol, West had the best view of them. Setting his burden aside, he unslung his rifle from his shoulder and sighted on the enemy. Though suffering sharp pain from the shrapnel in his eye, West brought the North Koreans down with three carefully aimed shots. Then he finished dragging the unconscious officer to the small depression along the trail serving as a temporary aid station.

A medic pulled West aside. "Let me look at that eye," he insisted. "There's no time," West replied. "There's a couple more wounded guys out there I've gotta get. You guys head back. I'll be all right." Spurning all attempts at aid and continually urging the others to start back, West made his way back down the trail through enemy fire. Ignoring the rifle shots fired at him and the occasional crash of an enemy grenade, West patiently searched through the thick underbrush, calling softly for the two casualties. At last he found them, sheltered at the base of a rock outcropping.

West hastily bound the two men's wounds. One casualty had taken several machine-gun bullets in the legs and couldn't walk. West slipped an arm around the man's shoulders and, with the help of the other casualty, started back down the trail.

By now enemy activity had dwindled to sporadic firing. West and his two charges shuffled hurriedly down the path. Suddenly, three figures appeared on the trail in front of them, blocking their way to safety.

Unsure who they were, West issued a challenge, then waited for the password. No response. Whipping his rifle to his hip, West pumped off three quick rounds. North Korean screams filled the night as the rounds cut into them. They fell in a heap alongside the trail. Then West calmly led the casualties to safety.

Because of West's unflinching loyalty to his comrades, all three men received timely medical attention and their lives were saved. The doctors were unable to save West's eye, though; it was too badly damaged. The quiet, unassuming soldier spent ten months in various hospitals before finally being medically discharged in August 1953. Five months later, on January 12, 1954, West was summoned to the White House to receive his Medal of Honor from President Eisenhower. Then West returned to his modest home in the rolling hills overlooking the Ohio River. West has avoided the glare of the limelight that frequently floods war heroes. He prefers to live a quiet life. "I didn't do anything special," he insists.

In early October General Van Fleet communicated to General Clark his desire to launch a limited objective attack north of Kumhwa in the IX Corps area of responsibility. Van Fleet proposed Operation *Showdown*, designed to improve the corps defensive line. Van Fleet explained to Clark that in the hills beyond Kumhwa IX Corps and enemy troops manned positions that were often less than two hundred yards apart. On Hill 598 and Sniper Ridge, about one mile northeast of Hill 598, the opposing forces looked down each other's throats. As a result, U.N. casualties were unnecessarily, and unacceptably, high.

The objective of Van Fleet's plan was to throw the enemy off these two high points. Once dislodged, the Chinese would be forced to pull back 1,250 yards to the next defensive positions, giving IX Corps units the needed breathing room. Counting heavily on massive firepower from the ground troops and maximum close-air support, General Van Fleet was optimistic about *Showdown*'s chances for success.

Clark had recently demonstrated an unwillingness to approve of similar costly hill-taking expeditions. Evidently, though, he felt that *Showdown* was not only tactically necessary but could be achieved without excessive casualties. He approved Van Fleet's proposal.

As conceived, *Showdown* would use two battalions of infantry, one from the U.S. 7th Infantry Division and one from the ROK 2d Division. There would be five days of preparatory air and artillery bombardments. Van Fleet estimated the operation would take five days and incur about two hundred casualties.

As it turned out, commitments elsewhere on the battlefield reduced the air strikes and artillery preparations against the hills to just two days. Moreover, early recon efforts clearly demonstrated the Chinese had no intention of easily relinquishing their hold on Hill 598. Accordingly, the 7th Division commander assigned a second battalion to the assault. The 1st Battalion, 31st Infantry Regiment, would assault the right arm of the Hill 598 complex, dubbed "Jane Russell Hill." The left arm of the V-shaped hill mass was assigned to the 3d Battalion, 31st Infantry. The ROK unit would stand by in reserve.

The 3d Battalion jumped off shortly after dawn on October 14, 1952. They immediately ran into fierce enemy resistance. The Chinese unleashed a vicious barrage of hand grenades, shaped charges, and mortar fire on the attackers. By mid-afternoon the assault company had been reinforced by two more companies. They did little better.

On the right flank, Company A, 1st Battalion, 31st Infantry Regiment, stood poised to begin its assault against Jane Russell Hill. At its helm was a twenty-four-year-old first lieutenant determined to take his company to the top of the ridge.

EDWARD R. SCHOWALTER

A few weeks before Operation *Showdown* began, 1st Lt. Edward R. Schowalter overheard a conversation between his battalion commander and the 7th Infantry Division's assistant commander. The brigadier general commented to the major as they strolled past Schowalter's tent in a reserve area, "Looks like we'll be getting some Chinese real estate pretty soon."

The battalion commander responded, "I'd sure like to be part of that, sir."

With that remark Schowalter's battalion was chosen to lead the attack on Jane Russell Hill. Because he was the battalion's most experienced company commander, Schowalter's Company A would go up the hill first.

Born in New Orleans on Christmas Eve 1927, Schowalter grew up in nearby Metairie, the son of a prosperous attorney. Like many youngsters of that era, Schowalter was gripped by patriotic fever during World War II. He begged to be allowed to enlist but his sensible father declined to let his underage son join the military. Not until he'd graduated from high school in June 1944, then attained his seventeenth birthday, did Schowalter's father relent to the pressure and sign his son's enlistment papers.

The service branch selected by young Schowalter was the merchant marine, operating during World War II under the U.S. Coast Guard. He'd completed his training and was preparing to ship out to Europe aboard a Liberty ship when Germany surrendered. Schowalter spent the next year as a galley helper, ferrying veterans of the European fighting back to the United States.

Though the work was boring and uninspiring, Schowalter did come away with one positive impression from his year's service aboard the Liberty ship: He found the soldiers to be men he admired and respected. He determined to become an officer and make the army his career.

With his father's help Schowalter entered the Virginia Military Institute in the fall of 1947. He immersed himself in all his college classes, but especially the ROTC courses; he simply wanted to be the best soldier possible.

Upon graduation in June 1951 Schowalter's hard work paid off: He was offered, and immediately accepted, a regular army commission. Six months of stateside troop duty followed the completion of the officers' basic course at Fort Benning, Georgia, before 2d Lt. Schowalter headed for Korea in March 1952.

The trip to Korea from the replacement depot in Japan was made by ferry boat across the Sea of Japan, then via a coal-fired train to 7th Infantry Division headquarters near Kumhwa. Once there, Schowalter's first priority was to shower off the dirt and grime of the week's journey. After checking into the transient officer's tent, Schowalter headed off to the nearest shower. While marveling at the efficiency of the shower, its unending gallons of hot water, and its excellent construction, Schowalter's bath was interrupted by a nervous sergeant major who informed the young second lieutenant he was using the commanding general's personal stall! Schowalter beat a hasty retreat.

Schowalter began his career with Company A as a platoon leader. Because of the high casualty rates in line outfits, he became the executive officer within three months. In August 1952 his CO was evacuated and Schowalter took over the company.

Once his company was selected to be the first up Jane Russell Hill, Schowalter spent the available time training his men for the upcoming battle.

He selected terrain that closely resembled Jane Russell Hill and repeatedly led his company in practice assaults. He arranged for L-19 artillery spotter planes to fly him and his platoon leaders over the Chinese positions. He even led several night recon patrols to the base of Jane Russell Hill, seeking all available information on the enemy's disposition. By the time Company A was ready to leave the MLR at daybreak on October 14, it was as ready for the upcoming fight as any unit could be.

At the base of the hill Schowalter sent one of his platoons against adjacent Sandy Ridge. He kept one platoon in reserve then personally led the other two against an enemy strong point midway up Jane Russell Hill.

Within fifty yards of their jumping-off point, the Chinese hit Schowalter and his platoons with a fury they had not previously encountered. From their trenches farther up the hill, the Chinese unloaded on the GIs with dozens of small arms, burp guns, machine guns, and mortars. Grenade after grenade flew through the air, exploding among the Americans. Men barked in pain as they were hit by shrapnel from the enemy missiles.

At the head of the two platoons, Schowalter was shocked by the volume of fire. The air around his head was alive with the buzz of bullets. For a moment he hesitated; to advance into that maelstrom seemed to invite death. "But then," Schowalter later recalled, "I realized this is what I'd trained for for over a year, what I'd wanted to do for over five years. These men depended on me. I couldn't let them down. And most importantly, I couldn't let myself down."

With a shout to those around him, Schowalter jumped forward. Within the first few steps an enemy bullet ripped across the back of his hand while another grazed an ankle. Their impact only stung Schowalter, so he kept going.

Above the platoon line U.N. artillery crashed into the enemy positions, pinning the Chinese down. Back on the MLR U.S. tanks and quad .50s poured a lethal dose of fire into the Chinese trenches. Moving as close to this fire as he dared, "leaning into" the friendly fire as the GIs said, Schowalter boldly led his men into the enemy strong point.

As he charged upward one of his BAR men moved alongside him, blasting away at the Chinese. Schowalter looked on in stunned horror as an enemy round slammed square into the man's face, horribly wounding him. Then he watched in awe as the young soldier, blood pouring from his hideous wound, kept right on going, never letting up on his firing. "Where do we get such men?" Schowalter wondered.

Around him Schowalter's soldiers admired his courage. One man said, "Right through the hail of grenades and small-arms fire he led us." By his tremendous display of leadership, Schowalter set an example of stamina and courage his men strove to emulate.

While providing cover fire for the men wiping out the first strong point, Schowalter was hit directly in the head by a sniper's bullet. He went down, out cold from the impact of the round. Fortunately, Schowalter's steel helmet deflected the bullet. It tore halfway around his head between his helmet and its liner before exiting and lodging between the skin and bone above his right ear.

When Schowalter came to a few minutes later, he found himself being dragged to a protected area by a medic. Once he realized his wound wasn't that serious, Schowalter shrugged off the efforts of the medic and returned to the fight.

As he followed his two platoons up the hill, Schowalter was amazed at the tremendous increase in enemy fire. He hadn't thought it possible, but the Chinese fire seemed twice as strong as before. As a result, the GIs were stalled in their attack. Schowalter bounded to the front, shouting for everyone to follow him. His chest swelled with pride when his men rose and charged. Together they overwhelmed the next line of Chinese.

Seconds later an enemy grenade erupted right next to the indomitable lieutenant. Despite his protective flak jacket, shards of razor sharp steel tore into his right side. Again a medic tried to treat the wounds. Again Schowalter refused. "Take care of my men first. They need it worse than I do," is all he said.

Below him Schowalter watched the walking wounded streaming downhill, their fight over. His platoons were nearly cut in half, but he had a job to do. He wasn't about to give up.

About this time the battalion commander radioed Schowalter that two marine corps planes were available for a rocketing and strafing run on the main Chinese trenches. Could Schowalter use them? Absolutely, he answered. He had his radiomen mark the platoon's lines with panels, then called the planes in.

"They came in so low I felt I could reach up and touch their bellies," Schowalter remembered. "The air force guys wouldn't come in below two thousand feet. The marines were great. They zoomed in just feet above the ground."

The Corsairs made two runs, blasting the Chinese positions with rockets and .50-caliber machine guns. "Those babies blew a path right through the center of the Chinese," Schowalter said. "We followed right into the trenches just as soon as the planes peeled off."

The GIs poured into the enemy's works, turning left and right down the trenches in pursuit of the foe. The crackle of rifle fire resounded throughout the trenchworks as the GIs hunted down the enemy. Hand-to-hand fighting broke out as the two sides closed.

Schowalter led one squad down a trench, firing his pistol at the enemy with his left hand while he tossed grenades into bunkers with his right. After clearing out a number of positions, Schowalter rounded a blind curve in the trench. He froze.

"Rushing right at me was a Chinaman, his bayoneted rifle pointed at my chest," Schowalter said. "I was scared to death. Then, suddenly, I thought my whole head was blown off as a large explosion went off right next to my ear."

Behind Schowalter, one of his riflemen had spotted the enemy soldier. The GI raised his rifle, pointed it over the lieutenant's shoulder and fired. The report startled Schowalter. The bullet stopped the Chinese, who dropped at Schowalter's feet.

Schowalter continued down the trench, firing at any remaining enemy. Around him the surviving platoon members were winning, pushing the Chinese off Jane Russell Hill. Schowalter had nearly accomplished his objective. Then a Chinese machine gun, hidden in a cave dug into the trench wall, spat out a short burst. A slug slammed into Schowalter's right forearm, shattering the bone. The shock of the injury knocked him out.

When he came to for the second time that morning, Schowalter found he could not move. Heavy weights pressed down on his legs and back. As he slowly regained his senses he realized where he was. Someone had stacked him in a pile of dead Chinese. He squirmed and struggled for what seemed like an eternity before he finally broke free of the ghastly trap.

Staggering under the pain of his wounds, Schowalter assured himself the platoons had secured their objective. Only then did he turn to head downhill. On the way down he bumped into the commander of a reinforcing company. The commander queried Schowalter, "How's it going up there?"

"Okay, I guess," Schowalter answered. "I've been out for a while."

A short time later Schowalter was in the hands of medics. Within a few days he was on his way to an army hospital in Japan and, eventually, one in the United States. He would spend a total of six months in the hospital while bone specialists rebuilt his arm. They did an excellent job. A year after being wounded, Schowalter completed airborne training to qualify as an army parachutist.

On January 12, 1954, President Eisenhower placed the blue ribbon of the Medal of Honor around Schowalter's neck. Schowalter was always amazed he was nominated for the august award. "I was just doing my job," he says with genuine humility. "I saw other guys do things I'd never have the guts to do and they received no medals. I always figured I was awarded the medal as the representative of a superb fighting team. We took that hill together. I wear the Medal of Honor on behalf of all the men who fought and died on that hill. It's really theirs."

Schowalter's subsequent military career included the command of a battalion in the 82d Airborne Division and two tours of duty in Vietnam, where he was wounded three more times. Along the way he married and fathered five children. He retired as a full colonel on July 1, 1977. He has devoted the years since then to enjoying his retirement.

While Lieutenant Schowalter was being ferried by half-track to an aid station, the fight continued for Hill 598 and its various ridges and spurs. At the end of the day the CCF counterattacked, forcing the 1st Battalion to withdraw its forces back to the MLR. It was brutally obvious the Chinese had no intention of surrendering Hill 598.

Over the next several days the U.S. 7th Infantry Division commander threw one fresh battalion after another into the fray. Time after time the intrepid U.S. infantrymen took the high ground during the day only to be counterattacked and forced off the hill at night. Not until October 23 were the Americans finally able to hold on to some of the hilltops. Two days later the ROK 2d Infantry Division relieved the U.S. 7th Infantry Division. On October 30 the CCF swept the ROK defenders off Hill 598 and the nearby hills, including Jane Russell. Though the ROKs repeatedly counterattacked, they were unable to retake the Chinese-held real estate. Thus, after nine weeks of fighting, the U.N. command held none of the Hill 598 complex. The original two-battalion attack, planned to last five days and cost two hundred casualties, had instead drawn in two divisions and cost over nine thousand casualties. The seemingly endless war in Korea dragged on.

In the United States the Korean problem dominated the closing days of the presidential campaign. Both candidates, Gen. Dwight D. Eisenhower for the Republicans and Adlai E. Stevenson for the Democrats, made peace on the embattled peninsula the mainstay of their respective platforms. Neither, though, actually presented a workable solution to end the war.

When Eisenhower emerged as the victor, the more hawkish U.S. military planners anticipated the architect of the Allied victory in Europe would approve a plan for a major U.N. offensive. In anticipation of such approval, General Clark approached the Joint Chiefs of Staff with a proposal to launch a seven-division offensive against Pyongyang. However, when President-elect Eisenhower visited Korea in early December, fulfilling a much-repeated campaign pledge, General Clark had no opportunity to present his plan. Eisenhower never once brought up the matter of seeking a military victory in Korea.

In fact, at a press conference on December 5, his last day in Korea, Eisenhower admitted he had "no panaceas, no tricks," for ending the war. To Clark it was obvious the new president would follow the same course set by Mr. Truman and seek an honorable peace. The last hope for a purely military settlement thus died. It was evident that the country's political leaders, regardless of party, intended to negotiate an end to the war. And, unless the U.N. decided to capitulate to the enemy's demands for prisoner repatriation, the initiative for breaking the stalemate rested with the Communists.

After the sharp clashes along the MLR in October and early November, the advent of another brutal Korean winter saw a decline in operations at the front. The combatants retreated to their bunkers, seeking protection from the icy stab of the Korean winter wind. Though both sides kept up the old routine of raids and patrols, they seemed more content to watch each other warily along the battle lines and conserve their energy.

The relative lull continued through January 1953. The Chinese did attempt to gobble up a number of U.N. outposts but were repeatedly repulsed. Most of these attacks were still undoubtedly political in nature, designed solely to pressure the U.S. to get out of the war.

The U.N. utilized the same tactics. By wresting a few key positions from the enemy, General Van Fleet hoped to convince them they could not win a military victory, either. The I Corps planned such an operation for the U.S. 1st Marine Division in early February.

Ungok, or to the Marines Hill 101, sat just north of Bunker Hill and south of the Nevada Complex: Reno, Carson, and Vegas. A massive, formidable peak of granite, Ungok was held by several companies of experienced Chinese infantry. The I Corps planners did not expect to be able to conquer Ungok; the cost would be far too high. However, they did feel a company-sized raiding party with the mission of snatching a few prisoners would prove to the enemy the U.N. forces still had some fight in them after a long, hard winter.

RAYMOND G. MURPHY

To 2d Lt. Raymond G. Murphy, Ungok looked like the Rock of Gibraltar. It sat across the MLR from the bunker positions of his Third Platoon, Company A, 1st Battalion, 5th Marines. From its heights the Chinese frequently fired mortars and light artillery barrages on Murphy's marines, causing frequent casualties. Murphy's men eagerly anticipated the chance to repay the Chinese in kind.

Lieutenant Murphy had been due to rotate from Korea on January 31, 1953. But as soon as he learned of the upcoming mission, he volunteered to extend his tour. He was not about to let the marines of his platoon be led on such a potentially dangerous mission by anyone else. That's the way Murphy was—extremely protective of those under his care. He'd demonstrated that care more than once during his nearly eight months in Korea.

Born January 14, 1930, in Pueblo, Colorado, Murphy was an outstanding athlete in high school, excelling in baseball, basketball, and football. His exceptional ability on the gridiron earned him a college scholarship. He graduated from Adams State College, Alamosa, Colorado, with a degree in physical education; his goal was to coach high school athletes. Before that goal could be realized, though, Uncle Sam beckoned him.

Two of Murphy's brothers had served in World War II, one as an officer. Based on their experiences, Murphy, who faced the draft upon graduation, opted to take advantage of a special Marine Corps program.

Because of the high casualty rates among frontline junior officers in Korea, the Marine Corps offered qualified candidates a temporary commission upon successfully completing the rugged boot camp at Parris Island, South Carolina. Then the new second lieutenants would take the officers' basic course at Quantico, Virginia. If they graduated they retained their commission; if not, they reverted to enlisted status.

Murphy entered the Marine Corps in May 1951 as soon as he graduated from college. He successfully completed all phases of his training and was transferred to Camp Pendleton, California, for duty with troops. He was supposed to be part of a replacement battalion then forming at Camp Pendleton that would go to Korea as a unit, but the critical need for platoon leaders after the heavy spring fighting altered that plan. Murphy and several other new lieutenants were hustled off to Korea in June 1952.

Upon arrival in Korea, Murphy was assigned command of a platoon in Company C, 1st Battalion, 5th Marines. In August he transferred to Company A. He took over the Third Platoon, the same unit that 1st Lt. Baldemoro Lopez had led ashore at Inchon two years earlier.

Just as Lopez had exhibited a high degree of concern for his men, so did Murphy. Because he clearly understood that the war would not be won or lost based on his men's sacrifices, Murphy took every precaution to reduce casualties. He knew some losses were inevitable, but he wanted to do all he could to keep them to a minimum. One time he was convinced his actions would result in a court-martial.

On the brisk night of November 22, 1952, Murphy led a patrol deep into Chinese territory north of Panmunjom. As they neared their objective a nervous corpsman on his first patrol threw a white phosphorous grenade at what he thought was an enemy position. The intense white light instantly silhouetted the patrol members, bringing down a barrage of Chinese mortars.

Murphy instantly reacted to the dangerous situation by hustling his men to cover. Despite his best efforts, a number of his marines were wounded by the enemy shells, several quite seriously. Murphy knew if he delayed in getting them medical aid they'd die. He couldn't allow that. Rather than hike over the rugged mountains he decided to take the quickest route back to the MLR—down the neutral peace zone extending between Panmunjom and Munsan-ni.

Though Murphy's actions created quite a stir among those charged with overseeing the neutrality of the corridor, the seriously wounded marines survived. For several weeks he sweated over the consequences of his violation of the neutral zone. He felt for sure he'd be brought up on charges. He wasn't. Instead, his concern for his men resulted in a Silver Star award.

Once word of the prisoner-snatching raid on Ungok was revealed to Murphy's company commander, he established a schedule of dry runs—practices for the raid. For nearly two weeks the entire company went over the plan time after time. Simulated assaults with live ammo honed the marines to a keen fighting edge. By the time the company filed out of the MLR on the night of February 2, they could run through the assault in their sleep.

The third platoon had the assignment of acting as both the evacuation platoon and the company reserve. Murphy's men would aid casualties from the assault platoons and be available to join the battle as needed.

Company A assumed its jump-off positions in the predawn darkness of February 3. As soon as it became light the assault platoons started up Ungok.

From his position below the attacking platoons Murphy could hear the sounds of the bitter fight raging above him. The sharp crack of M-1s and the crash of grenades seemed to be a nearly constant roar. A steady stream of wounded marines filtered down Ungok. Murphy's marines gathered them up and guided them to the rear.

After the fight had continued for over an hour, Murphy began to feel that something was wrong. By now enemy prisoners should have been rounded up and the company should have been on its way back to the MLR. Instead, the casualties had stopped coming down the hill and the sounds of a brisk firefight continued to fill the air. Murphy decided to go forward and find out for himself what was going on.

What he found was chaos. The Chinese resistance had proven to be much stronger than anticipated. As a result, the attack had stalled. Almost all the officers and senior NCOs were killed or wounded. The surviving marines had sought shelter. Murphy saw immediately that the attack had fallen apart. He had to act now to save what was left of the company.

He led his platoon in an attack on a key enemy strong point. At the front of his men, Murphy maneuvered them with words of encouragement and praise. Bounding from one position to the next, he brought his platoon to the rescue of the others.

Several times Murphy deliberately exposed himself to enemy fire to pull wounded men to safety. They were still his responsibility and he couldn't let them down.

The gallant lieutenant was hit and painfully wounded when an enemy mortar exploded near him while going to the aid of one casualty. Blood poured from the numerous holes that dotted his left side but Murphy hardly felt the enemy metal; he was intent only on getting the marine to safety. While several of his men provided covering fire, Murphy made uncounted trips across open ground to save the wounded. One of the sergeants who witnessed Murphy's heroics said "it would be impossible to know how many trips Murphy made under enemy fire to pull guys to safety."

As the wounded picked their way downhill through the rocky ground, Murphy noticed an enemy detachment pouring a deadly stream of fire at them. Determined to protect the casualties to the fullest extent possible, he stalked the enemy soldiers. He cornered them and, in a lightning-fast duel, killed them.

Through his radioman Murphy had kept the battalion commander apprised of the situation. Based on his reports it was decided to break off the attack. Murphy moved across the bullet-swept hillside, passing the word to withdraw. As the others pulled back, the young lieutenant covered their movement with deadly accurate fire from his carbine. At one point he picked up a discarded BAR and used it with telling effect to repulse a vicious enemy attack.

At the base of Ungok Murphy quickly started the casualties on their way to the MLR. Then he organized a search party to sweep the battleground for any overlooked marines. He located and helped carry down the hill the bodies of a machine-gun crew. Only when he was convinced all the marines had been accounted for did Murphy leave the battlefield.

On the way back to the MLR Murphy helped carry the stretcher of one badly wounded marine. As he did so, the Chinese dropped harassing artillery fire on the retreating marines. A piece of shrapnel from one round tore into Murphy's right hand but he maintained his grip on the stretcher, preventing further injury to the man.

Once back in the friendly confines of the MLR, Murphy steadfastly refused treatment for his wounds until he was assured all the other casualties had been treated. Only then did he allow the corpsman to treat him.

The attack on Ungok had been a near disaster. Eighteen marines died; another seventy were wounded. If Murphy had not repeatedly risked his life to save others the casualty list would undoubtedly have been higher.

Murphy's numerous wounds forced his evacuation. He ended up at the Naval Hospital at Mare Island, California. On April 12, 1953, fully recovered, he was released from active duty. He took advantage of the GI Bill of Rights to enroll in graduate school in Massachusetts. It was while he was there he received word of his Medal of Honor.

"I was shocked," Murphy recalled. "It didn't seem to me I'd done anything to warrant this high honor."

Those whose lives he'd saved felt otherwise. Their recommendations had brought this ultimate distinction to the Coloradan. President Eisenhower made the presentation on October 27, 1953.

Murphy then returned to his studies, earning his master's degree in education in December 1954. He worked as the recreational director for Natick, Massachusetts, for four years before joining his brother in a business venture in Santa Fe, New Mexico. In 1974, after selling the business, Murphy joined the Veterans Administration as a benefits counselor, where he remains today helping other veterans.

As February progressed there was growing concern in General Clark's headquarters that the Chinese might launch a major offensive before the spring thaw. United Nations intelligence estimated the CCF and NKPA now had nearly 1,100,000 men available and had been stockpiling massive amounts of ammo and supplies throughout the relatively quiet winter. Several badly bloodied Communist units had been replaced at the front lines by full-strength, well-equipped, fresh units.

General Van Fleet was not worried. He remained confident that his Eighth Army could meet anything the enemy threw at them. Despite the frustration he'd experienced in fighting a limited war, Van Fleet had lost none of his desire to deal the Communists a crushing blow.

But he would have to be satisfied with aggressive patrols and raids into enemy territory. The American state of mind for getting out of Korea as painlessly as possible had not changed.

Van Fleet would never be able to carry out his longed-for offensive operation against the enemy. On February 11, 1953, he turned over command of the Eighth Army to Lt. Gen. Maxwell D. Taylor, the famed World War II commander of the 101st Airborne Division. While Van Fleet returned to the United States and retirement, Taylor instituted a rigid training schedule for all his troops. Under it, all patrols vigorously rehearsed their battle plans. Reserve units underwent an eight-week training cycle before reentering the line.

Taylor's new programs resulted in increased penetration of the enemy's lines. Nearly every unit in each corps sent heavy raiding parties after enemy hill positions. In early March the enemy began hitting back. Attacks in full battalion strength fell on U.N. positions. Particularly hard hit were the U.S. 2d Infantry Division's positions on Little Gibraltar; the U.S. 7th Infantry Division's outposts on Old Baldy and Porkchop Hill; and the ROK 9th Infantry Division's hilltops near Kumhwa. But the brunt of the Chinese attacks hit the U.S. 1st Marine Division.

An outpost of a Korean marine regiment serving with the U.S. 1st Marine Division was overrun by two Chinese platoons on the night of March 18. The next day two full Chinese companies hit positions held by the 5th

Marines. The attackers were beaten off after several hours of bitter fighting. The marines responded to these attacks with a raid into enemy territory. This, in turn, brought retaliatory attacks from the Chinese. On the night of March 22, two Chinese companies, supported by a seventeen-hundred-round artillery barrage, hit Bunker Hill. Savage hand-to-hand combat erupted before the Chinese were driven off.

Over the next several nights sporadic diversionary attacks struck a number of marine outposts. Then, on the night of March 26, 1953, an entire Chinese regiment struck a series of outposts manned by units of the 5th Marines. These outposts—Vegas, Reno, and Carson—sat about ten miles northeast of Panmunjom. Chinese POWs later told their interrogators their mission was to seize these three outposts before an anticipated U.N. spring offensive got under way.

Both Reno and Vegas fell after close, heavy fighting. The surviving marines pulled back and hastily set up blocking positions between the lost outposts and the MLR. Reinforcements for Carson were sent out. The response unit was Company F, 2d Battalion, 5th Marines. From their positions on the MLR they hastened forward in the inky blackness toward Carson. They didn't make it.

Less than halfway to Carson a vicious enemy artillery and mortar barrage dropped on the marines. Right behind the rolling wall of lethal steel came a column of Chinese troops. The marines dived for cover. A brisk firefight erupted as the leathernecks took the enemy under fire.

Casualties were heavy as the marines defended their impromptu positions, keeping the company's corpsmen busy. One of them, Hospital Corpsman Francis C. Hammond, a twenty-one-year-old from Alexandria, Virginia, continually ignored the crashing explosions to go to the aid of stricken marines. Even after he himself was severely wounded, Hammond kept on moving across the fire-swept area to reach casualties.

For over four hours the embattled company held its positions, unable to reach Carson and unwilling to concede the hotly contested ground. Finally, though, word came from the battalion to pull back under the covering fire of another unit; Carson would be abandoned, too. Hammond, though suffering from great pain, refused to be evacuated. Instead, he oversaw the evacuation of the others. Several times he led litter-bearer teams across open, fire-swept areas to get to isolated casualties.

One casualty lay directly exposed to the enemy's rifle fire. Without hesitation, Hammond, who had a pregnant wife back in Alexandria, dashed from cover toward the writhing form. Suddenly, an earth-shattering roar split the night. A mortar shell had landed at Hammond's feet, killing him before he could complete his mission of mercy.

The U.N. efforts to retake the three outposts were continually repulsed, despite rushing heavy reinforcements to the battleground. Altogether, supporting U.N. artillery units fired over 100,000 rounds, mortar units fired over fifty-four thousand shells, and tanks directed seven thousand 90mm cannon rounds at the enemy. These barely fazed the CCF. They stubbornly clung to their hard-won positions and, in turn, sent nearly fifty thousand artillery rounds flying back toward the marines.

As it became obvious the marines could not dislodge the Chinese from all three outposts, it was decided to concentrate the counterattacks against Vegas Hill, the highest of the three hilltops. To strengthen the marines' counterattack the 2d Battalion, 7th Marines, was attached to the 5th Marines. Trucked from their reserve position behind the MLR, they arrived ready to do battle. While it was still dark on the morning of March 27, the marines started toward Vegas. Across the rugged, sloping ground, the shrubs and trees almost completely destroyed by shellfire, they moved on Vegas. In Company F, 2d Battalion, 7th Marines, was a navy corpsman, a friend of Francis Hammond's, whose personal heroism over the next twenty-four hours would bring him two special honors.

WILLIAM R. CHARETTE

When he was four years old William R. Charette lost his parents. His aunt and uncle raised him, seeing him through high school in his hometown of Ludington, Michigan. After graduating from high school in June 1950, Charette found a job on one of the ferry boats crossing Lake Michigan between Ludington and Milwaukee, Wisconsin. From that experience Charette developed a fondness for the sea. Thus, when Charette realized the draft was rapidly approaching him, he decided to enlist in the navy.

Charette took basic training at the Great Lakes Naval Base starting in January 1951. Because his sister was a nurse, he elected to attend hospital corpsman school. Six months of intensive medical training, where he and the other trainees took courses in anatomy, physiology, and advanced first aid, followed at Bainbridge, Maryland. From there he was assigned to the Naval Hospital at Charleston, South Carolina.

By the time Charette had spent a year on ward duty he wanted a change. The only way to effect a transfer was to volunteer for service as a field medic with the marines in Korea. In October 1952 he did so. From Charleston he headed cross-country to Camp Pendleton, a marine corps base in southern California. There the navy trained its corpsmen in the rugged task of field medicine, the treatment of combat casualties.

One of Charette's buddies in training was Francis Hammond. They spent a good deal of their off-duty time together. Most of the time Hammond talked about his wife, Phyllis, and their plans for their first child. Charette and Hammond became fast friends and hoped they'd serve together in Korea.

After he'd completed the six-week course Charette spent the holidays of 1952 with his family in Michigan. Then he started the long journey to Korea. Upon arrival in the war-torn country in January 1953, he drew an assignment to the 7th Marines. His buddy Hammond went to the 5th Marines. Charette was sure they'd see each other again, perhaps even take a leave together.

Charette's first two months in Korea were relatively uneventful. When his company was on the MLR he accompanied a number of barbed-wire-laying patrols into enemy territory. Though there were a few casualties from enemy shelling, those were about the only shots Charette heard fired in anger. When off the line, duty was routine and boring, the days filled with work details and training problems.

The inactivity ended when the call came for Company F to reinforce the 5th Marines fighting to regain Vegas Hill. As Charette boarded a truck for the ride to the front, he wondered how Hammond was doing. He wouldn't find out for several days that his good friend had fallen on the battlefield.

The drive to retake Vegas began at noon, March 27. The advancing marines encountered heavy concentrations of enemy artillery as they made their way forward. Men dropped, cut down by the flying shrapnel. Charette and the other corpsmen in his company were kept busy patching the guys up as best they could and getting them evacuated.

Progress in the drive up Vegas was slow. The Chinese put up a stubborn resistance. Not until late afternoon had the marines fought their way into the lower trenches of Vegas Hill. Charette was so busy he didn't notice the passage of time. It was nearly dusk when he caught up with the rest of his company. They were by then providing covering fire for the lead company in the next trench line about seventy-five yards farther up the hill.

Charette had barely time to organize himself before the cry came down the hill, "Corpsman! Corpsman up! CORPSMAN!"

The lead company was taking heavy casualties, more than their overworked corpsmen could handle. They needed help. Charette went forward without hesitation.

He bounded up the badly scarred hill, oblivious to the bullets zipping by his head, the crunch of mortars and grenades going off nearby. Once in the forward trenches Charette was directed to a casualty. Before he knew it he found himself with the point squad. One of its members lay at the bottom of the trench, severely wounded. Charette went to work.

"The Chinese above us were rolling grenades downhill onto us," Charette remembered. "There were so many going off there was no way to count them. It was just a constant roar."

While working on the marine, Charette wondered, "What the hell am I doing here? I don't even know these guys. Then I realized my job was to save people. That's what I was there for. That's what I tried to do."

While he was treating the man, grenades continued to fall into the trench, detonating every few seconds. One landed right near Charette and his patient. "I couldn't see it in the dark. I knew it was there. It was going to go off," Charette said. "The guy I was working on was pretty bad. If he were hit again I didn't think he'd make it.

"I was scared. I knew I couldn't jump on the grenade. So I grabbed my medical bag and tried to push it away. I think it went into the bag."

Desiring only to protect the marine, Charette crouched over his inert form. The grenade exploded with a violent roar. The blast drove shrapnel deep into Charette's face. The concussion blew his helmet off, deafened him, and temporarily blinded him. But his patient was alive.

With the fighting raging all around him, and since he was the only corpsman that far forward, casualties drifted toward Charette. Before he knew it five badly wounded marines were under his care. When one of them was brought in with his flak jacket blown off, Charette quickly pulled one off a dead marine and put it on the man. At one point, with his medical supplies nearly exhausted, Charette tore his own clothing into strips to use as bandages.

Grenades and artillery shells pounded the marines continually throughout the hellish night. Eventually, the constant pounding collapsed the trench wall around Charette. By this time it was close to dawn, March 28. Word came for the lead company to pull back. Several marines helped carry Charette's patients out of the battered trench.

One casualty's leg was nearly severed, hanging on only by a thin strip of flesh. Because of the collapsed trench walls it was nearly impossible for the marines, huddled down to avoid the brisk enemy fire, to pull the man out from the trench without injuring him further. Charette solved the dilemma by picking the man up in his arms and, standing fully upright, carrying him downhill to safety.

"I could hear the bullets zipping by my head," Charette says, "but I had no choice. I couldn't leave the guy there."

It was about 5:00 A.M., March 28, when Charette came down off Vegas Hill. "I looked like a butcher," he said. "I was covered with blood. Not my own, but that of the fellows I'd treated."

Enemy fire was still so heavy a smoke screen was necessary to allow the marines to pull back. Charette had his facial wounds treated at an aid station, then rejoined his company. After the mauling they'd taken the company was again placed in reserve.

Charette spent several more months with Company F, then was reassigned to a field hospital. For his valor on Vegas he had been recommended for the

Navy Cross. As the paperwork made its way up the chain of command, the reviewing authorities questioned whether the Navy Cross was an appropriate award for the corpsman. They decided it was not. Instead, they approved a Medal of Honor for him.

Charette was still in Korea when he received word of the prestigious award in late 1953. He quickly found himself on a plane bound for the United States. After seeing his family for the first time in nearly a year, Charette traveled to Washington. There, on January 12, 1954, he received his award from President Eisenhower.

When Charette's enlistment expired he took his discharge. After ninety days as a married civilian with a pregnant wife, he decided to reenlist and make the navy his career. He also volunteered for submarine duty and ended up spending the next twenty years in the sub fleet.

On May 26, 1958, Charette experienced the second greatest honor of his life. As the only active duty navy enlisted Medal of Honor holder he was chosen to select the World War II Unknown Soldier. Aboard the USS *Canberra* off the Virginia Capes, he placed a wreath in front of the casket containing the remains of an American unknown that would lie forever in Arlington National Cemetery as a symbol of America's dead from that war.

"This was a tremendous honor for me," Charette says. "My grandchildren and their grandchildren will be able to visit the Tomb of the Unknowns and realize I had a small role in this national monument."

Charette retired from the navy in 1977.

Another member of Charette's company earned a Medal of Honor in the fighting for Vegas Hill. Sgt. Daniel P. Matthews, a twenty-one-year-old from San Fernando, California, saw that the devastating fire from a Chinese machine gun was preventing a corpsman from reaching a casualty lying in the open. Snaking his way forward, he arrived undetected at the base of the rock fortification surrounding the gun. He leaped up, stood on the lip of the machine-gun nest, and fired down into the pit. A burst of fire from another enemy automatic weapon tore into Matthews but he held his position. Three Chinese fell under his fire. Then Matthews collapsed on the embankment. Below him the corpsman pulled the wounded marine to safety.

For the rest of March 28 fresh marine companies were fed into the fight for Vegas Hill. Late that afternoon they finally succeeded in gaining the crest of the hill. Almost immediately the Chinese counterattacked. For the rest of that bloody day and well into the next day, the CCF tried to retake Vegas. The marines made skillful use of artillery to box in the enemy formations, breaking up several attacks before they could begin. Finally, the Chinese broke off their attacks on the afternoon of March 29. Their efforts in the Nevada complex cost them over thirteen hundred casualties. The marines, too, paid a heavy price for their victory: 118 dead, 801 wounded, and 98 missing in action.

While the fight for Vegas still raged, the first major break in the aborted armistice negotiations occurred, giving rise to an optimistic attitude that hostilities in Korea might finally end.

Chapter Thirteen
Final Months

When Gen. William K. Harrison and his associates walked out of the truce tent at Panmunjom on October 8, 1952, they did not know if they would ever return. The Communists' stance on prisoner repatriation appeared implacable. And since the U.N. command had offered its final negotiating position, the discussion phase was over. Until a break appeared in the adamant fronts presented by both sides, the prospects for a settlement remained remote.

During the winter months of 1952–53 various proposals aimed at breaking the impasse had been put forth by different members of the United Nations. None of the suggestions was acceptable to the U.S.; several were rejected by the Soviet delegation.

Those who had hoped the inauguration of Dwight D. Eisenhower would bring peace to Korea were disappointed. The new administration had no plans for ending the war and no intention of expanding the military pressure to force a settlement upon the Communists. The best proposal they could put forth was an old one: simply release those POWs who did not desire repatriation and present the Communists with a *fait accompli*. General Clark opposed that plan and it soon faded away.

The first break in this frustrating deadlock came in response to a communications General Clark had sent to the Communists in February. Reacting to a recommendation from the International Red Cross, Clark suggested the opponents exchange their sick and wounded prisoners. He expected no response and received none. Until March 28, 1953.

On that day the Communists unexpectedly agreed to an exchange of sick and wounded captives. They further surprised the U.N. command when they said they felt the exchange could "lead to the smooth settlement of the entire question of prisoners of war, thereby achieving an armistice in Korea . . ."

Two days later, in a statement covering the course of the armistice negotiations, Chinese Foreign Minister Chou En-lai offered a key concession. Referring to the POW issue, he said both sides "should undertake to repatriate immediately after the cessation of hostilities all those prisoners of war in their custody who insist upon repatriation and to hand over the remaining prisoners of war to a neutral state so as to ensure a just solution to the question of repatriation."

With that ray of hope in the air, preparations for the exchange of the sick and wounded POWs began at Panmunjom on April 6, 1953, when liaison officers for the two sides met to discuss the details of the swap. On April 11, the two sides signed an agreement completing the general arrangements. Operation *Little Switch* began at Panmunjom on April 20, 1953. The U.N. Command delivered POWs in batches of five hundred; the Communists a hundred. By the time the exchange was completed on May 3, 6,670 Communist POWs had been exchanged for 684 U.N. prisoners.

Based on the initial success of Operation *Little Switch*, the U.N. suggested a reconvening of the armistice talks on April 26. The Communists concurred. At the meetings over the next few weeks both sides presented proposals and counterproposals for the repatriation of prisoners. Most centered on selecting the neutral nation to which the nonrepatriates would be sent and how long they would be held.

The armistice discussions ebbed and flowed throughout the spring, with each side making concessions. Finally, at the end of May, the major details for handling POWs desiring repatriation and those who did not were ironed out. On June 8, 1953, the chief delegates signed an agreement settling this issue.

The final stumbling block to peace in Korea was the establishment of a demarcation line. The U.N. wanted the line to be the one originally agreed upon in November 1951. As the Communists had seized some key terrain features since then, they insisted on using the current positions. Because of their overwhelming desire to end the war, the U.N. negotiators soon agreed to accept the current disposition of the front line as the final demarcation line. The major considerations for an armistice agreement thus were successfully negotiated by June 17, 1953.

In the meantime, during these intense negotiations, the war had gone on. The Communists had launched major attacks at various points along the MLR, most falling against ROK divisions. Heavy pressure, however, was felt at the Nevada complex, now manned by the U.S. 25th Infantry Division, while the marines were in reserve, at the end of May. Earlier, the Communists had struck repeatedly at much-fought-over Porkchop Hill, defended by units of the U.S. 7th Infantry Division. The Chinese were repulsed, but Porkchop, west of Chorwon overlooking the historical invasion route to Seoul, remained a hotbed of activity.

Such was the case in the early morning hours of June 4, 1953. An eleven-man patrol from Company K, 17th Infantry, 7th Infantry Division, moved out from its position on Porkchop Hill to screen the north finger of the hill where enemy activity had been reported. As it moved through the darkness in a diamond formation, the man on the left flank, Pvt. Charles H. Barker, alerted the patrol leader to sounds coming from his left.

The patrol leader silently maneuvered the men into position. Soon he spotted a platoon of Chinese digging in on the finger. The GIs opened fire. The enemy broke for cover and their weapons. A brisk firefight erupted.

To the amazement of all who witnessed his actions, Barker, an eighteen-year-old from Pickens, South Carolina, crawled forward to within twenty yards of the enemy. From there he poured a withering hail of fire from his BAR into the Chinese, allowing the patrol to shift to a more advantageous position from which to fire on the enemy. While the higher ground occupied by the patrol enabled it to concentrate more deadly fire on the Chinese, it soon began to run low on ammo. Accordingly, the patrol leader ordered the men to pull out.

The Chinese quickly responded to the resulting slackening in fire by coming out of their holes and rushing forward. Rather than retreat, Barker held his ground. He rose to one knee, triggering bursts from his BAR into the charging enemy. When they continued coming, Barker stood up and slowly, deliberately, walked straight at them, firing his weapon, throwing grenades.

When the patrol members last saw Barker he was grappling hand-to-hand with an enemy soldier. Because of Barker's willing self-sacrifice, the rest of the patrol safety returned to their outpost.

Even though an armistice agreement was all but complete, the CCF and NKPA continued to mount attacks on the U.N. and its outposts in front of the MLR. There was no military justification for the vicious assaults. The final demarcation line had virtually been agreed upon. Any terrain the Communists captured would have to be relinquished when the armistice went into effect.

But still they came. Vicious clashes erupted nightly along the MLR. Some U.N. commanders felt their Communist counterparts across the MLR simply were not aware of the progress at Panmunjom; thus, for them, it was a matter of business as usual. Others felt the enemy applied the pressure in order to force the U.N. to accept the less desirable proposals put forth by the Communists in the truce talks. Some simply felt the enemy wanted to kill.

Whatever the reason, the fighting in June and July 1953 was brutal and bloody. United Nations casualties in those two months were the heaviest in nearly two years.

Following the agreement on June 8 concerning a general exchange of prisoners, the Communists mounted their biggest drive since the spring of 1951. The primary targets were those sectors in the Eighth Army's center guarded by the ROKs. In nine days of hard fighting the ROKs were driven back more than three thousand yards along a thirteen-thousand-yard front.

U.S. troops were not immune to these attacks. Northeast of Chorwon, in the IX Corps zone held by the U.S. 3d Infantry Division, two battalions of Chinese infantry opened a succession of attacks against Outpost *Harry*. The valiant defense of the outpost produced a Medal of Honor hero whose personal courage was reminiscent of the fabled Horatio at the Bridge.

OLA L. MIZE

Two platoons from Company K, 3d Battalion, 15th Infantry, moved out from the MLR on the morning of June 4, 1953. Heavily laden with their weapons, ammo, and equipment, the forty-eight GIs moved slowly, cautiously across the broad valley floor. Into the humpbacked hills, around winding ridges, through thick stands of trees and dense clumps of underbrush, the long column of green-clad GIs made their way to the finger-shaped hill that was their objective.

Outpost *Harry* was one of three key outposts—the others were *Tom* and *Dick*—protecting the 3d Infantry Division's main positions. When the Company K platoons reached *Harry* late in the afternoon, the outfit it relieved reported that it had had little or no activity during the week it held the position.

As the relieved GIs filed down the hill on their way back to the MLR, the men of Company K deployed among the bunkers and trenches on Outpost *Harry*. The second platoon moved into bunkers near the crest of the hill. Its assistant platoon leader, Sgt. Ola L. Mize, placed his squads into bunkers and issued orders. A soft-spoken Alabaman, Mize had only been with the company since Easter but had already earned a reputation as a first-class fighting man.

Born in Marshall County, Alabama, on August 28, 1931, Mize grew up in nearby Gadsden, where he attended grade and high school. When his parents split up, Mize quit school in the tenth grade to help support his mother and brothers by working at a variety of jobs. In April 1950 Mize fulfilled a longtime dream by enlisting in the army.

Following basic training, Mize volunteered for airborne training, thus beginning a nearly thirty-year career with America's elite fighting forces.

He spent over two years assigned to the 82d Airborne Division with duty in the United States. As a trained infantryman Mize wanted to go to Korea and do his part in the war. He volunteered several times for a transfer to Korea, specifically asking for duty with a line company. It took awhile but he finally got what he wanted. In December 1952 Mize received orders for Korea.

In April 1953, after a leave at home and a long journey across the Pacific and through the replacement depots in Japan and Korea, Pfc. Mize was assigned to Company K. Most of the following weeks with the company were spent in routine maneuvers; to Mize the war was similar to training exercises in the United States. There were some skirmishes and minor clashes with the enemy while Company K was on patrols, to be sure. Mize exhibited such a high degree of coolness and fearlessness during these encounters his superiors rapidly promoted him to sergeant.

After the elements of Company K took over Outpost *Harry*, they aggressively patrolled the surrounding area looking for signs of the enemy. They found them nearly everywhere. Enemy patrols were frequently spotted sneaking throughout the sector. On several occasions Mize even witnessed dozens of Chinese trucks unloading men and equipment behind their positions less than three thousand yards away. He requested artillery barrages on the vehicles but was denied because no one believed him.

Daytime hours on Outpost *Harry* were particularly dangerous. Enemy artillery rounds fell on the hill sporadically throughout the day. One minute the trenches and bunkers dotting Harry would be filled with the normal sounds of GIs on garrison duty. Suddenly, the scream of an incoming artillery shell would catch the men's attention. Someone would yell, "Incoming!" They would all dive for cover, hoping they had enough time to scramble to safety.

Some didn't make it. "Not a day went by while we were on *Harry* that we didn't lose a couple of guys to enemy artillery," Mize said. Since there were no replacements sent out, the strength of the garrison was slowly whittled down.

June 10 was the second to last day on Outpost *Harry* for the two understrength platoons. The next night they would be relieved. Sergeant Mize took four others out on a patrol that afternoon, reconnoitering routes for the next day's withdrawal. They returned to their positions just before 6:00 P.M. A short time later enemy artillery began falling on *Harry*. Thundering crashes roared across the barren hill, rocking the men huddled deep in their bunkers. The night air was filled with hundreds of thousands of shards of jagged steel, making movement above ground suicidal.

Nonetheless, when Mize learned a wounded man lay in an LP 150 yards downslope, he rounded up a volunteer medic and went after the man. Through the near-ceaseless explosions, the pair threaded their way to the LP. Incredibly, they made it back safely with the wounded man.

By this time the enemy infantry had joined the attack. Some were already jumping into the trenches, killing GIs as they raced down the earthen works. Mize gunned down several Chinese as he worked his way down the main trench, intent on checking on the remaining men of the second platoon.

He found one bunker—actually a cave dug into the hillside through the rear trench wall—almost completely collapsed from several near hits from the enemy shelling. The sandbagged front wall was a shambles, nearly destroyed by artillery blasts. The few survivors were half-buried in dirt, splintered wood, and rocks. Mize pulled several men clear of the debris.

"How many weapons are still working?" Mize asked them.

"Just yours," replied Pvt. Allan K. England, pointing to Mize's carbine. The others were clogged with dirt.

"That's not good," Mize observed. "They'll be on us in a few minutes."

Mize went to the bunker door where he posted himself in the shadows at the entrance. And none too soon. Within minutes the Chinese were pouring into the trench. England saw them and figured there must have been over a hundred of them working their way toward their bunker.

"I thought I'd bought the farm," Mize recalls somberly. "I just knew I was going to die. I knew it. I accepted it. All I wanted to do was take as many of them with me as I could."

Mize waited until the first of the mob of Chinese came within grenade range. Then he tossed a missile down the trench. It shook the Chinese up and killed a few, but the rest came on. Behind them, fresh enemy troops dropped one after the other into the trench.

At the bunker entrance Mize moved his carbine's selector to full automatic and started spraying hot lead down the trench. Behind him, England and Cpl. James J. Kelly loaded magazines as fast as they could and passed them to Mize. Whenever any Chinese neared the bunker, Mize cut them down. "They were so close I could smell 'em," he recalled.

At one point, while he was reloading his carbine, a group of Chinese rushed him. He slammed home the fresh clip and opened fire just in time. The closest enemy soldier dropped right at Mize's feet.

Out of the lifeless enemy's hand rolled a concussion grenade. Before Mize could jump out of the way the grenade went off. The blast blew him back into the bunker. Momentarily stunned, he groped in the darkness for his carbine, found it, and returned to his post.

All through Mize's gallant stand at the bunker, enemy artillery continued to rock the hill. Twice in one ten-minute period shells whistled in and blew Mize from his post; one blast actually blew him completely out of the trench. As a result, Mize's pants were blown nearly completely off, his helmet was gone, his flak jacket was smoldering, his body was perforated by a dozen holes, his skin was black with soot and dirt, and he suffered a deep, biting pain from his wounds and the repeated concussions. But each time he scrambled back to his position.

For over two hours Mize held his post. Then England warned him they were running low on ammo.

"Come on," Mize told the others, "let's head for the platoon CP."

On the way out England gazed at the pile of enemy bodies littering the trench. "There were dozens of them," he later said. Forty-seven dead Chinese were later counted in that spot.

As the little group pushed down the trench toward the CP, they were attacked by fresh Chinese troops. Mize, still the only man with a weapon, killed five more of the enemy.

They found the CP bunker battered and out of action, dead GIs and Chinese scattered everywhere. But they also found working weapons and ammo. Together they built a barricade using broken timbers and ration crates. Time after time the Chinese hurled themselves at the makeshift barrier. Each time the little band, operating under Mize's bold direction, threw them off.

About 10:30 P.M. somebody brought Mize a radio he'd found buried in the rubble of the CP. Mize called the artillery fire direction center (FDC).

"Lay it on me," he shouted over the gunfire. "Right on top of us!"

The man refused. "There's GIs up there," he said.

"Not many," Mize yelled into the handset. "There's a lot more of them than there is of us. Fire away!"

Within minutes friendly fire began breaking over the hill. The firing continued for over half an hour, catching many Chinese in the open. The barrage also killed some Americans. Mize deeply regretted that but it couldn't be helped.

Several shells slammed into Mize's position. One wrecked his radio. When the sergeant at the FDC failed to raise Mize, he turned to his lieutenant, "Everyone on *Harry*'s dead, sir. Only Chinese left up there now."

The officer reported that fact to battalion.

But it wasn't true. Tough, indestructible Ola Mize and about fifteen others still fought on. Oblivious to the carnage all around him, Mize moved calmly among his men, offering words of encouragement, urging them to keep fighting.

By 2:00 A.M., June 11, the enemy attack had slackened. A short time later Mize decided to make his way to the company CP. He hoped to find another radio and any other survivors. He and one other man slipped down the trench line. All about them they could hear the Chinese jabbering and chattering away.

Stealthily, they moved along, a foot or two at a time. Passing a curve in the trench, the pair suddenly stumbled on a group of thirty or more Chinese. "They were just standing there," Mize said, "smoking cigarettes and talking. I don't think they saw us."

Mize's companion instantly hit the dirt. Mize whipped his carbine up and started pumping rounds into the Chinese.

"It was hell," Mize said. "Here I'm trying to shoot all these Chinese and I keep stepping on this guy laying between my feet. I was afraid I'd fall down and they'd get us. Finally, I yanked him to his feet and we got out of there."

The two returned to the platoon CP bunker where they spent the rest of the night fighting off periodic probes by the Chinese.

With the dawn the Chinese began pulling back from Outpost *Harry*. Mize moved his men from behind the barricade and began clearing out any Chinese remaining in the bunkers.

About 8:00 A.M. a friendly relief company finally arrived on *Harry*. They swept over the hill, mopping up any remaining enemy. The scene around them was incredible. Not a bunker remained intact. A good portion of the trench line had collapsed from the constant pounding of artillery. And everywhere were the dead. Frozen in the grotesque grip of death, they lay in piles three and four deep.

Of the roughly forty Americans on Outpost *Harry* at the start of the fight, twelve survived. Mize attributed his being alive to two factors. "For two years while with the 82d Airborne I had the best training possible from highly experienced World War II veterans," he said. "Plus, the Good Lord was looking after me."

Mize's wounds proved to be not serious. After several weeks' rest in the hospital he returned to Company K. He stayed with it for over a year, extending his tour in Korea several times to remain with the company. In fact, he refused to leave Korea until ordered back to the United States to receive his Medal of Honor.

The presentation ceremony took place at the summer White House in Denver on September 7, 1954. Mize then was reassigned to his old outfit, the 82d Airborne. Two years later he received a commission.

In the early 1960s Mize joined the fledgling Special Forces. He would serve with the elite Green Berets for the next twenty years, rising to the rank of colonel and command of the Special Forces Schools at Fort Bragg, North Carolina, before retiring on June 1, 1981. In those two decades he spent nearly four years in Southeast Asia. Among his accomplishments was the formation of Project Sigma, an unconventional warfare group providing long-range reconnaissance and intelligence-gathering capabilities to the II Field Force Commander in Vietnam. On a later tour he commanded the 3d

Mobile Strike Force Command, composed of indigenous personnel. He also was shot three times during his Vietnam tours.

Mize returned home after retirement where he enjoys the grandchildren given to him by his two daughters.

While the Eighth Army units cleaned up the debris on the battlefield and prepared their dead for burial, the prospect for peace loomed brighter than ever before. At Panmunjom only relatively minor details remained to be ironed out. The United States, for example, was awaiting replies from those U.N. members asked to supervise the prisoner repatriations. Once those agreements were reached, the final stages of the negotiations could begin. Unfortunately, the United States had not counted on the defiance of Syngman Rhee.

The aging president of South Korea was completely dissatisfied with the agreement. He publicly stated several times he would not accept a treaty that left his country divided. He called for a complete military victory, driving the Chinese back across the Yalu. Further, he opposed the compromise reached on POWs and refused to allow any U.N. member selected to oversee the repatriations who had any Communist leanings to set foot in Korea.

General Clark met repeatedly with Rhee to assuage the old man's discontent, but made little headway. Rhee threatened to remove his army from U.N. command and fight on alone. Clark quietly pointed out to Rhee that his army was so dependent on U.S. supplies that its withdrawal would doom the ROK army to defeat.

That threat temporarily calmed Rhee, but then he threw a monkey wrench of monstrous proportions into the works. On June 18 he unilaterally released twenty-seven thousand alleged non-Communist Chinese and North Koreans from South Korean POW camps.

At Panmunjom the Chinese reacted with predictable outrage. They demanded to know if the United States could control its ally, then broke off the talks. General Clark immediately flew from Tokyo to confer with Rhee but again made little progress in persuading the old man to accept the armistice.

Finally, President Eisenhower dispatched Assistant Secretary of State Walter S. Robertson to Seoul. From June 25 to July 12, 1953, Robertson met with Rhee in what came to be called the Little Truce Talks. Despite the fact that South Korea had no hope of going north without the U.S. Army, Rhee's price for accepting the armistice was high.

In return for his acquiescence, Rhee extracted from Robertson a pledge of a U.S.-ROK Mutual Security Treaty, an agreement for the U.S. to fund an expansion of the ROK Army to twenty divisions from its present strength of twelve, and massive long-term economic aid, with a down payment of two hundred million dollars and foodstuffs worth nine million more.

Once he'd extorted all he could, Rhee signed a letter to Eisenhower assuring the president "he would not obstruct in any way the implementation of the terms of the armistice . . ."

In exchange for peace the United States had adopted a permanent ward.

While Robertson negotiated with Rhee, the Communists continued their attacks against the Eighth Army. Most of the pressure again fell on the ROKs, apparently to impress on them their vulnerability without American aid. In addition, the Communists apparently wanted the world to be aware of their military might before the armistice ended the fighting. Because the Americans worked so closely with the ROKs, hundreds of GIs became casualties while Rhee worked out his own armistice package with Robertson. These men, the survivors, and the families of those who died in these final days would never be fans of Syngman Rhee.

The heaviest Chinese attack on an American sector once again fell on the bitterly contested Porkchop Hill. On the night of July 6, 1953, in a driving summer thunderstorm, the Chinese fell on Porkchop. Company A, 17th Infantry, U.S. 7th Infantry Division, garrisoned the hill.

RICHARD T. SHEA

During his last three years as a cadet at the U.S. Military Academy, Richard T. Shea was known as "the greatest track and field star in West Point history." For three years in a row he ruled indoor and outdoor collegiate track and field. He won sixteen major middle distance and cross-country championships. He also set seven indoor and outdoor West Point records in track and field. For his efforts the Army Athletic Association named him its "Outstanding Athlete" in the Class of 1952.

Shea's arrival on the West Point scene followed a rather circuitous route. Born on a farm outside of Portsmouth, Virginia, on January 3, 1927, he attended Virginia Polytechnic Institute for one and a half years before enlisting in the army in April 1945 and opening a door to an entirely new way of life.

Although he'd always enjoyed sports, not until he was in the army did Shea take them seriously. He boxed for a short period, then abandoned the ring for the cinder path. Shea trained hard and devoted nearly all of his off-duty hours to building his prowess. While stationed in Germany he won the European championship for the five-thousand-meter run. He was a leading candidate for the U.S. Olympic Team but he had ideas of his own for the future.

In 1947 Shea entered the army's prep school for West Point. He successfully completed the tough course of instruction, entering the Military Academy in June 1948 as a member of the Class of 1952. When he graduated he selected the infantry as his service branch. He went through the basic infantry officers' course at Fort Benning, Georgia, trained troops in the States for several months, got married, then was posted to Korea in the spring of 1953.

By early July 1953 Shea had worked his way from platoon leader in Company A to its executive officer. When the company rotated to duty on Porkchop, Shea supervised the construction of fighting positions. He attacked the task with the same enthusiasm he'd shown for a track event. Later, his intimate knowledge of Porkchop's terrain would prove invaluable.

Shea was making his rounds of the positions on Porkchop on the evening of July 6 when the Chinese hit. Company A was vastly outnumbered. It seemed for awhile the CCF would overwhelm the defenders. Because he knew the terrain so well, Shea organized and led several local counterattacks. Despite his efforts, the Chinese fought their way into the trenches and established squatters' rights on a part of the crest.

Throughout the first night reinforcements flowed onto Porkchop from the enemy's main positions. They threw repeated charges against the bunkers and trenches held by the remnants of Company A. Shea stood out among the defenders for the way he bounded from position to position, pointing out targets to his men, passing out ammo, calming the men with optimistic words.

"Don't worry," he reassured the young infantrymen. "Help will be here in the morning. We've just got to hang on 'til then. We can make it."

Not long before dawn a cluster of Chinese riflemen pushed their way down a trench line, overrunning the GIs there. Reacting instantly to the threat, Shea pulled his .45-caliber pistol from its holster and brazenly ran right at the enemy.

He dropped four or five with pistol shots. When the Colt's hammer clicked on an empty chamber, Shea slipped his trench knife from its sheath. Slashing and kicking, Shea drove into the remaining Chinese with a violent fury. The steel blade killed two of the enemy while the rest backpedaled furiously to escape Shea's cold steel.

Shea and a handful of men chased the Chinese down the trench, clearing the sector of enemy. From these newly won positions he directed rifle fire on the enemy throughout the night, helping to throw back numerous attacks at heavy cost to the Chinese.

When dawn broke Shea led several attacks on enemy-held bunkers, adding new and vital positions to the company's sector.

Shea spent most of the daylight hours of July 7 organizing Company A for the attacks everyone knew would be coming as soon as night fell.

That afternoon Company G, 17th Infantry, tried to reach Porkchop. Chinese artillery pummelled them as they came forward, killing and wounding nearly half their number. Shea rounded up a number of Company G survivors and swiftly integrated them into his command.

Repeatedly that afternoon Shea went after the Chinese still holding out on Porkchop. Even after an enemy round cut a deep furrow across his face, Shea kept up the fight. At one point a particularly stubborn Chinese machine gun threw Shea and his men back. Determined to wipe it out, Shea cautiously worked his way under fire to within a few yards of the emplacement. First, he tossed two grenades at the enemy. Then he jumped to his feet, his carbine at his hip, and walked straight at the enemy, pulling the trigger as fast as he could. Three Chinese fell under his onslaught. The gun was silenced.

During the night, the second straight night of unrelenting combat, Shea coordinated his sector's holding action.

At about 9:00 A.M., July 8, the third day of attacks on Porkchop, Company A's commander, Capt. William S. Roberts, received word the enemy was assembling for a massive attack. He passed that information to his XO. Shea immediately went to work checking on the men's fighting position. "They're coming," he told them, "but we can hold."

When the Chinese came a little after 3:00 P.M. Shea and his battered band were waiting. Under a hail of enemy small-arms fire the GIs battled back. Several times the CCF nearly overran the thin line of Americans. Each time Shea rallied his men to throw them off. Only through Shea's forceful leadership and tremendous personal courage were the GIs able to hold out.

Later, when he sensed a weakness in the enemy's attacks, Shea went from man to man, preparing them for a counterattack.

"Okay," he told them. "We're ready. Let's go!"

Screaming at the tops of their lungs, the men charged out of the trench, catching the Chinese by surprise. Sprinting at the forefront of the attack was former cross-country star Richard T. Shea.

He was hit and temporarily stopped, but only temporarily. In seconds Shea was back on his feet, yelling at those around him to "get going!"

Captain Roberts witnessed Shea's last minutes. "He was almost a one-man assault," Roberts later said. "He was again wounded, but continued with a courage I have never seen displayed by any man. He continued fighting and gaining terrain."

But now enemy reinforcements burst on the scene. Only a handful of men remained with Shea. They disappeared in the onslaught. Roberts watched in horror as the counterattack disintegrated. It tore him apart to write in his after-action report, "Lieutenant Shea was last seen in close hand-to-hand combat with the enemy."

Two days after twenty-six-year-old Shea fell on the meaningless hill in west central Korea, his son was born back in Portsmouth. Nearly two years later, on May 16, 1955, young Richard T. Shea III stood proudly at his mother's side in the Pentagon while she accepted his father's posthumous Medal of Honor.

Among the men from Company G, 17th Infantry Regiment, to reach Porkchop Hill on July 7 was nineteen-year-old Cpl. Dan D. Schoonover of Boise, Idaho. Though actually assigned to Company A, 13th Engineer Combat Battalion, Schoonover and his squad were attached to Company G as a demolition team.

Because of the heavy volume of enemy fire, the engineers were unable to carry out their original assignment. Instead, Schoonover turned his men into an infantry squad. Later, he also took command of an infantry squad whose leader was shot down.

Over the next three days Schoonover led his impromptu fighting team like a "seasoned infantry noncommissioned officer," according to one witness. He repeatedly disregarded enemy fire to direct his team's fire on the onrushing force. On one occasion he personally stormed an enemy-held bunker, killing or capturing the Chinese manning the position.

One man said, "Schoonover did not seem to have any fear at all as he stood in the open, directing the rifle fire of his men in spite of enemy artillery and mortar fire," crashing around him. At one point he took over a machine gun after its gunner had been cut down. He stayed in that position for over four hours, delivering a mass of tremendously accurate fire on enemy formations.

On the afternoon of July 9, the survivors of Company G were pulled off Porkchop. Schoonover voluntarily remained with the relieving unit. On the morning of July 10, while pouring a devastating blast of BAR fire into an enemy bunker, he died in a mortar blast.

General Taylor and Gen. Bruce C. Clarke, the I Corps commander, conferred on July 10 and agreed that the Chinese disregard for casualties and their obvious desire to maintain their hold on Porkchop Hill outweighed the tactical value of the U.N. holding the position. Accordingly, on July 11 the U.N. abandoned Porkchop.

The armistice negotiations resumed on July 10. China's primary concern was the willingness of Syngman Rhee to accept and adhere to the terms of the agreement. At that time the discussions between Rhee and Robertson were not completed, so the U.N. negotiators were unable to give the Communists the assurances they demanded. After several days of inconsequential discussions the Communists suggested an adjournment until July 19. The U.S. agreed. This recess would also give the CCF and NKPA time to consolidate their gains along the front.

When the conferees returned to Panmunjom on July 19, the enemy offensive was over and the battle line had once again stabilized. The U.N. negotiators also gave the Communists solemn assurances that Syngman Rhee would not upset the terms already agreed upon. With that last major hurdle overcome, the adversaries agreed to have their respective staffs work out the myriad of minor, but important, details that would lead to a cease-fire. As the U.N. negotiating team departed Panmunjom on the afternoon of July 19 there was an optimistic attitude that they had at last entered the home stretch.

That same night, in the Punchbowl area in the X Corps sector, a six-man patrol from Company F, 2d Battalion, 223d Infantry Regiment, U.S. 40th Infantry Division, moved out from the MLR. Its mission: contact the enemy.

GILBERT G. COLLIER

At the point of the patrol was Cpl. Gilbert G. Collier. Born in Hunter, Arkansas, on December 30, 1930, he grew up in Tichnor, Arkansas. He lived there until his marriage in May 1950. He and his wife then moved to Chicago, Illinois, in search of better employment opportunities.

Two years later, on July 25, 1952, Collier was drafted. He trained as an infantryman, then received his orders to Korea. In February 1953 he joined Company F. In the next five months Collier proved himself to be an able, competent soldier who carried out his orders swiftly and efficiently. His abilities earned him a meritorious promotion to corporal and command of a rifle squad.

During the briefing for the patrol on July 19, its leader, 2d Lt. Richard S. Agnew, outlined the patrol's makeup, order of march, radio frequencies, and escape route. He also detailed Collier to take the point. Collier's job was to lead the patrol on a predetermined course, all the while keeping a sharp eye open for signs of the enemy. It was a dangerous job, reserved for those experienced soldiers with nerves of steel.

Collier was all that and more.

The night of July 19 was pitch black. A heavy cloud cover blocked any light from the moon and stars. Occasional showers limited visibility. Collier and the other patrol members had difficulty seeing more than a few feet away.

The patrol had proceeded more than two miles across the no-man's land between the opposing forces and was walking out of a small valley when suddenly the ground in front of Collier disappeared. With an involuntary yell he plummeted down the craggy face of a sixty-foot cliff. A few steps behind him Lieutenant Agnew came forward to investigate Collier's scream. Seconds later, he, too, stepped into space. His body twisted and tumbled as it bounced off rocks and small trees, stopping only when he reached bottom.

At the base of the cliff the two men lay within arm's length of each other. Collier whispered, "You okay, lieutenant?"

"Twisted my ankle," the officer painfully responded. "I don't think I can stand on it. How about you?"

Collier reported he'd wrenched his back. Like Agnew, he was covered with scrapes and bruises but had no broken bones.

The two men conferred. Since daylight, with its inherent dangers, would be on them before a rescue party could reach and recover them, Agnew decided to send the rest of the patrol back to the MLR. Collier would crawl back up the cliff and join them. Agnew would hide until a rescue party came out the next night.

Collier refused to abandon his leader. "I won't do it, lieutenant," he said. "You need help. I'll stay and get you out."

Though Agnew tried to dissuade Collier he made no headway. Finally, reluctantly, Agnew radioed the patrol members still waiting above to return to the MLR. They assured him they'd be back the next night with more men. Then they were gone.

Alone in the pitch dark, the two injured soldiers took stock of their situation. Each man had held on to his carbine during the fall. Agnew still had his radio. They each had a canteen. That was it.

It didn't take Agnew and Collier long to conclude they were helpless at the bottom of the cliff. If a Chinese patrol should discover them there they would have no chance at all. They decided to try to climb up from the cliff bottom and conceal themselves on higher ground.

Despite their painful cuts, scrapes, and bruises, the two young soldiers stoically attacked the cliff face. In total darkness, ignoring the biting hurt of their damaged limbs, the pair inched their way upward. Unable to see handholds, they frequently slid downwards in a shower of stones and dirt. On one occasion Agnew slid nearly all the way back down to the bottom. In the fall he lost his carbine and the radio.

Collier worked his way down to Agnew. Though the pain from his wrenched back frequently brought tears to his eyes, Collier tugged and pulled Agnew back up the cliff face. Offering words of encouragement and praise, he persuaded the lieutenant to keep moving.

At last, after hours of torturous climbing, the pair crested the cliff top. Crawling downhill, they made their way to a thick stand of underbrush. They scurried into the center of the bushes, concealing themselves as best they could.

The hot day passed slowly. They had no food and only the brackish water in their canteens to sustain them. Agnew's ankle had swollen to over twice its normal size; he was unable to put any weight on it. Collier's back throbbed with a constant, dull pain he was unable to relieve in any position.

When the sun finally disappeared behind the western horizon, the two decided to continue crawling toward American lines; they didn't want to risk being overlooked by a rescue patrol. They had worked their way to within three hundred yards of their own lines when a six-man Chinese patrol discovered them.

Collier shouted a warning, "Lieutenant!" then blazed away with his carbine at the enemy. Two Chinese soldiers fell. The other four dispersed and moved toward the Americans. One threw several grenades. Shrapnel bit into Collier's side. Agnew screamed in pain as hot metal tore into his legs.

Sensing the danger to Agnew, Collier crawled in the opposite direction, firing his carbine, drawing the Chinese away from the injured officer. Then he ran out of ammo. The Chinese rushed him.

Collier later said, "I realized that my only chance for survival was to stand my ground and fight off the enemy."

From his position Agnew saw the enemy soldiers fall on Collier. "Two of them started dragging him off," he said. "He fought valiantly as they beat him with their rifles."

It was the worst kind of street brawl; a no-holds-barred fight to the death. With four Chinese surrounding him, kicking him, hitting him, stabbing him, Collier fought back with the fury of a cornered animal.

He lashed out with his fists, feeling the satisfying collapse of cartilage beneath his knuckles. One Chinese began pounding Collier in the head with the butt of his rifle. Twisting to the side, Collier pulled his bayonet free from its sheath and stabbed upward. The thick steel blade slipped into the man's heart. He fell.

Now on his knees, with the three remaining Chinese continuing to beat and stab him, Collier lunged at the nearest enemy. He buried his bayonet in that man's throat.

That was enough for the two remaining Chinese. They took off for their own lines. Collier collapsed in a heap, bleeding from more than a dozen stab wounds.

The sounds of the fight caught the attention of the rescue patrol. Within minutes they were on the scene. A medic patched up Collier, then loaded him on a stretcher for the short trip to the MLR. Lieutenant Agnew also received medical attention before being carried to safety. All the way to the aid station he kept praising Collier's gallant conduct.

Maj. Charles A. Brown, the battalion commander, spoke with Collier in the aid station. He tried to get the youngster to talk of his ordeal. Collier related some details but had concerns of his own. "Although he was dying," Brown said, "Sergeant Collier kept asking me if Lieutenant Agnew had been rescued and if he was all right."

The doctors tried as hard as they could but Collier had been beaten too badly. He died that night.

Collier's widow, Peggy, accepted his posthumous Medal of Honor in a Pentagon ceremony on January 12, 1955. Corporal Collier was the last soldier to earn this high award in Korea.

Four areas remained for the two sides to finalize before a cease-fire could be instituted: the place of delivery of the nonrepatriated prisoners; the inception of activities for the various commissions established by the armistice; the finalization of the line of demarcation and the demilitarized zone; and the physical arrangements for the actual signing ceremony.

Staff officers quickly agreed to deliver nonrepatriated POWs to the repatriation commission in their respective halves of the DMZ. The Communists agreed to allow the commissions to commence their appointed activities the day after the armistice was signed.

Establishing a final demarcation line was, in most places, a relatively simple matter because there had been little or no action in those locales. Where recent fighting had shifted the front line from the previously drawn demarcation line, intense bargaining proved necessary. Neither side wanted to surrender terrain but, with each giving some and taking some, the staff members finally reached an agreement on July 21.

The originally scheduled date for signing the armistice was July 24. However, complicating factors made this choice overly optimistic. Maps of the demarcation line and DMZ had to be printed and verified, the construction of the building for the ceremony was not yet complete, and differences of opinion had broken out over the actual signing procedure. The ceremony was postponed until July 27.

The delay gave the Communists time to throw one last punch at the U.N. They could not resist the opportunity to claim they had won a military victory. Men died needlessly on both sides; one became America's last Medal of Honor hero in this frustrating war.

AMBROSIO GUILLEN

Born in La Junta, Colorado, on December 7, 1929, Ambrosio Guillen grew up in El Paso, Texas. He left school to join the marines when he was eighteen. It didn't take him long to recognize he'd found a home. The esprit de corps of the marines appealed most to him. There was a bonding among marines that made Guillen feel part of a big family.

Guillen's pride in the Marine Corps prompted him to apply for drill instructor school. He felt if he could train recruits to become marines his Marine Corps would be that much better. He did so well he received a special commendation for his "outstanding ability as a leader." When he left San Diego, California, for Korea in the spring of 1953 he would have ample opportunity to demonstrate that leadership ability.

Guillen drew an assignment to Company F, 2d Battalion, 7th Marines, the same outfit that produced Medal of Honor heroes William Barber, Hector Cafferata, William Charette, and Daniel Matthews.

On the night of July 25 Guillen was the sergeant in charge of his company's reaction platoon. If the enemy attacked any of the battalion's outposts near the old Nevada complex, his platoon would be dispatched as reinforcements.

That's what happened about nine o'clock that night.

Reacting quickly, Guillen rushed his platoon forward across unfamiliar ground, encouraging his men to ignore the bursts of mortar fire. Once at the threatened outpost, the thin Hispanic sergeant expertly placed his men in fighting positions. Under his command they battled the Chinese to a halt.

Repeatedly exposing himself to the enemy's small-arms and automatic-weapons fire, Guillen rushed to the weak spots along the outpost's perimeter, adding his fire to its defense. To his marines Guillen was a pillar of strength and calm on a hellish night.

Several times Guillen moved across bullet-swept ground to go to the aid of wounded marines. He pulled them to safety, applied first aid, then saw them to the evacuation point.

Just when it seemed the Chinese had been repulsed, they rallied for a final attack. Storming through the night, they hit the marines with a ferocious intensity. Some Chinese overran the positions, dropping into bunkers and trenches, wrestling with the marines.

Guillen gathered the men around him and led them in a classic infantry attack right down the trench. The crash of close-quarters rifle shots and the clank of cold steel on metal filled the night as the marines tore into the enemy. A savage fight raged for nearly fifteen minutes as the marines cleared the trenches of Chinese.

During the fighting Guillen was mortally wounded. One of his men tried to pull him to cover. Guillen shrugged him off. "That can wait," he insisted, "until we push 'em the hell back where they came from!"

It took another two hours of brutal fighting before the Chinese finally withdrew. By that time it was too late for Guillen. His life blood had poured from his body for too long. Before his men could carry him back to the aid station he died. To those marines who survived this last vicious battle, they knew they owed their lives to the valiant leadership of Sergeant Guillen.

Guillen's family accepted his Medal of Honor August 18, 1954.

*   *   *

Less than thirty-six hours after Guillen led his platoon into battle, the final armistice papers were signed at Panmunjom. At 10:00 A.M., July 27, 1953, the chief negotiators for the two sides began the process of fixing their signatures to the eighteen copies of the truce. At 10:12 A.M. they were finished. All fighting in Korea would halt in twelve hours. After more than three years of combat, two of which had been along a virtually unchanged battle line, the war was finally over.

The Korean War was America's first limited-commitment war. From the very beginning of hostilities, America's political and military leaders expected to swiftly conclude the conflict. In their minds, a quick, surgically precise application of American military might would free South Korea of its invaders. Then the hostiles would be chased all the way out of Korea, returning the entire country to freedom.

Once it became obvious the war would not go as envisioned, the U.S. still refused to commit all of its resources. That was primarily because it was worried about further aggression in Europe. Further, the U.S. economy was at last prospering after more than a decade of stagnation and war. America's leaders had no desire to return the country to a war footing.

In addition, President Truman's doctrine of containment dictated that the U.S. not make a major military commitment in combating communism. According to his principle, all America had to do was retard communism's growth, hold it to acceptable levels, and not become embroiled in another devastating worldwide conflict.

For most of the American public, limited commitment in Korea was completely acceptable. Consumer goods were flowing freely for the first time in years. Jobs were plentiful; there was good money to be made. Sure it was a good idea to stop communism, but not if it cost too much.

Limited commitment also meant limited objectives. Once it became clear the Communists could not be forced out of North Korea the war bogged down. There were no more towns to liberate or peoples to free. There were only hills to defend and attack. As a result, many of America's fighting men questioned their role in this seemingly endless war. Why did they have to fight and die for the preservation of this little country halfway around the world? During the final two years of the war, when some men were dying while others argued over the settlement of the war, it was especially difficult for the GIs to understand why they had to risk their lives in and for Korea.

The only aspect of the Korean War that was not limited was the intensity and brutality of its combat. Fighting in Korea rivaled any of the fighting witnessed in World War II. From the house-to-house street fighting in Seoul and other cities to the trenches cut into the face of nearly every hill in Korea, America's fighting men faced a resourceful, determined foe who neither asked nor gave quarter.

It was in the midst of such horrible combat that America's fighting men, despite the lack of objectives and clear motivations, repeatedly demonstrated their ability to meet any challenge, defeat any enemy. On hundreds of nameless, desolate hilltops soldiers, sailors, and marines fought as valiantly as their ancestors had at Bunker Hill, Gettysburg, the Little Big Horn, the Argonne, Normandy, and Iwo Jima. They gave their all, and 33,643 of them gave their lives, in fighting this unpopular war.

One hundred thirty-one of these brave American men fought so valiantly they earned the Medal of Honor. In a moment of extreme danger they were able to rise above the questions which surrounded the war and exhibit a courage, a selflessness, a heroism that went far above and beyond the call of duty. Because of that extraordinary gallantry, these men can truly be called "the bravest of the brave."

Appendix:
Korean War
Medal of Honor
Recipients

Name Rank, Branch	Unit	Date	Place	Hometown
*Abrell, Charles G. Cpl, USMC	Co E, 2nd Bn, 1st Mar, 1st Mar Div	Jun 10, 1951	the Punchbowl	Terre Haute, IN
Adams, Stanley T. Sfc, USA	Co A, 1st Bn, 19th Inf, 24th Inf Div	Feb 4, 1951	Sesim-ri	Olathe, KS
Barber, William E. Capt, USMC	Co F, 2nd Bn, 7th Mar, 1st Mar Div	Nov 28– Dec 2, 1950	Toktong Pass	W. Liberty, KY
*Barker, Charles H. Pvt, USA	Co K, 3rd Bn, 17th Inf, 7th Inf Div	Jun 4, 1953	Porkchop Hill	Pickens, SC
*Baugh, William B. Pfc, USMC	Co G, 3rd Bn, 1st Mar, 1st Mar Div	Nov 29, 1950	near Koto-ri	Harrison, OH
*Benfold, Edward C. HC3c, USN	Co L, 3rd Bn, 5th Mar, 1st Mar Div	Sep 5, 1952	Bunker Hill	Camden, NJ
*Bennett, Emory L. Pfc, USA	Co B, 1st Bn, 15th Inf, 3rd Inf Div	Jun 24, 1951	Sobangsan	Cocoa, FL
Bleak, David B. Sgt, USA	Med Co, 223rd Inf, 40th Inf Div	Jun 14, 1952	near Minari-gol	Shelley, ID
*Brittin, Nelson V. Sfc, USA	Co I, 3rd Bn, 19th Inf, 24th Inf Div	Mar 7, 1951	near Yonggong-ni	Audubon, NJ
*Brown, Melvin L. Pfc, USA	Co D, 8th Eng Combat Bn	Sep 4, 1950	Kasan	Mahaffey, PA
Burke, Lloyd L. 1Lt, USA	Co G, 2nd Bn, 5th Cav, 1st Cav Div	Oct 28, 1951	near Chong-dong	Stuttgart, AR
*Burris, Tony K. Sfc, USA	Co L, 3rd Bn, 38th Inf, 2nd Inf Div	Oct 8–9, 1951	near Heartbreak Ridge	Blanchard, OK

*Posthumous award

Name, Rank, Branch	Unit	Date	Place	Hometown
Cafferata, Hector A., Jr. Pvt, USMC	Co F, 2nd Bn, 7th Mar, 1st Mar Div	Nov 28, 1950	Toktong Pass	Montville, NJ
*Champagne, David B. Cpl, USMC	Co A, 1st Bn, 7th Mar, 1st Mar Div	May 28, 1952	near Panmunjom	Wakefield, RI
Charette, William R. HC3c, USN	Co F, 2nd Bn 7th Mar, 1st Mar Div	Mar 27, 1953	Vegas Hill	Ludington, MI
*Charlton, Cornelius H. Sgt, USA	Co C, 1st Bn, 24th Inf, 25th Inf Div	Jun 2, 1951	near Chipo-ri	Bronx, NY
*Christianson, Stanley R. Pfc, USMC	Co E, 2nd Bn, 1st Mar, 1st Mar Div	Sep 29, 1950	Seoul	Mindoro, WI
*Collier, Gilbert C. Cpl. USA	Co F, 2nd Bn, 223rd Inf, 40th Inf Div	Jul 19–20, 1953	near the Punchbowl	Tichnor, AR
*Collier, John W. Cpl. USA	Co C, 1st Bn, 27th Inf, 25th Inf Div	Sep 19, 1950	near Chindong-ni	Worthington, KY
Commiskey, Henry A., Sr. 2Lt, USMC	Co C, 1st Bn, 1st Mar, 1st Mar Div	Sep 20, 1950	Yongdungp'o	Hattiesburg, MS
*Coursen, Samuel S. 1Lt, USA	Co C, 1st Bn, 5th Cav, 1st Cav Div	Oct 12, 1950	near Kaesong	Madison, NJ
*Craig, Gordon M. Cpl, USA	Recon Co, 1st Cav Div	Sep 10, 1950	near Kasan	E. Bridgewater, MA
Crump, Jerry K. Cpl, USA	Co L, 3rd Bn, 7th Inf, 3rd Inf Div	Sep 6–7, 1951	near Chorwon	Forest City, NC
*Davenport, Jack A. Cpl, USMC	Co G, 3rd Bn, 5th Mar, 1st Mar Div	Sep 21, 1951	Songnae-dong	Mission, KS
*Davis, George A., Jr. Maj, USAF	334th Fighter Squadron, 4th Fighter Group	Feb 10, 1952	Yalu River area	Lubbock, TX
Davis, Raymond G. Lt Col, USMC	1st Bn, 7th Mar, 1st Mar Div	Dec 1–4, 1950	near Yudam-ni	Goggins, GA
Dean, William F. Maj Gen, USA	24th Inf Div	Jul 20–21, 1950	Taejon	Berkeley, CA
*Desiderio, Reginald B. Capt, USA	Co E, 2nd Bn, 27th Inf, 25th Inf Div	Nov 27, 1950	near Ipsok	El Monte, CA
*Dewert, Richard D. HC3c, USN	Co D, 2nd Bn, 7th Mar, 1st Mar Div	Apr 5, 1951	Mapyang-ni	Taunton, MA
Dewey, Duane E. Cpl, USMC	Co E, 2nd Bn, 5th Mar, 1st Mar Div	Apr 16, 1952	near Panmunjom	South Haven, MI
Dodd, Carl H. 2Lt, USA	Co E, 2nd Bn, 5th Inf, 24th Inf Div	Jan 30–31, 1951	near Subuk	Kenvir, Ky
*Duke, Ray E. Sfc, USA	Co C, 1st Bn, 21st Inf, 24th Inf Div	Apr 26, 1951	near Mugok	Whitwell, TN

Name, Rank, Branch	Unit	Date	Place	Hometown
*Edwards, Junior D. Sfc, USA	Co E, 2nd Bn, 23rd Inf, 2nd Inf Div	Jan 2, 1951	near Changbong-ni	Indianola, IA
*Essebagger, John, Jr. Cpl, USA	Co A, 1st Bn, 7th Inf, 3rd Inf Div	Apr 25, 1951	near Popsu-dong	Holland, MI
*Faith, Don C., Jr. Lt Col, USA	1st Bn, 32nd Inf, 7th Inf Div	Nov 27– Dec 1, 1950	near Hagaru-ri	Washington, IN
*Garcia, Fernando L. Pfc, USMC	Co I, 3rd Bn, 5th Mar, 1st Mar Div	Sep 5, 1952	Bunker Hill	Utado, PR
*George, Charles Pfc, USA	Co C, 1st Bn, 179th Inf, 45th Inf Div	Nov 30, 1952	near Songnae-dong	Cherokee, NC
*Gilliland, Charles L. Pfc, USA	Co I, 3rd Bn, 7th Inf, 3rd Inf Div	Apr 25, 1951	near Tongmang-ni	Yellville, AR
*Gomez, Edward Pfc, USMC	Co E, 2nd Bn, 1st Mar, 1st Mar Div	Sep 14, 1951	the Punchbowl	Omaha, NB
*Goodblood, Clair Cpl, USA	Co D, 1st Bn, 7th Inf, 3rd Inf Div	Apr 24–25, 1951	near Popsu-dong	Burnham, ME
*Guillen, Ambrosio SSgt, USMC	Co F, 2nd Bn, 7th Mar, 1st Mar Div	Jul 25, 1953	near Panmunjom	El Paso, TX
*Hammond, Francis C. HC3c, USN	Co F, 2nd Bn, 5th Mar, 1st Mar Div	Mar 26–27, 1953	Carson Hill	Alexandria, VA
*Hammond, Lester, Jr. Cpl, USA	Co A, 1st Bn, 187th Airborne Regt	Aug 14, 1952	near Kumhwa	Quincy, IL
*Handrich, Melvin O. MSgt, USA	Co C, 1st Bn, 5th Inf, 25th Inf Div	Aug 25–26, 1950	near Sobuk-son	Manawa, WI
*Hanson, Jack G. Pfc, USA	Co F, 2nd Bn, 31st Inf, 7th Inf Div	Jun 7, 1951	near Pachi-dong	Escatawpa, MS
*Hartell, Lee R. 1Lt, USA	Battery A, 15th FA, 2nd Inf Div	Aug 27, 1951	Bloody Ridge	Danbury, CT
Harvey, Raymond Capt, USA	Co C, 1st Bn, 17th Inf, 7th Inf Div	Mar 9, 1951	near Taemi-dong	Pasadena, CA
*Henry, Frederick F. 1Lt, USA	Co F, 2nd Bn, 28th Inf, 2nd Inf Div	Sep 1, 1950	near Am-dong	Clinton, OK
Hernandez, Rodolfo P. Cpl, USA	Co G, 2nd Bn, 187th Airborne Regt	May 31, 1951	near Wontong-ni	Fowler, CA
Hudner, Thomas J., Jr. Lt(jg), USN	Fighter Squadron 32	Dec 4, 1950	Chosin Reservoir	Fall River, MA
Ingman, Einar H., Jr. Cpl, USA	Co E, 2nd Bn, 17th Inf, 7th Inf Div	Feb 26, 1951	near Malta-ri	Tomahawk, WI
*Jecelin, William R. Sgt, USA	Co C, 1st Bn, 35th Inf, 25th Inf Div	Sep 19, 1950	near Sага	Baltimore, MD

Name, Rank, Branch	Unit	Date	Place	Hometown
*Johnson, James E. Sgt, USMC	Co J, 3rd Bn, 7th Mar, 1st Mar Div	Dec 2, 1950	Yudam-ni	Pocatello, ID
*Jordan, Mack A. Pfc, USA	Co K, 3rd Bn, 21st Inf, 24th Inf Div	Nov 15, 1951	near Kumsong	Collins, MS
*Kanell, Billie G. Pvt, USA	Co I, 3rd Bn, 35th Inf, 25th Inf Div	Sep 7, 1951	near Pyonggang	Poplar Bluff, MO
*Kaufman, Loren R. Sfc, USA	Co G, 2nd Bn, 9th Inf, 2nd Inf Div	Sep 4–5, 1950	near Yongsan	The Dalles, OR
*Kelly, John D. Pfc, USMC	Co C, 1st Bn, 7th Mar, 1st Mar Div	May 28, 1952	near Panmunjom	Homestead, PA
*Kelso, Jack W. Pfc, USMC	Co I, 3rd Bn, 7th Mar, 1st Mar Div	Oct 2, 1952	Detroit Hill	Fresno, CA
Kennemore, Robert S. SSgt, USMC	Co E, 2nd Bn, 7th Mar, 1st Mar Div	Nov 27–28, 1950	near Yudam-ni	Greenville, SC
*Kilmer, John E. HC3c, USN	H&S Co, 3rd Bn, 7th Mar, 1st Mar Div	Aug 13, 1952	Bunker Hill	San Antonio, TX
*Knight, Noah O. Pfc, USA	Co F, 2nd Bn, 7th Inf, 3rd Inf Div	Nov 23–24, 1951	near Kowang-san	Jefferson, SC
*Koelsch, John K. Lt(jg), USN	Helicopter Squadron 2	Jul 3–10, 1951	near Wonsan	Los Angeles, CA
Kouma, Ernest R. Sfc, USA	Co A, 72nd Tank Bn, 2nd Inf Div	Aug 31– Sep 1, 1950	near Agok	Dwight, NB
*Krzyzowski, Edward C. Capt, USA	Co B, 1st Bn, 9th Inf, 2nd Inf Div	Aug 31– Sep 3, 1951	Bloody Ridge	Cicero, IL
*Kyle, Darwin K. 2Lt, USA	Co K, 3rd Bn, 7th Inf, 3rd Inf Div	Feb 16, 1951	near Kamil-ni	Racine, WV
Lee, Hubert L. MSgt, USA	Co I, 3rd Bn, 23rd Inf, 2nd Inf Div	Feb 1, 1951	near Ipo-ri	Leland, MS
*Libby, George D. Sgt, USA	Co C, 3rd Eng Combat Bn, 24th Inf Div	Jul 20, 1950	Taejon	Casco, ME
*Littleton, Herbert A. Pfc, USMC	Co C, 1st Bn, 7th Mar, 1st Mar Div	Apr 22, 1951	Chunchon	Nampa, ID
*Long, Charles R. Sgt, USA	Co M, 3rd Bn, 38th Inf, 2nd Inf Div	Feb 12, 1951	near Hoeng-song	Kansas City, MO
*Lopez, Baldomero 1Lt, USMC	Co A, 1st Bn, 5th Mar, 1st Mar Div	Sep 15, 1950	Inchon	Tampa, FL
*Loring, Charles J., Jr. Maj, USAF	80th Fighter-Bomber Squad, 8th Fighter-Bomber Wing	Nov 22, 1952	near Sniper Ridge	Portland, ME
*Lyell, William F. Cpl, USA	Co F, 2nd Bn, 17th Inf, 7th Inf Div	Aug 31, 1951	near Chupa-ri	Old Hickory, TN

Name, Rank, Branch	Unit	Date	Place	Hometown
*Martinez, Benito Cpl, USA	Co A, 1st Bn, 27th Inf, 25th Inf Div	Sep 6, 1952	Heartbreak Ridge	Fort Hancock, TX
*Matthews, Daniel P. Sgt, USMC	Co F, 2nd Bn, 7th Mar, 1st Mar Div	Mar 28, 1953	Vegas Hill	Van Nuys, CA
*Mausert, Frederick W., III Sgt, USMC	Co B, 1st Bn, 7th Mar, 1st Mar Div	Sep 12, 1951	the Punchbowl	Dresher, PA
*McGovern, Robert M. 1Lt, USA	Co A, 1st Bn, 5th Cav, 1st Cav Div	Jan 30, 1951	near Kamyangjan-ni	Washington, DC
McLaughlin, Alford L. Pfc, USMC	Co L, 3rd Bn, 5th Mar, 1st Mar Div	Sep 4–5, 1952	Bunker Hill	Leeds, AL
*Mendonca, Leroy A. Sgt, USA	Co B, 1st Bn, 7th Inf, 3rd Inf Div	Jul 4, 1951	near Chich-on	Honolulu, HI
Millett, Lewis L. Capt, USA	Co E, 2nd Bn, 27th Inf, 25th Inf Div	Feb 7, 1951	near Soam-ni	So.Dartmouth, MA
*Mitchell, Frank N. 1Lt, USMC	Co A, 1st Bn, 7th Mar, 1st Mar Div	Nov 26, 1950	near Yudam-ni	Roaring Springs, TX
Miyamura, Hiroshi H. Cpl, USA	Co H, 2nd Bn, 7th Inf, 3rd Inf Div	Apr 24–25, 1951	near Taejon-ni	Gallup, NM
Mize, Ola L. Sgt, USA	Co K, 3rd Bn, 15th Inf, 3rd Inf Div	Jun 10–11, 1953	Outpost Harry	Gadsden, AL
*Monegan, Walter C., Jr. Pfc, USMC	Co F, 2nd Bn, 1st Mar, 1st Mar Div	Sep 17 & 20, 1950	near Sosa-ri	Seattle, WA
*Moreland, Whitt L. Pfc, USMC	Co C, 1st Bn, 5th Mar, 1st Mar Div	May 29, 1951	Kwagchi-dong	Austin, TX
*Moyer, Donald R. Sfc, USA	Co E, 2nd Bn, 35th Inf, 25th Inf Div	May 20, 1951	near Seoul	Keego Harbor, MI
Murphy, Raymond G. 2Lt, USMC	Co A, 1st Bn, 5th Mar, 1st Mar Div	Feb 3, 1953	near Panmunjom	Pueblo, CO
Myers, Reginald R. Maj, USMC	3rd Bn, 1st Mar, 1st Mar Div	Nov 29, 1950	Hagaru-ri	Boise, ID
*Obregon, Eugene A. Pfc, USMC	Co G, 3rd Bn, 5th Mar, 1st Mar Div	Sep 26, 1950	Seoul	Los Angeles, CA
O'Brien, George H., Jr. 2Lt, USMC	Co H, 3rd Bn, 7th Mar, 1st Mar Div	Oct 27, 1952	near Panmunjom	Big Spring, TX
*Ouellette, Joseph R. Pfc, USA	Co H, 2nd Bn, 9th Inf, 2nd Inf Div	Aug 31– Sep 3, 1950	near Yongsan	Lowell, MA
*Page, John U. D. Lt Col, USA	52nd Trans Bn, X Corps	Nov 29– Dec 10, 1950	near Koto-ri	St. Paul, MN
*Pendleton, Charles F. Cpl, USA	Co D, 1st Bn, 15th Inf, 3rd Inf Div	Jul 16–17, 1953	Choo Gung-dong	Ft. Worth, TX

Name, Rank, Branch	Unit	Date	Place	Hometown
*Phillips, Lee H. Cpl, USMC	Co E, 2nd Bn, 7th Mar, 1st Mar Div	Nov 4, 1950	near Sudong	Ben Hill, GA
*Pililaau, Herbert K. Pfc, USA	Co C, 1st Bn, 23rd Inf, 2nd Inf Div	Sep 17, 1951	Heartbreak Ridge	Waianae, HI
Pittman, John A. Sgt, USA	Co C, 1st Bn, 23rd Inf, 2nd Inf Div	Nov 26, 1950	near Kujang-dong	Tallula, MS
*Pomeroy, Ralph E. Pfc, USA	Co E, 2nd Bn, 31st Inf, 7th Inf Div	Oct 15, 1952	near Kumhwa	Quinwood, WV
*Porter, Donn F. Sgt, USA	Co G, 2nd Bn, 14th Inf, 25th Inf Div	Sep 7, 1952	Heartbreak Ridge	Baltimore, MD
*Poynter, James I. Sgt, USMC	Co A, 1st Bn, 7th Mar, 1st Mar Div	Nov 4, 1950	near Sudong	Downey, CA
*Ramer, George H. 2Lt, USMC	Co I, 3rd Bn, 7th Mar, 1st Mar Div	Sep 12, 1951	Punchbowl	Lewisburg, PA
*Red Cloud, Mitchell, Jr. Cpl, USA	Co E, 2nd Bn, 19th Inf, 24th Inf Div	Nov 5, 1950	near Chonghyon	Friendship, WI
*Reem, Robert D. 2Lt, USMC	Co H, 3rd Bn, 7th Mar, 1st Mar Div	Nov 6, 1950	near Chinhung-ni	Elizabethtown, PA
Rodriguez, Joseph C. Pfc, USA	Co F, 2nd Bn, 17th Inf, 7th Inf Div	May 21, 1951	near Munye-ri	San Bernardino, CA
Rosser, Ronald E. Cpl, USA	Heavy Mortar Co, 38th Inf, 2nd Inf Div	Jan 12, 1952	Ponggilli	Crooksville, OH
*Schoonover, Dan D. Cpl, USA	Co A, 13th Eng Combat Bn 7th Inf Div	Jul 8–10, 1953	Porkchop Hill	Boise, ID
Schowalter, Edward R., Jr. 1Lt, USA	Co A, 1st Bn, 31st Inf, 7th Inf Div	Oct 14, 1952	near Kumhwa	Metairie, LA
*Sebille, Louis J. Maj, USAF	67th Fighter-Bomber Squad, 18th Fighter-Bomber Group	Aug 5, 1950	near Hamchang	Chicago, IL
*Shea, Richard T., Jr. 1Lt, USA	Co A, 1st Bn, 17th Inf, 7th Inf Div	Jul 6–8, 1953	Porkchop Hill	Portsmouth, VA
*Shuck, William E., Jr. SSgt, USMC	Co G, 3rd Bn, 7th Mar, 1st Mar Div	Jul 3, 1952	Bunker Hill	Cumberland, MD
Simanek, Robert E. Pfc, USMC	Co F, 2nd Bn, 5th Mar, 1st Mar Div	Aug 17, 1952	Bunker Hill	Detroit, MI
*Sitman, William S. Sfc, USA	Co M, 3rd Bn, 23rd Inf, 2nd Inf Div	Feb 14, 1951	near Chipyong-ni	Bedford, PA
Sitter, Carl L. Capt, USMC	Co G, 3rd Bn, 1st Mar, 1st Mar Div	Nov 29–30, 1950	Hagaru-ri	Pueblo, CO
*Skinner, Sherrod E., Jr. 2Lt, USMC	Battery F, 2nd Bn, 11th Mar, 1st Mar Div	Oct 26, 1952	near Panmunjom	E. Lansing, MI

Name, Rank, Branch	Unit	Date	Place	Hometown
*Smith, David M. Pfc, USA	Co E, 2nd Bn, 9th Inf, 2nd Inf Div	Sep 1, 1950	near Yongsan	Livingston, KY
*Speicher, Clifton T. Cpl, USA	Co F, 2nd Bn, 223rd Inf, 40th Inf Div	Jun 14, 1952	near Minari-gol	Gray, PA
Stone, James L. 1Lt, USA	Co E, 2nd Bn, 8th Cav, 1st Cav Div	Nov 21–22, 1951	near Sokkogae	Pine Bluff, AR
*Story, Luther H. Pfc, USA	Co A, 1st Bn, 9th Inf, 2nd Inf Div	Sep 1, 1950	near Agok	Americus, GA
*Sudut, Jerome A. 2Lt, USA	Co B, 1st Bn, 27th Inf, 25th Inf Div	Sep 12, 1951	near Kumhwa	Wausau, WI
*Thompson, William Pfc, USA	Co M, 3rd Bn, 24th Inf, 25th Inf Div	Aug 6, 1950	near Haman	Bronx, NY
*Turner, Charles W. Sfc, USA	2nd Recon Co, 2nd Inf Div	Sep 1, 1950	near Yongsan	Boston, MA
Van Winkle, Archie SSgt, USMC	Co B, 1st Bn, 7th Mar, 1st Mar Div	Nov 2, 1950	near Sudong	Everett, WA
*Vittori, Joseph Cpl, USMC	Co F, 2nd Bn, 1st Mar, 1st Mar Div	Sep 15–16, 1951	Punchbowl	Beverly, MA
*Walmsley, John S., Jr. Capt, USAF	8th Bombardment Squad, 3rd Bomb Group	Sep 14, 1951	near Yangdok	Baltimore, MD
*Watkins, Lewis G. SSgt, USMC	Co I, 3rd Bn, 7th Mar, 1st Mar Div	Oct 7, 1952	Detroit Hill	Seneca, SC
*Watkins, Travis E. MSgt, USA	Co H, 2nd Bn, 9th Inf, 2nd Inf Div	Aug 31– Sep 3, 1950	near Yongsan	Gladewater, TX
West, Ernest E. Pfc, USA	Co L, 3rd Bn, 14th Inf, 25th Inf Div	Oct 12, 1952	near Heartbreak Ridge	Wurtland, KY
Wilson, Benjamin F. MSgt, USA	Co I, 3rd Bn, 31st Inf, 7th Inf Div	Jun 5, 1951	near Hwachon	Vashon, WA
Wilson, Harold E. TSgt, USMC	Co G, 3rd Bn, 1st Mar, 1st Mar Div	Apr 23–24, 1951	near Chunchon	Birmingham, AL
*Wilson, Richard G. Pfc, USA	Co I, 3rd Bn, 187th Airborne Regt	Oct 21, 1950	Opa-ri	Cape Girardeau, MO
*Windrich, William G. SSgt, USMC	Co I, 3rd Bn, 5th Mar, 1st Mar Div	Dec 1, 1950	near Yudam-ni	East Chicago, IN
*Womack, Bryant H. Pfc, USA	Medical Co, 14th Inf, 25th Inf Div	Mar 12, 1952	near the Punchbowl	Rutherfordton, SC
*Young, Robert H. Pfc, USA	Co E, 2nd Bn, 8th Cav, 1st Cav Div	Oct 9, 1950	near Kaesong	Vallejo, CA

Bibliography

Appleman, Roy E., *Escaping the Trap*. College Station, Tex.: Texas A and M Univ. Press, 1990.

—, *South to the Naktong, North to the Yalu*. Washington, D.C.: Govt. Printing Office, 1961.

—, *East of Chosin*. College Station, Tex.: Texas A and M Univ. Press, 1987.

Blair, Clay, *The Forgotten War*. New York: Times Books, 1987.

Dept. of the Army, Office of the Chief of Military History, *Korea–1950*. Washington, D.C.: Govt. Printing Office, 1952.

Editors, Boston Publishing Co., *Above and Beyond—A History of the Medal of Honor from the Civil War to Vietnam*. Boston: Boston Publishing Co., 1985.

Fehrenbach, T. R., *This Kind of War*. New York: The Macmillan Company, 1963.

Giangreco, D. M., *War in Korea, 1950–53*. Novato, Calif.: Presidio Press, 1990.

Hammel, Eric M., *Chosin*. New York: The Vanguard Press, 1981.

Hermes, Walter G., *Truce Tent and Fighting Front*. Washington, D.C.: Govt. Printing Office, 1966.

Hoyt, Edwin P., *On to the Yalu*. New York: Stein and Day, 1984.

—, *Pusan Perimeter*. New York: Stein and Day, 1984.

Leckie, Robert, *The March to Glory*. New York: Bantam Books, 1960.

Miller, John, et al., *Korea 1951–1953*. Washington, D.C.: Govt. Printing Office, 1982.

Murphy, Edward F., *Vietnam Medal of Honor Heroes*. New York: Ballantine Books, 1987.

U.S. Senate, Committee on Veterans Affairs, *Medal of Honor Recipients 1863–1978*. Washington, D.C.: Govt. Printing Office, 1979.

Ward, Orland, *Korea—1950*. Washington, D.C.: Govt. Printing Office, 1952.

Whelan, Richard, *Drawing the Line, Korea 1950–1953*. Boston: Little, Brown and Co., 1990.

Wilson, Jim, *Retreat Hell!* New York: William Morrow and Co., 1988.

Index